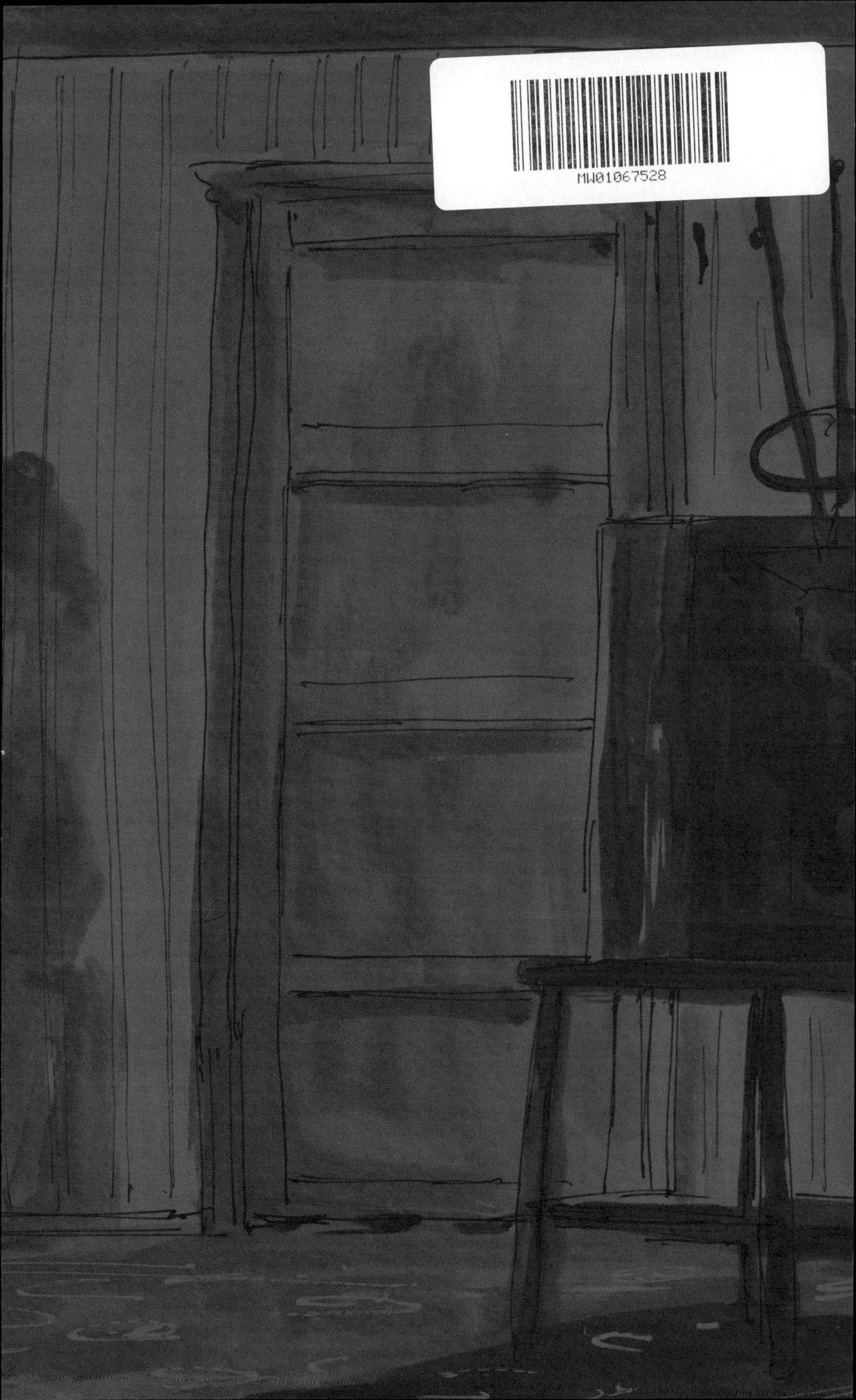

TUMOR

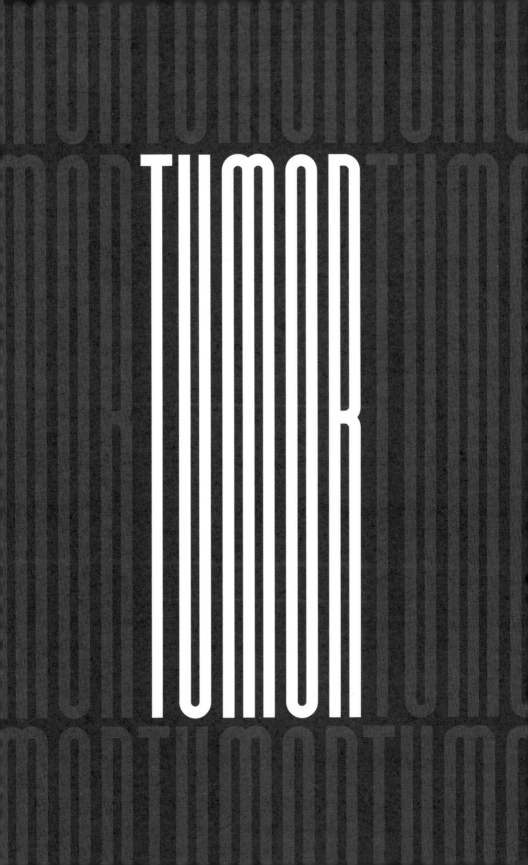

TUMOR

A Medical
Noir

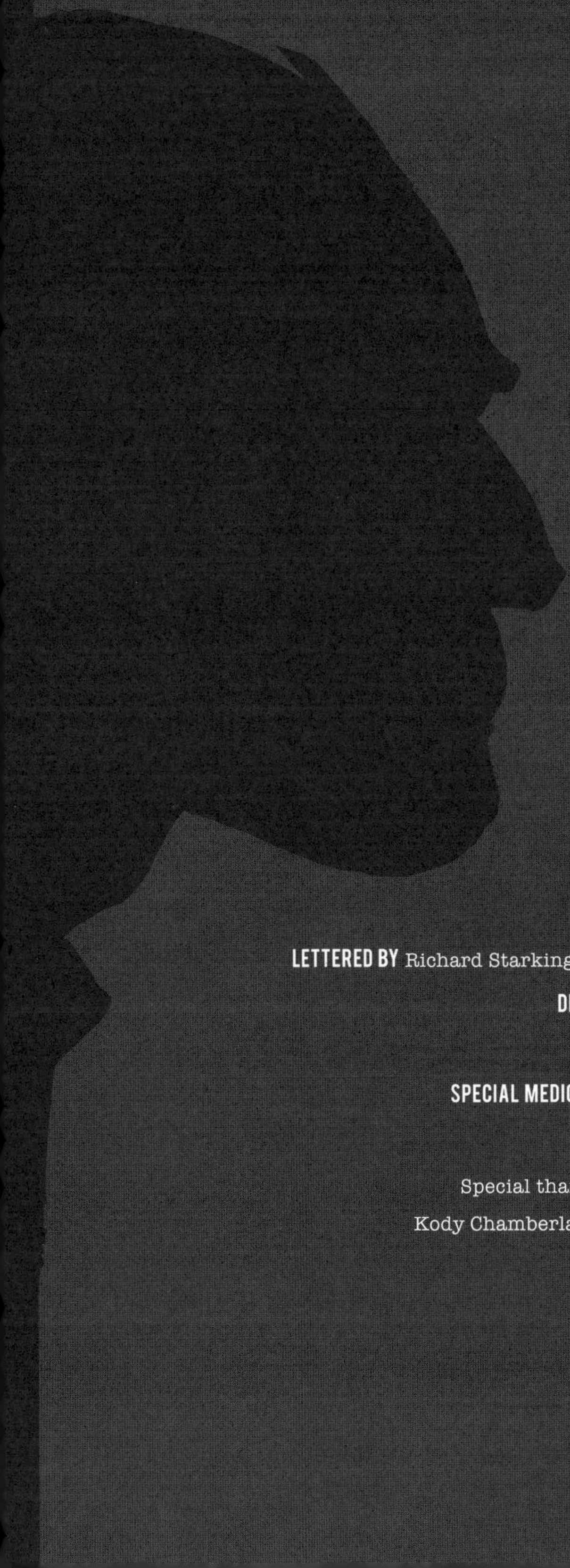

AN ONI PRESS PUBLICATION

WRITTEN BY Joshua Hale Fialkov

ILLUSTRATED BY Noel Tuazon

LETTERED BY Richard Starkings & Comicraft's Jimmy Betancourt

DESIGNED BY Catherine Renee Dimalla

EDITED BY Ari Yarwood

SPECIAL MEDICAL CONSULTANT Arnold Schiebel, MD

Special thanks to original edition contributors
Kody Chamberlain, Marlen Moore & Scott Newman

PUBLISHED BY ONI PRESS, INC.

JOE NOZEMACK publisher

JAMES LUCAS JONES editor in chief

ANDREW MCINTIRE V.P. of marketing & sales

CHEYENNE ALLOTT director of sales

RACHEL REED publicity coordinator

TROY LOOK director of design & production

HILARY THOMPSON graphic designer

JARED JONES digital art technician

ARI YARWOOD managing editor

CHARLIE CHU senior editor

ROBIN HERRERA editor

BESS PALLARES editorial assistant

BRAD ROOKS director of logistics

JUNG LEE logistics associate

ONIPRESS.COM

onipress.tumblr.com

instagram.com/onipress

facebook.com/onipress

twitter.com/onipress

---

thefialkov.com / @joshfialkov

noeltuazon.blogspot.com / @NoelMTuazon

First edition: August 2016

ISBN 978-1-62010-326-5 | eISBN 978-1-62010-327-2

PRINTED IN CHINA.

Library of Congress Control Number: 2015959960

1 2 3 4 5 6 7 8 9 10

SAPPED

An Introduction to TUMOR

BY DUANE SWIERCZYNSKI

One of the time-honored traditions of private detective literature—and by "time-honored" I mean completely ridiculous and overused to the point of screaming cliché—is the sharp blow to the head that makes everything go bye-bye.

Some believe that Carroll John Daly's Three Gun Terry—making his debut in the first-ever hardboiled P.I. story—started this long, painful trend:

"Something like a ton of bricks comes down and... after that... everything goes black."

Any Raymond Chandler fan can tell you that Phillip Marlowe was frequently walloped in the noggin. Consider this beaut from *Lady in the Lake:*

"The scene exploded into fire and darkness. I didn't even remember being slugged. Fire and darkness and just before the darkness a sharp flash of nausea."

Even modern-day crime writers can't resist a good cosh to the brainpan. Check out George Pelecanos' Nick Stefanos in *Down by the River Where the Dead Men Go:*

"I felt a blunt shock to the back of my head and a short, sharp pain. The floor dropped out from beneath my feet, and

I was falling, diving toward a pool of cool black water."

The problem, of course, is that such blows to the head are completely ridiculous. It's not easy to bounce back from a severe concussion. And even if you do, it's unlikely that you'll remember the blow in any kind of detail ("...fire and darkness and just before the darkness...") thanks to retrograde amnesia. Plus, it's kind of hard to knock someone out with a single blow. Just ask my younger brother.

But private eye writers, man... they do love their bumps to the ol' brainpan.

Then along comes Joshua Hale Fialkov, who has done something remarkable with his hardboiled P.I. graphic novel, *Tumor*. He's taken this "time-honored tradition" and turned it on its you-know-what. In short, he's given hardboiled fiction a brand new blow to the head.

I'd call it a "masterstroke," but you all might groan.

In a few pages you're going to meet Frank Armstrong, Los Angeles P.I. He's pressed into a search for the daughter of a mob boss—but he's also just started to suffer the effects of a brain tumor. (Sucky day for Frank, all around.) Now no malign tumor is fun, but a brain tumor can fuck up your life in very interesting ways. Moments after agreeing to take a case, Frank's sense of time suddenly becomes—as he puts it—"fluid." For example, Frank wakes up in a hospital bed and tell us:

"20 seconds ago, I was standing outside a noodle factory with a convicted felon, and now I'm here."

From its opening pages, *Tumor* treats you to life inside Frank's skull, and it's about as noir as you can get. Think you have problems focusing? In issue #2, Frank tells us:

"My head's ringing, and I keep losing my place. Like I'm reading a book while the TV's on and there's someone knockin' at the door."

Like Phillip Marlowe and Three Gun Terry before him, P.I. Frank Armstrong is reeling from a blow, and describing it to us in grisly detail. Unlike Marlowe and Terry, however, Frank's blow is much more realistic—clearly, Fialkov did his brain tumor homework—and for that reason, utterly horrifying. Cancer knocks you out, you're not just going to pull yourself up off the floor and go searching your desk drawer to an unopened bottle of rail whiskey. You're going to feel it. It's probably going to kill you.

All the while Frank's still got a case to unravel, which is no mean feat when he's in an alley with a slimy suspect one minute, and on his deathbed the next.

Here's the best thing, though: Frank refuses to give up. Private eyes are almost always on the losing end of the sociological spectrum: broke, drunk, weary, maimed—you name it. Despite this, they're often the only agents of good, whether they like it or not. Frank Armstrong is one seriously fucked-up human being, but I think you're going to like Frank—even if you'd never want to be Frank.

Here's another cliché for you: When you die, your life flashes before your eyes. Again, Fialkov takes this shopworn idea, spins it around, and makes it do something cool. Frank's life doesn't so much flash so much as rewind and fast-forward, as if you're playing DVD chapters on random—often to heartbreaking effect. And that's the twisty genius of *Tumor*. Punches and kicks and bullet wounds hurt, but not as bad as glimpses of the city you used to love—or more important, the woman you used to love—now gone forever.

Tumor may call to mind (sorry) some other brain-bending classics—the fractured, reverse narrative of Christopher Nolan's *Memento* and Dalton Trumbo's horrifying *Johnny Got His Gun,* with its helpless protagonist at war with his own immobile, nearly senseless body. But it's utterly original and completely addictive (and I should add that Noel Tuazon's art is beautifully gritty and woozy and stark). Just when you think a genre staple been done to death, some mad genius like Joshua Hale Fialkov comes along, kicks the corpse, and makes it breakdance.

Ain't that a kick in the head.

DUANE SWIERCZYNSKI

November 2009

Duane Swierczynski is the bestselling author of *Severance Package* and *Expiration Date*, both available from St. Martin's Press, as well as *Level 26: Dark Origins* with CSI creator Anthony E. Zuiker. He has also written the X-Men series *Cable* for Marvel Comics, and has written stories featuring the Punisher, Immortal Iron Fist, Wolverine, Werewolf By Night and Deadpool. Swierczynski has never been knocked unconscious. At least, not that he remembers.

For my wife, who gives me
happiness that a bum like me
doesn't rightly deserve.

JOSHUA HALE FIALKOV

For Jeffrey Catherine Jones.

NOEL TUAZON

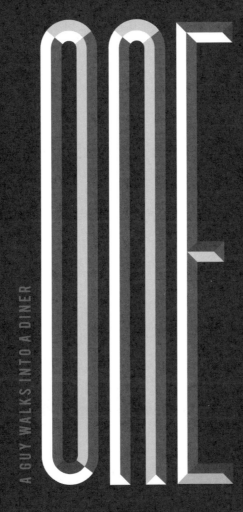

ONE

A GUY WALKS INTO A DINER

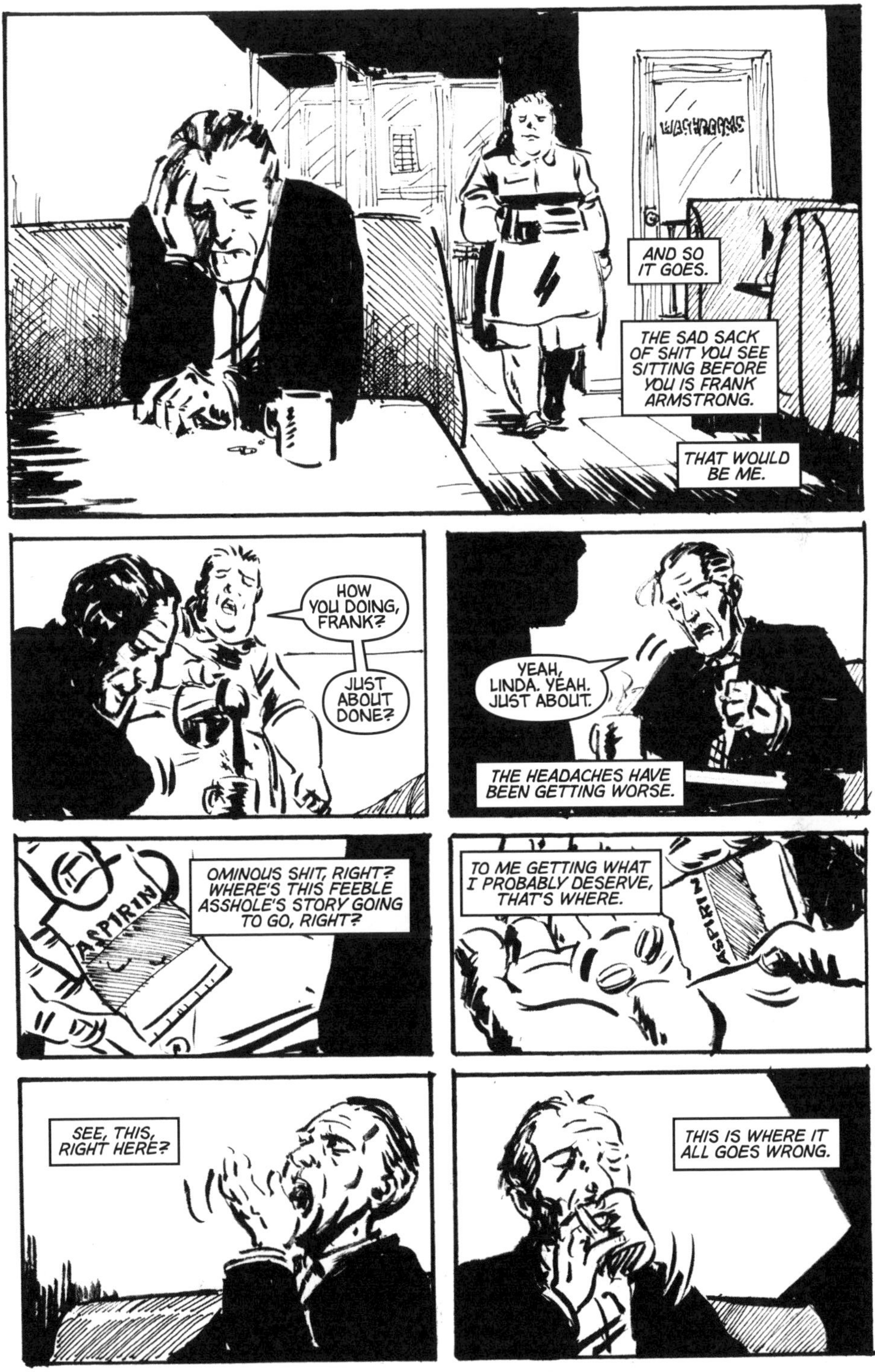

WASHROOMS
AND SO IT GOES.
THE SAD SACK OF SHIT YOU SEE SITTING BEFORE YOU IS FRANK ARMSTRONG.
THAT WOULD BE ME.
HOW YOU DOING, FRANK?
JUST ABOUT DONE?
YEAH, LINDA. YEAH. JUST ABOUT.
THE HEADACHES HAVE BEEN GETTING WORSE.
OMINOUS SHIT, RIGHT? WHERE'S THIS FEEBLE ASSHOLE'S STORY GOING TO GO, RIGHT?
ASPIRIN
TO ME GETTING WHAT I PROBABLY DESERVE, THAT'S WHERE.
ASPIRIN
SEE, THIS, RIGHT HERE?
THIS IS WHERE IT ALL GOES WRONG.

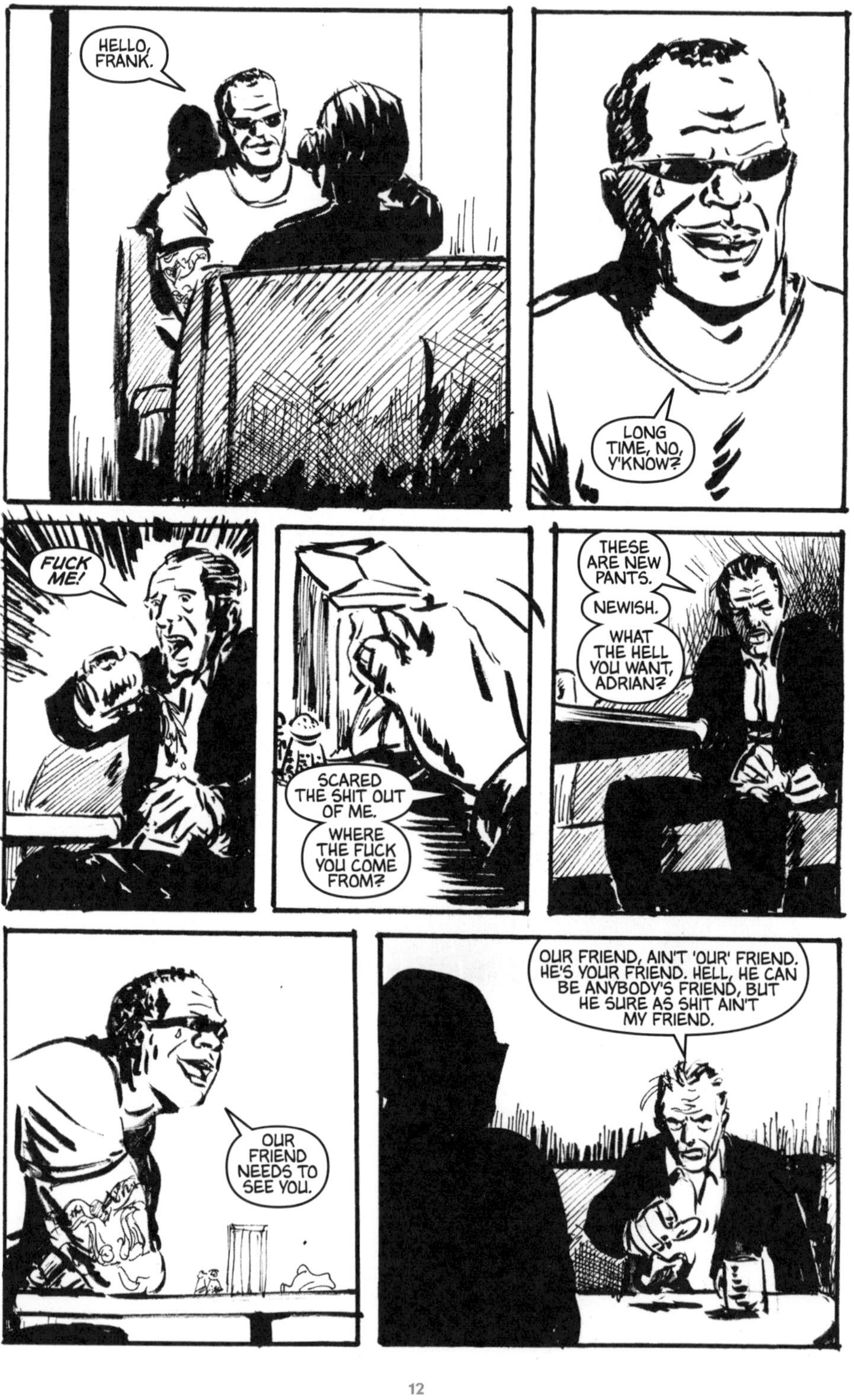
HELLO, FRANK.
LONG TIME, NO, Y'KNOW?
FUCK ME!
SCARED THE SHIT OUT OF ME.
WHERE THE FUCK YOU COME FROM?
THESE ARE NEW PANTS.
NEWISH.
WHAT THE HELL YOU WANT, ADRIAN?
OUR FRIEND NEEDS TO SEE YOU.
OUR FRIEND, AIN'T 'OUR' FRIEND. HE'S YOUR FRIEND. HELL, HE CAN BE ANYBODY'S FRIEND, BUT HE SURE AS SHIT AIN'T MY FRIEND.

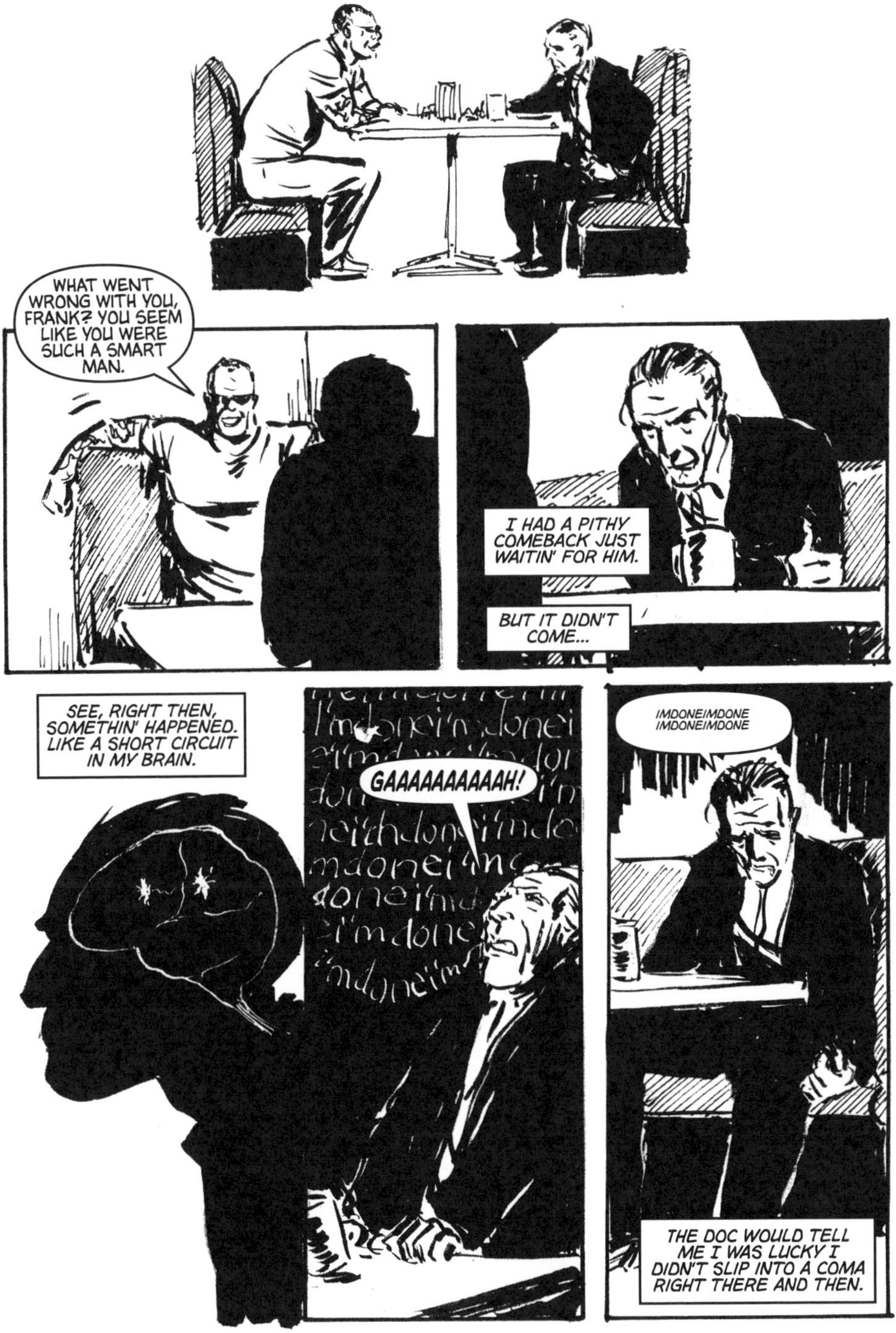
WHAT WENT WRONG WITH YOU, FRANK? YOU SEEM LIKE YOU WERE SUCH A SMART MAN.
I HAD A PITHY COMEBACK JUST WAITIN' FOR HIM.
BUT IT DIDN'T COME...
SEE, RIGHT THEN, SOMETHIN' HAPPENED. LIKE A SHORT CIRCUIT IN MY BRAIN.
GAAAAAAAAAAH!
IMDONEIMDONE IMDONEIMDONE
THE DOC WOULD TELL ME I WAS LUCKY I DIDN'T SLIP INTO A COMA RIGHT THERE AND THEN.

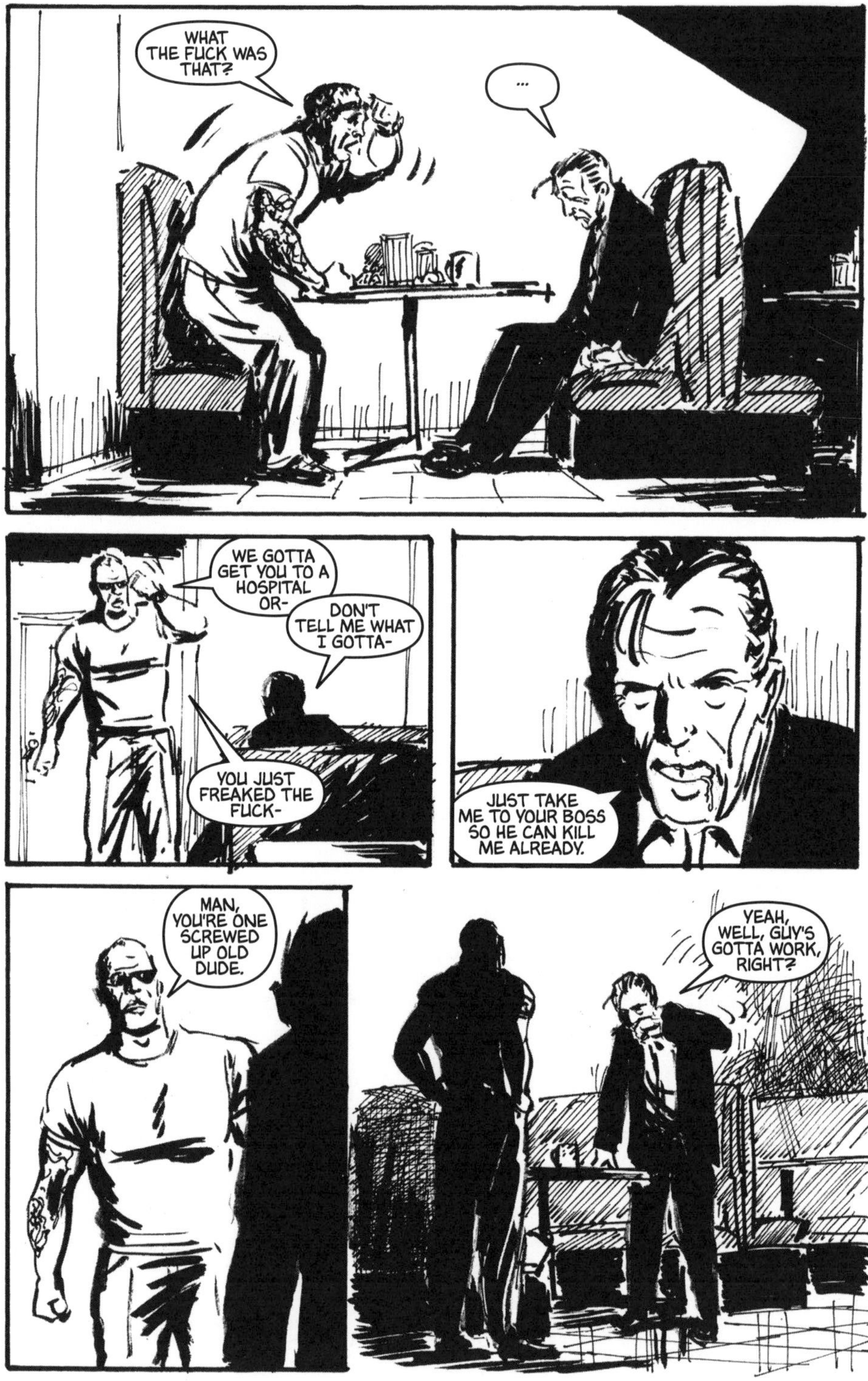
WHAT THE FUCK WAS THAT?
...
WE GOTTA GET YOU TO A HOSPITAL OR-
DON'T TELL ME WHAT I GOTTA-
YOU JUST FREAKED THE FUCK-
JUST TAKE ME TO YOUR BOSS SO HE CAN KILL ME ALREADY.
MAN, YOU'RE ONE SCREWED UP OLD DUDE.
YEAH, WELL, GUY'S GOTTA WORK, RIGHT?

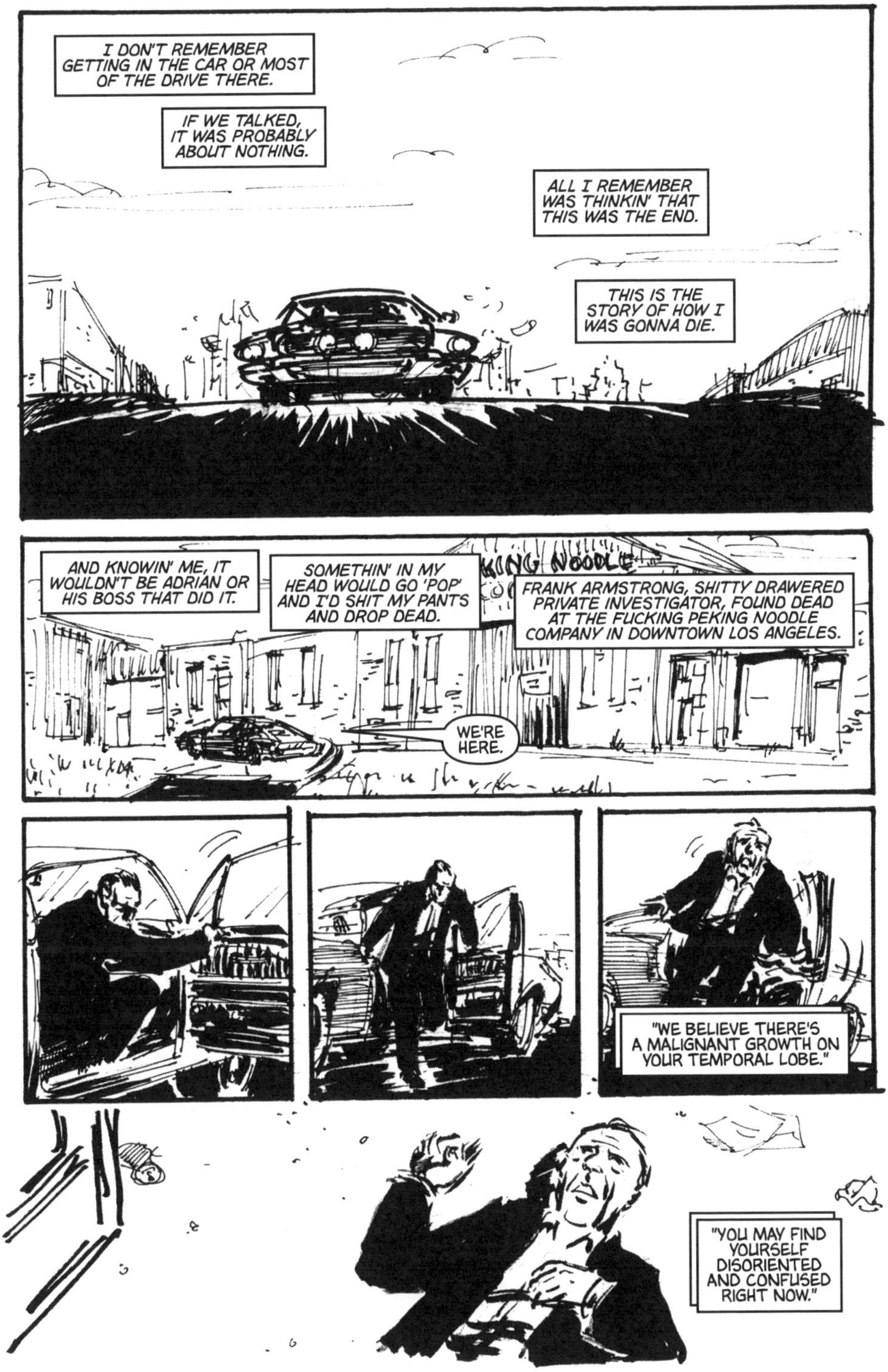

I DON'T REMEMBER GETTING IN THE CAR OR MOST OF THE DRIVE THERE.
IF WE TALKED, IT WAS PROBABLY ABOUT NOTHING.
ALL I REMEMBER WAS THINKIN' THAT THIS WAS THE END.
THIS IS THE STORY OF HOW I WAS GONNA DIE.
AND KNOWIN' ME, IT WOULDN'T BE ADRIAN OR HIS BOSS THAT DID IT.
SOMETHIN' IN MY HEAD WOULD GO 'POP' AND I'D SHIT MY PANTS AND DROP DEAD.
FRANK ARMSTRONG, SHITTY DRAWERED PRIVATE INVESTIGATOR, FOUND DEAD AT THE FUCKING PEKING NOODLE COMPANY IN DOWNTOWN LOS ANGELES.
WE'RE HERE.
"WE BELIEVE THERE'S A MALIGNANT GROWTH ON YOUR TEMPORAL LOBE."
"YOU MAY FIND YOURSELF DISORIENTED AND CONFUSED RIGHT NOW."

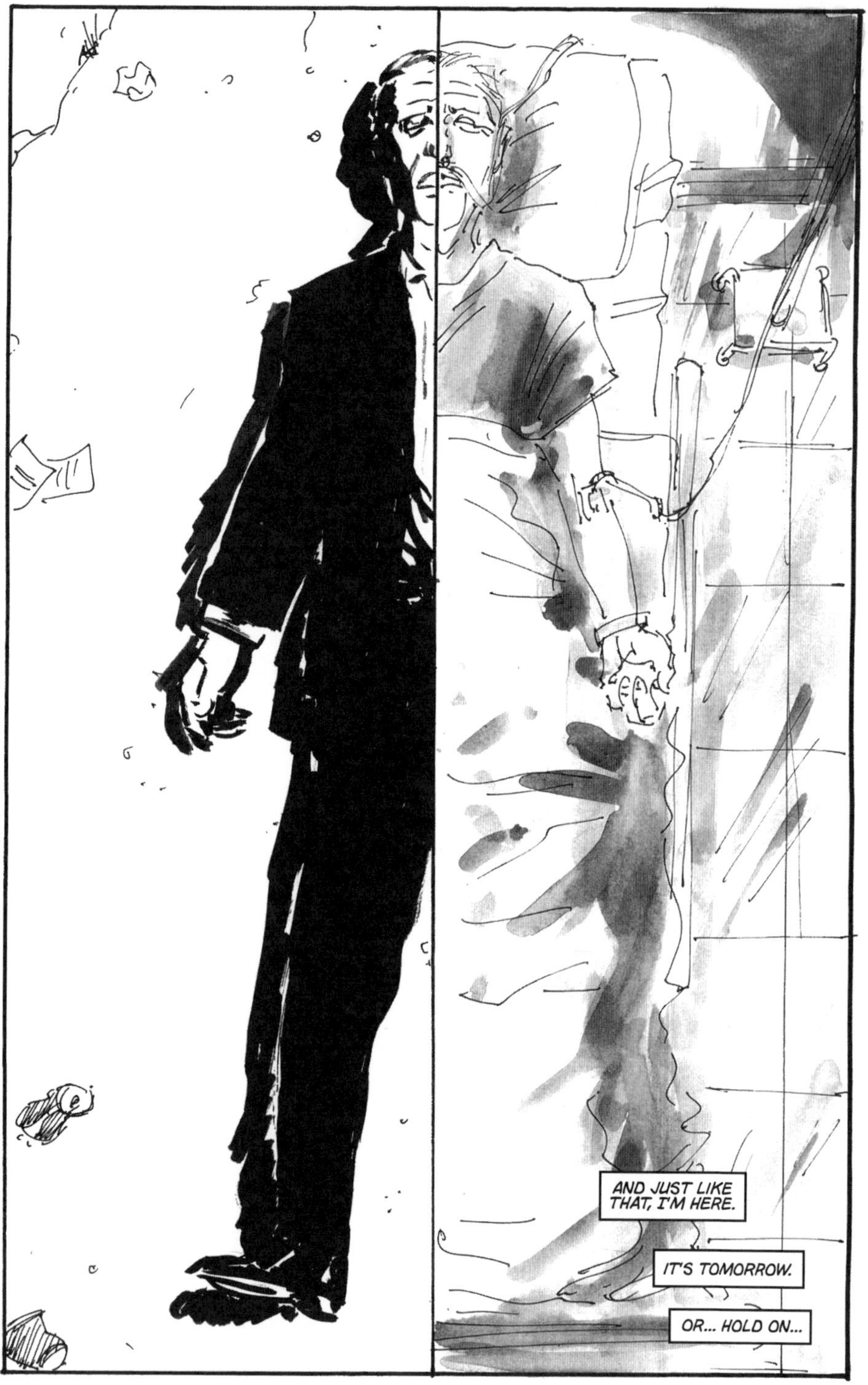
AND JUST LIKE THAT, I'M HERE.
IT'S TOMORROW.
OR... HOLD ON...

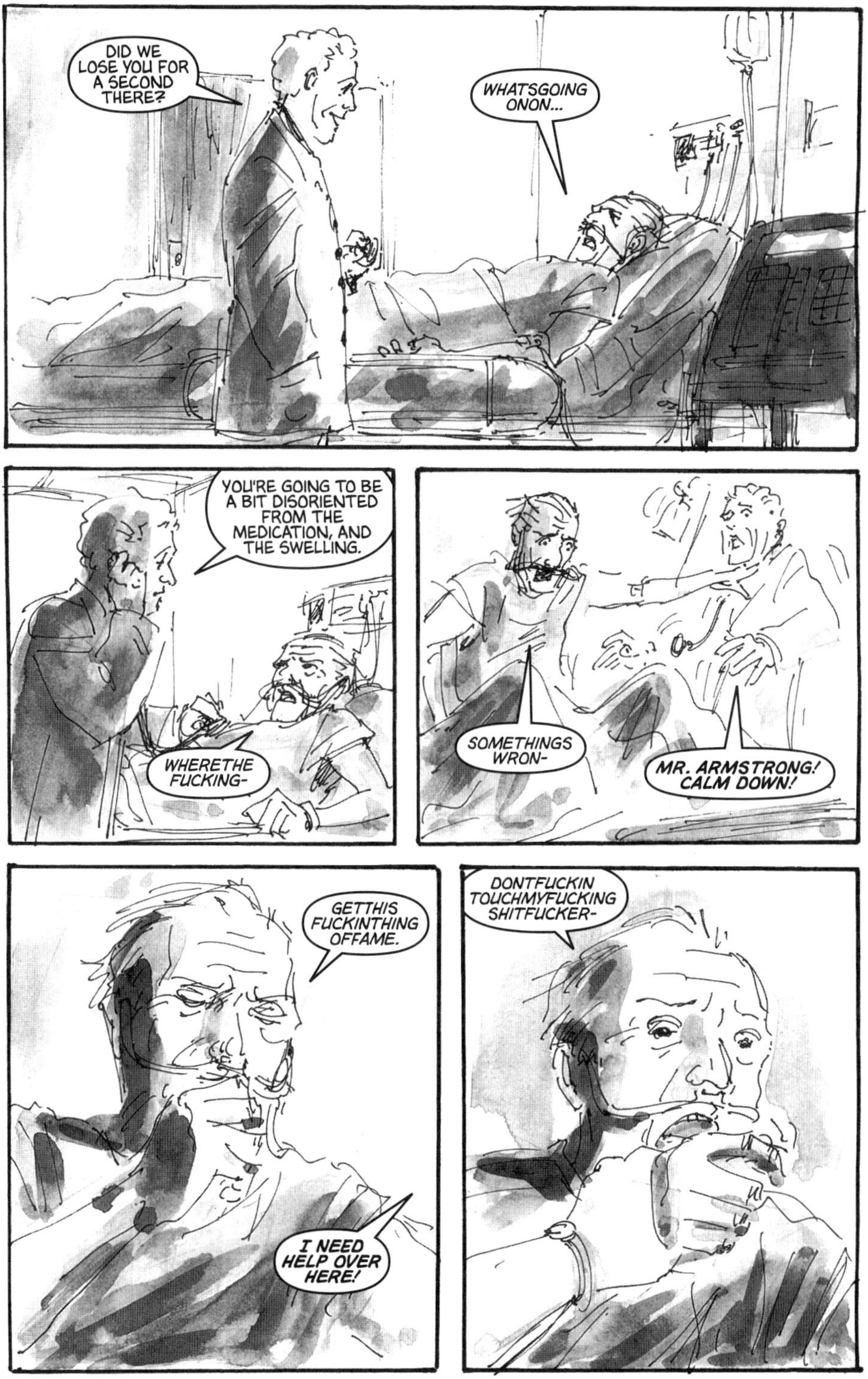
DID WE LOSE YOU FOR A SECOND THERE?
WHATSGOING ONON...
YOU'RE GOING TO BE A BIT DISORIENTED FROM THE MEDICATION, AND THE SWELLING.
WHERETHE FUCKING-
SOMETHINGS WRON-
MR. ARMSTRONG! CALM DOWN!
GETTHIS FUCKINTHING OFFAME.
I NEED HELP OVER HERE!
DONTFUCKIN TOUCHMYFUCKING SHITFUCKER-

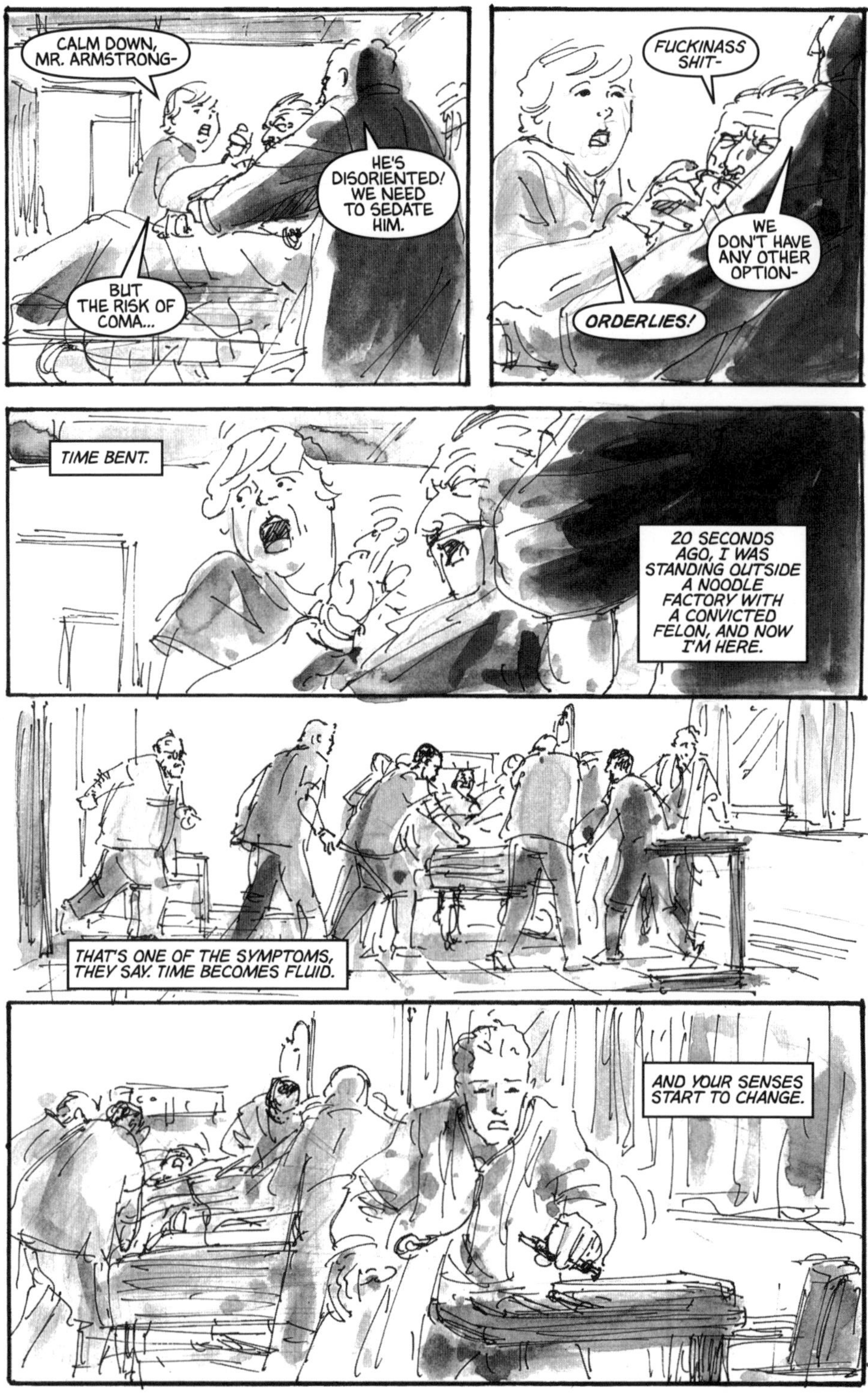
CALM DOWN, MR. ARMSTRONG-
HE'S DISORIENTED! WE NEED TO SEDATE HIM.
BUT THE RISK OF COMA...
FUCKINASS SHIT-
WE DON'T HAVE ANY OTHER OPTION-
ORDERLIES!
TIME BENT.
20 SECONDS AGO, I WAS STANDING OUTSIDE A NOODLE FACTORY WITH A CONVICTED FELON, AND NOW I'M HERE.
THAT'S ONE OF THE SYMPTOMS, THEY SAY. TIME BECOMES FLUID.
AND YOUR SENSES START TO CHANGE.

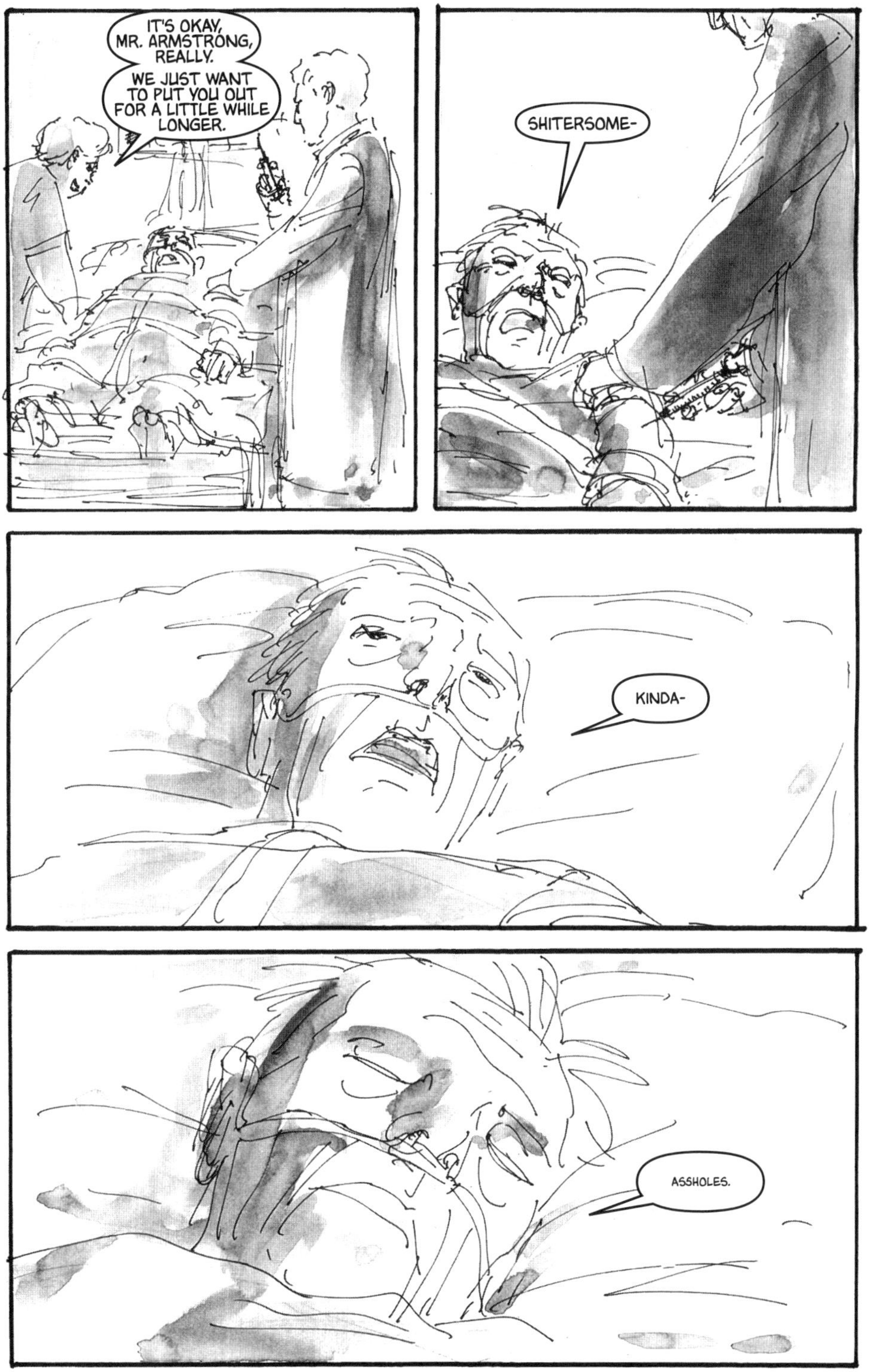
IT'S OKAY, MR. ARMSTRONG, REALLY.
WE JUST WANT TO PUT YOU OUT FOR A LITTLE WHILE LONGER.
SHITERSOME-
KINDA-
ASSHOLES.

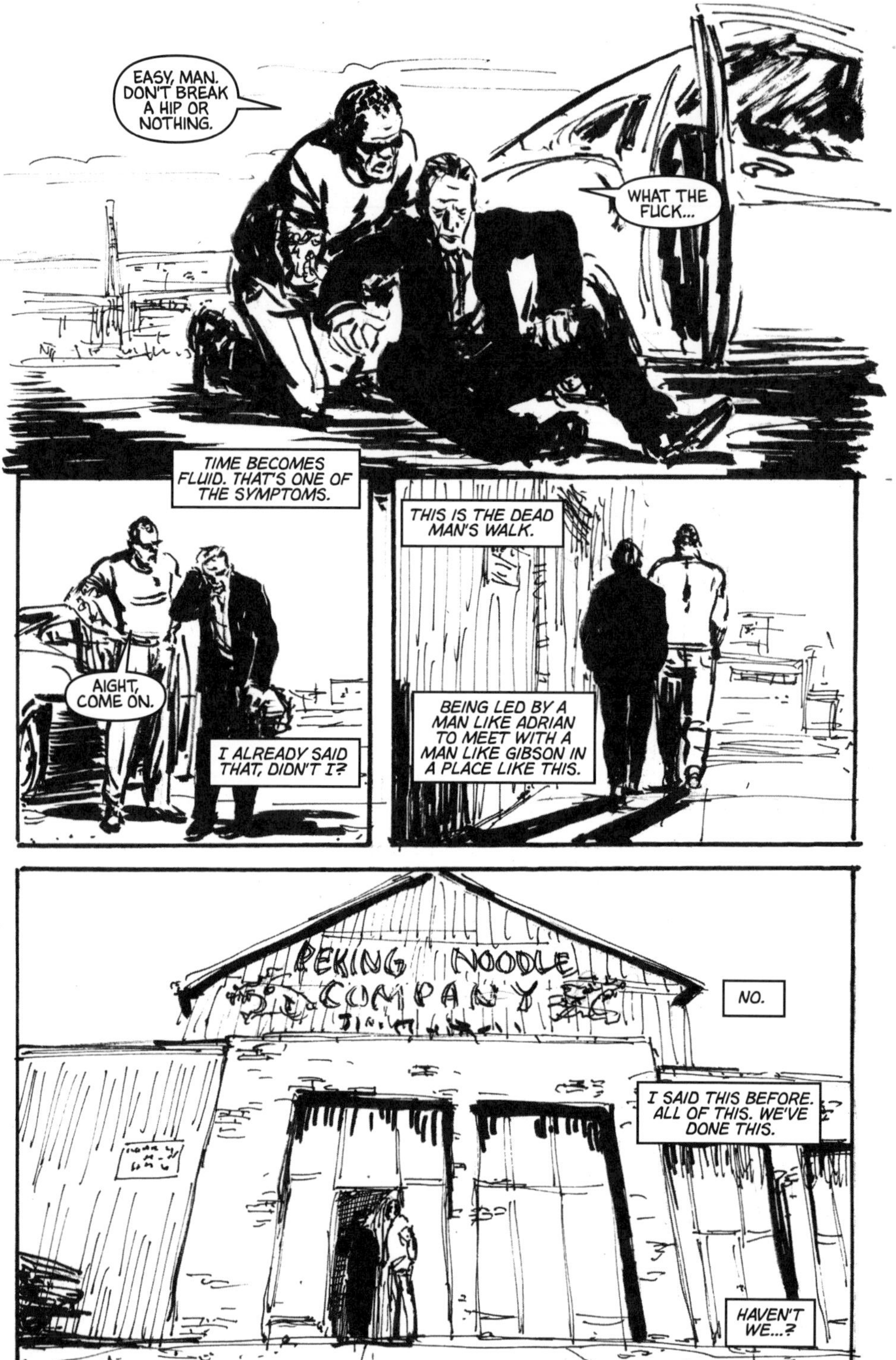
EASY, MAN. DON'T BREAK A HIP OR NOTHING.
WHAT THE FUCK...
TIME BECOMES FLUID. THAT'S ONE OF THE SYMPTOMS.
AIGHT, COME ON.
I ALREADY SAID THAT, DIDN'T I?
THIS IS THE DEAD MAN'S WALK.
BEING LED BY A MAN LIKE ADRIAN TO MEET WITH A MAN LIKE GIBSON IN A PLACE LIKE THIS.
PEKING NOODLE COMPANY
NO.
I SAID THIS BEFORE. ALL OF THIS. WE'VE DONE THIS.
HAVEN'T WE...?

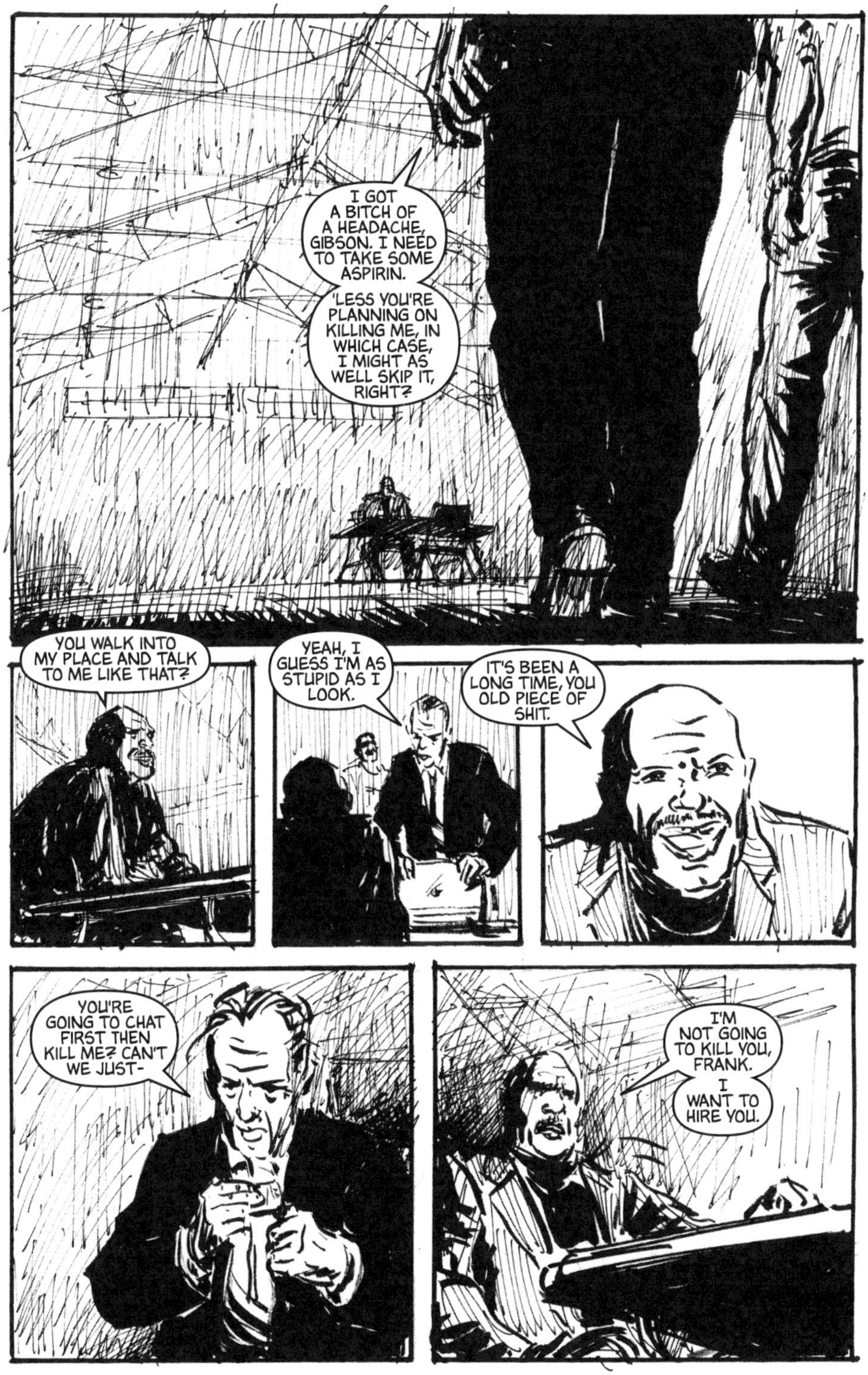

I GOT A BITCH OF A HEADACHE, GIBSON. I NEED TO TAKE SOME ASPIRIN.
'LESS YOU'RE PLANNING ON KILLING ME, IN WHICH CASE, I MIGHT AS WELL SKIP IT, RIGHT?
YOU WALK INTO MY PLACE AND TALK TO ME LIKE THAT?
YEAH, I GUESS I'M AS STUPID AS I LOOK.
IT'S BEEN A LONG TIME, YOU OLD PIECE OF SHIT.
YOU'RE GOING TO CHAT FIRST THEN KILL ME? CAN'T WE JUST-
I'M NOT GOING TO KILL YOU, FRANK.
I WANT TO HIRE YOU.

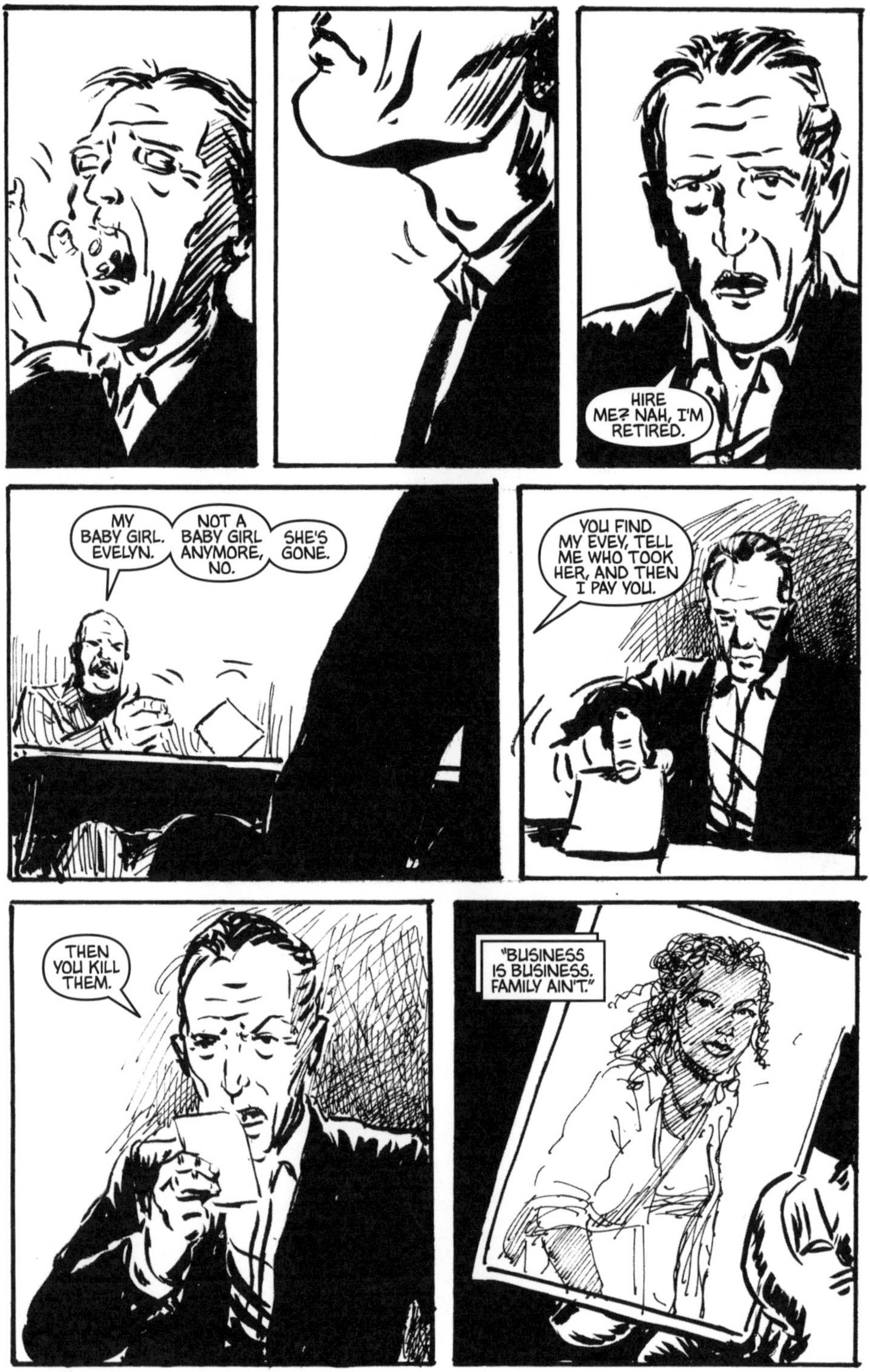
HIRE ME? NAH, I'M RETIRED.
MY BABY GIRL. EVELYN.
NOT A BABY GIRL ANYMORE, NO.
SHE'S GONE.
YOU FIND MY EVEY, TELL ME WHO TOOK HER, AND THEN I PAY YOU.
THEN YOU KILL THEM.
"BUSINESS IS BUSINESS. FAMILY AIN'T."

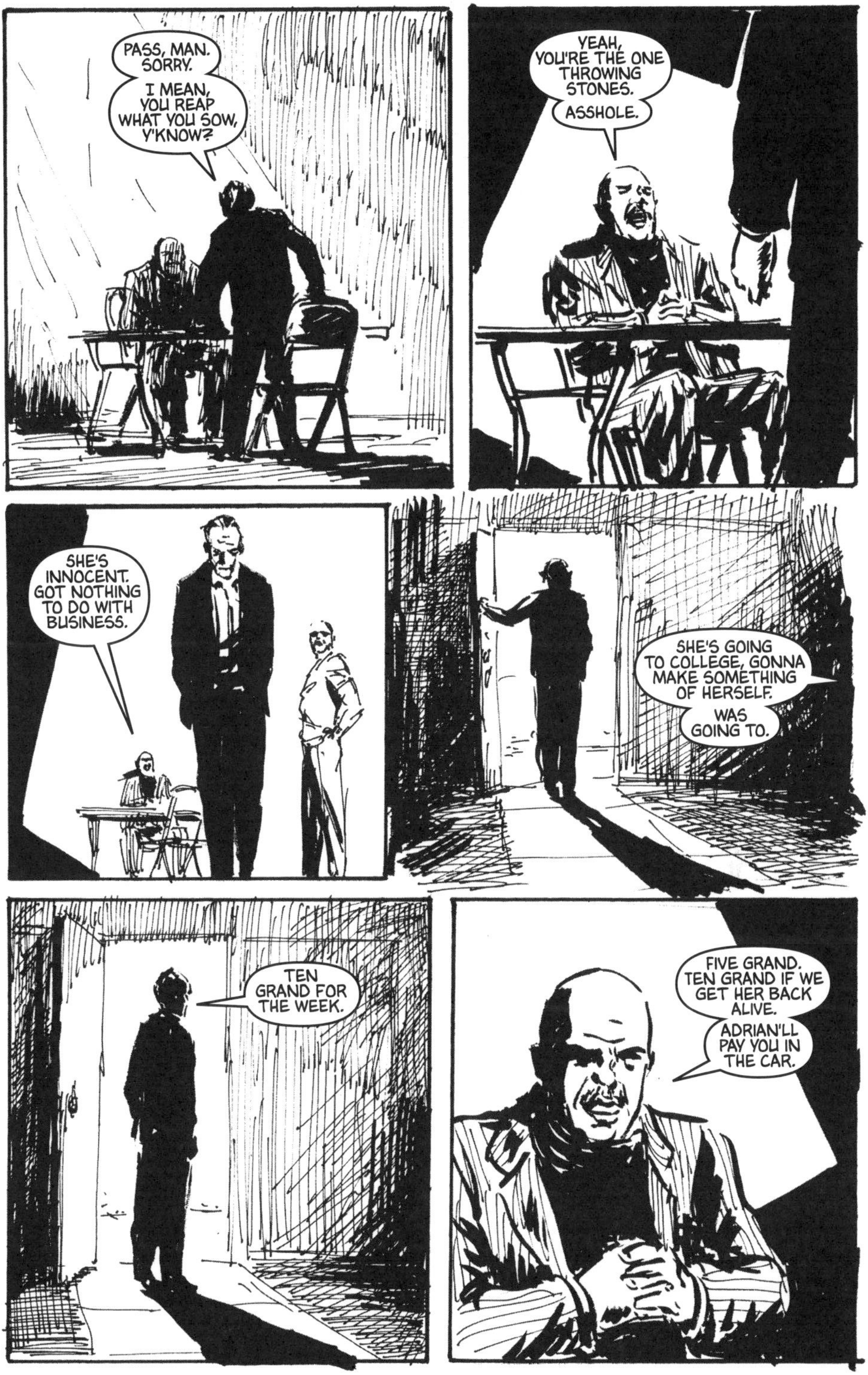
PASS, MAN. SORRY.
I MEAN, YOU REAP WHAT YOU SOW, Y'KNOW?
YEAH, YOU'RE THE ONE THROWING STONES.
ASSHOLE.
SHE'S INNOCENT. GOT NOTHING TO DO WITH BUSINESS.
SHE'S GOING TO COLLEGE, GONNA MAKE SOMETHING OF HERSELF.
WAS GOING TO.
TEN GRAND FOR THE WEEK.
FIVE GRAND. TEN GRAND IF WE GET HER BACK ALIVE.
ADRIAN'LL PAY YOU IN THE CAR.

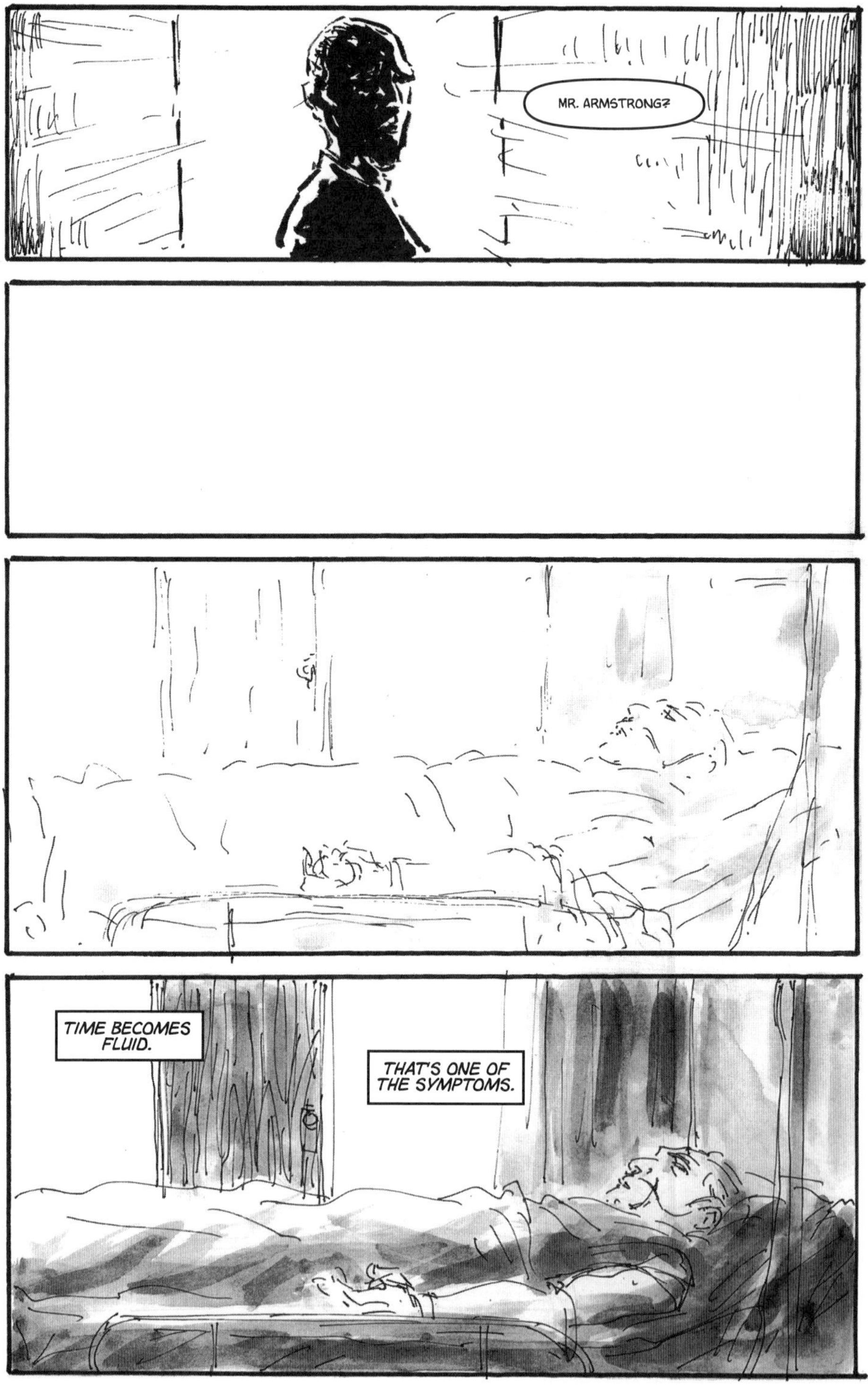
MR. ARMSTRONG?
TIME BECOMES FLUID.
THAT'S ONE OF THE SYMPTOMS.

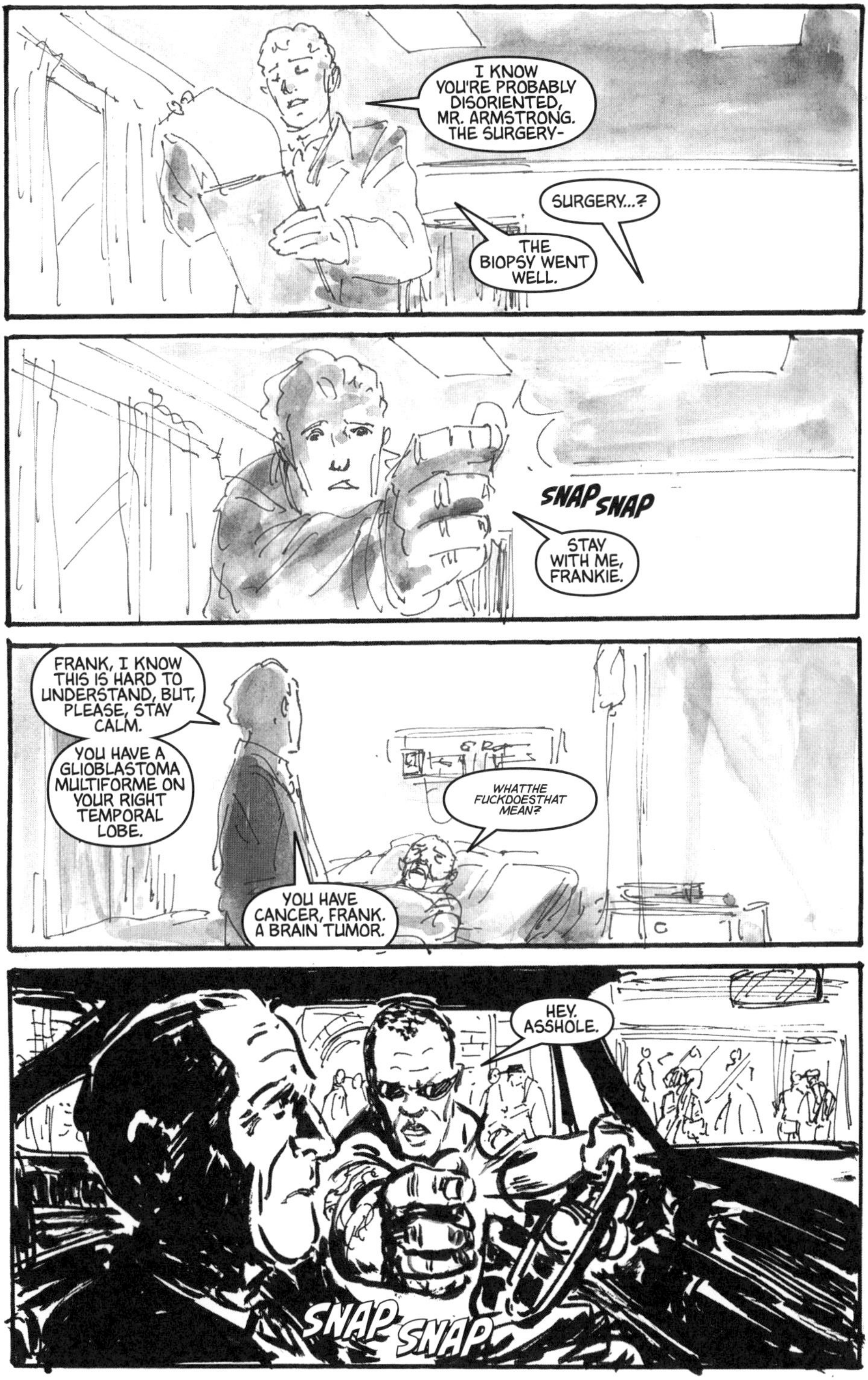
I KNOW YOU'RE PROBABLY DISORIENTED, MR. ARMSTRONG. THE SURGERY-
SURGERY...?
THE BIOPSY WENT WELL.
SNAP SNAP
STAY WITH ME, FRANKIE.
FRANK, I KNOW THIS IS HARD TO UNDERSTAND, BUT, PLEASE, STAY CALM.
YOU HAVE A GLIOBLASTOMA MULTIFORME ON YOUR RIGHT TEMPORAL LOBE.
WHATTHE FUCKDOESTHAT MEAN?
YOU HAVE CANCER, FRANK. A BRAIN TUMOR.
HEY. ASSHOLE.
SNAP SNAP

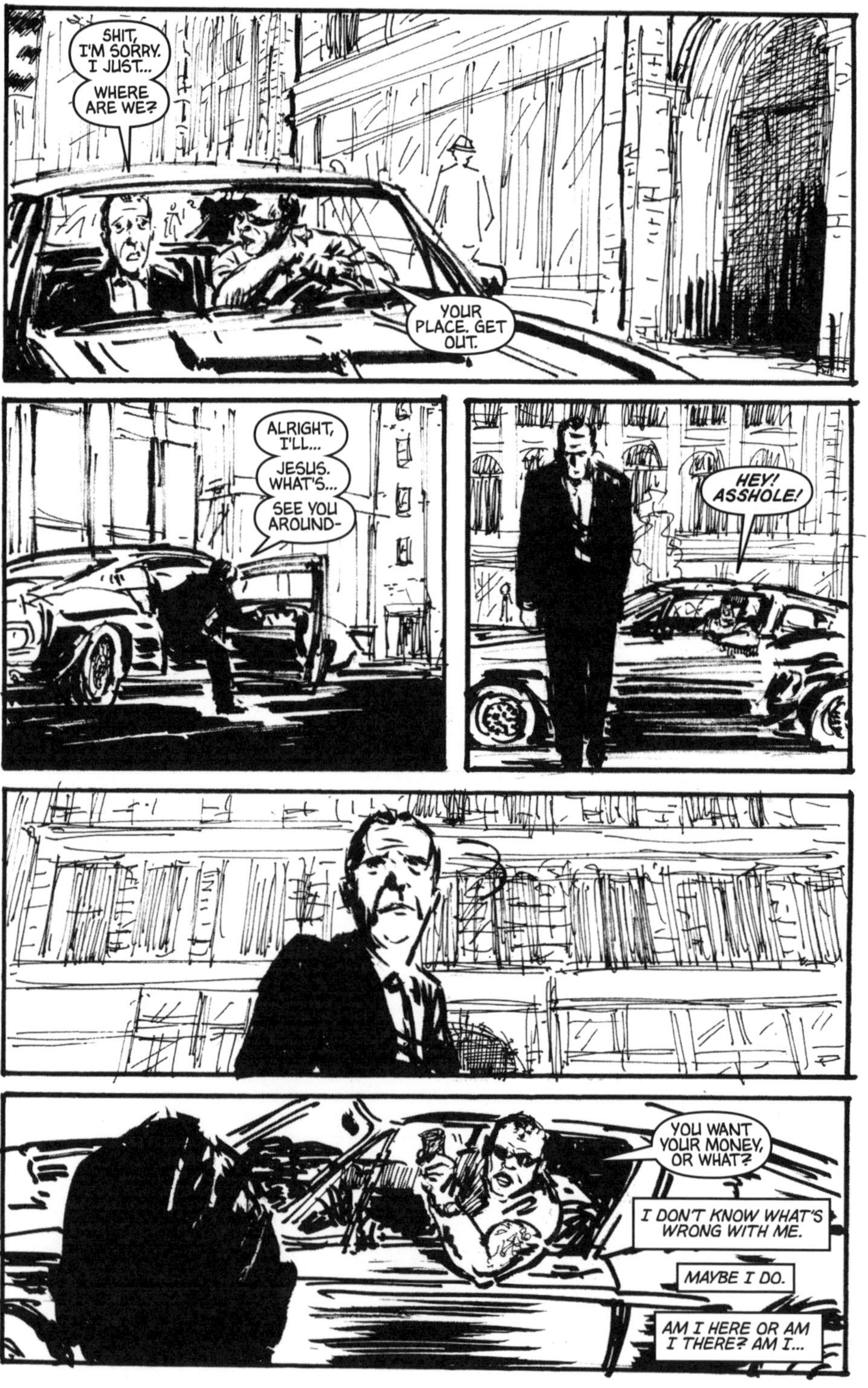
SHIT, I'M SORRY. I JUST...
WHERE ARE WE?
YOUR PLACE. GET OUT.
ALRIGHT, I'LL...
JESUS. WHAT'S...
SEE YOU AROUND-
HEY! ASSHOLE!
YOU WANT YOUR MONEY, OR WHAT?
I DON'T KNOW WHAT'S WRONG WITH ME.
MAYBE I DO.
AM I HERE OR AM I THERE? AM I...

I USED TO JUST WORK HERE.

FRANK ARMSTRONG INVESTIGATIVE SERVICES

I USED TO HAVE CLIENTS.

FRANK ARMSTRONG INVESTIGATIVE SERVICES

ONES THAT WEREN'T DRUG DEALERS AND GUN SMUGGLERS.

NOT LOCKED.

DAMMIT.

I CHECK FOR A GUN.

THERE HASN'T BEEN ONE THERE SINCE I LOST MY LICENSE.

BUT I STILL CHECK.

27

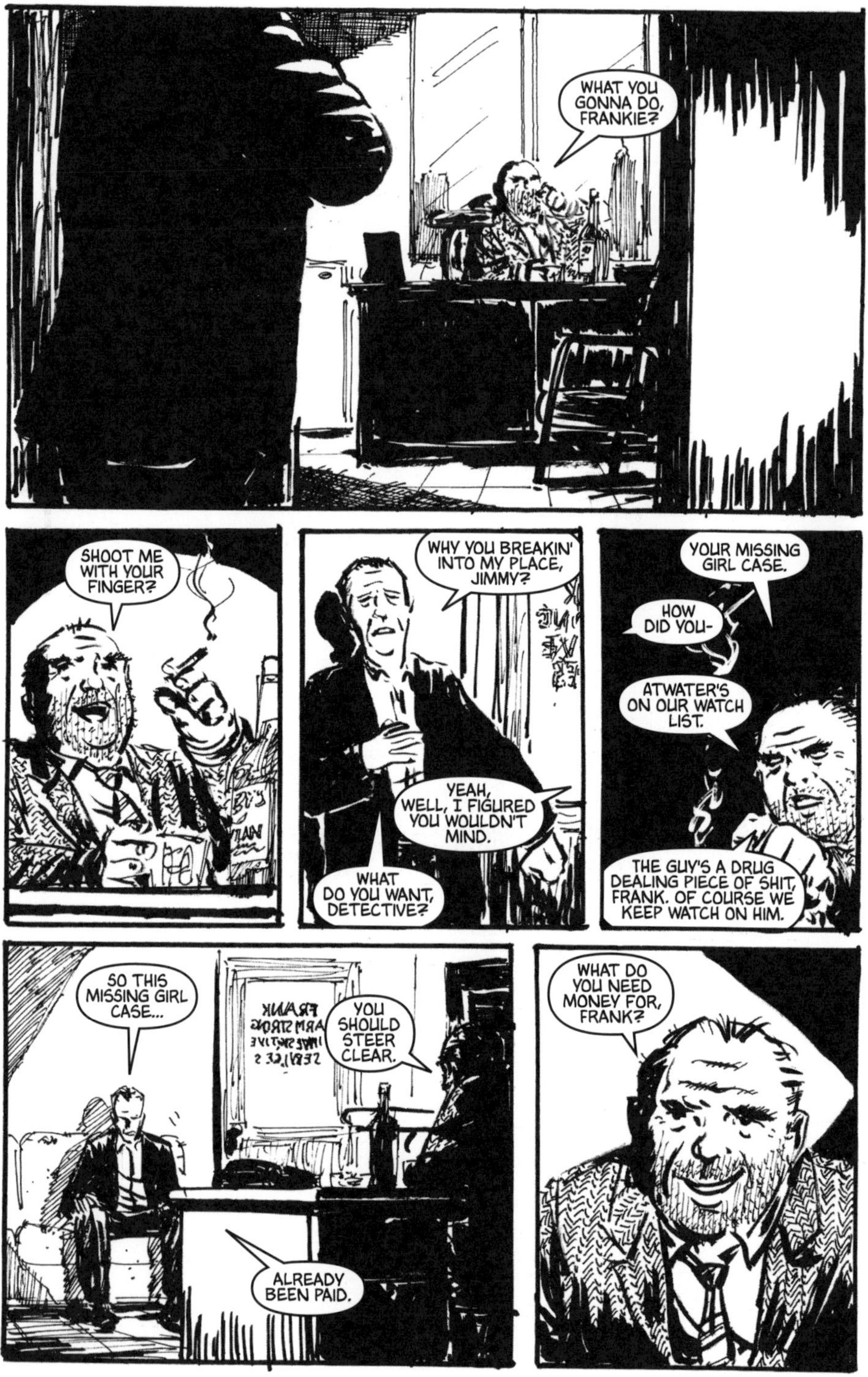
WHAT YOU GONNA DO, FRANKIE?
SHOOT ME WITH YOUR FINGER?
WHY YOU BREAKIN' INTO MY PLACE, JIMMY?
YEAH, WELL, I FIGURED YOU WOULDN'T MIND.
WHAT DO YOU WANT, DETECTIVE?
YOUR MISSING GIRL CASE.
HOW DID YOU-
ATWATER'S ON OUR WATCH LIST.
THE GUY'S A DRUG DEALING PIECE OF SHIT, FRANK. OF COURSE WE KEEP WATCH ON HIM.
SO THIS MISSING GIRL CASE...
YOU SHOULD STEER CLEAR.
ALREADY BEEN PAID.
WHAT DO YOU NEED MONEY FOR, FRANK?

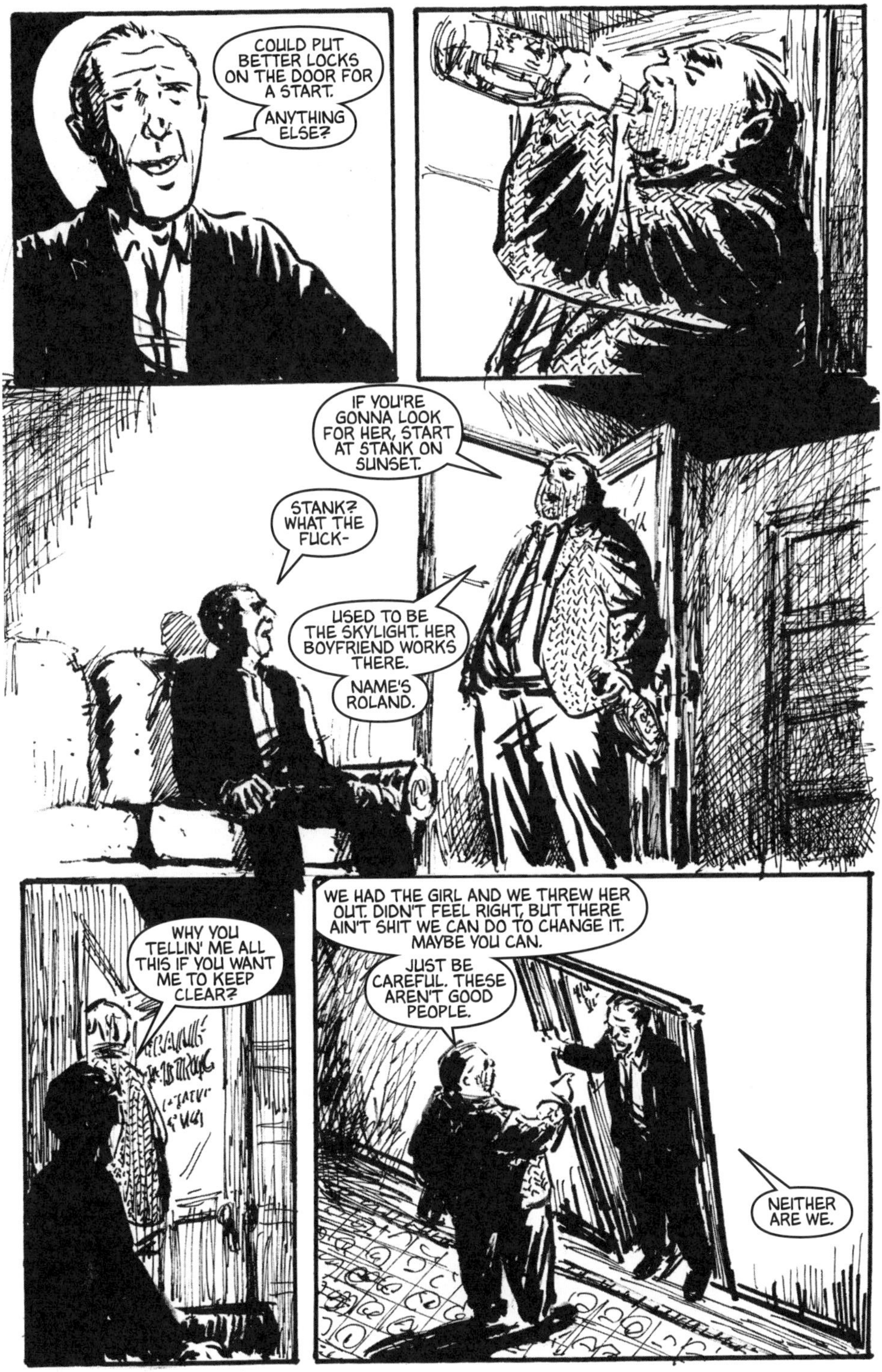
COULD PUT BETTER LOCKS ON THE DOOR FOR A START.
ANYTHING ELSE?
IF YOU'RE GONNA LOOK FOR HER, START AT STANK ON SUNSET.
STANK? WHAT THE FUCK-
USED TO BE THE SKYLIGHT. HER BOYFRIEND WORKS THERE.
NAME'S ROLAND.
WHY YOU TELLIN' ME ALL THIS IF YOU WANT ME TO KEEP CLEAR?
WE HAD THE GIRL AND WE THREW HER OUT. DIDN'T FEEL RIGHT, BUT THERE AIN'T SHIT WE CAN DO TO CHANGE IT. MAYBE YOU CAN.
JUST BE CAREFUL. THESE AREN'T GOOD PEOPLE.
NEITHER ARE WE.

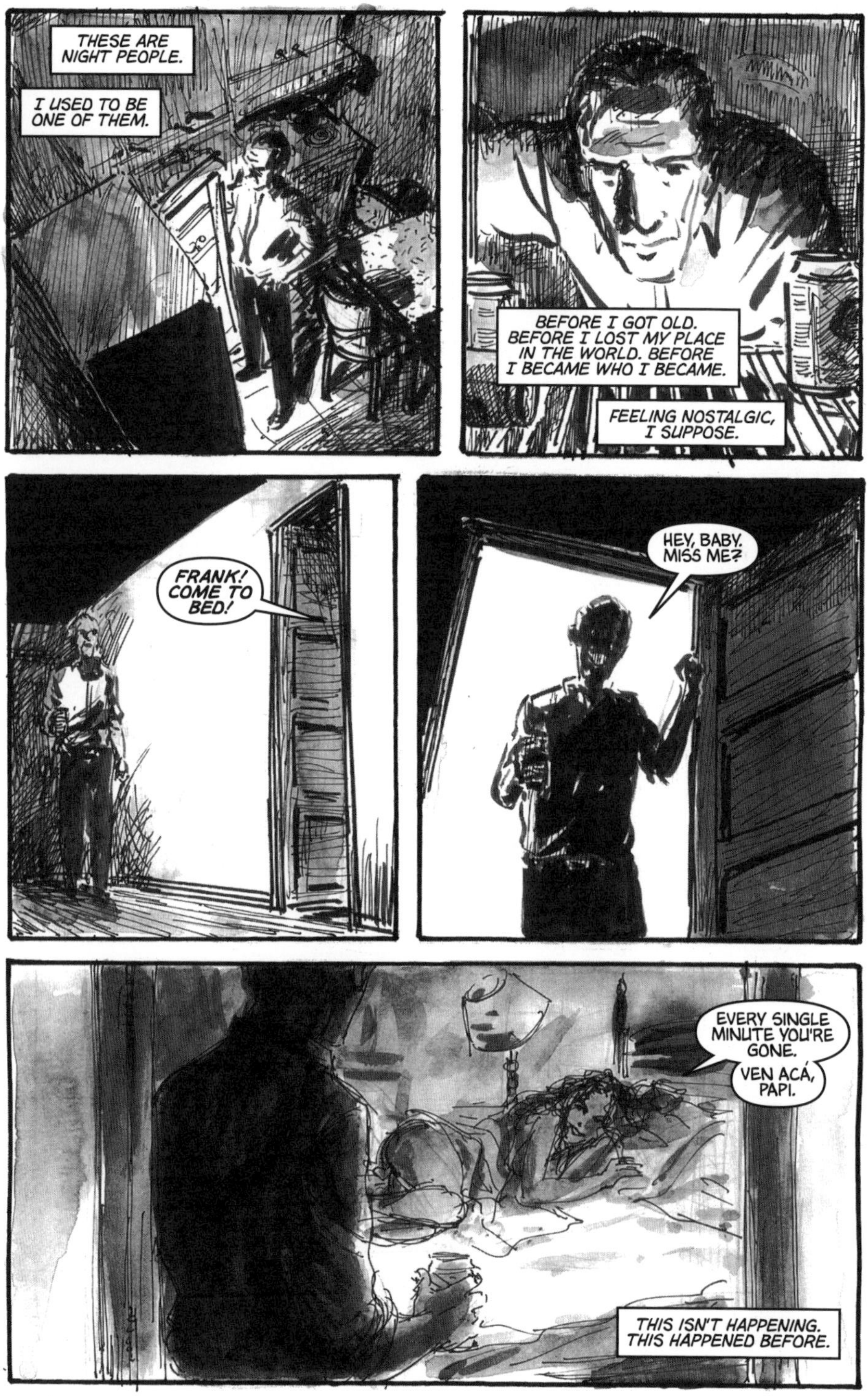
THESE ARE NIGHT PEOPLE.
I USED TO BE ONE OF THEM.
BEFORE I GOT OLD. BEFORE I LOST MY PLACE IN THE WORLD. BEFORE I BECAME WHO I BECAME.
FEELING NOSTALGIC, I SUPPOSE.
FRANK! COME TO BED!
HEY, BABY. MISS ME?
EVERY SINGLE MINUTE YOU'RE GONE.
VEN ACÁ, PAPI.
THIS ISN'T HAPPENING. THIS HAPPENED BEFORE.

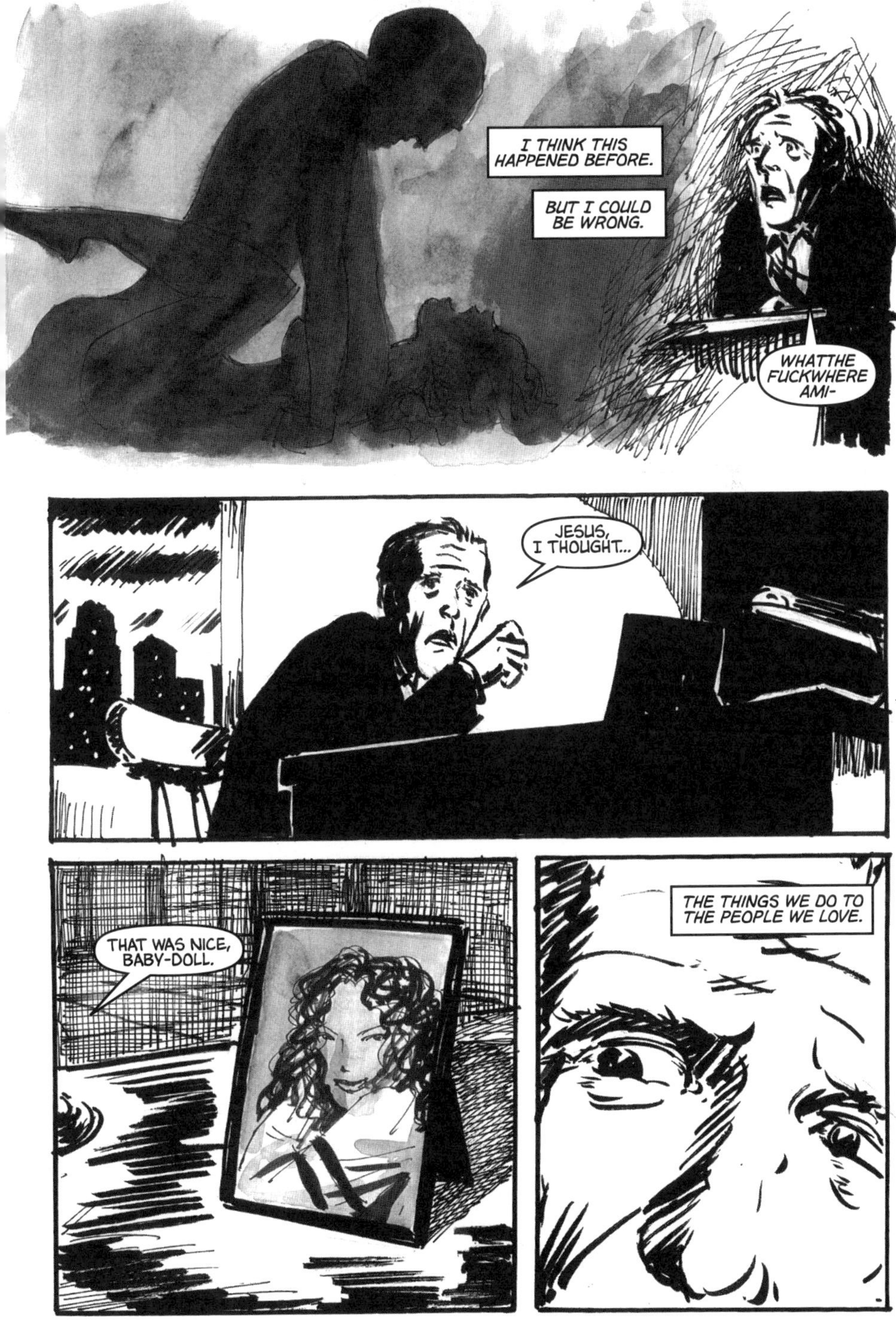
I THINK THIS HAPPENED BEFORE.
BUT I COULD BE WRONG.
WHATTHE FUCKWHERE AMI-
JESUS, I THOUGHT...
THAT WAS NICE, BABY-DOLL.
THE THINGS WE DO TO THE PEOPLE WE LOVE.

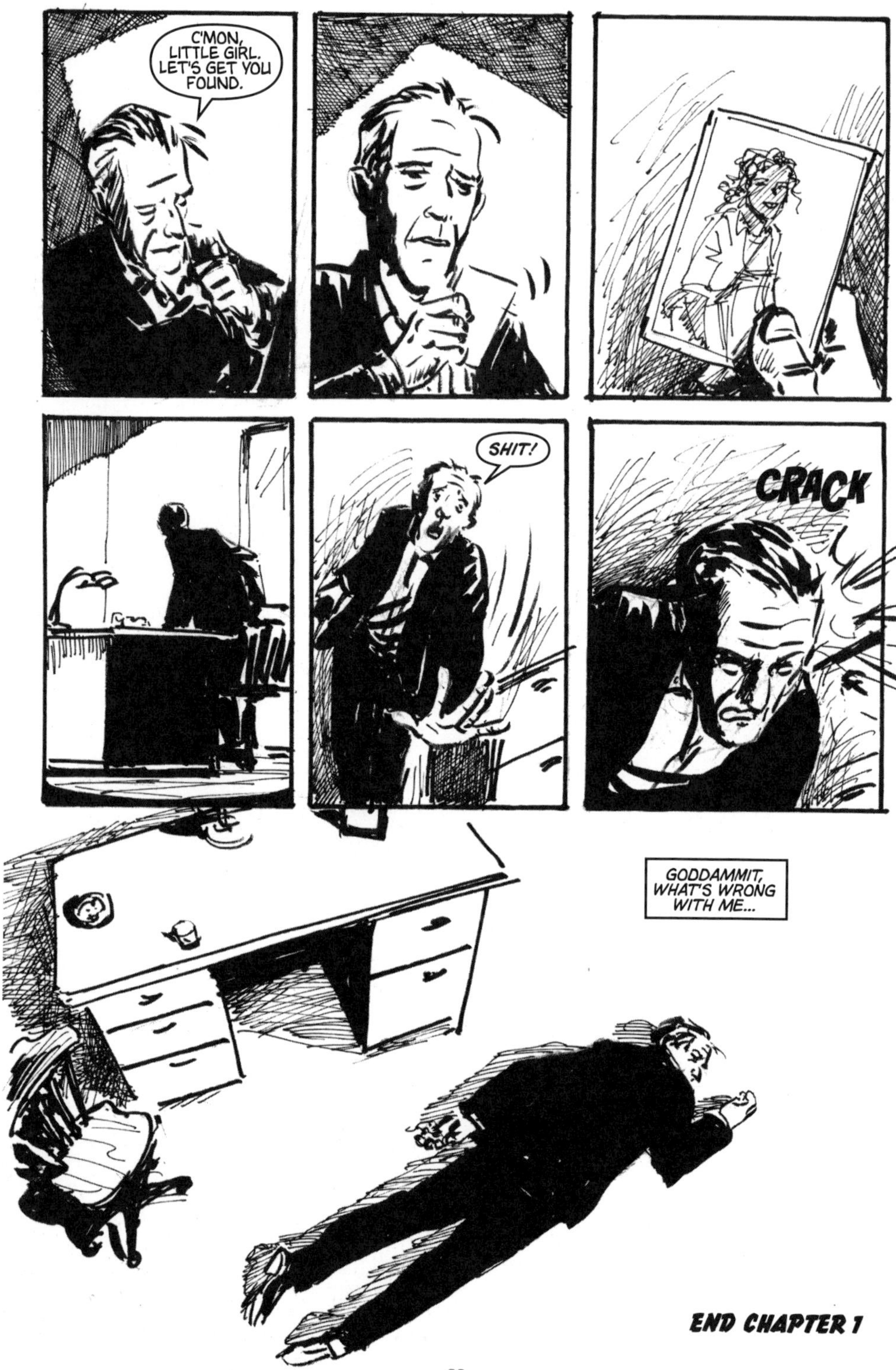
C'MON, LITTLE GIRL. LET'S GET YOU FOUND.
SHIT!
CRACK
GODDAMMIT, WHAT'S WRONG WITH ME...
END CHAPTER 1

TWO

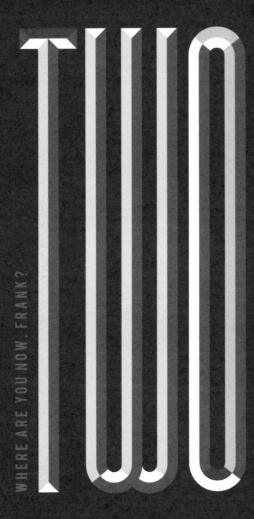

WHERE ARE YOU NOW, FRANK?

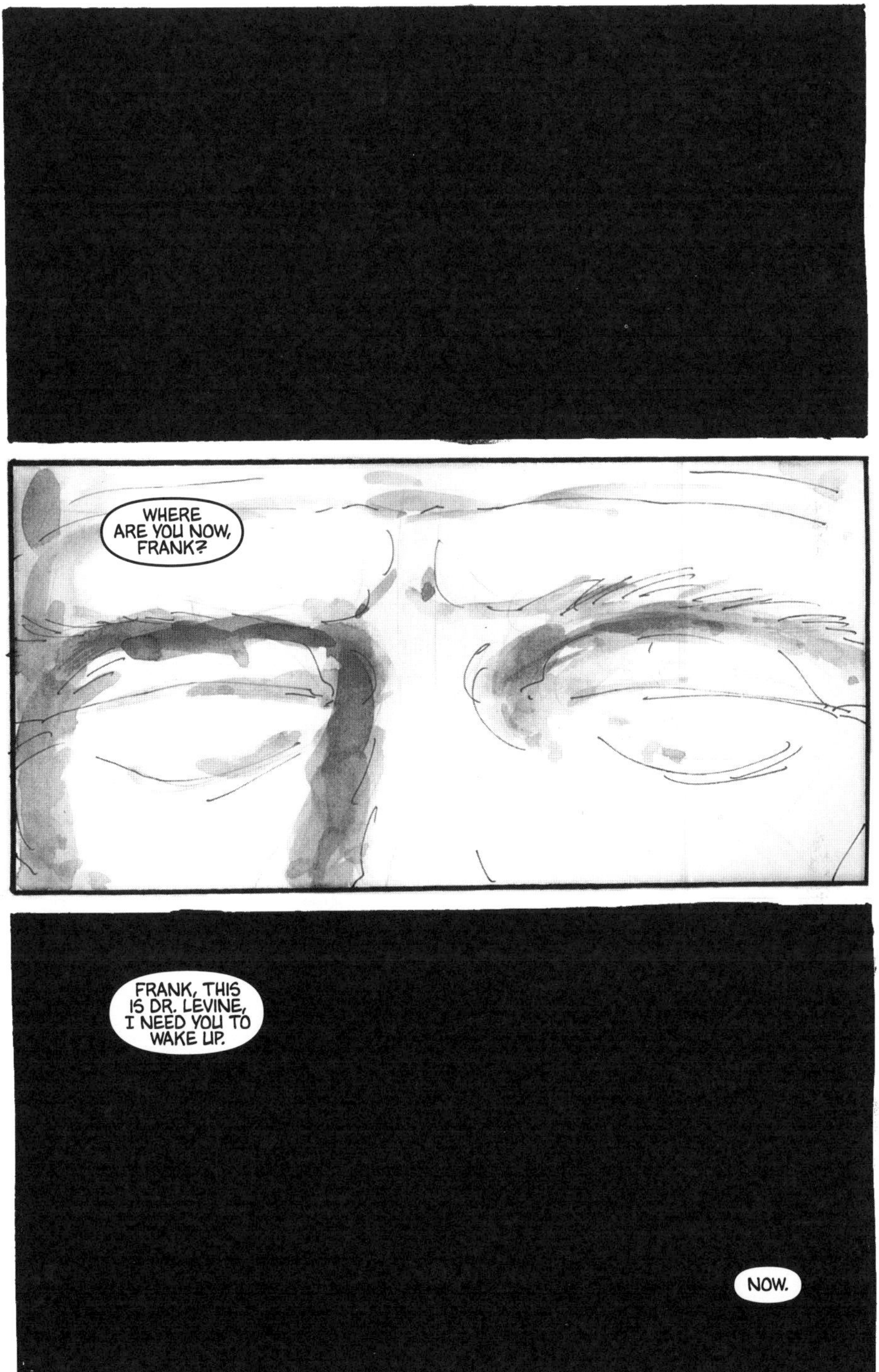
WHERE ARE YOU NOW, FRANK?
FRANK, THIS IS DR. LEVINE, I NEED YOU TO WAKE UP.
NOW.

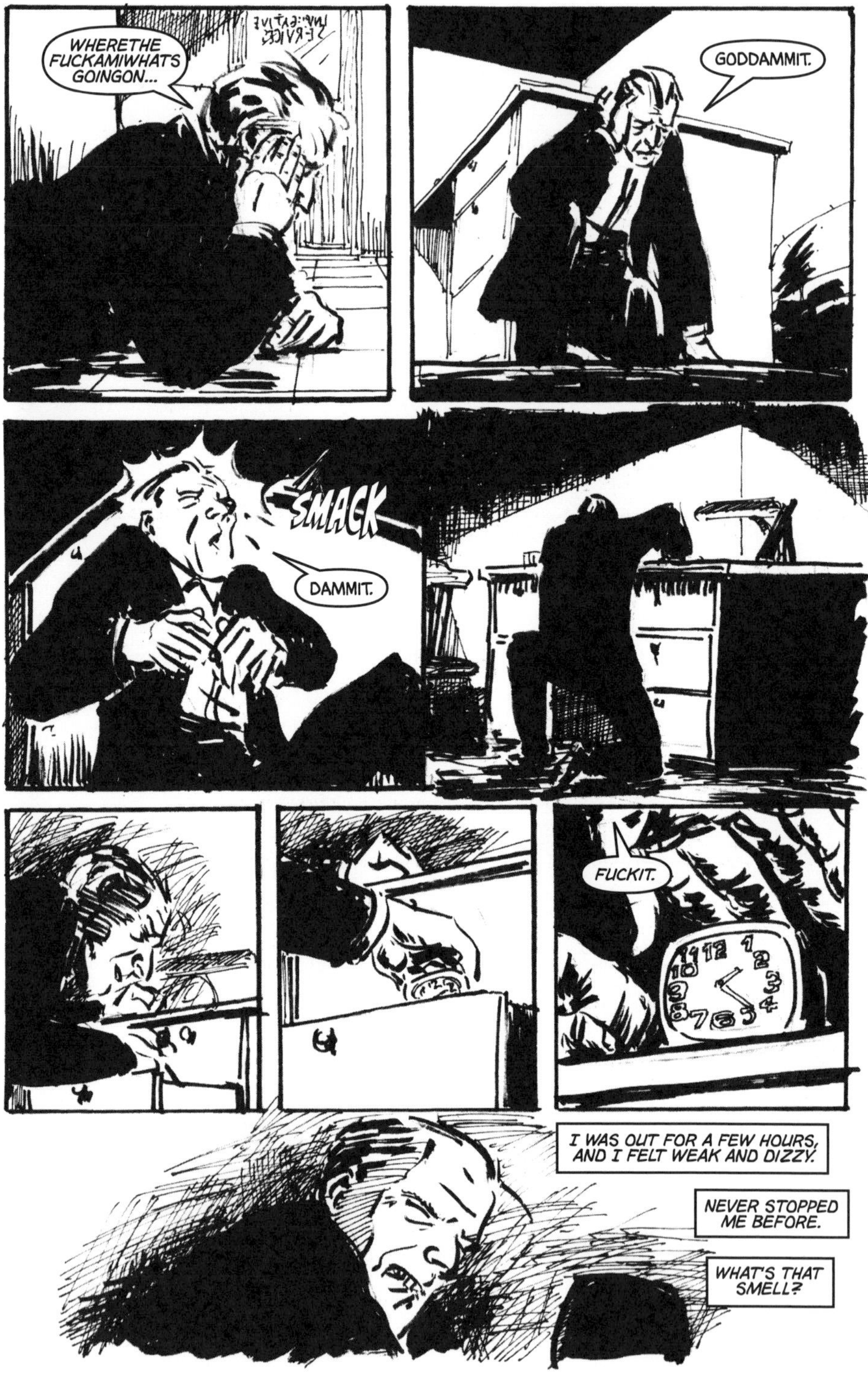
WHERETHE FUCKAMIWHATS GOINGON...
GODDAMMIT.
SMACK
DAMMIT.
FUCKIT.
I WAS OUT FOR A FEW HOURS, AND I FELT WEAK AND DIZZY.
NEVER STOPPED ME BEFORE.
WHAT'S THAT SMELL?

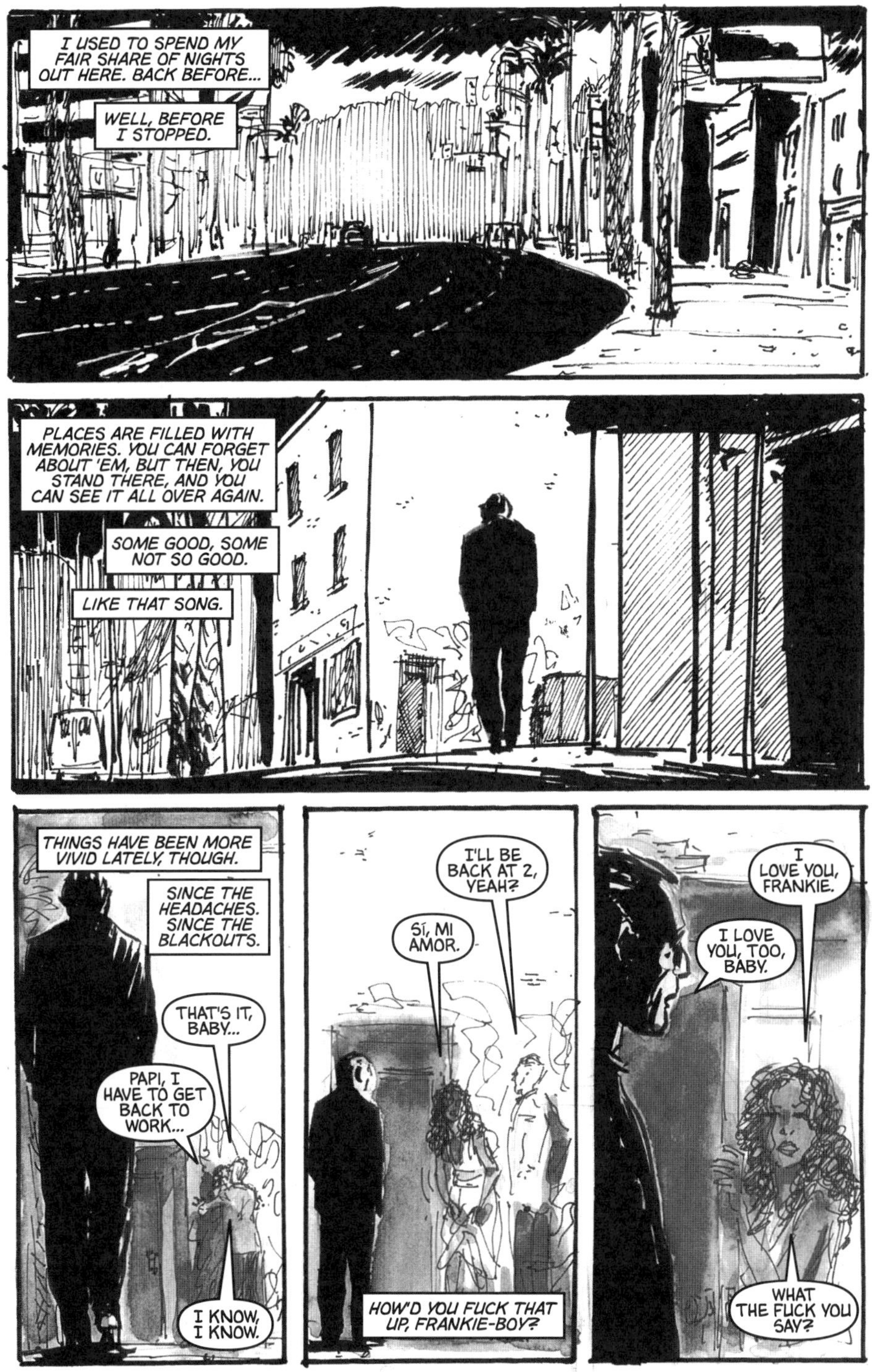
I USED TO SPEND MY FAIR SHARE OF NIGHTS OUT HERE. BACK BEFORE...
WELL, BEFORE I STOPPED.
PLACES ARE FILLED WITH MEMORIES. YOU CAN FORGET ABOUT 'EM, BUT THEN, YOU STAND THERE, AND YOU CAN SEE IT ALL OVER AGAIN.
SOME GOOD, SOME NOT SO GOOD.
LIKE THAT SONG.
THINGS HAVE BEEN MORE VIVID LATELY, THOUGH.
SINCE THE HEADACHES. SINCE THE BLACKOUTS.
THAT'S IT, BABY...
PAPI, I HAVE TO GET BACK TO WORK...
I KNOW, I KNOW.
I'LL BE BACK AT 2, YEAH?
SÍ, MI AMOR.
HOW'D YOU FUCK THAT UP, FRANKIE-BOY?
I LOVE YOU, FRANKIE.
I LOVE YOU, TOO, BABY.
WHAT THE FUCK YOU SAY?

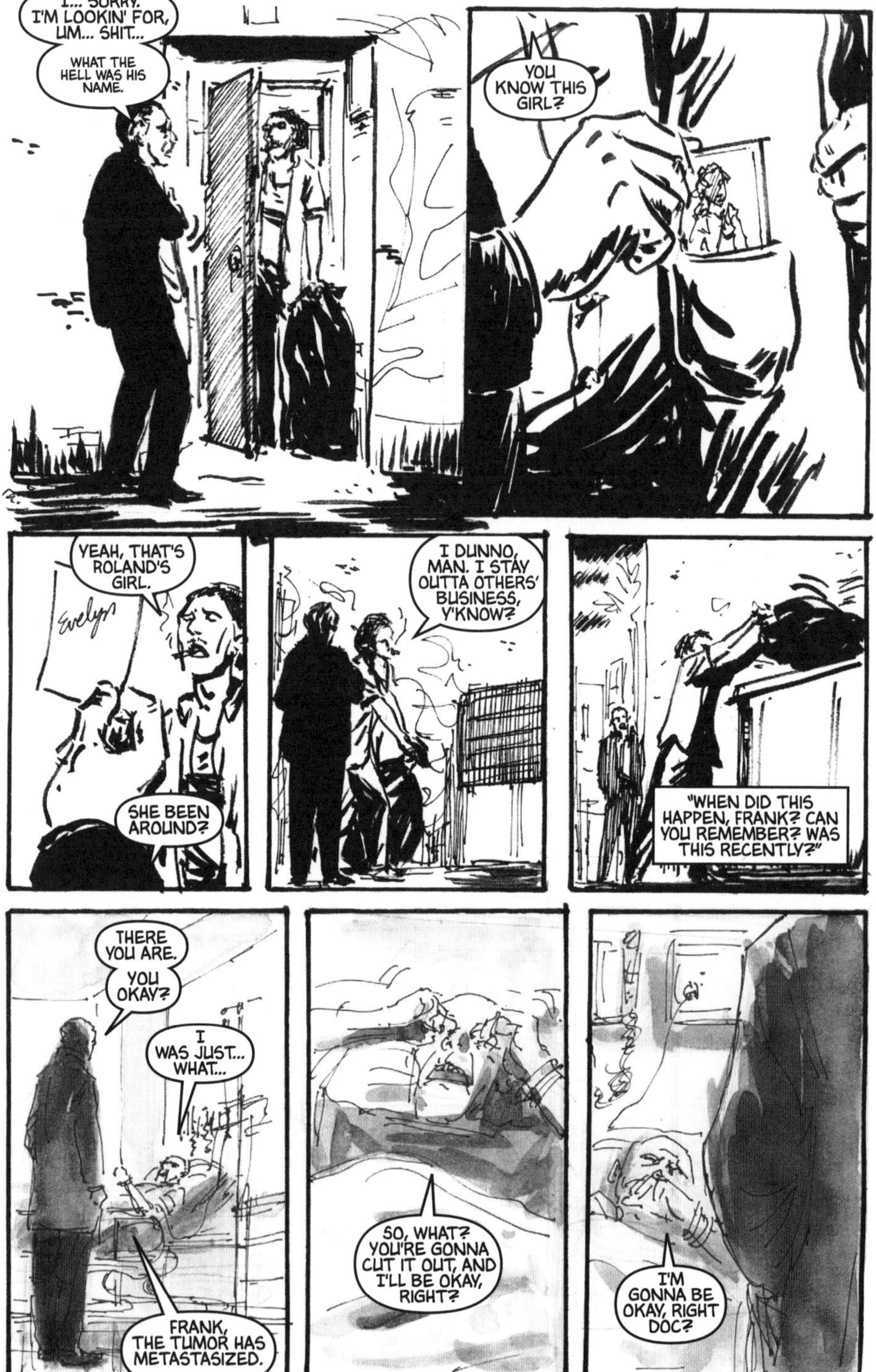

I... SORRY. I'M LOOKIN' FOR, UM... SHIT...
WHAT THE HELL WAS HIS NAME.
YOU KNOW THIS GIRL?
YEAH, THAT'S ROLAND'S GIRL.
Evelyn
SHE BEEN AROUND?
I DUNNO, MAN. I STAY OUTTA OTHERS' BUSINESS, Y'KNOW?
"WHEN DID THIS HAPPEN, FRANK? CAN YOU REMEMBER? WAS THIS RECENTLY?"
THERE YOU ARE.
YOU OKAY?
I WAS JUST... WHAT...
FRANK, THE TUMOR HAS METASTASIZED.
SO, WHAT? YOU'RE GONNA CUT IT OUT, AND I'LL BE OKAY, RIGHT?
I'M GONNA BE OKAY, RIGHT DOC?

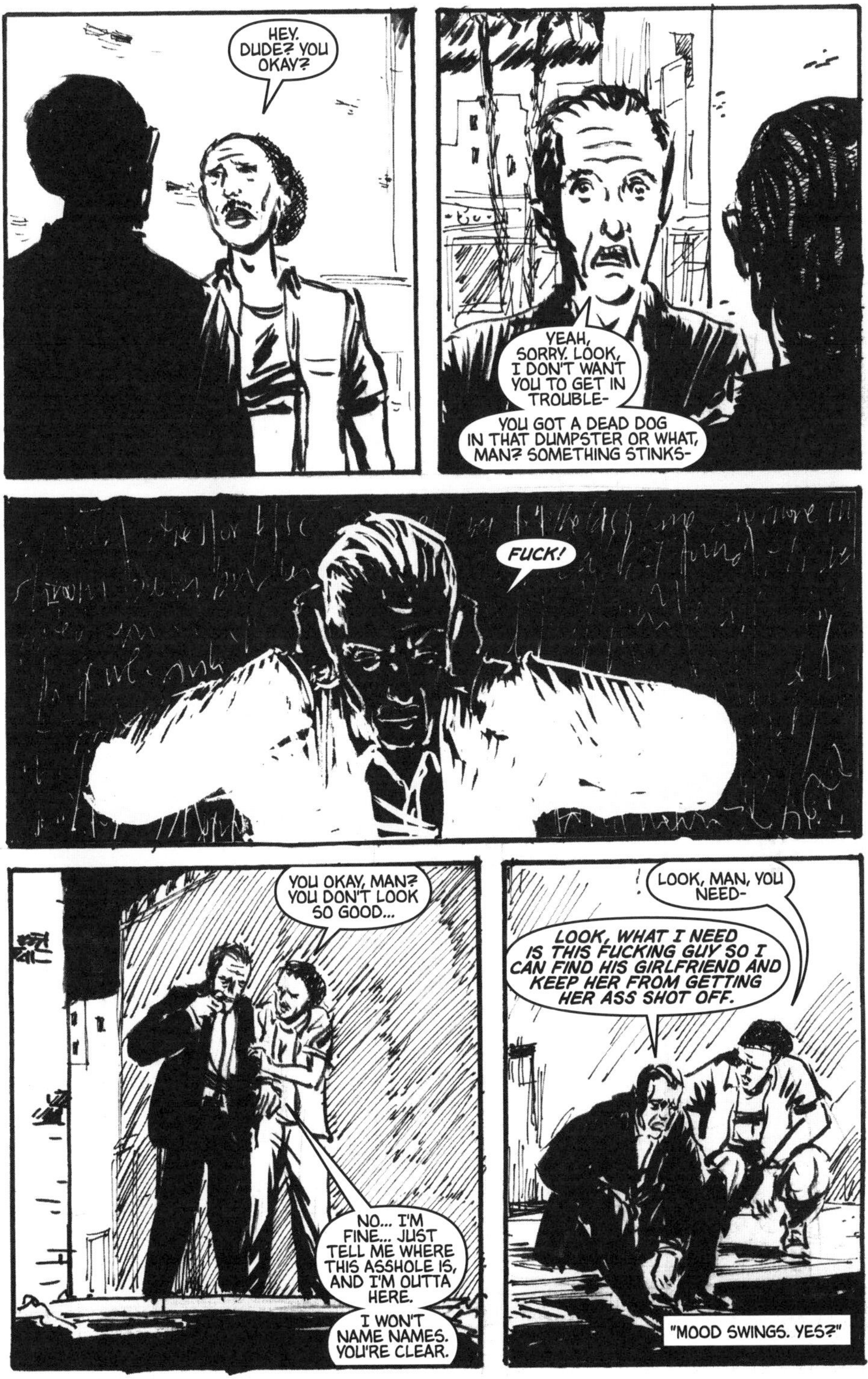
HEY. DUDE? YOU OKAY?
YEAH, SORRY. LOOK, I DON'T WANT YOU TO GET IN TROUBLE-
YOU GOT A DEAD DOG IN THAT DUMPSTER OR WHAT, MAN? SOMETHING STINKS-
FUCK!
YOU OKAY, MAN? YOU DON'T LOOK SO GOOD...
NO... I'M FINE... JUST TELL ME WHERE THIS ASSHOLE IS, AND I'M OUTTA HERE.
I WON'T NAME NAMES. YOU'RE CLEAR.
LOOK, MAN, YOU NEED-
LOOK, WHAT I NEED IS THIS FUCKING GUY SO I CAN FIND HIS GIRLFRIEND AND KEEP HER FROM GETTING HER ASS SHOT OFF.
"MOOD SWINGS. YES?"

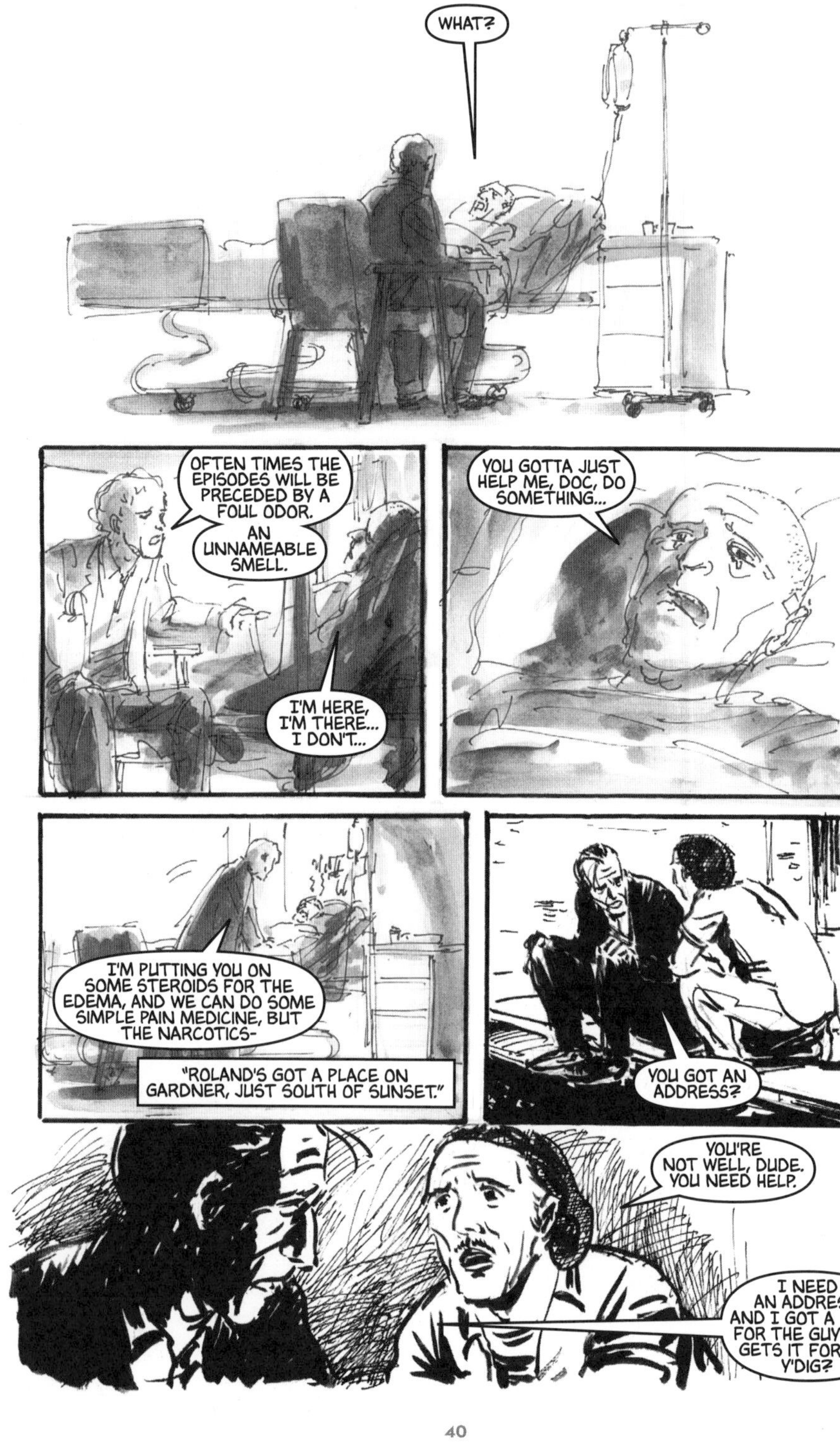
WHAT?
OFTEN TIMES THE EPISODES WILL BE PRECEDED BY A FOUL ODOR.
AN UNNAMEABLE SMELL.
I'M HERE, I'M THERE... I DON'T...
YOU GOTTA JUST HELP ME, DOC, DO SOMETHING...
I'M PUTTING YOU ON SOME STEROIDS FOR THE EDEMA, AND WE CAN DO SOME SIMPLE PAIN MEDICINE, BUT THE NARCOTICS-
"ROLAND'S GOT A PLACE ON GARDNER, JUST SOUTH OF SUNSET."
YOU GOT AN ADDRESS?
YOU'RE NOT WELL, DUDE. YOU NEED HELP.
I NEED AN ADDRESS, AND I GOT A FIFTY FOR THE GUY WHO GETS IT FOR ME. Y'DIG?

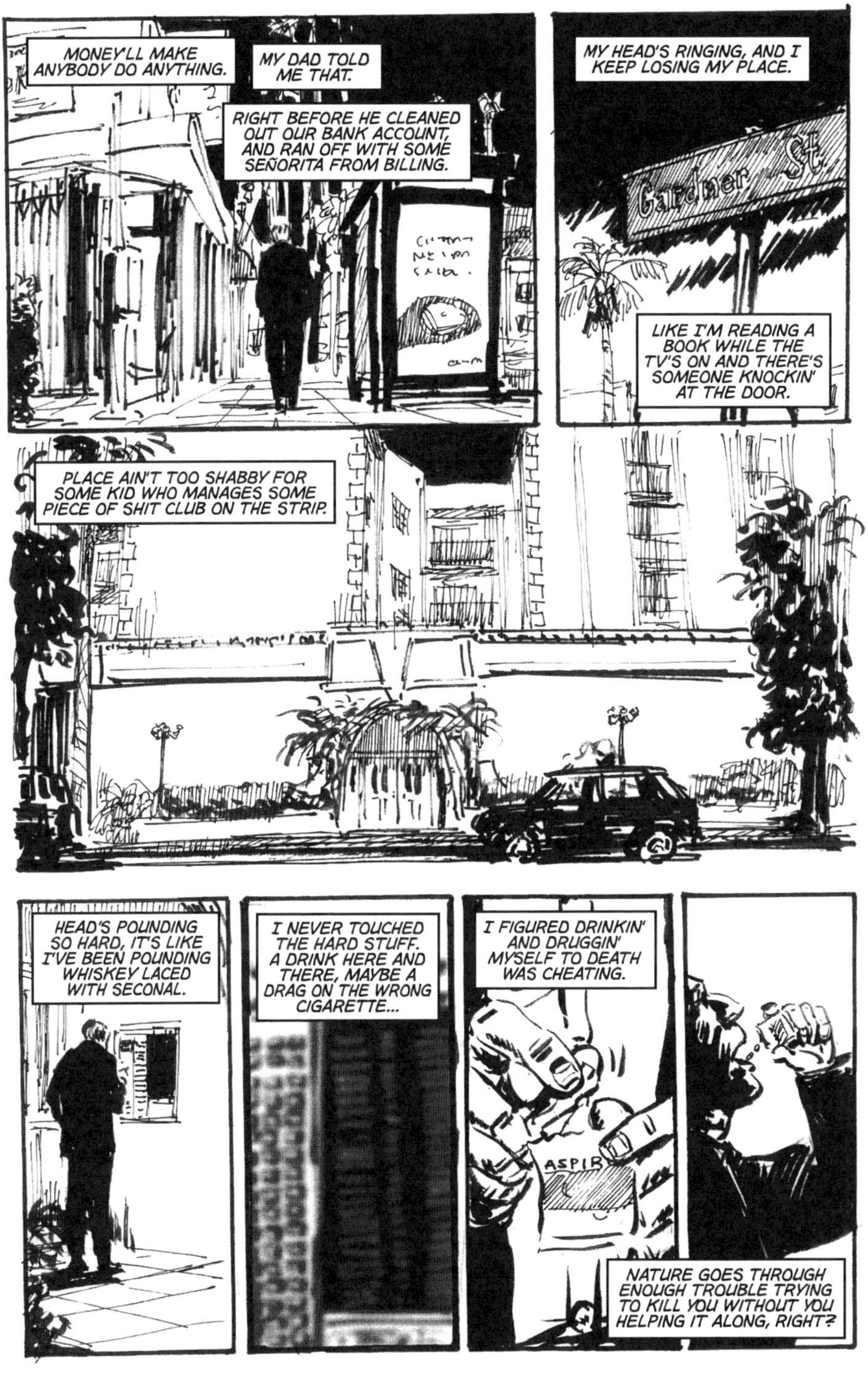
MONEY'LL MAKE ANYBODY DO ANYTHING.
MY DAD TOLD ME THAT.
RIGHT BEFORE HE CLEANED OUT OUR BANK ACCOUNT, AND RAN OFF WITH SOME SEÑORITA FROM BILLING.
MY HEAD'S RINGING, AND I KEEP LOSING MY PLACE.
Gardner St
LIKE I'M READING A BOOK WHILE THE TV'S ON AND THERE'S SOMEONE KNOCKIN' AT THE DOOR.
PLACE AIN'T TOO SHABBY FOR SOME KID WHO MANAGES SOME PIECE OF SHIT CLUB ON THE STRIP.
HEAD'S POUNDING SO HARD, IT'S LIKE I'VE BEEN POUNDING WHISKEY LACED WITH SECONAL.
I NEVER TOUCHED THE HARD STUFF. A DRINK HERE AND THERE, MAYBE A DRAG ON THE WRONG CIGARETTE...
I FIGURED DRINKIN' AND DRUGGIN' MYSELF TO DEATH WAS CHEATING.
ASPIR
NATURE GOES THROUGH ENOUGH TROUBLE TRYING TO KILL YOU WITHOUT YOU HELPING IT ALONG, RIGHT?

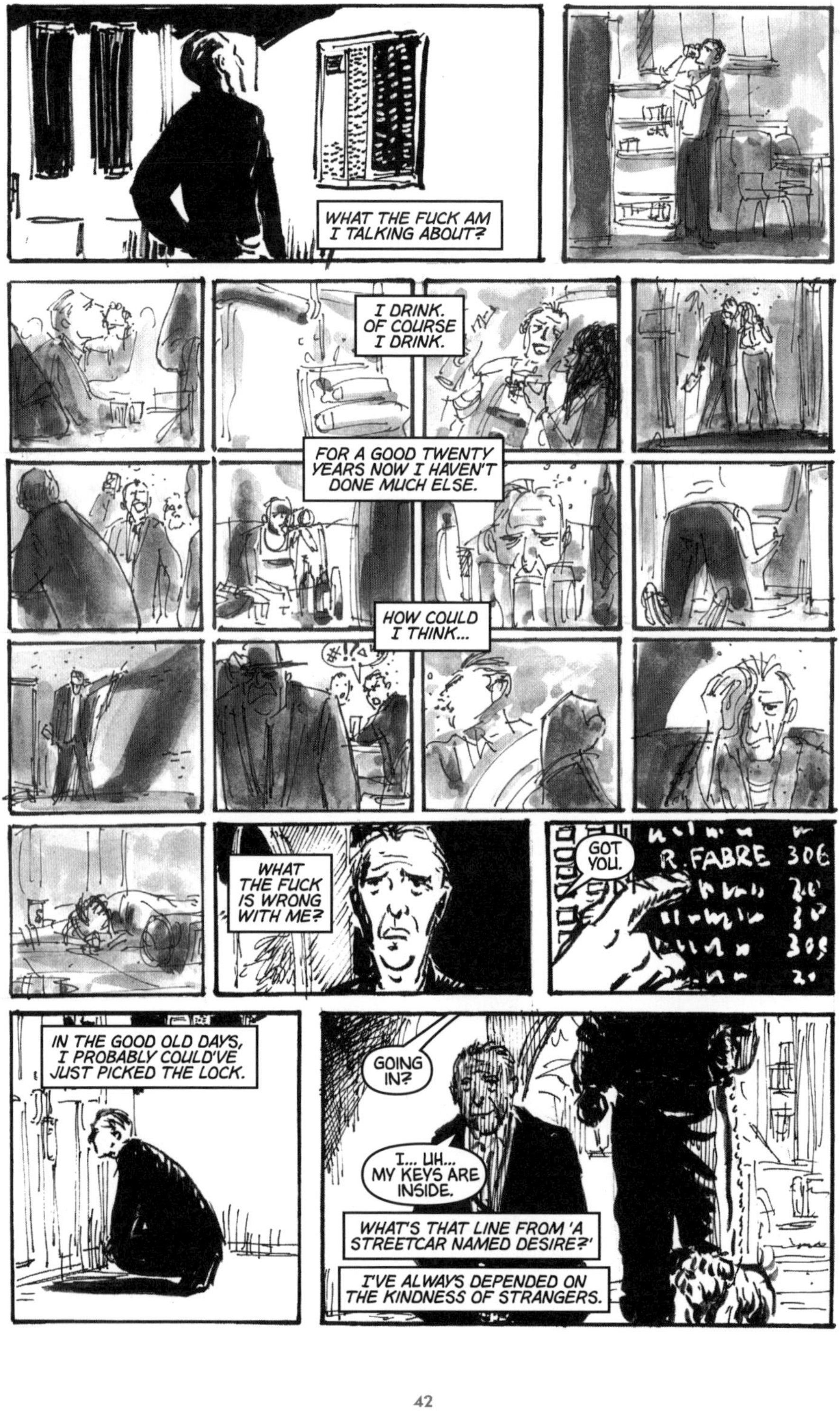

WHAT THE FUCK AM I TALKING ABOUT?
I DRINK. OF COURSE I DRINK.
FOR A GOOD TWENTY YEARS NOW I HAVEN'T DONE MUCH ELSE.
HOW COULD I THINK...
WHAT THE FUCK IS WRONG WITH ME?
GOT YOU.
R. FABRE 306
IN THE GOOD OLD DAYS, I PROBABLY COULD'VE JUST PICKED THE LOCK.
GOING IN?
I... UH... MY KEYS ARE INSIDE.
WHAT'S THAT LINE FROM 'A STREETCAR NAMED DESIRE?'
I'VE ALWAYS DEPENDED ON THE KINDNESS OF STRANGERS.

I'MDONEI'MDONEI'MDONE I'MDONEI'MDONETAKEI'M DONETAKEI'MDONE- FUUUUCK
HE'S SEIZING AGAIN! GET ME 10 C.C.'S OF DIAZEPAM!
I'MDONE I'MDONEI'MDONE I'MDONEI'MDONETAKE I'MDONETAKE I'MDONE I'MDONEI'MDONE-
MY FATHER WAS A DOCTOR.
CAME OVER FROM RUSSIA WHEN HE WAS A KID, AND HIS FOLKS PUSHED HIM TO BE SOMETHING.
I SUPPOSE HE RESENTED IT, 'CAUSE THE GUY BARELY TOOK A LICK OF INTEREST IN ME.
NOT THAT I BLAME HIM.
ANYWAY, I USED TO PLAY FOOTBALL. AND I WAS OKAY AT IT.
NOT GREAT. NOT LYNN SWANN, BUT NOT ALEX HAWKINS, EITHER.

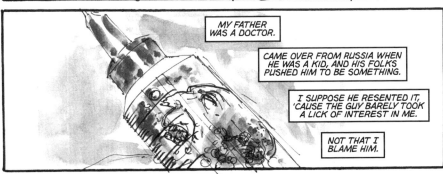

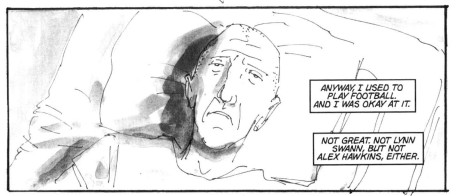

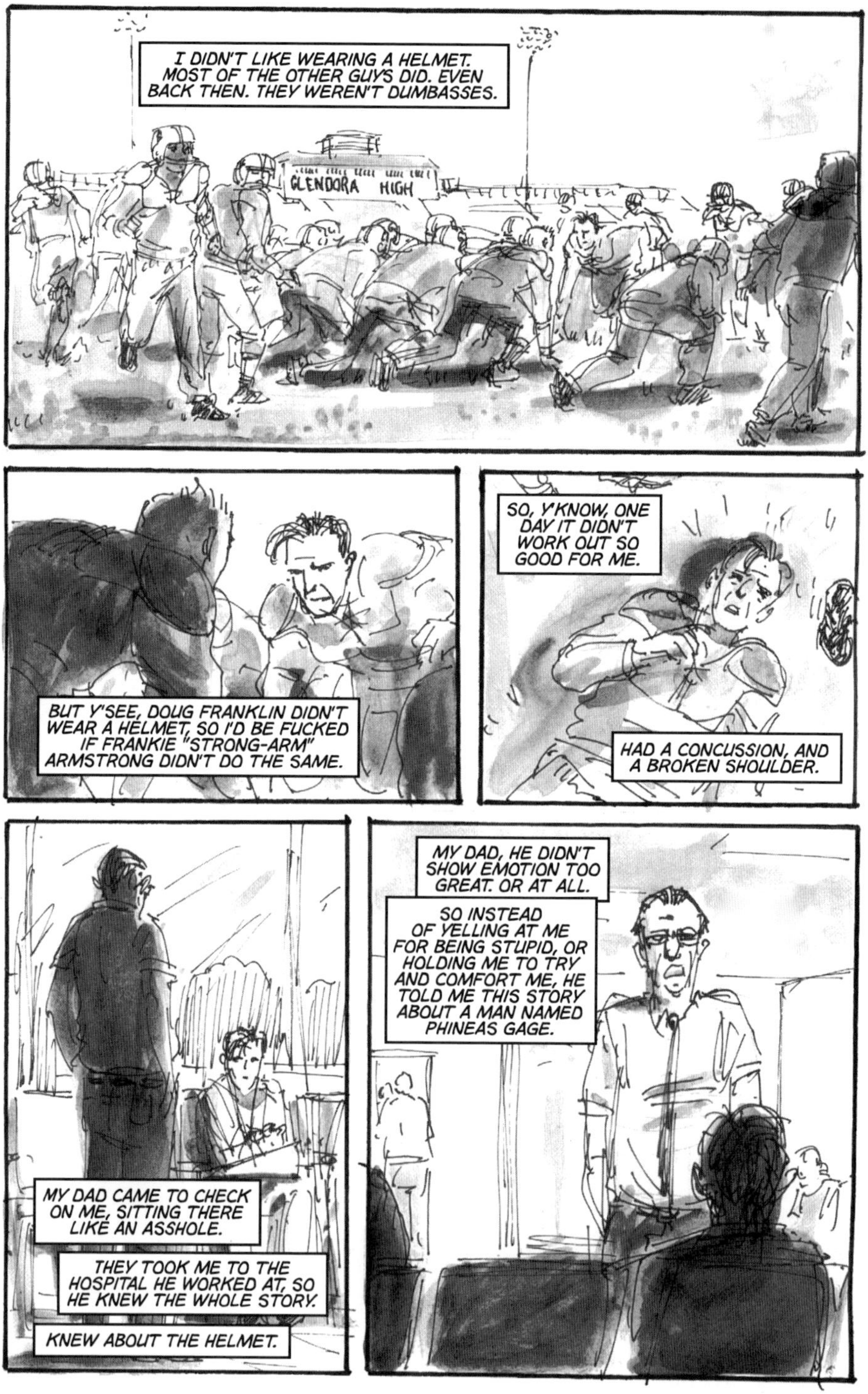
I DIDN'T LIKE WEARING A HELMET. MOST OF THE OTHER GUYS DID. EVEN BACK THEN. THEY WEREN'T DUMBASSES.
GLENDORA HIGH
BUT Y'SEE, DOUG FRANKLIN DIDN'T WEAR A HELMET, SO I'D BE FUCKED IF FRANKIE "STRONG-ARM" ARMSTRONG DIDN'T DO THE SAME.
SO, Y'KNOW, ONE DAY IT DIDN'T WORK OUT SO GOOD FOR ME.
HAD A CONCUSSION, AND A BROKEN SHOULDER.
MY DAD CAME TO CHECK ON ME, SITTING THERE LIKE AN ASSHOLE.
THEY TOOK ME TO THE HOSPITAL HE WORKED AT, SO HE KNEW THE WHOLE STORY.
KNEW ABOUT THE HELMET.
MY DAD, HE DIDN'T SHOW EMOTION TOO GREAT. OR AT ALL.
SO INSTEAD OF YELLING AT ME FOR BEING STUPID, OR HOLDING ME TO TRY AND COMFORT ME, HE TOLD ME THIS STORY ABOUT A MAN NAMED PHINEAS GAGE.

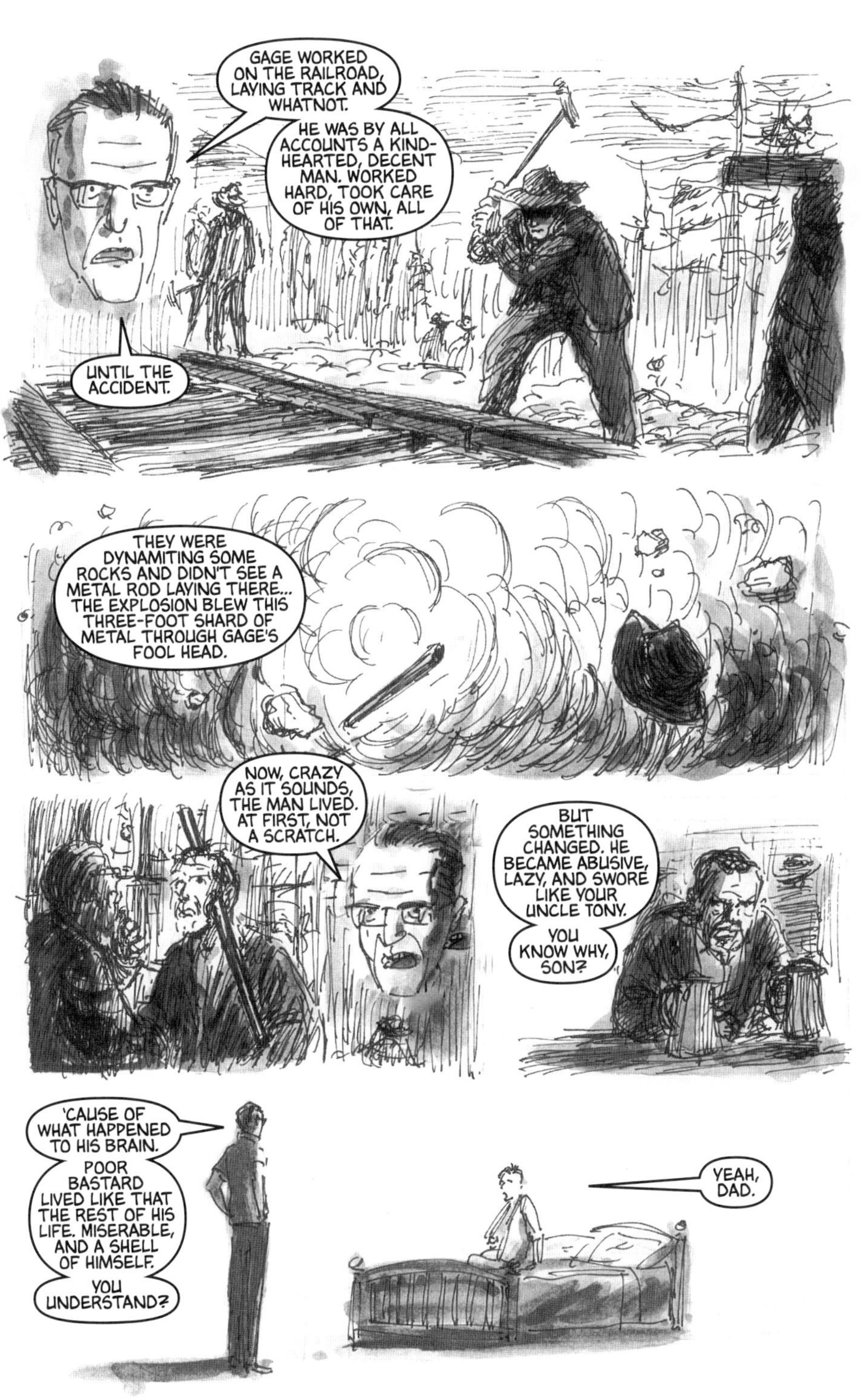
GAGE WORKED ON THE RAILROAD, LAYING TRACK AND WHATNOT.
HE WAS BY ALL ACCOUNTS A KIND-HEARTED, DECENT MAN. WORKED HARD, TOOK CARE OF HIS OWN, ALL OF THAT.
UNTIL THE ACCIDENT.
THEY WERE DYNAMITING SOME ROCKS AND DIDN'T SEE A METAL ROD LAYING THERE... THE EXPLOSION BLEW THIS THREE-FOOT SHARD OF METAL THROUGH GAGE'S FOOL HEAD.
NOW, CRAZY AS IT SOUNDS, THE MAN LIVED. AT FIRST, NOT A SCRATCH.
BUT SOMETHING CHANGED. HE BECAME ABUSIVE, LAZY, AND SWORE LIKE YOUR UNCLE TONY.
YOU KNOW WHY, SON?
'CAUSE OF WHAT HAPPENED TO HIS BRAIN.
POOR BASTARD LIVED LIKE THAT THE REST OF HIS LIFE. MISERABLE, AND A SHELL OF HIMSELF.
YOU UNDERSTAND?
YEAH, DAD.

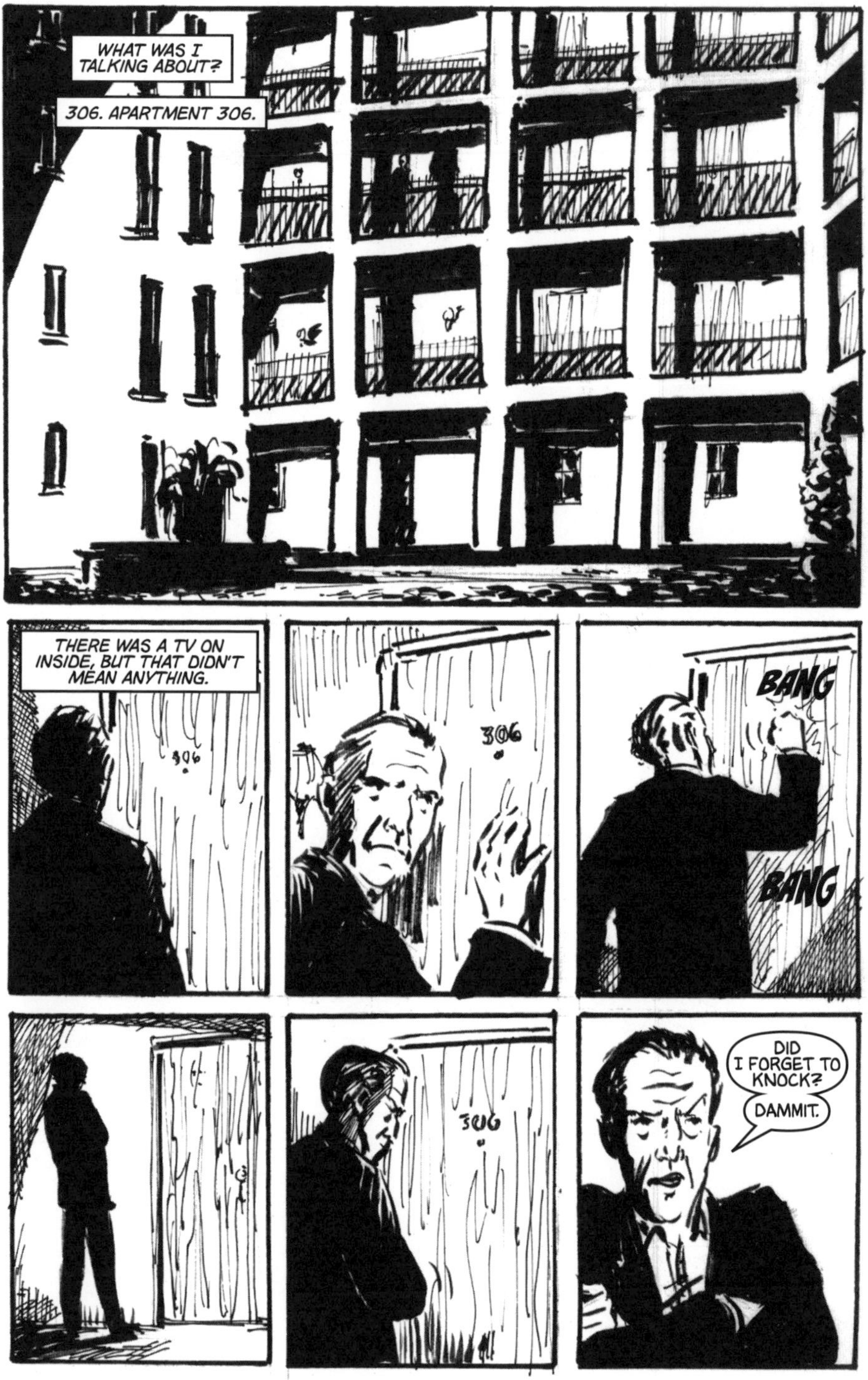
WHAT WAS I TALKING ABOUT?
306. APARTMENT 306.
THERE WAS A TV ON INSIDE, BUT THAT DIDN'T MEAN ANYTHING.
306
306
BANG
BANG
306
DID I FORGET TO KNOCK?
DAMMIT.

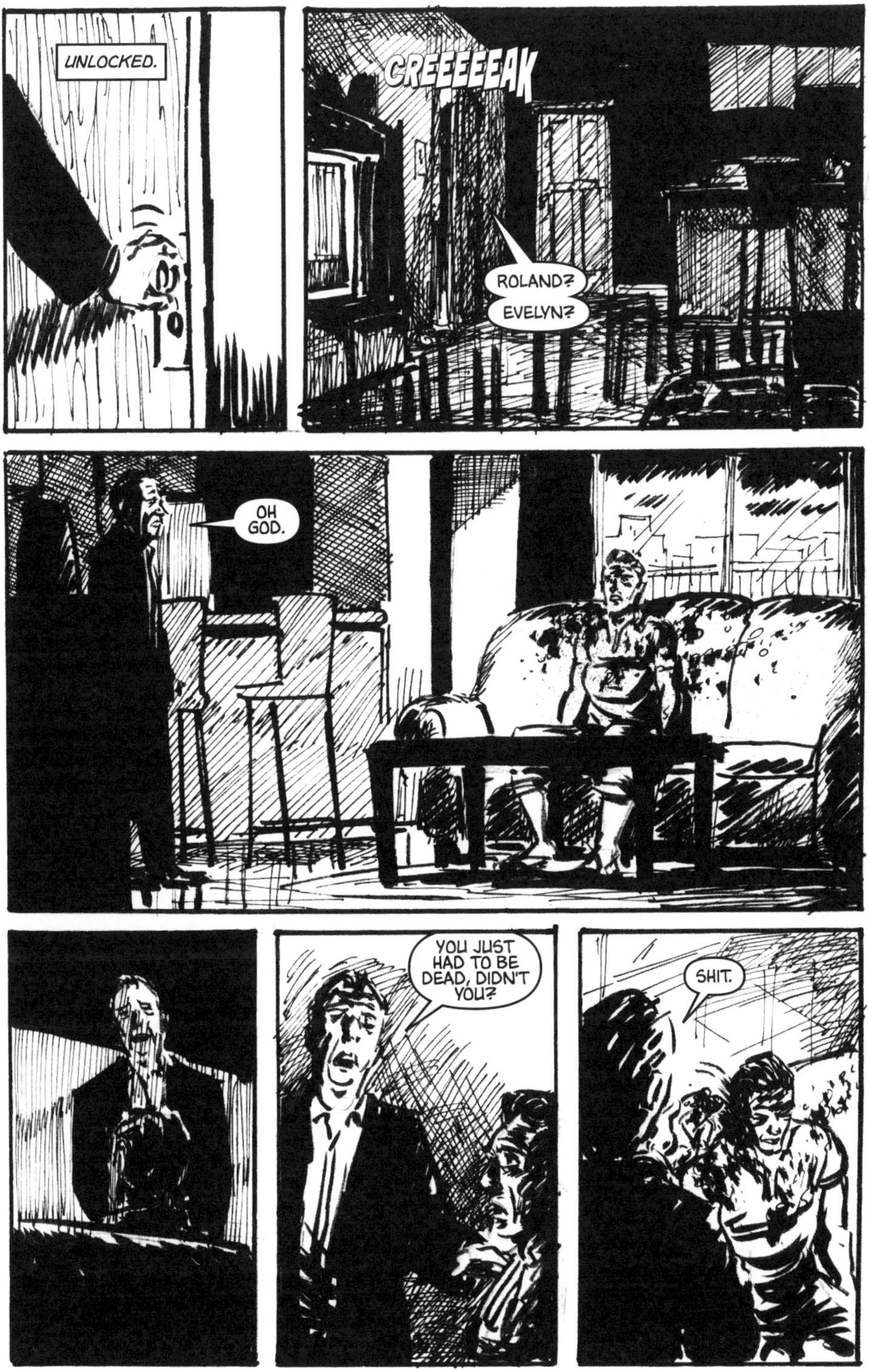
UNLOCKED.
CREEEEEAK
ROLAND?
EVELYN?
OH GOD.
YOU JUST HAD TO BE DEAD, DIDN'T YOU?
SHIT.

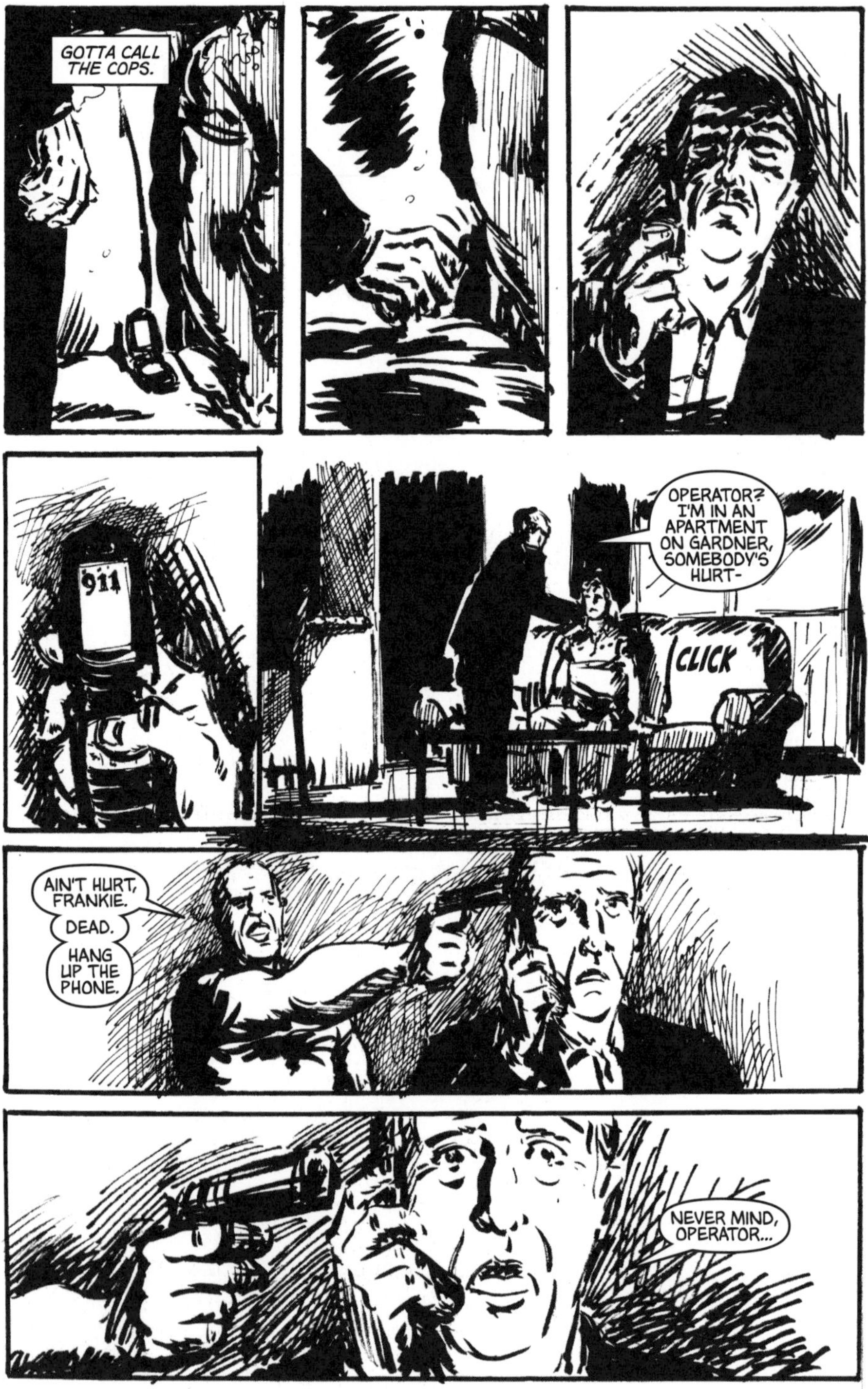
GOTTA CALL THE COPS.
911
OPERATOR? I'M IN AN APARTMENT ON GARDNER, SOMEBODY'S HURT-
CLICK
AIN'T HURT, FRANKIE.
DEAD.
HANG UP THE PHONE.
NEVER MIND, OPERATOR...

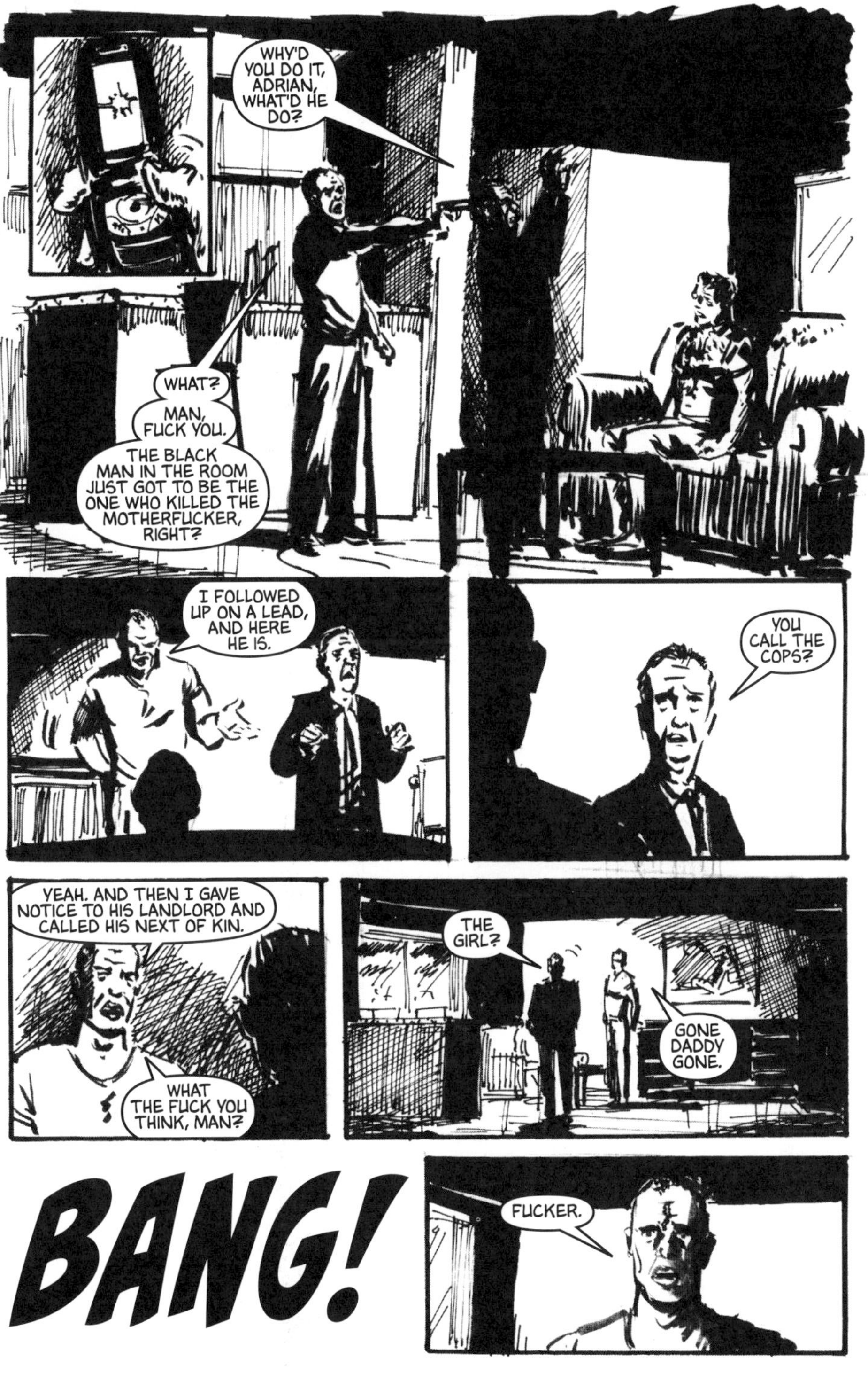
WHY'D YOU DO IT, ADRIAN, WHAT'D HE DO?
WHAT?
MAN, FUCK YOU.
THE BLACK MAN IN THE ROOM JUST GOT TO BE THE ONE WHO KILLED THE MOTHERFUCKER, RIGHT?
I FOLLOWED UP ON A LEAD, AND HERE HE IS.
YOU CALL THE COPS?
YEAH. AND THEN I GAVE NOTICE TO HIS LANDLORD AND CALLED HIS NEXT OF KIN.
WHAT THE FUCK YOU THINK, MAN?
THE GIRL?
GONE DADDY GONE.
BANG!
FUCKER.

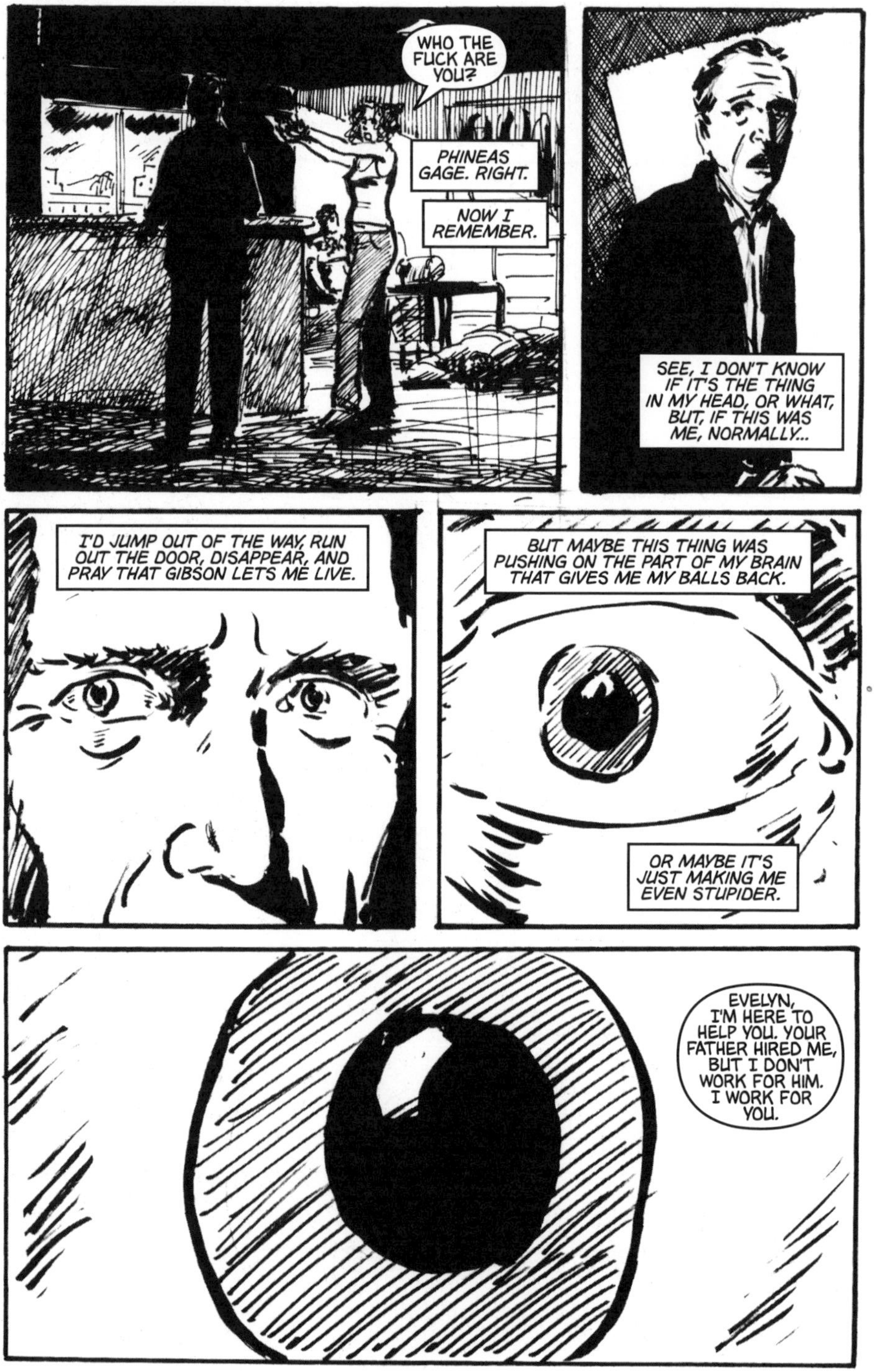
WHO THE FUCK ARE YOU?
PHINEAS GAGE. RIGHT.
NOW I REMEMBER.
SEE, I DON'T KNOW IF IT'S THE THING IN MY HEAD, OR WHAT, BUT, IF THIS WAS ME, NORMALLY...
I'D JUMP OUT OF THE WAY, RUN OUT THE DOOR, DISAPPEAR, AND PRAY THAT GIBSON LETS ME LIVE.
BUT MAYBE THIS THING WAS PUSHING ON THE PART OF MY BRAIN THAT GIVES ME MY BALLS BACK.
OR MAYBE IT'S JUST MAKING ME EVEN STUPIDER.
EVELYN, I'M HERE TO HELP YOU. YOUR FATHER HIRED ME, BUT I DON'T WORK FOR HIM. I WORK FOR YOU.

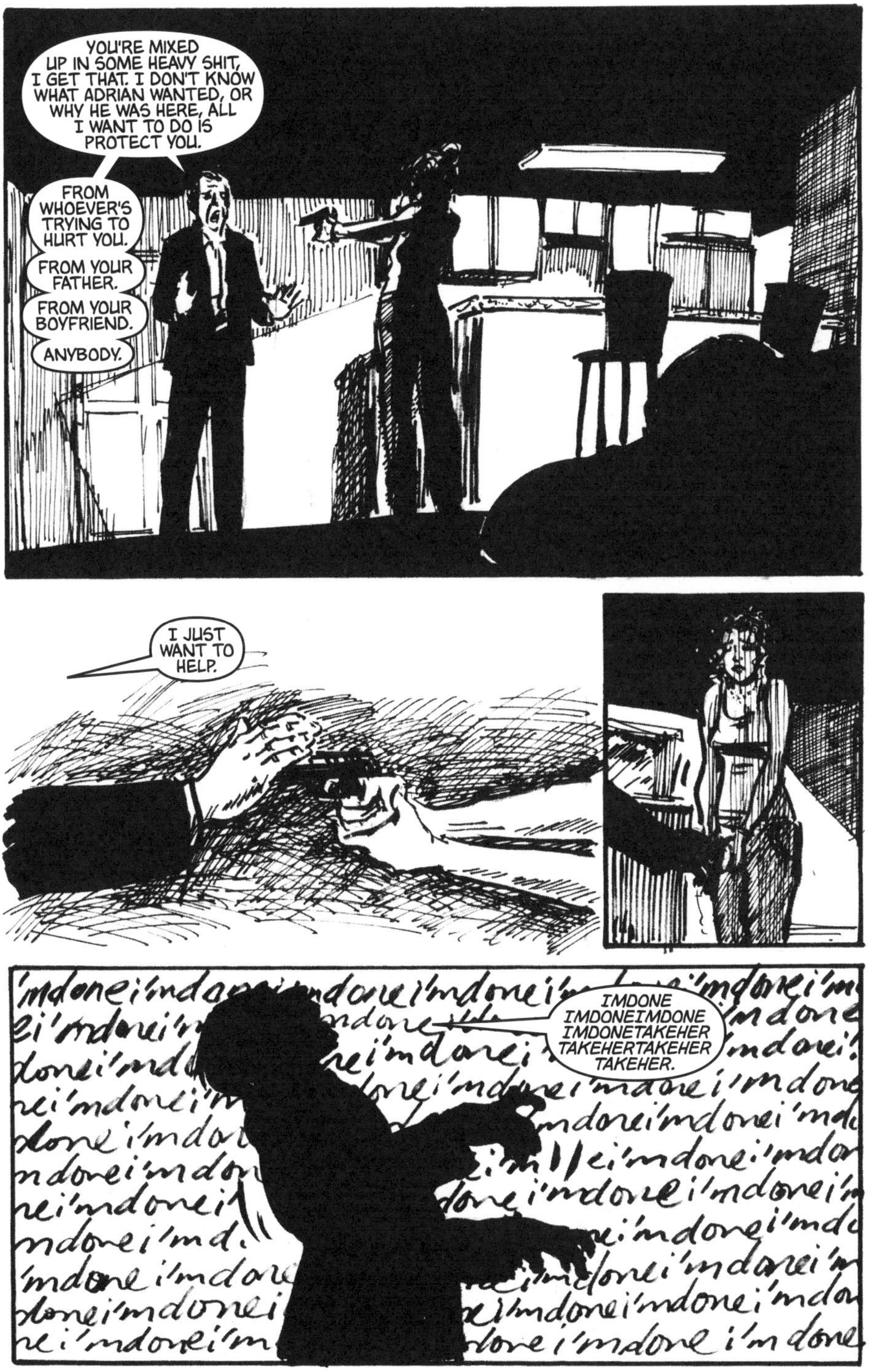
YOU'RE MIXED UP IN SOME HEAVY SHIT, I GET THAT. I DON'T KNOW WHAT ADRIAN WANTED, OR WHY HE WAS HERE, ALL I WANT TO DO IS PROTECT YOU.
FROM WHOEVER'S TRYING TO HURT YOU.
FROM YOUR FATHER.
FROM YOUR BOYFRIEND.
ANYBODY.
I JUST WANT TO HELP.
IMDONE IMDONEIMDONE IMDONETAKEHER TAKEHERTAKEHER TAKEHER.

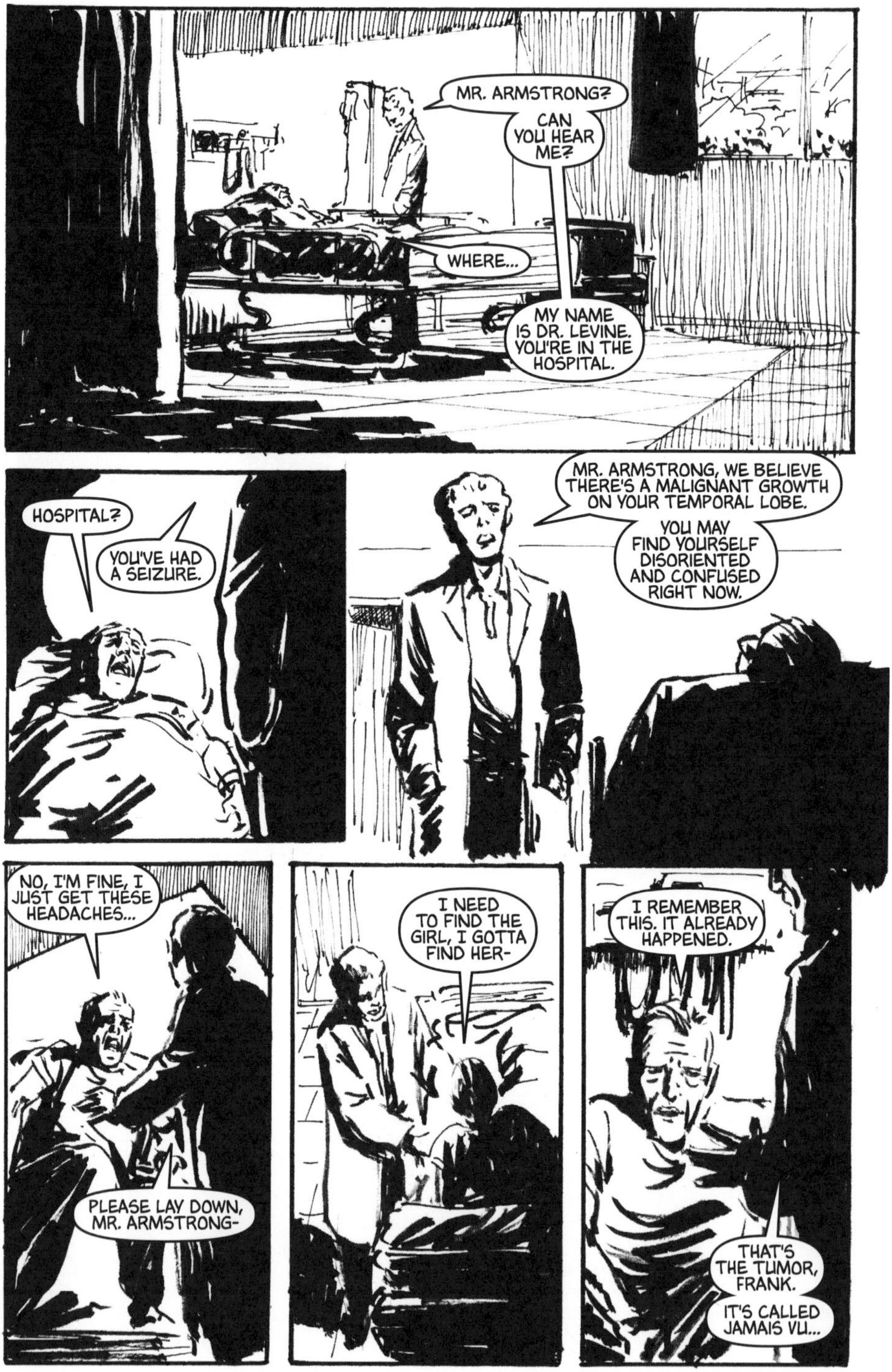
MR. ARMSTRONG?
CAN YOU HEAR ME?
WHERE...
MY NAME IS DR. LEVINE. YOU'RE IN THE HOSPITAL.
HOSPITAL?
YOU'VE HAD A SEIZURE.
MR. ARMSTRONG, WE BELIEVE THERE'S A MALIGNANT GROWTH ON YOUR TEMPORAL LOBE.
YOU MAY FIND YOURSELF DISORIENTED AND CONFUSED RIGHT NOW.
NO, I'M FINE, I JUST GET THESE HEADACHES...
PLEASE LAY DOWN, MR. ARMSTRONG-
I NEED TO FIND THE GIRL, I GOTTA FIND HER-
I REMEMBER THIS. IT ALREADY HAPPENED.
THAT'S THE TUMOR, FRANK.
IT'S CALLED JAMAIS VU...

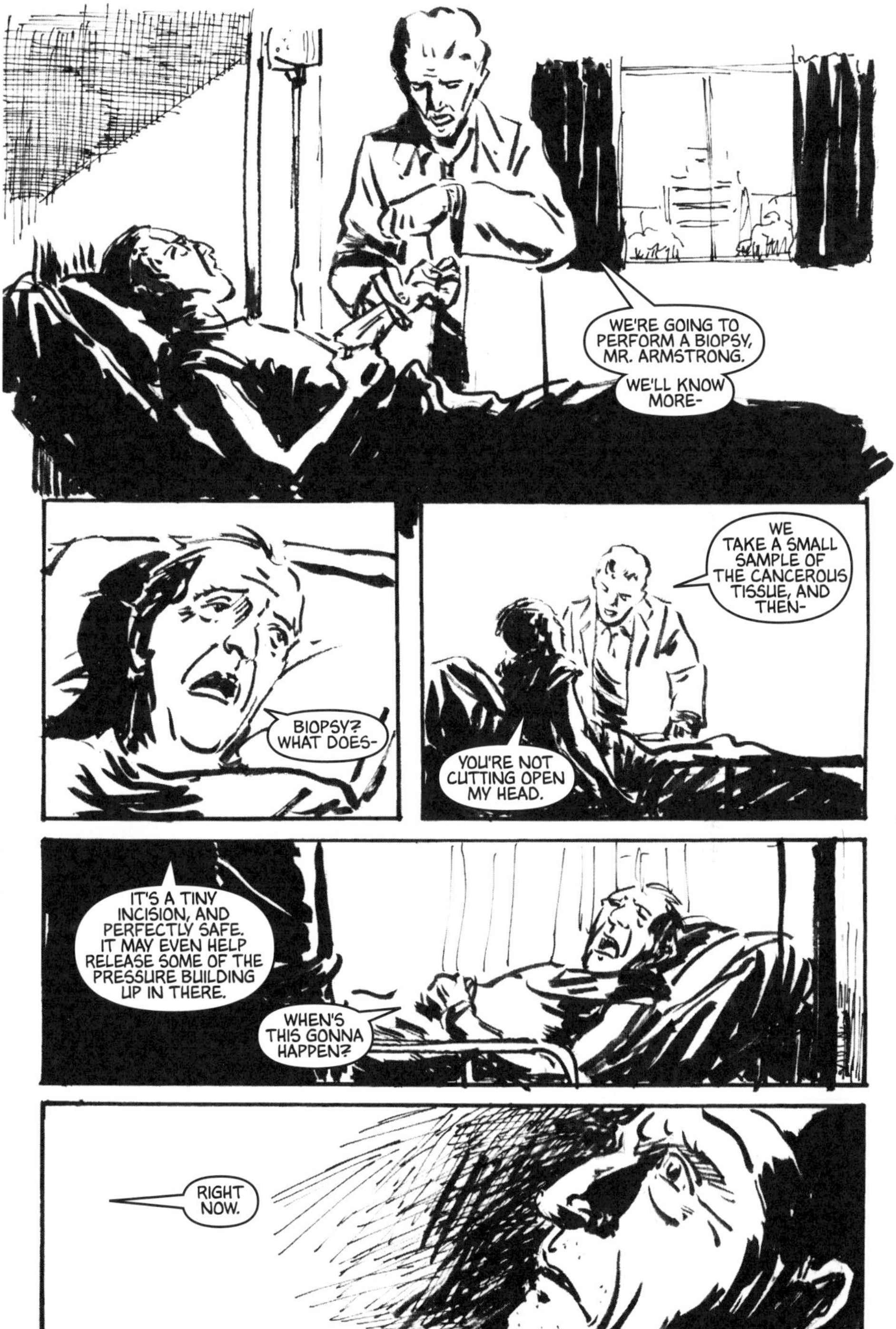

WE'RE GOING TO PERFORM A BIOPSY, MR. ARMSTRONG.
WE'LL KNOW MORE-
BIOPSY? WHAT DOES-
WE TAKE A SMALL SAMPLE OF THE CANCEROUS TISSUE, AND THEN-
YOU'RE NOT CUTTING OPEN MY HEAD.
IT'S A TINY INCISION, AND PERFECTLY SAFE. IT MAY EVEN HELP RELEASE SOME OF THE PRESSURE BUILDING UP IN THERE.
WHEN'S THIS GONNA HAPPEN?
RIGHT NOW.

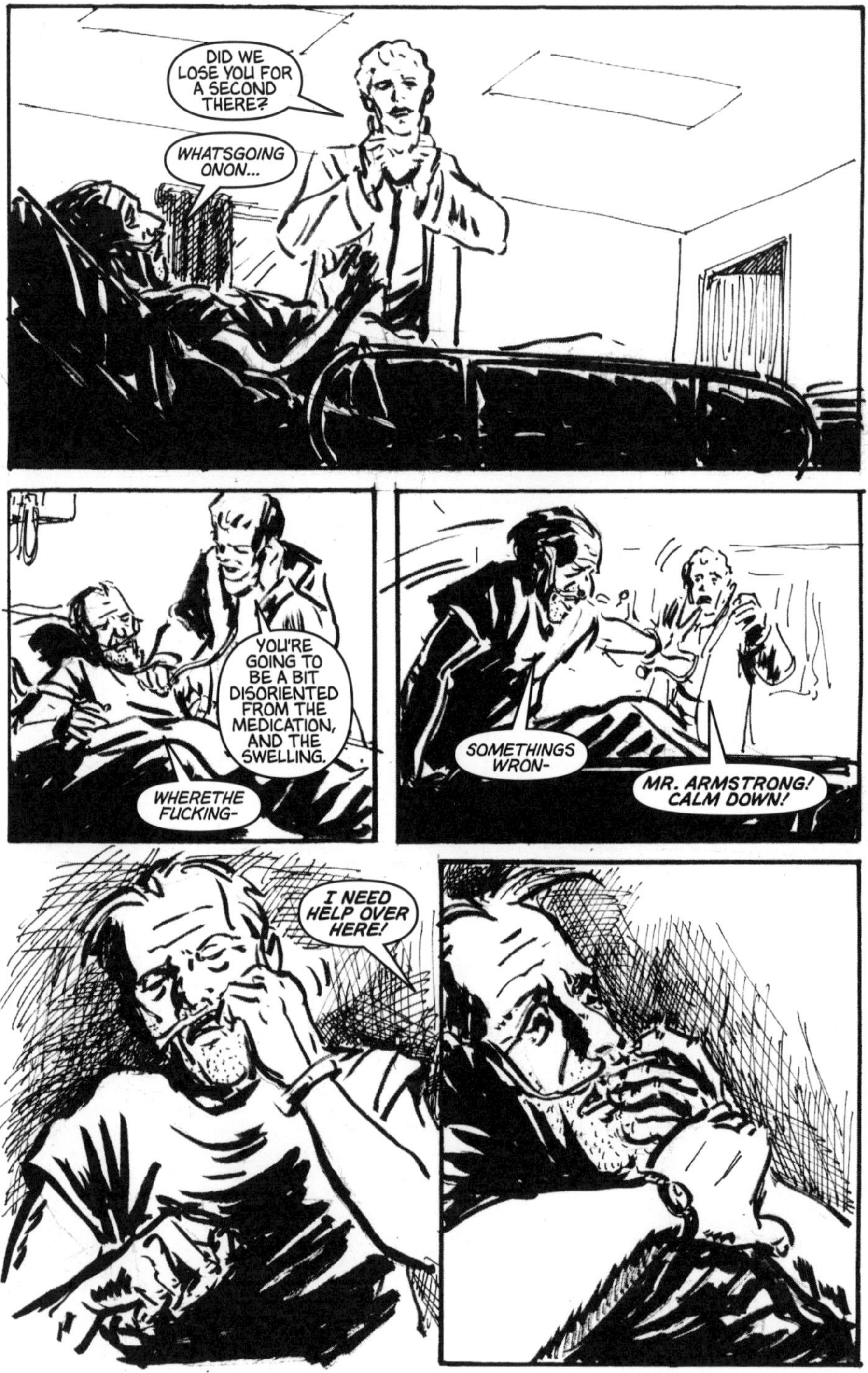
DID WE LOSE YOU FOR A SECOND THERE?
WHATSGOING ONON...
YOU'RE GOING TO BE A BIT DISORIENTED FROM THE MEDICATION, AND THE SWELLING.
WHERETHE FUCKING-
SOMETHINGS WRON-
MR. ARMSTRONG! CALM DOWN!
I NEED HELP OVER HERE!

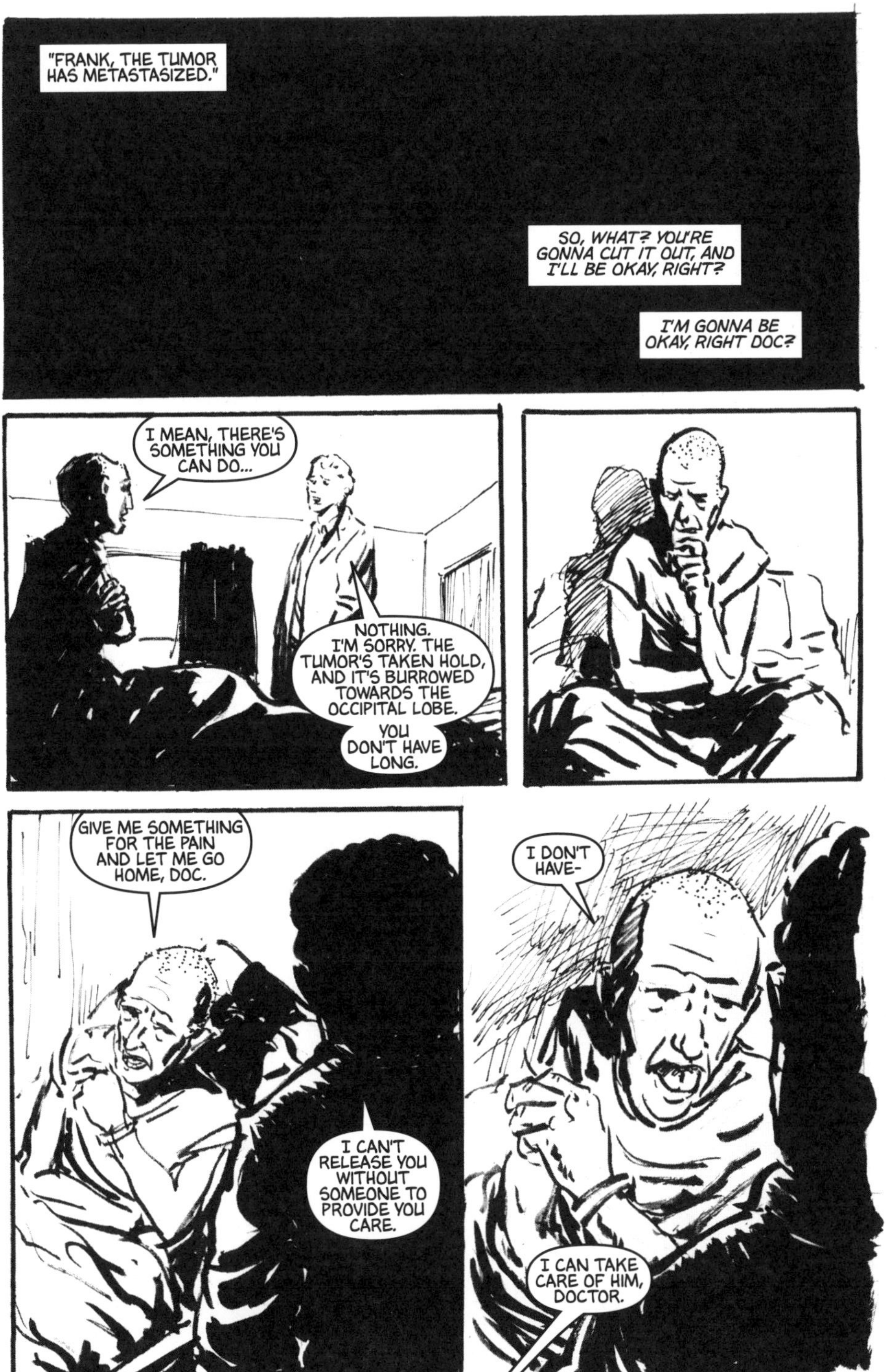
"FRANK, THE TUMOR HAS METASTASIZED."
SO, WHAT? YOU'RE GONNA CUT IT OUT, AND I'LL BE OKAY, RIGHT?
I'M GONNA BE OKAY, RIGHT DOC?
I MEAN, THERE'S SOMETHING YOU CAN DO...
NOTHING. I'M SORRY. THE TUMOR'S TAKEN HOLD, AND IT'S BURROWED TOWARDS THE OCCIPITAL LOBE.
YOU DON'T HAVE LONG.
GIVE ME SOMETHING FOR THE PAIN AND LET ME GO HOME, DOC.
I CAN'T RELEASE YOU WITHOUT SOMEONE TO PROVIDE YOU CARE.
I DON'T HAVE-
I CAN TAKE CARE OF HIM, DOCTOR.

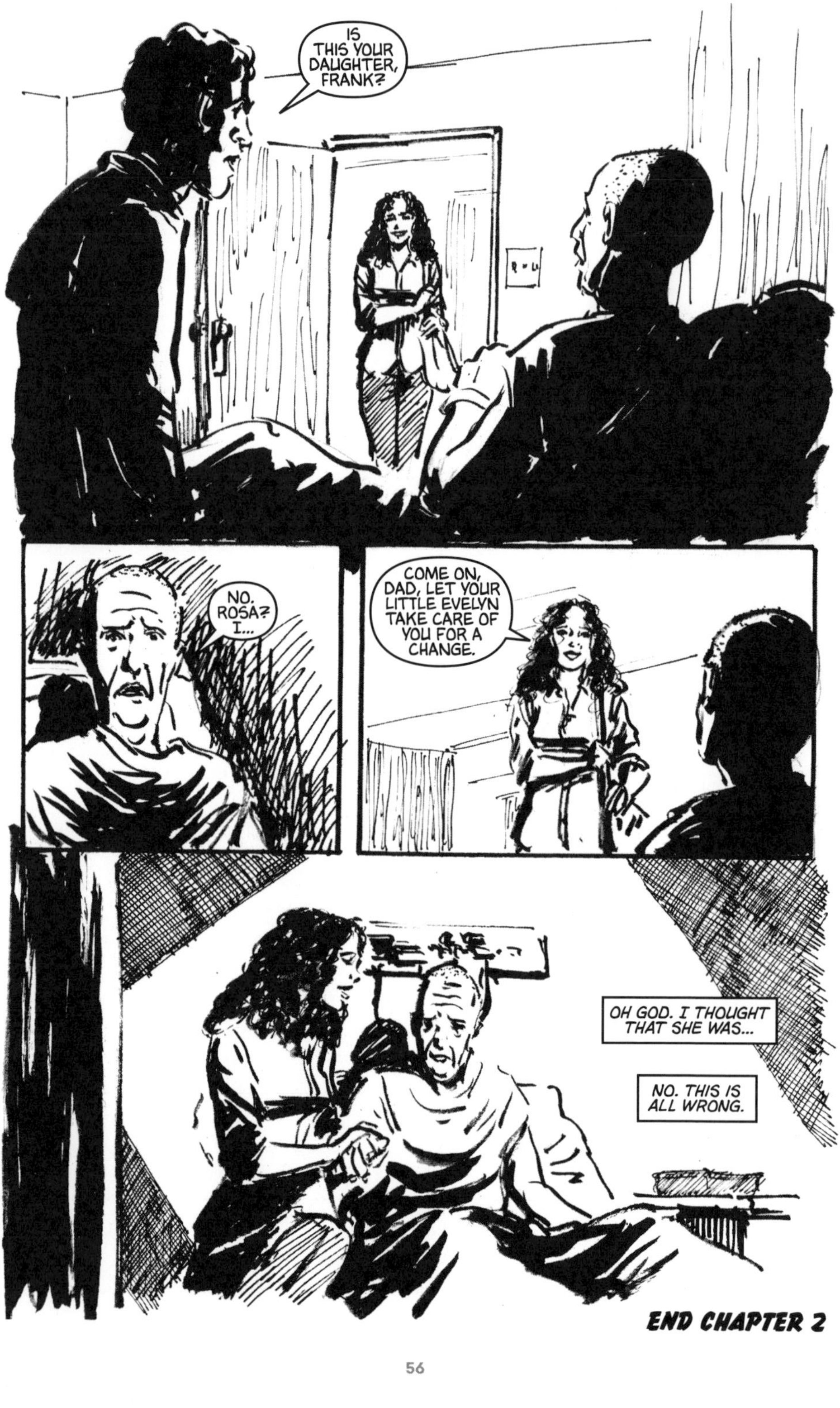
IS THIS YOUR DAUGHTER, FRANK?
NO. ROSA? I...
COME ON, DAD, LET YOUR LITTLE EVELYN TAKE CARE OF YOU FOR A CHANGE.
OH GOD. I THOUGHT THAT SHE WAS...
NO. THIS IS ALL WRONG.

END CHAPTER 2

THREE

OFF TO THE RACES

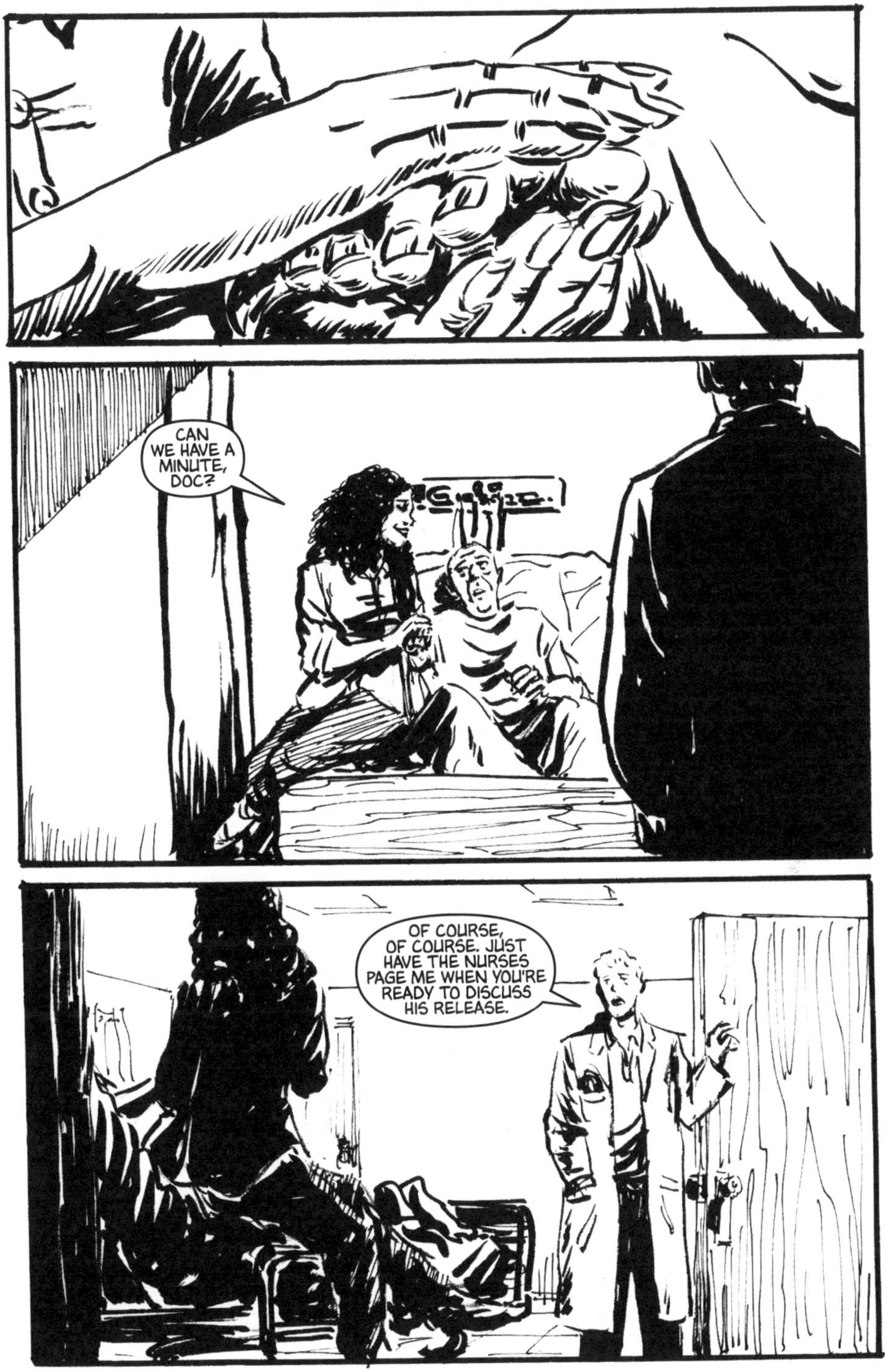
CAN WE HAVE A MINUTE, DOC?
OF COURSE, OF COURSE. JUST HAVE THE NURSES PAGE ME WHEN YOU'RE READY TO DISCUSS HIS RELEASE.

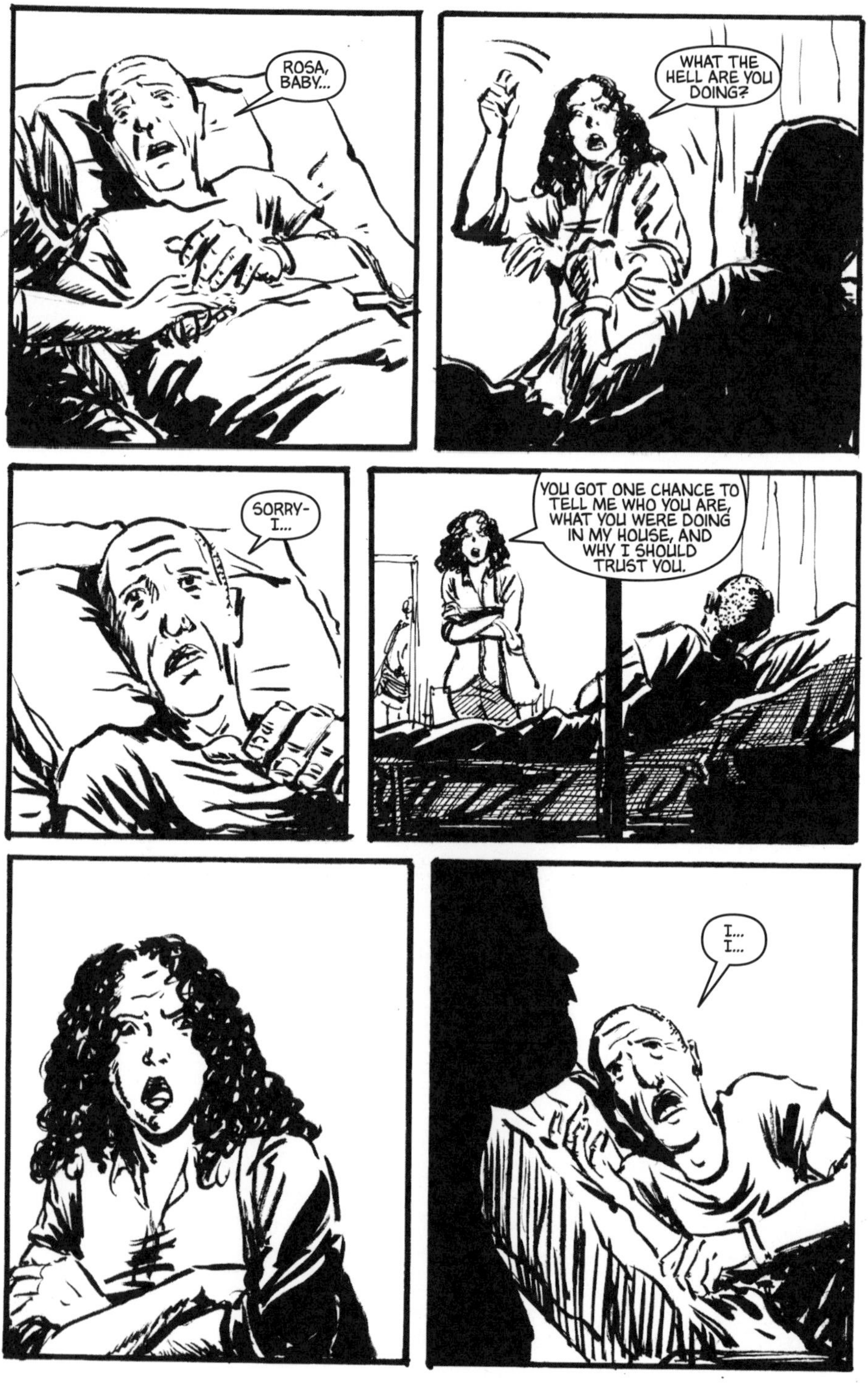
ROSA, BABY...
WHAT THE HELL ARE YOU DOING?
SORRY- I...
YOU GOT ONE CHANCE TO TELL ME WHO YOU ARE, WHAT YOU WERE DOING IN MY HOUSE, AND WHY I SHOULD TRUST YOU.
I... I...

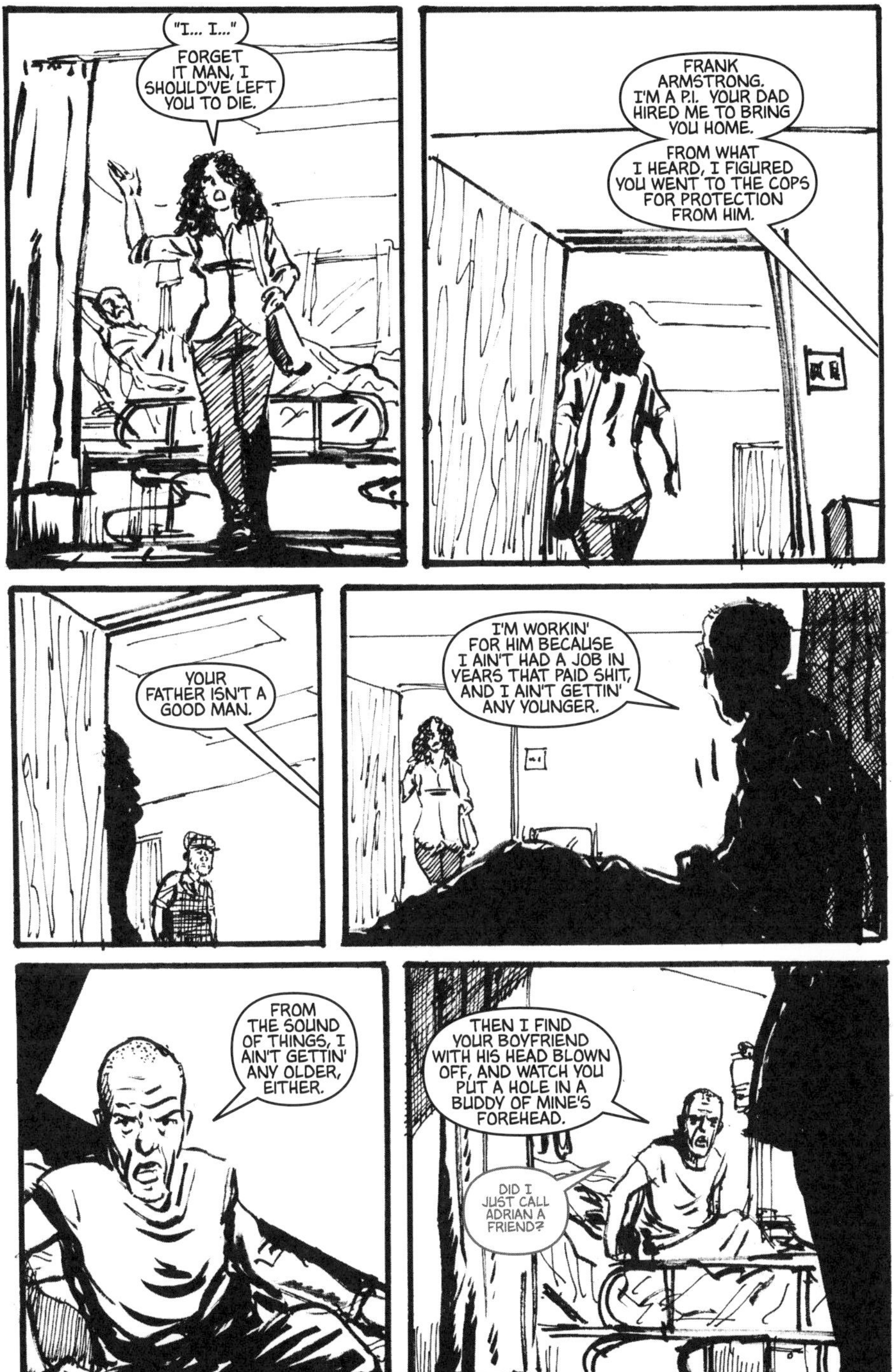
"I... I..."
FORGET IT MAN, I SHOULD'VE LEFT YOU TO DIE.
FRANK ARMSTRONG. I'M A P.I. YOUR DAD HIRED ME TO BRING YOU HOME.
FROM WHAT I HEARD, I FIGURED YOU WENT TO THE COPS FOR PROTECTION FROM HIM.
YOUR FATHER ISN'T A GOOD MAN.
I'M WORKIN' FOR HIM BECAUSE I AIN'T HAD A JOB IN YEARS THAT PAID SHIT, AND I AIN'T GETTIN' ANY YOUNGER.
FROM THE SOUND OF THINGS, I AIN'T GETTIN' ANY OLDER, EITHER.
THEN I FIND YOUR BOYFRIEND WITH HIS HEAD BLOWN OFF, AND WATCH YOU PUT A HOLE IN A BUDDY OF MINE'S FOREHEAD.
DID I JUST CALL ADRIAN A FRIEND?

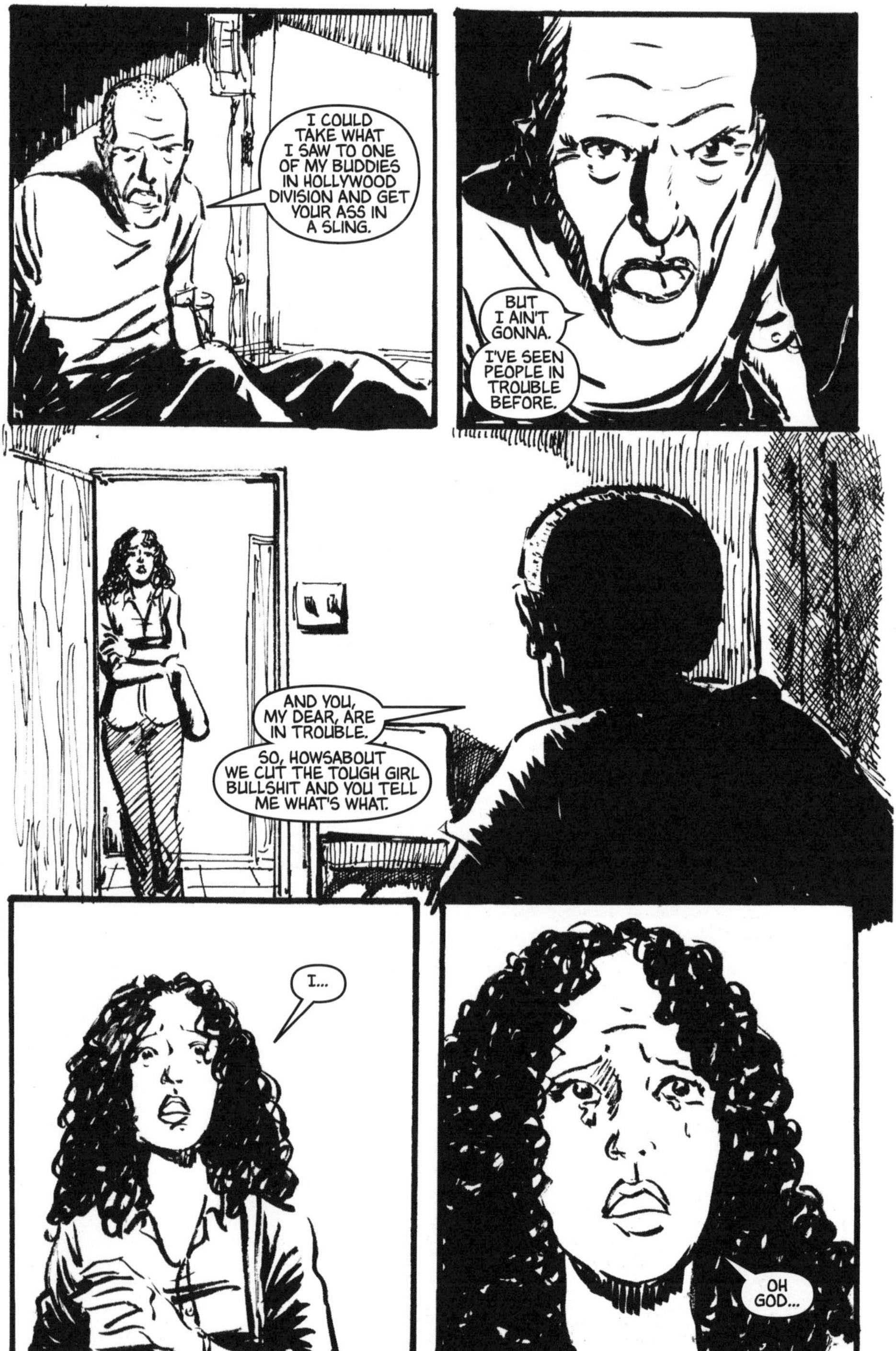
I COULD TAKE WHAT I SAW TO ONE OF MY BUDDIES IN HOLLYWOOD DIVISION AND GET YOUR ASS IN A SLING.
BUT I AIN'T GONNA.
I'VE SEEN PEOPLE IN TROUBLE BEFORE.
AND YOU, MY DEAR, ARE IN TROUBLE.
SO, HOWSABOUT WE CUT THE TOUGH GIRL BULLSHIT AND YOU TELL ME WHAT'S WHAT.
I...
OH GOD...

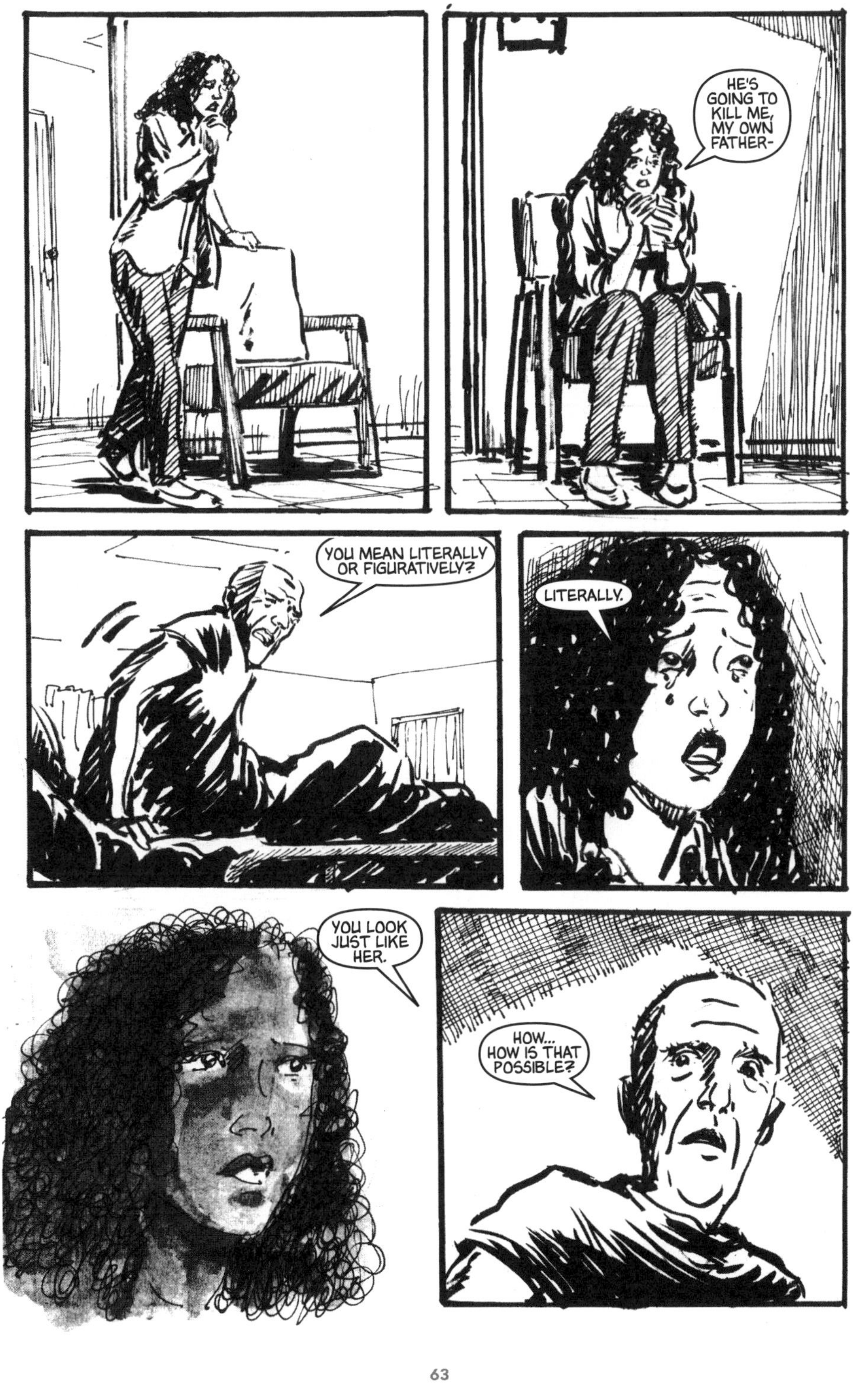
HE'S GOING TO KILL ME, MY OWN FATHER-
YOU MEAN LITERALLY OR FIGURATIVELY?
LITERALLY.
YOU LOOK JUST LIKE HER.
HOW... HOW IS THAT POSSIBLE?

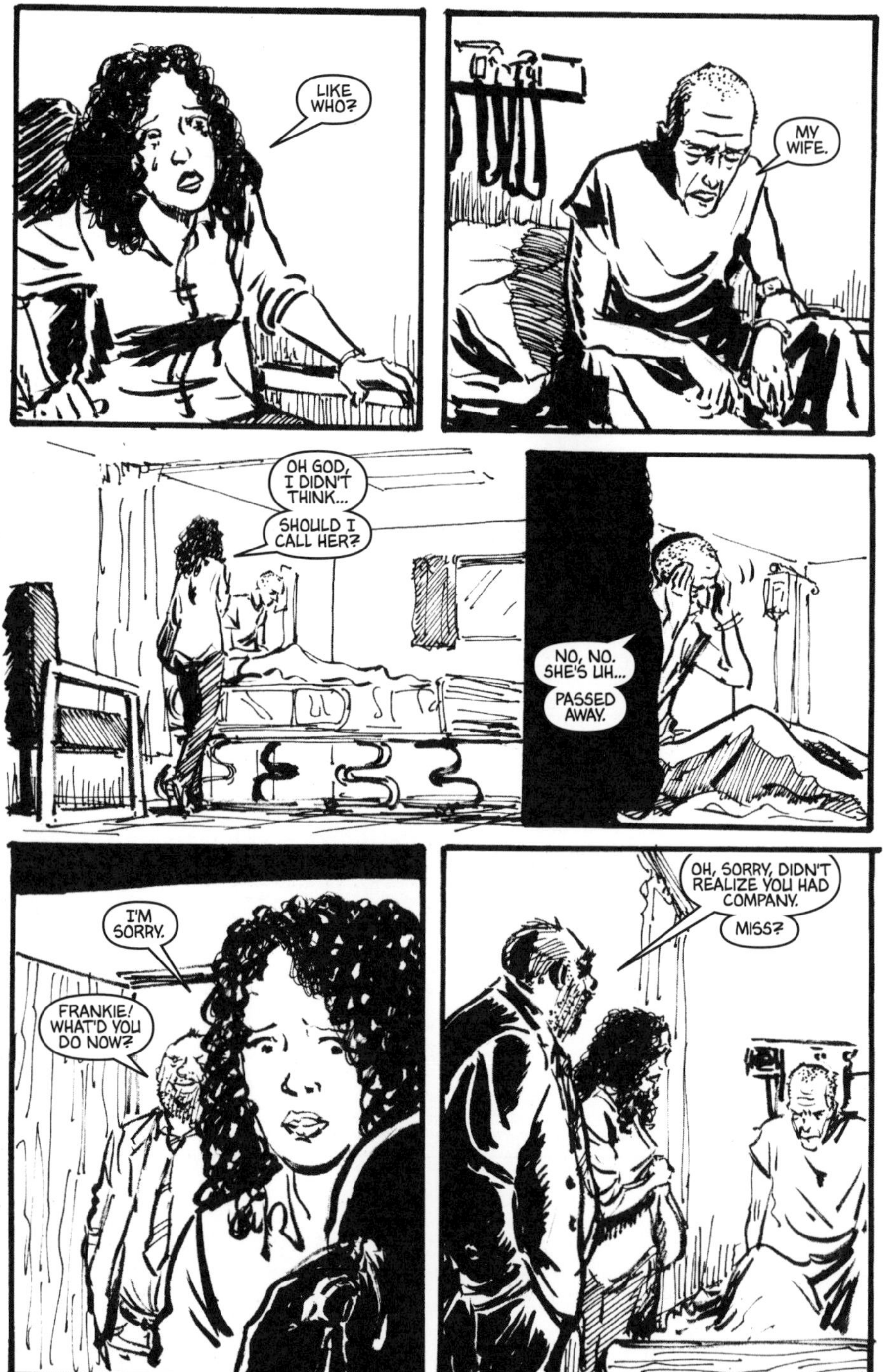
LIKE WHO?
MY WIFE.
OH GOD, I DIDN'T THINK...
SHOULD I CALL HER?
NO, NO. SHE'S UH...
PASSED AWAY.
I'M SORRY.
FRANKIE! WHAT'D YOU DO NOW?
OH, SORRY, DIDN'T REALIZE YOU HAD COMPANY.
MISS?

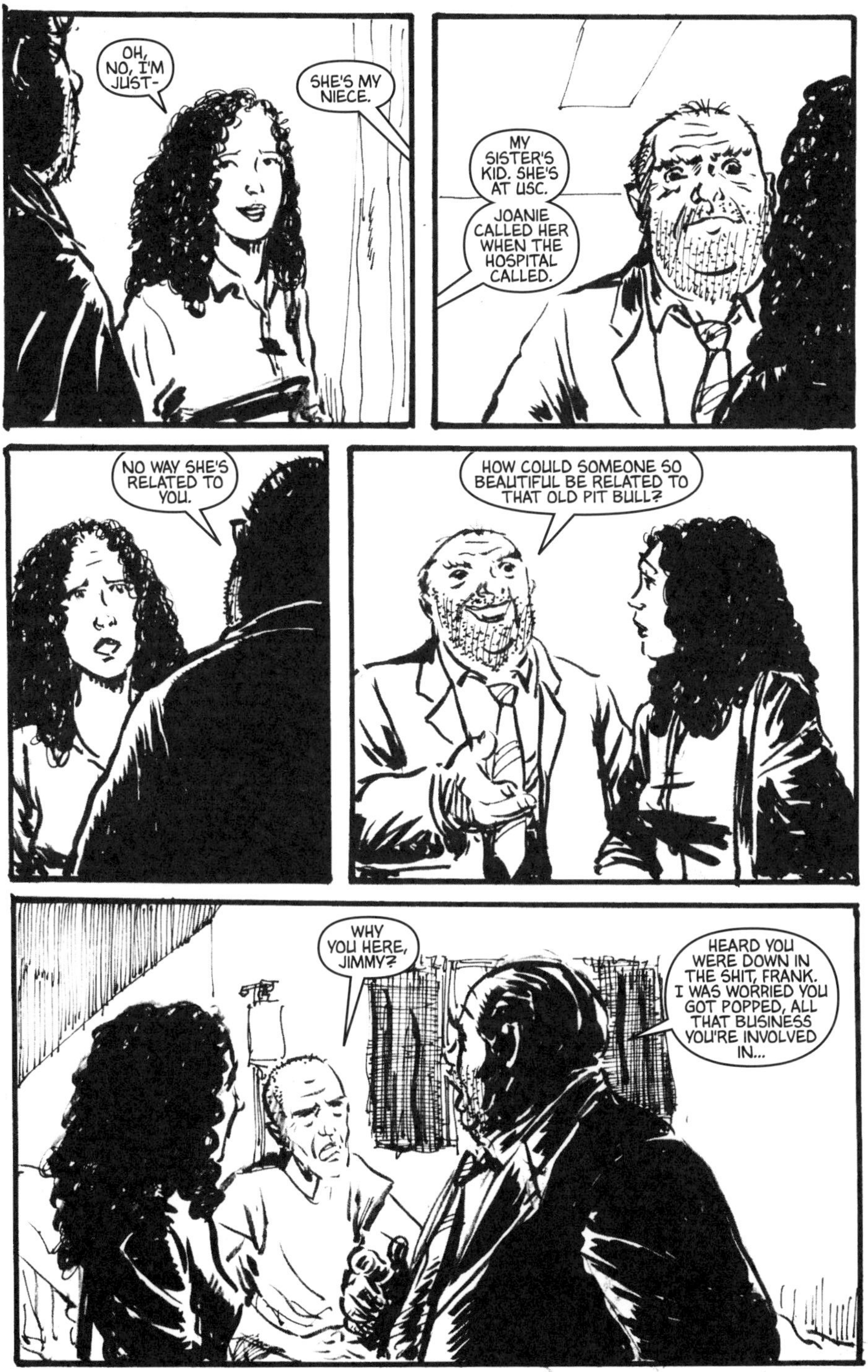
OH, NO, I'M JUST-
SHE'S MY NIECE.
MY SISTER'S KID. SHE'S AT USC.
JOANIE CALLED HER WHEN THE HOSPITAL CALLED.
NO WAY SHE'S RELATED TO YOU.
HOW COULD SOMEONE SO BEAUTIFUL BE RELATED TO THAT OLD PIT BULL?
WHY YOU HERE, JIMMY?
HEARD YOU WERE DOWN IN THE SHIT, FRANK. I WAS WORRIED YOU GOT POPPED, ALL THAT BUSINESS YOU'RE INVOLVED IN...

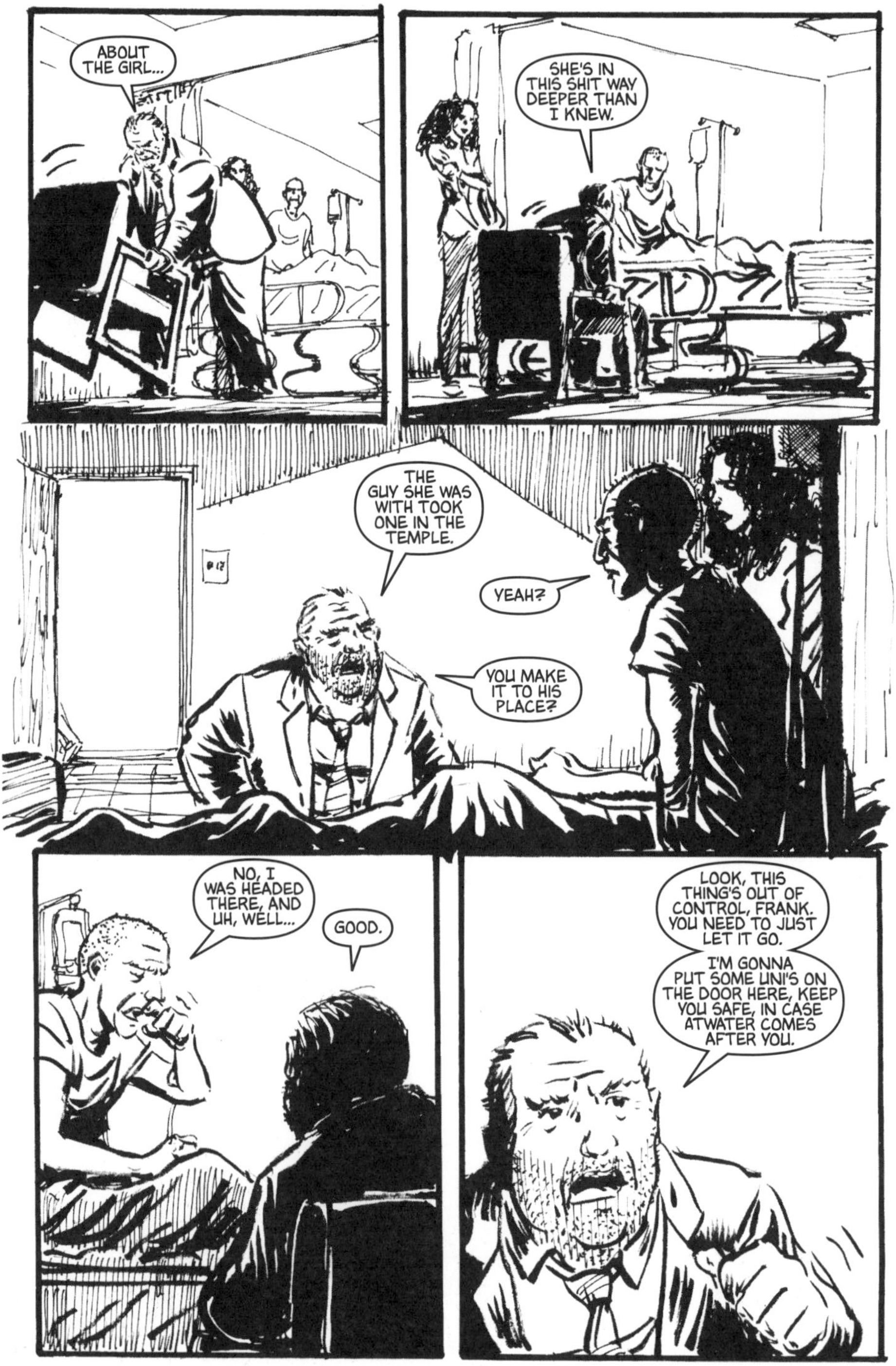
ABOUT THE GIRL...
SHE'S IN THIS SHIT WAY DEEPER THAN I KNEW.
THE GUY SHE WAS WITH TOOK ONE IN THE TEMPLE.
YEAH?
YOU MAKE IT TO HIS PLACE?
NO, I WAS HEADED THERE, AND UH, WELL...
GOOD.
LOOK, THIS THING'S OUT OF CONTROL, FRANK. YOU NEED TO JUST LET IT GO.
I'M GONNA PUT SOME UNI'S ON THE DOOR HERE, KEEP YOU SAFE, IN CASE ATWATER COMES AFTER YOU.

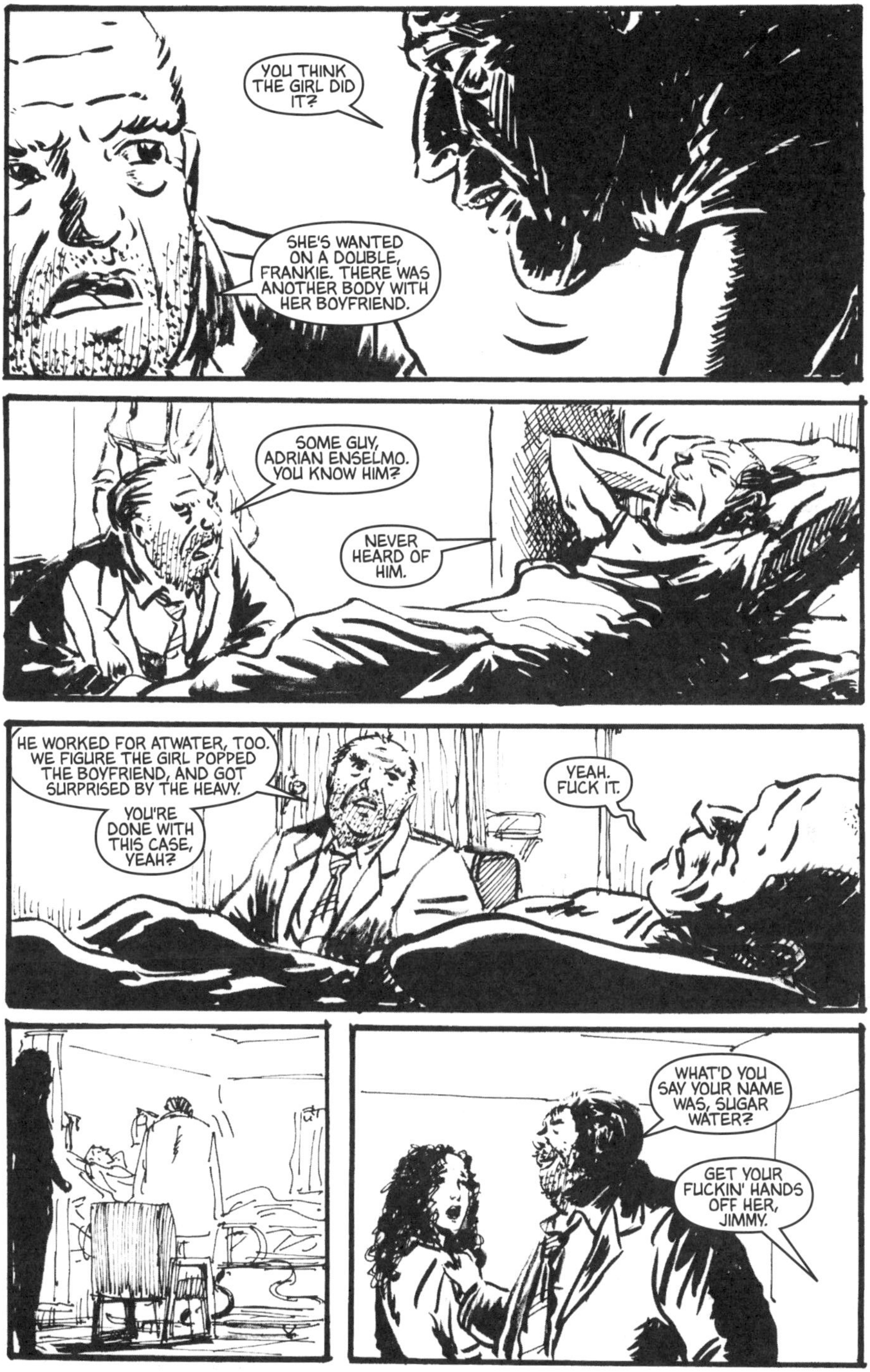
YOU THINK THE GIRL DID IT?
SHE'S WANTED ON A DOUBLE, FRANKIE. THERE WAS ANOTHER BODY WITH HER BOYFRIEND.
SOME GUY, ADRIAN ENSELMO. YOU KNOW HIM?
NEVER HEARD OF HIM.
HE WORKED FOR ATWATER, TOO. WE FIGURE THE GIRL POPPED THE BOYFRIEND, AND GOT SURPRISED BY THE HEAVY.
YOU'RE DONE WITH THIS CASE, YEAH?
YEAH. FUCK IT.
WHAT'D YOU SAY YOUR NAME WAS, SUGAR WATER?
GET YOUR FUCKIN' HANDS OFF HER, JIMMY.

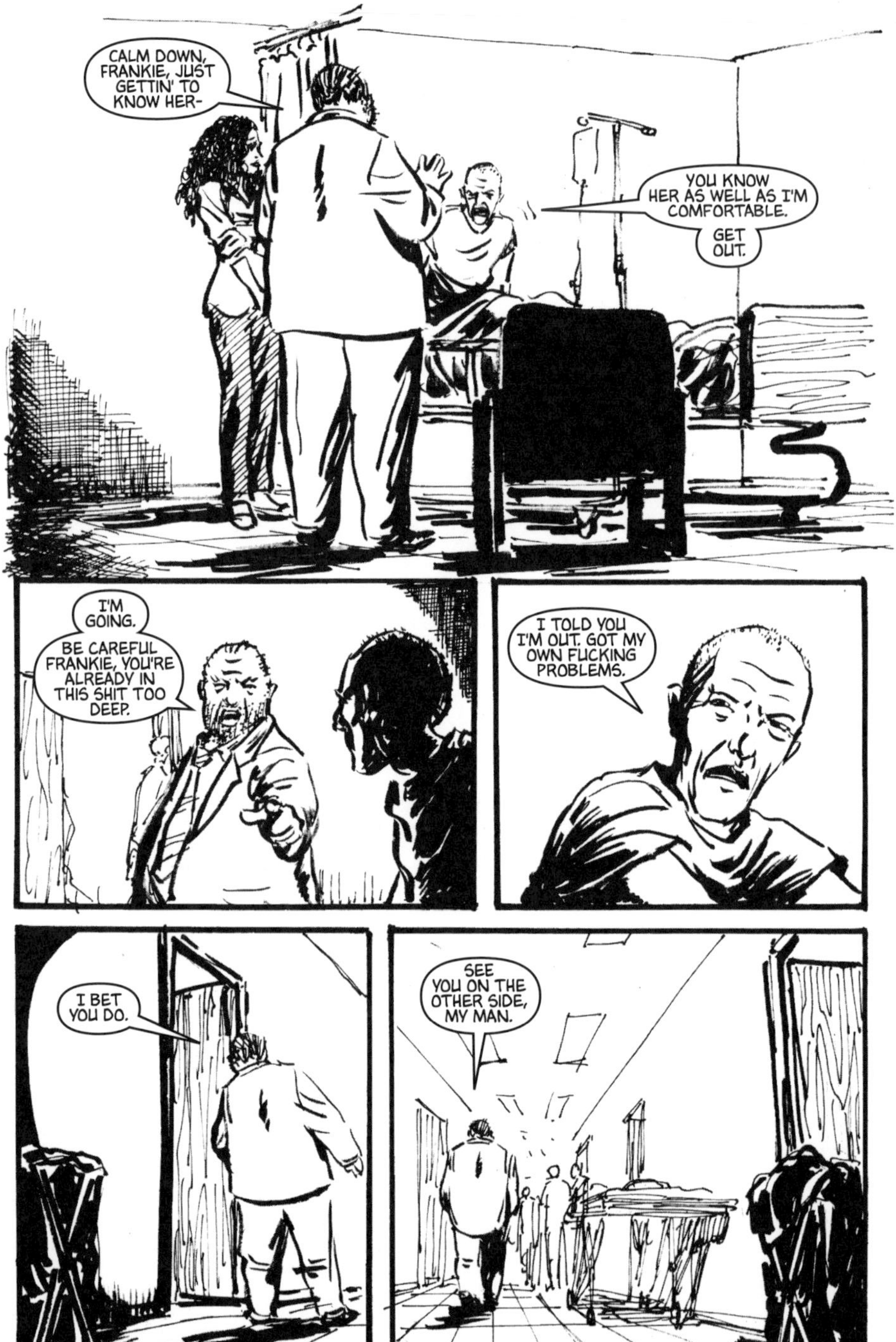
CALM DOWN, FRANKIE, JUST GETTIN' TO KNOW HER-
YOU KNOW HER AS WELL AS I'M COMFORTABLE.
GET OUT.
I'M GOING.
BE CAREFUL FRANKIE, YOU'RE ALREADY IN THIS SHIT TOO DEEP.
I TOLD YOU I'M OUT. GOT MY OWN FUCKING PROBLEMS.
I BET YOU DO.
SEE YOU ON THE OTHER SIDE, MY MAN.

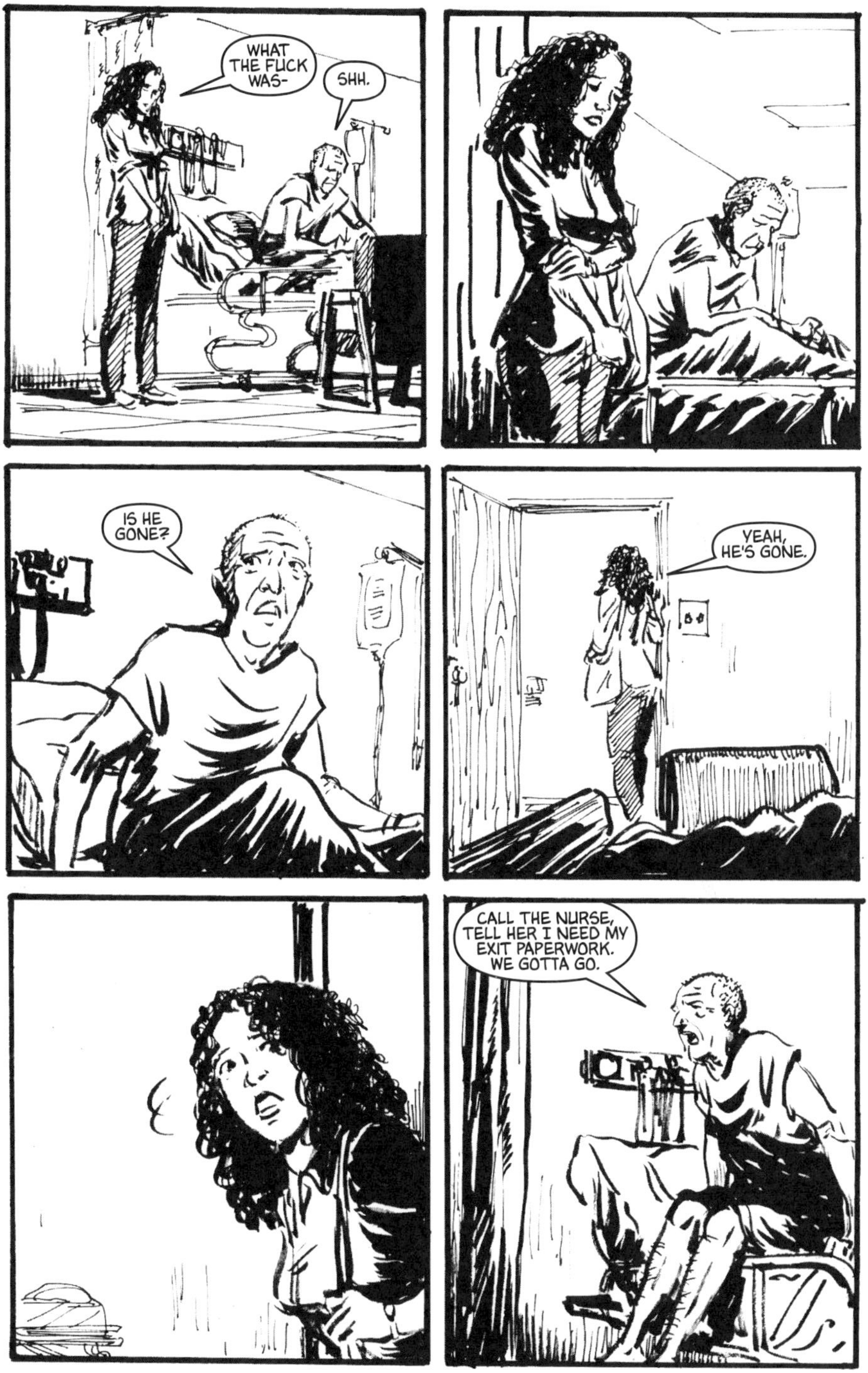
WHAT THE FUCK WAS-
SHH.
IS HE GONE?
YEAH, HE'S GONE.
CALL THE NURSE, TELL HER I NEED MY EXIT PAPERWORK. WE GOTTA GO.

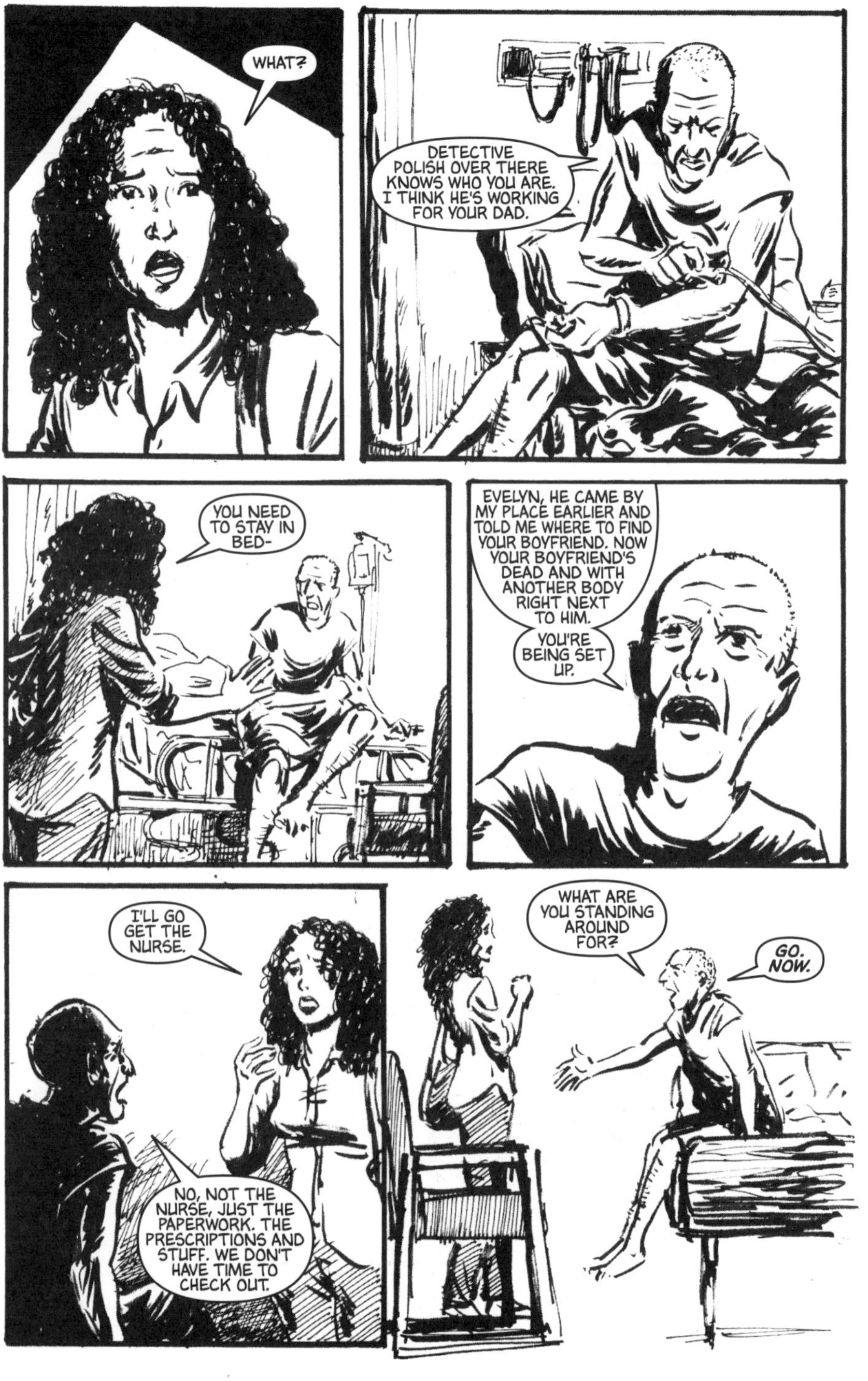
WHAT?
DETECTIVE POLISH OVER THERE KNOWS WHO YOU ARE. I THINK HE'S WORKING FOR YOUR DAD.
YOU NEED TO STAY IN BED-
EVELYN, HE CAME BY MY PLACE EARLIER AND TOLD ME WHERE TO FIND YOUR BOYFRIEND. NOW YOUR BOYFRIEND'S DEAD AND WITH ANOTHER BODY RIGHT NEXT TO HIM.
YOU'RE BEING SET UP.
I'LL GO GET THE NURSE.
NO, NOT THE NURSE, JUST THE PAPERWORK. THE PRESCRIPTIONS AND STUFF. WE DON'T HAVE TIME TO CHECK OUT.
WHAT ARE YOU STANDING AROUND FOR?
GO. NOW.

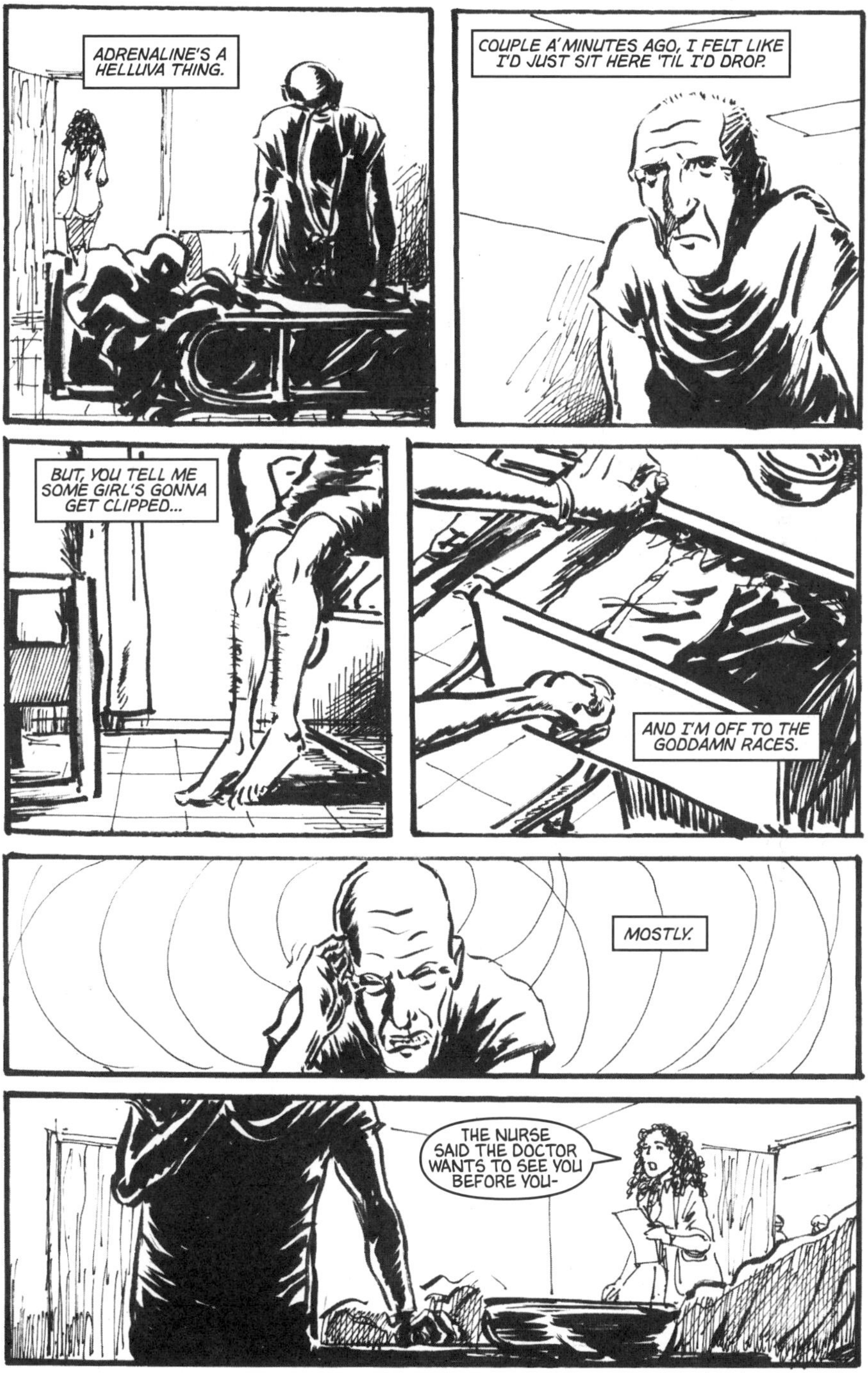
ADRENALINE'S A HELLUVA THING.
COUPLE A' MINUTES AGO, I FELT LIKE I'D JUST SIT HERE 'TIL I'D DROP.
BUT, YOU TELL ME SOME GIRL'S GONNA GET CLIPPED...
AND I'M OFF TO THE GODDAMN RACES.
MOSTLY.
THE NURSE SAID THE DOCTOR WANTS TO SEE YOU BEFORE YOU-

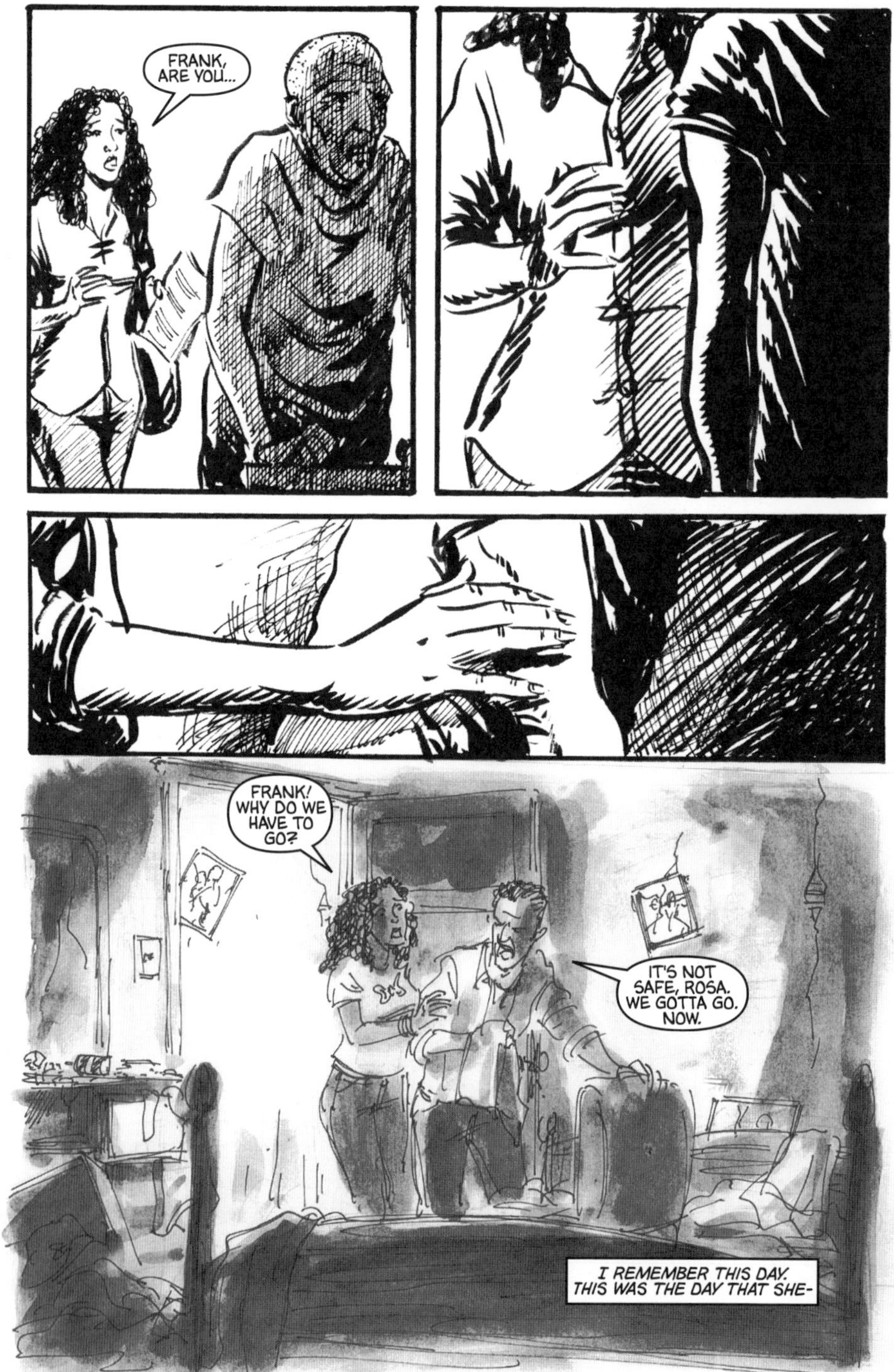
FRANK, ARE YOU...
FRANK! WHY DO WE HAVE TO GO?
IT'S NOT SAFE, ROSA. WE GOTTA GO. NOW.
I REMEMBER THIS DAY. THIS WAS THE DAY THAT SHE-

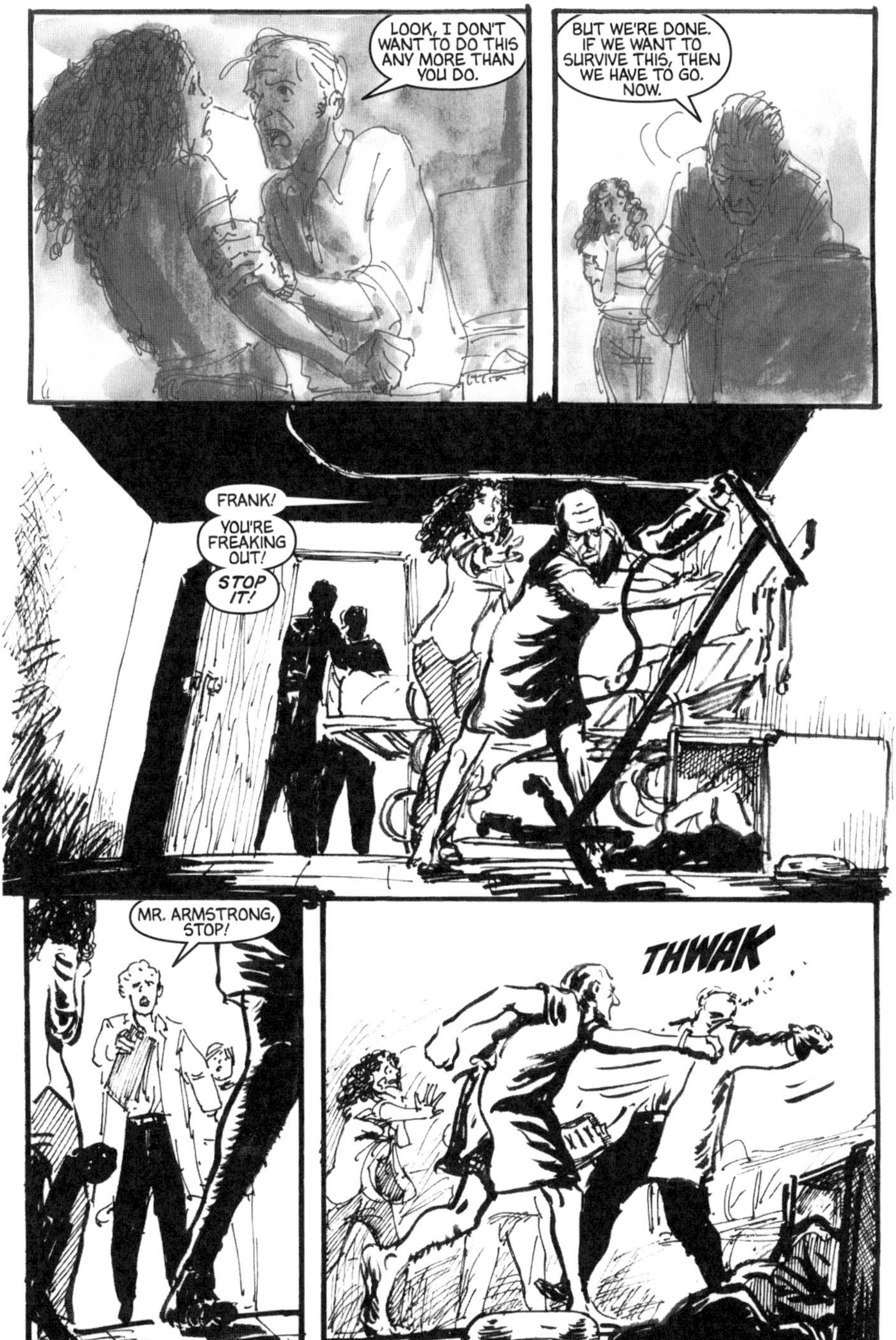
LOOK, I DON'T WANT TO DO THIS ANY MORE THAN YOU DO.
BUT WE'RE DONE. IF WE WANT TO SURVIVE THIS, THEN WE HAVE TO GO. NOW.
FRANK!
YOU'RE FREAKING OUT!
STOP IT!
MR. ARMSTRONG, STOP!
THWAK

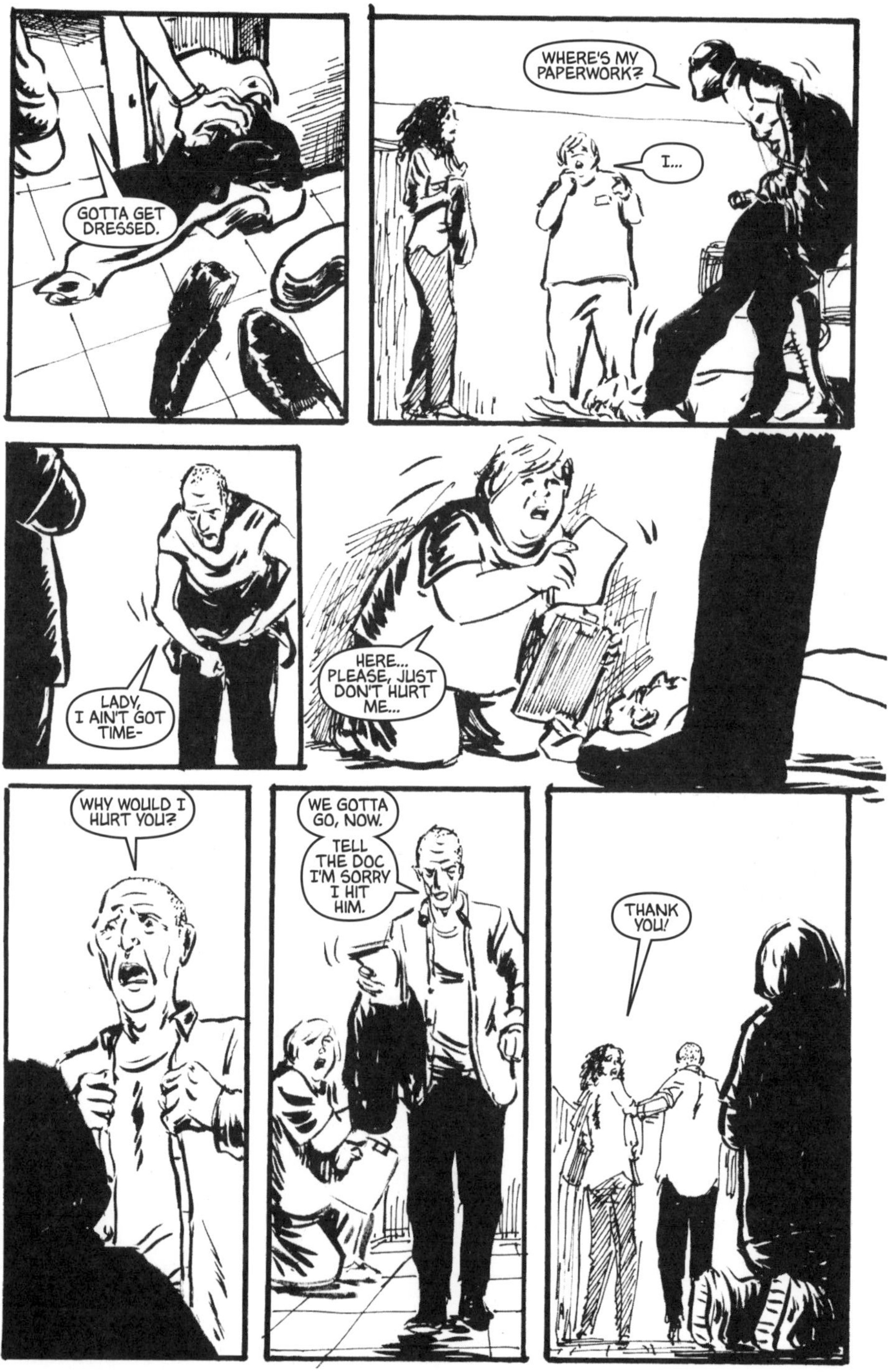
GOTTA GET DRESSED.
WHERE'S MY PAPERWORK?
I...
LADY, I AIN'T GOT TIME-
HERE... PLEASE, JUST DON'T HURT ME...
WHY WOULD I HURT YOU?
WE GOTTA GO, NOW.
TELL THE DOC I'M SORRY I HIT HIM.
THANK YOU!

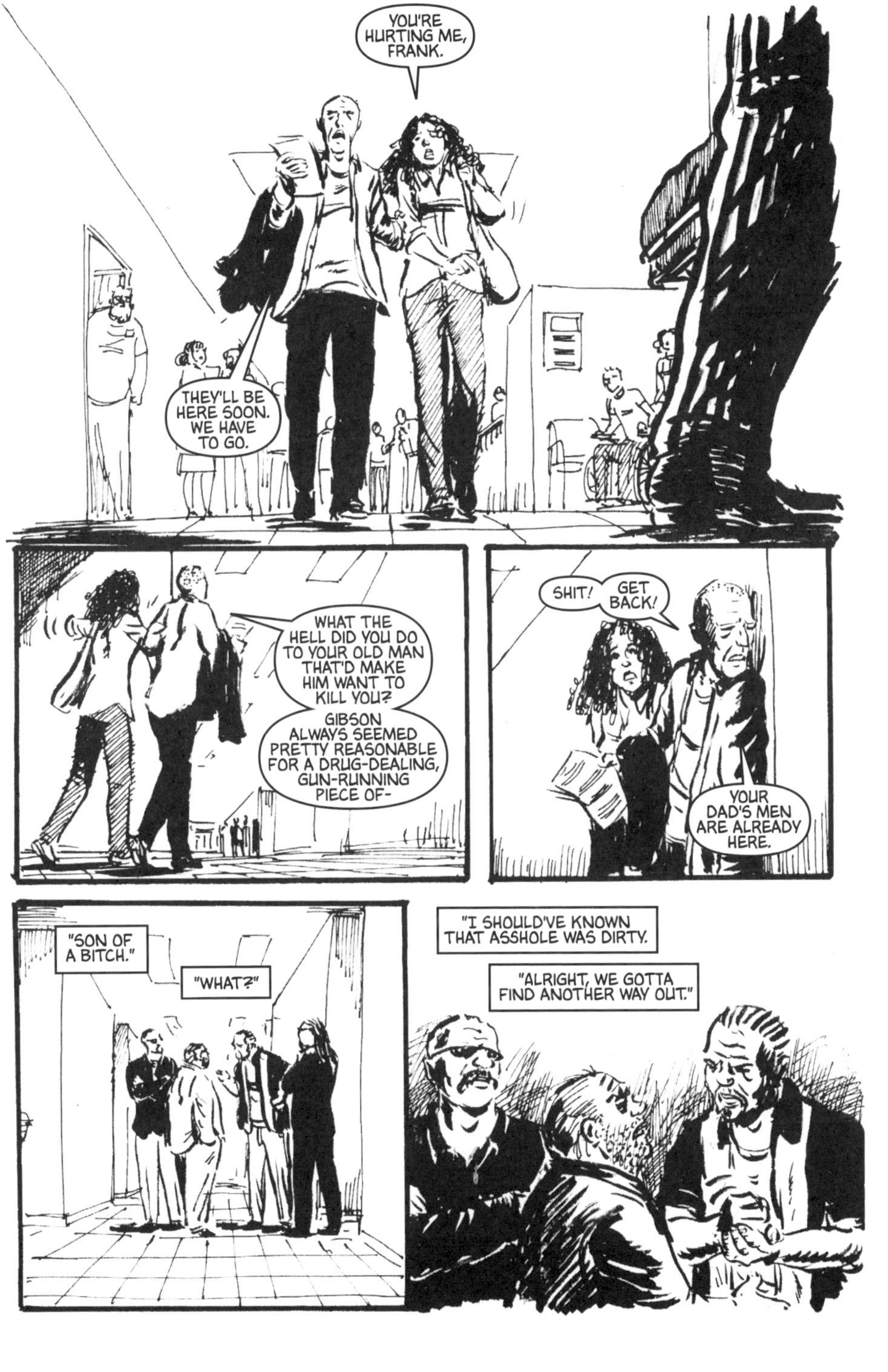

YOU'RE HURTING ME, FRANK.
THEY'LL BE HERE SOON. WE HAVE TO GO.
WHAT THE HELL DID YOU DO TO YOUR OLD MAN THAT'D MAKE HIM WANT TO KILL YOU?
GIBSON ALWAYS SEEMED PRETTY REASONABLE FOR A DRUG-DEALING, GUN-RUNNING PIECE OF-
SHIT!
GET BACK!
YOUR DAD'S MEN ARE ALREADY HERE.
"SON OF A BITCH."
"WHAT?"
"I SHOULD'VE KNOWN THAT ASSHOLE WAS DIRTY.
"ALRIGHT, WE GOTTA FIND ANOTHER WAY OUT."

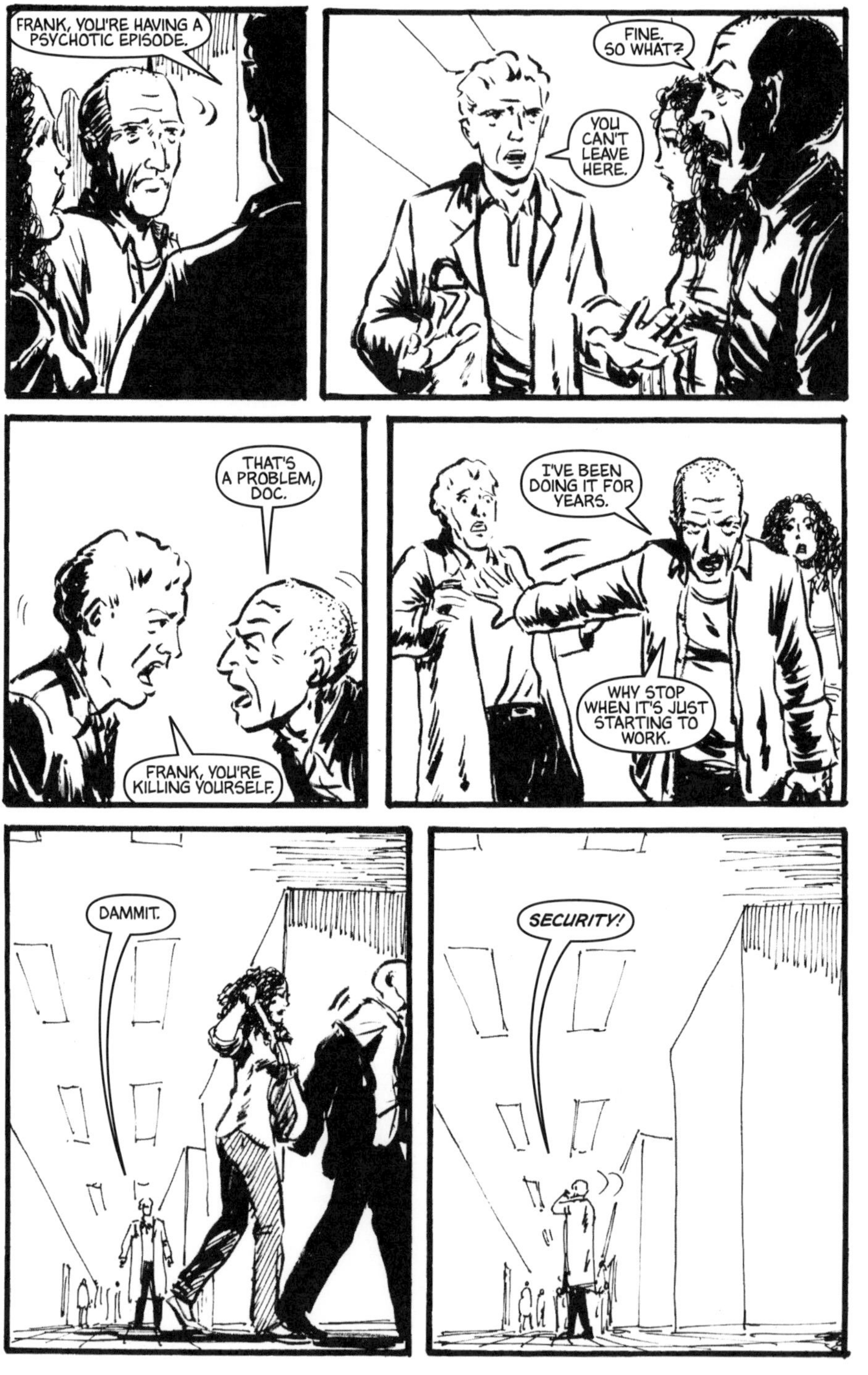
FRANK, YOU'RE HAVING A PSYCHOTIC EPISODE.
FINE. SO WHAT?
YOU CAN'T LEAVE HERE.
THAT'S A PROBLEM, DOC.
FRANK, YOU'RE KILLING YOURSELF.
I'VE BEEN DOING IT FOR YEARS.
WHY STOP WHEN IT'S JUST STARTING TO WORK.
DAMMIT.
SECURITY!

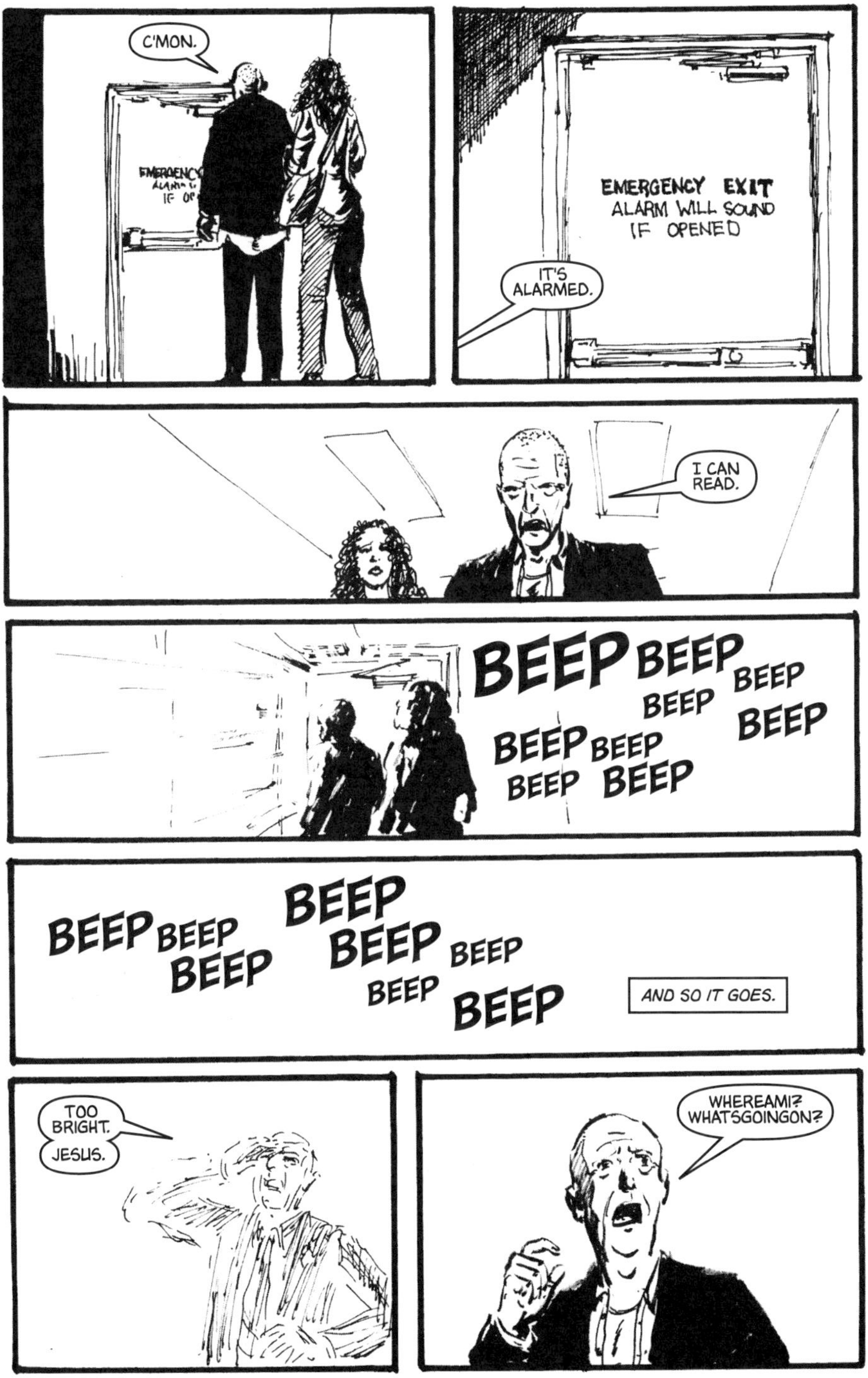
C'MON.
EMERGENCY EXIT
ALARM WILL SOUND
IF OPENED
IT'S ALARMED.
I CAN READ.
BEEP BEEP BEEP BEEP BEEP BEEP BEEP BEEP BEEP
BEEP BEEP BEEP BEEP BEEP BEEP BEEP BEEP
AND SO IT GOES.
TOO BRIGHT.
JESUS.
WHEREAMI? WHATSGOINGON?

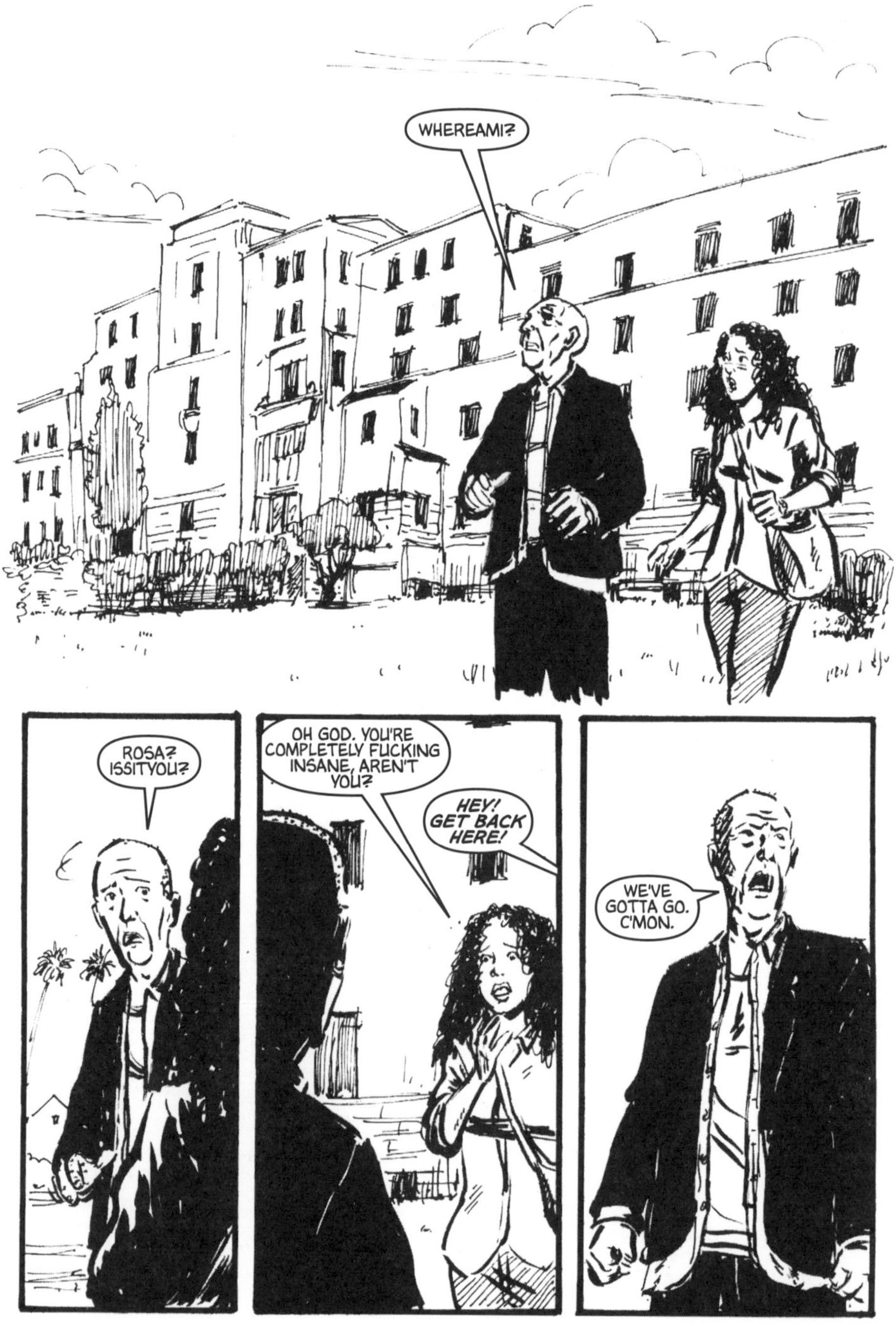
WHEREAMI?
ROSA? ISSITYOU?
OH GOD. YOU'RE COMPLETELY FUCKING INSANE, AREN'T YOU?
HEY! GET BACK HERE!
WE'VE GOTTA GO. C'MON.

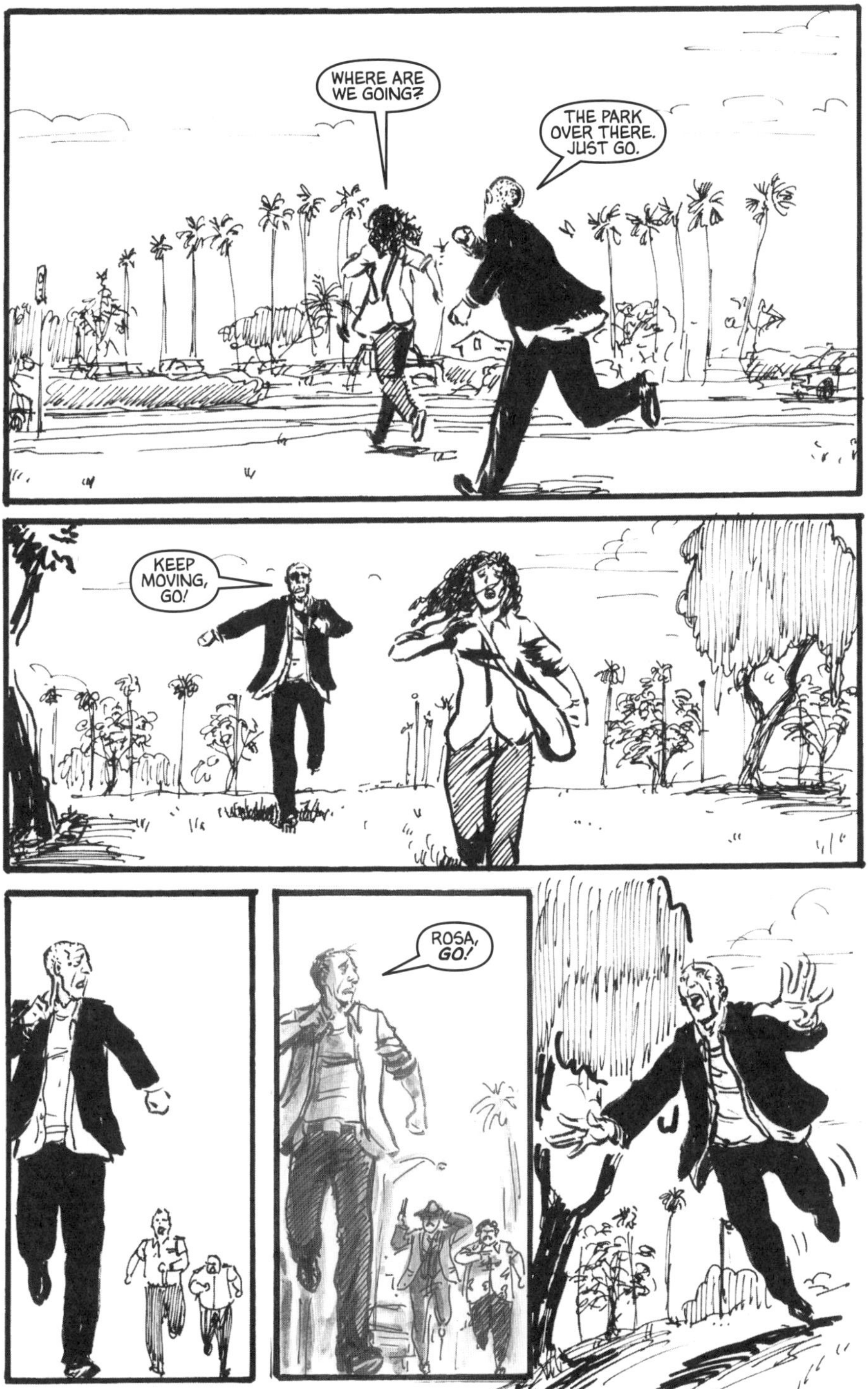
WHERE ARE WE GOING?
THE PARK OVER THERE. JUST GO.
KEEP MOVING, GO!
ROSA, GO!

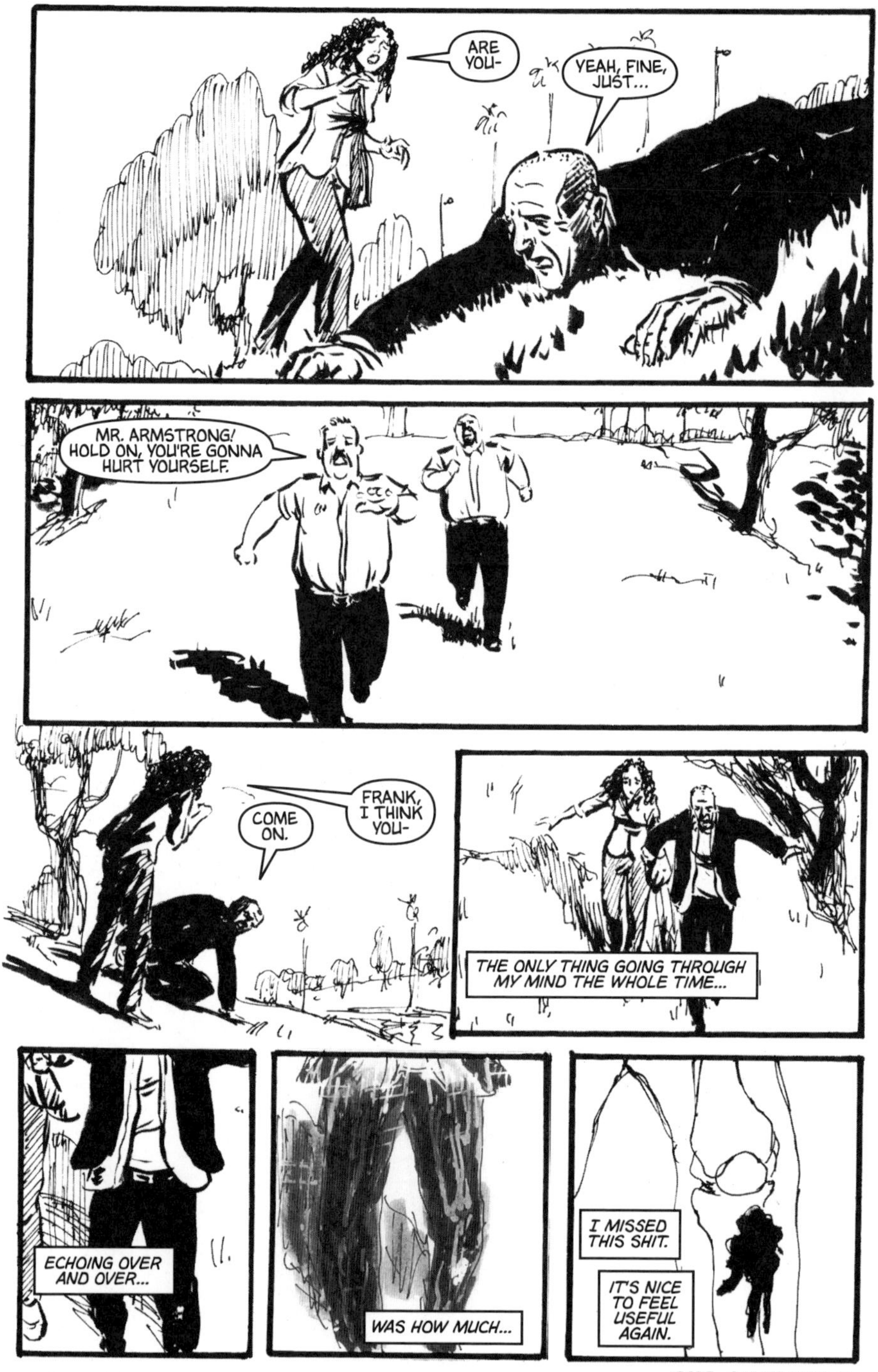
ARE YOU-
YEAH, FINE, JUST...
MR. ARMSTRONG! HOLD ON, YOU'RE GONNA HURT YOURSELF.
FRANK, I THINK YOU-
COME ON.
THE ONLY THING GOING THROUGH MY MIND THE WHOLE TIME...
ECHOING OVER AND OVER...
WAS HOW MUCH...
I MISSED THIS SHIT.
IT'S NICE TO FEEL USEFUL AGAIN.

END CHAPTER 3

FOUR

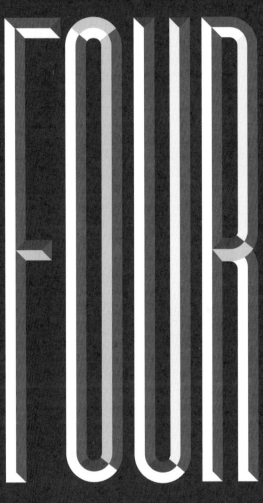

ANGEL'S FLIGHT

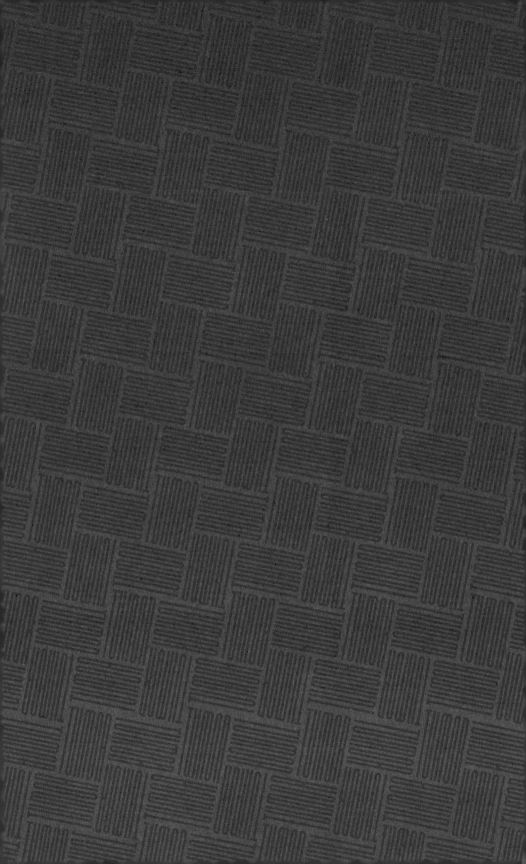

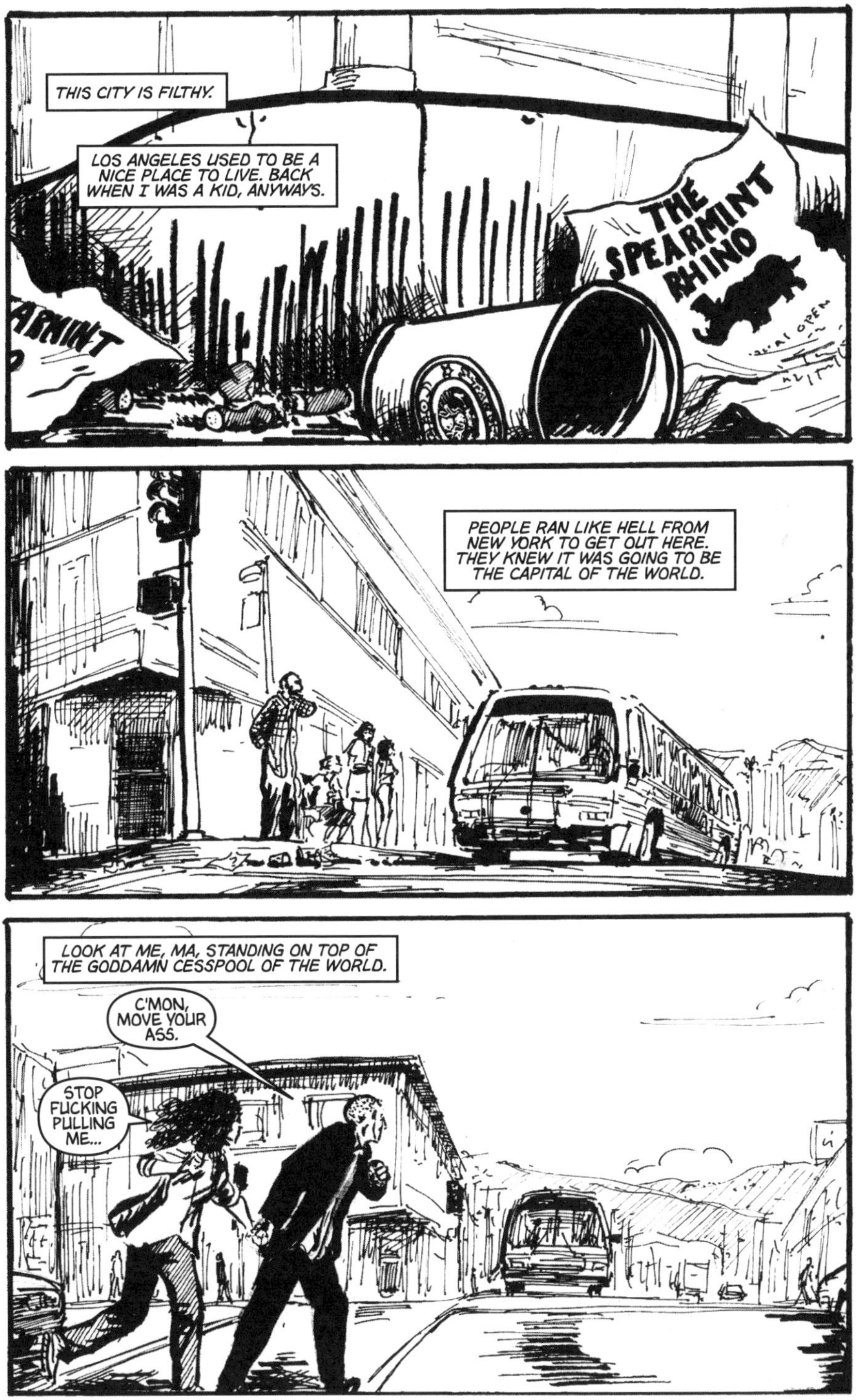

THIS CITY IS FILTHY.
LOS ANGELES USED TO BE A NICE PLACE TO LIVE. BACK WHEN I WAS A KID, ANYWAYS.
THE SPEARMINT RHINO
PEOPLE RAN LIKE HELL FROM NEW YORK TO GET OUT HERE. THEY KNEW IT WAS GOING TO BE THE CAPITAL OF THE WORLD.
LOOK AT ME, MA, STANDING ON TOP OF THE GODDAMN CESSPOOL OF THE WORLD.
C'MON, MOVE YOUR ASS.
STOP FUCKING PULLING ME...

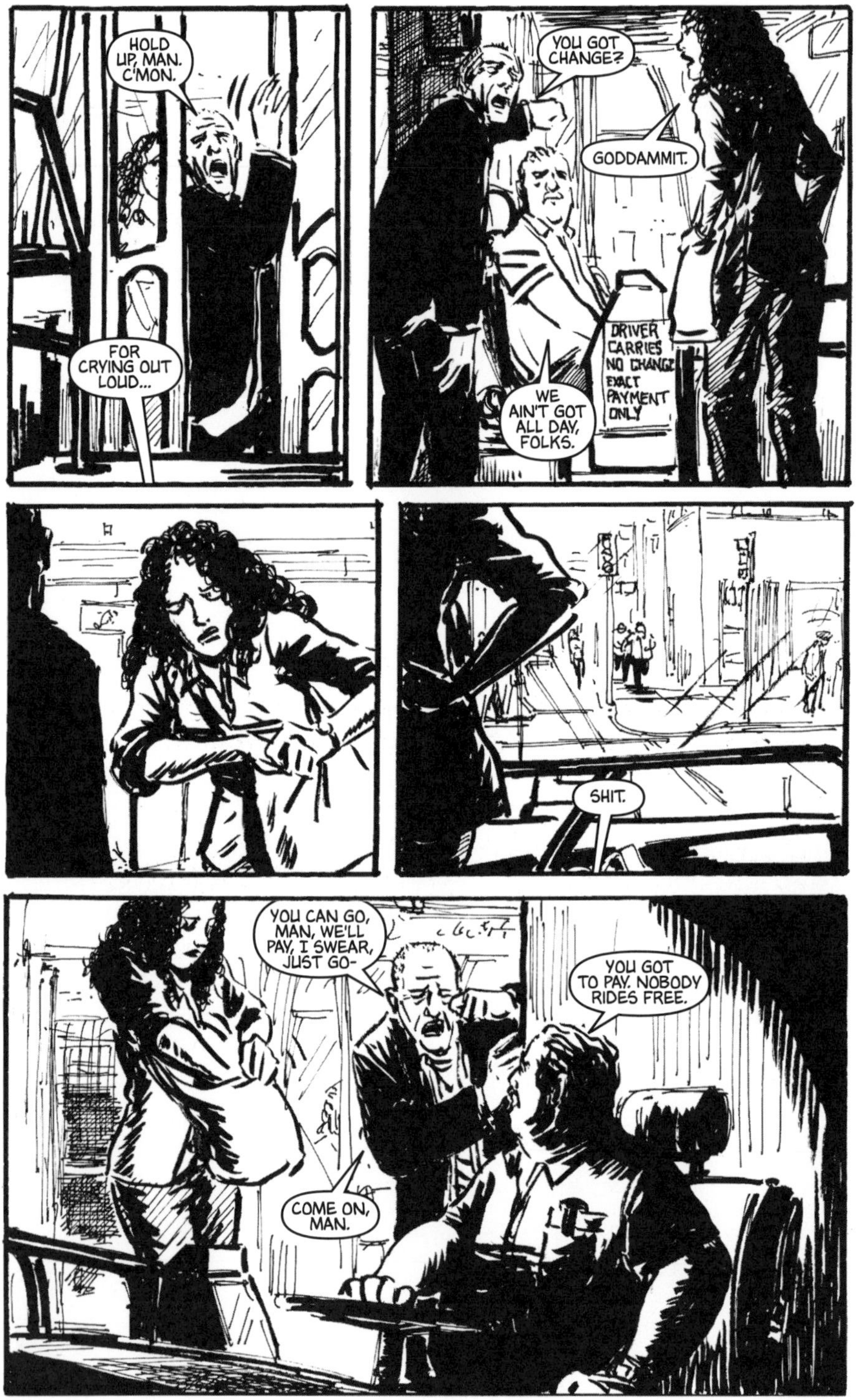
HOLD UP, MAN. C'MON.
FOR CRYING OUT LOUD...
YOU GOT CHANGE?
GODDAMMIT.
DRIVER CARRIES NO CHANGE EXACT PAYMENT ONLY
WE AIN'T GOT ALL DAY, FOLKS.
SHIT.
YOU CAN GO, MAN, WE'LL PAY, I SWEAR, JUST GO-
YOU GOT TO PAY. NOBODY RIDES FREE.
COME ON, MAN.

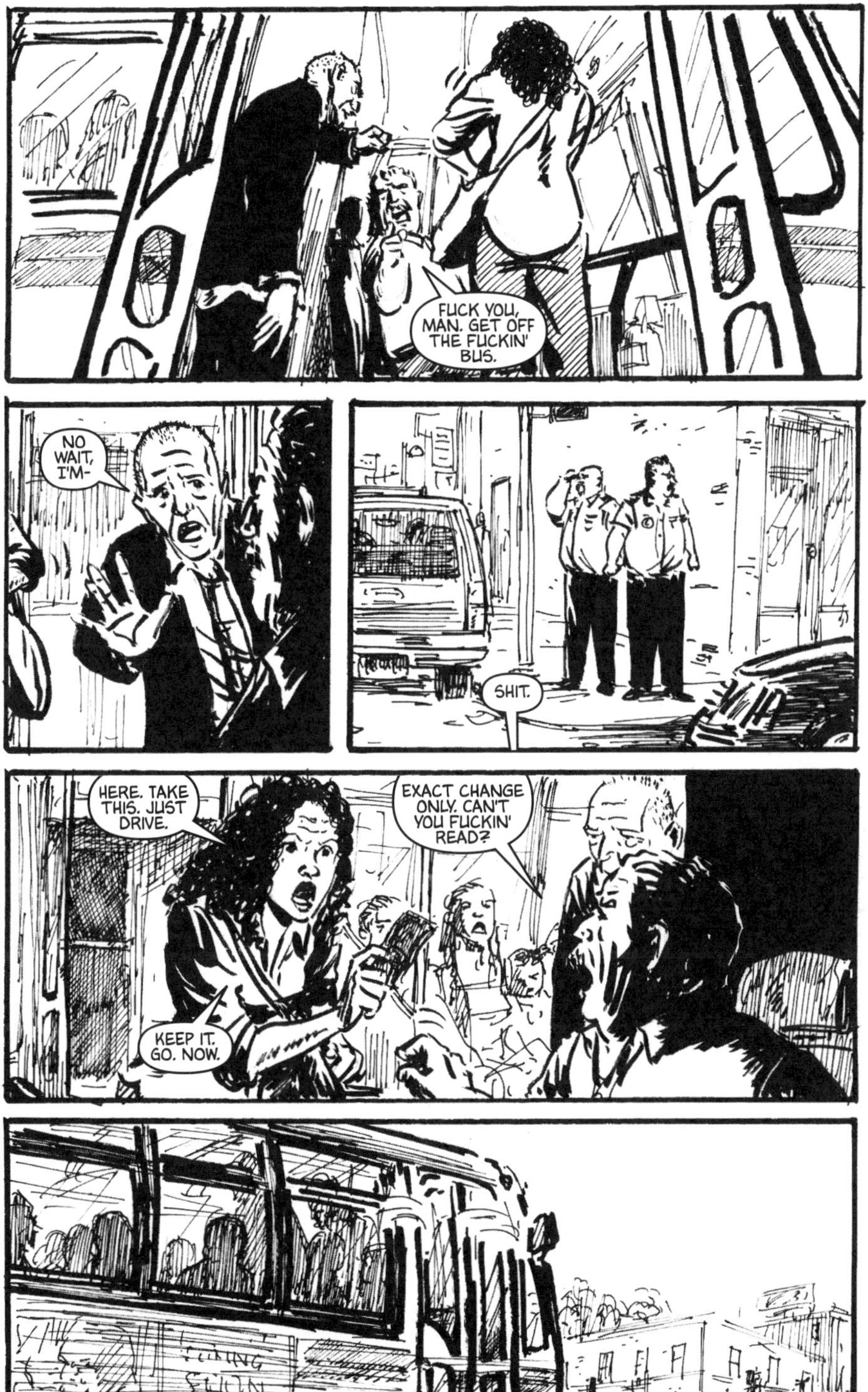
FUCK YOU, MAN. GET OFF THE FUCKIN' BUS.
NO WAIT, I'M-
SHIT.
HERE. TAKE THIS. JUST DRIVE.
EXACT CHANGE ONLY. CAN'T YOU FUCKIN' READ?
KEEP IT. GO. NOW.

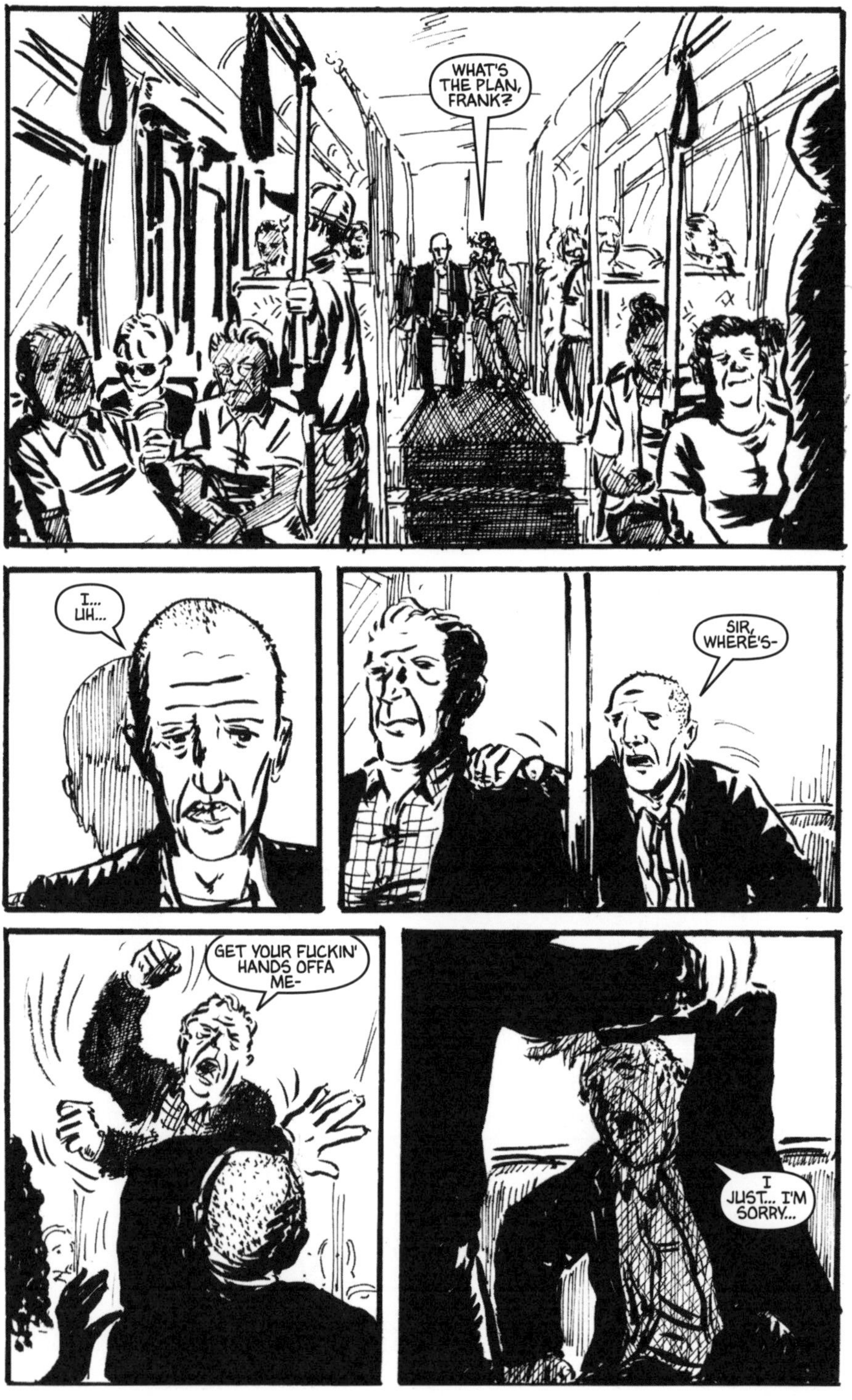
WHAT'S THE PLAN, FRANK?
I... UH...
SIR, WHERE'S-
GET YOUR FUCKIN' HANDS OFFA ME-
I JUST... I'M SORRY...

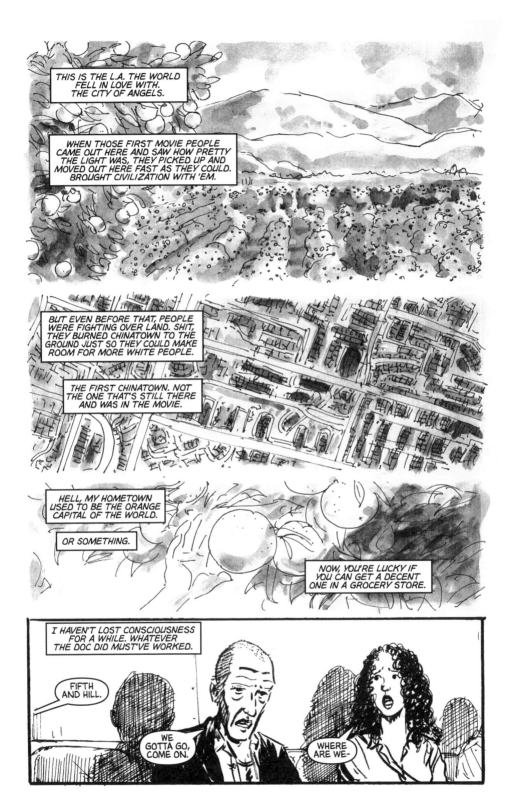

THIS IS THE L.A. THE WORLD FELL IN LOVE WITH. THE CITY OF ANGELS.

WHEN THOSE FIRST MOVIE PEOPLE CAME OUT HERE AND SAW HOW PRETTY THE LIGHT WAS, THEY PICKED UP AND MOVED OUT HERE FAST AS THEY COULD. BROUGHT CIVILIZATION WITH 'EM.

BUT EVEN BEFORE THAT, PEOPLE WERE FIGHTING OVER LAND. SHIT, THEY BURNED CHINATOWN TO THE GROUND JUST SO THEY COULD MAKE ROOM FOR MORE WHITE PEOPLE.

THE FIRST CHINATOWN. NOT THE ONE THAT'S STILL THERE AND WAS IN THE MOVIE.

HELL, MY HOMETOWN USED TO BE THE ORANGE CAPITAL OF THE WORLD.

OR SOMETHING.

NOW, YOU'RE LUCKY IF YOU CAN GET A DECENT ONE IN A GROCERY STORE.

I HAVEN'T LOST CONSCIOUSNESS FOR A WHILE. WHATEVER THE DOC DID MUST'VE WORKED.

FIFTH AND HILL.

WE GOTTA GO, COME ON.

WHERE ARE WE—

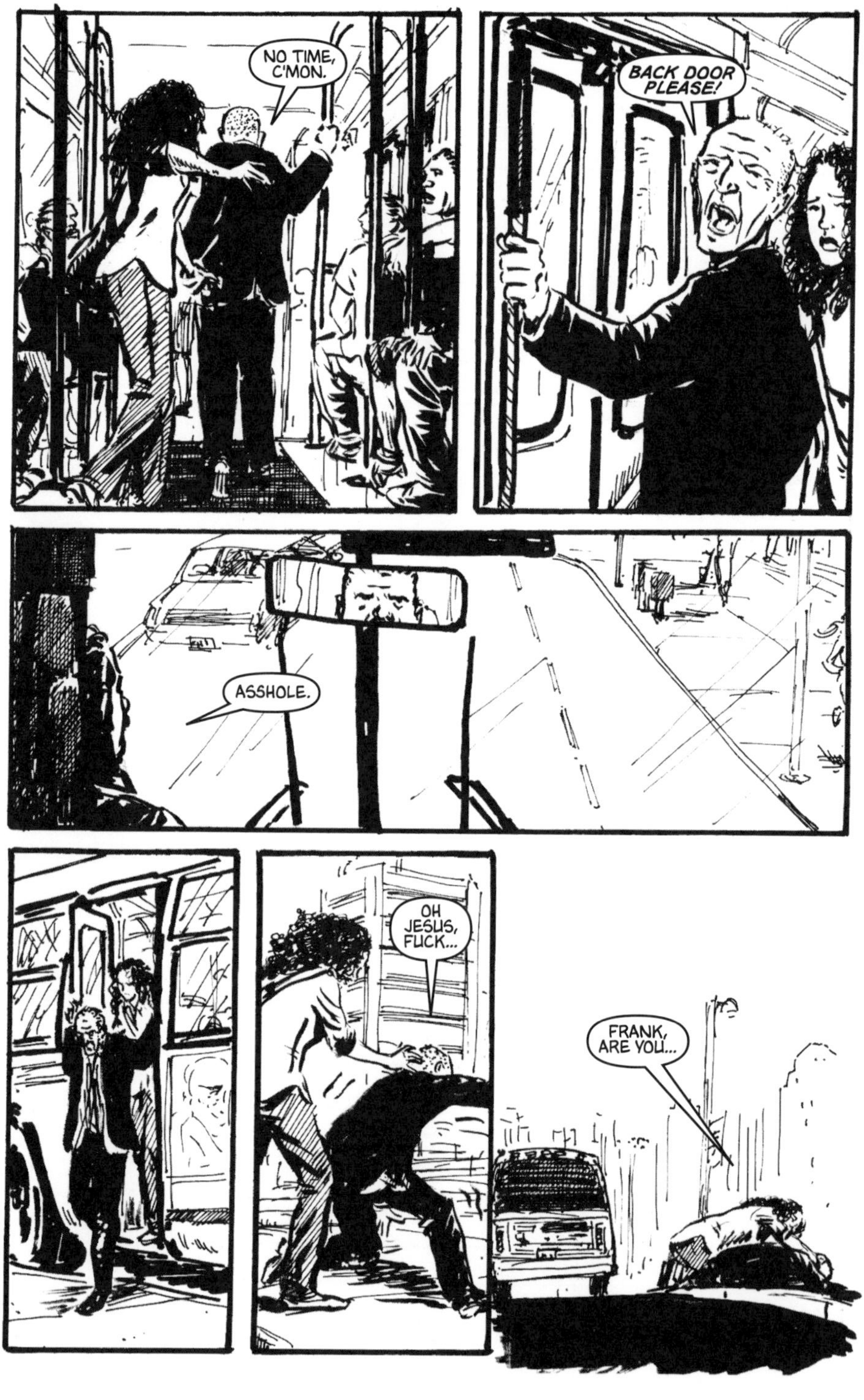
NO TIME, C'MON.
BACK DOOR PLEASE!
ASSHOLE.
OH JESUS, FUCK...
FRANK, ARE YOU...

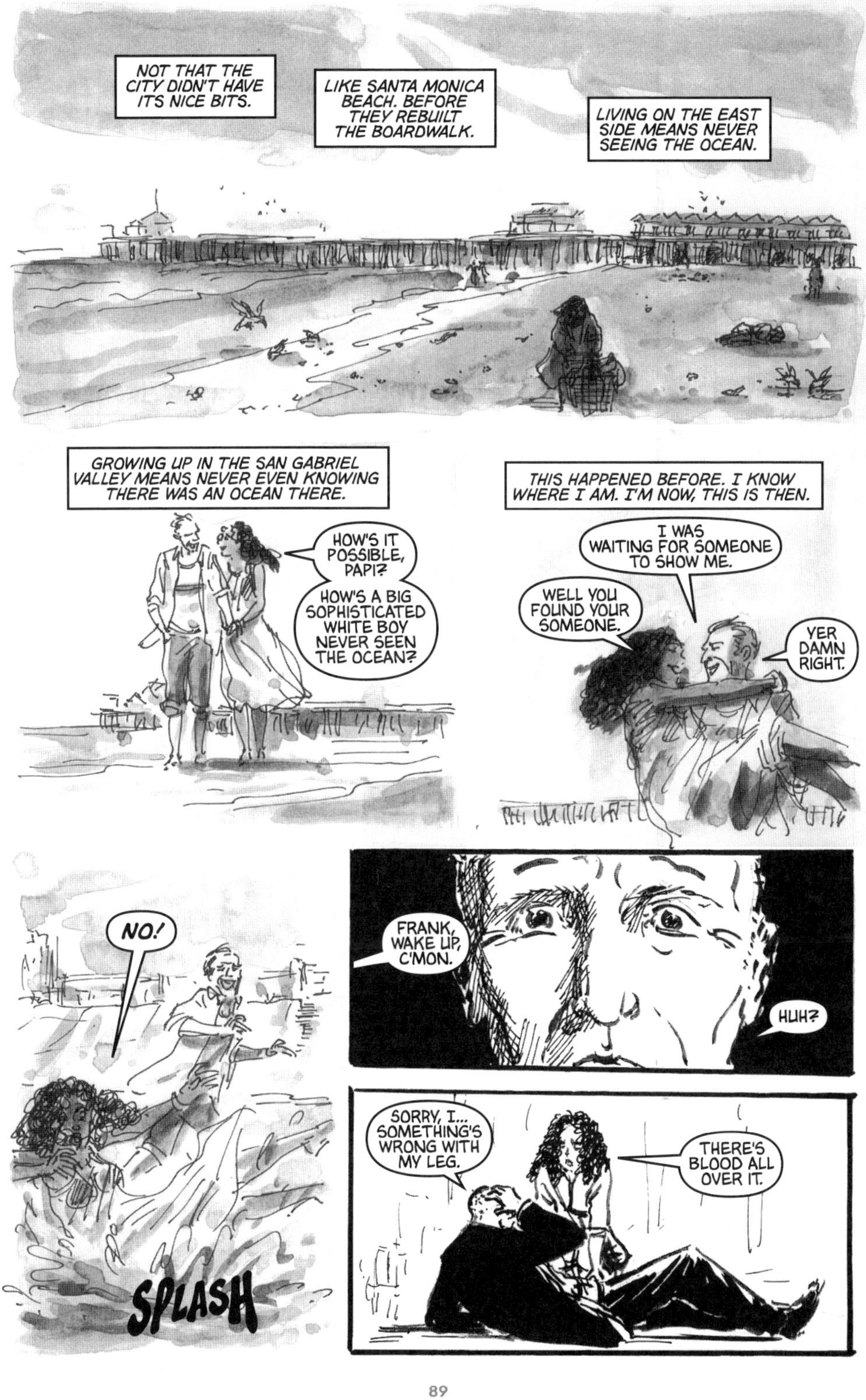
NOT THAT THE CITY DIDN'T HAVE ITS NICE BITS.
LIKE SANTA MONICA BEACH. BEFORE THEY REBUILT THE BOARDWALK.
LIVING ON THE EAST SIDE MEANS NEVER SEEING THE OCEAN.
GROWING UP IN THE SAN GABRIEL VALLEY MEANS NEVER EVEN KNOWING THERE WAS AN OCEAN THERE.
HOW'S IT POSSIBLE, PAPI?
HOW'S A BIG SOPHISTICATED WHITE BOY NEVER SEEN THE OCEAN?
THIS HAPPENED BEFORE. I KNOW WHERE I AM. I'M NOW, THIS IS THEN.
I WAS WAITING FOR SOMEONE TO SHOW ME.
WELL YOU FOUND YOUR SOMEONE.
YER DAMN RIGHT.
NO!
SPLASH
FRANK, WAKE UP, C'MON.
HUH?
SORRY, I... SOMETHING'S WRONG WITH MY LEG.
THERE'S BLOOD ALL OVER IT.

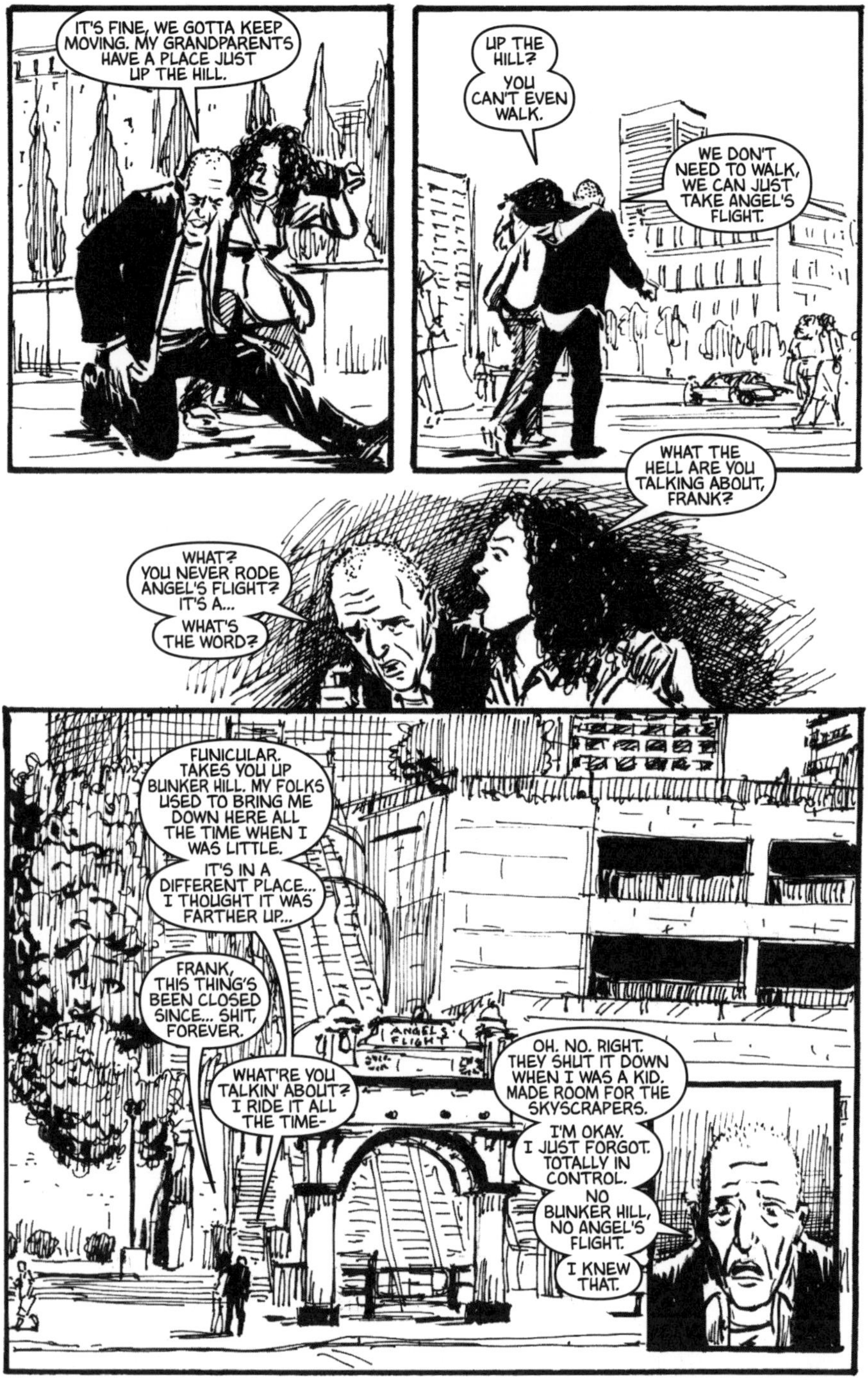
IT'S FINE, WE GOTTA KEEP MOVING. MY GRANDPARENTS HAVE A PLACE JUST UP THE HILL.
UP THE HILL?
YOU CAN'T EVEN WALK.
WE DON'T NEED TO WALK, WE CAN JUST TAKE ANGEL'S FLIGHT.
WHAT THE HELL ARE YOU TALKING ABOUT, FRANK?
WHAT? YOU NEVER RODE ANGEL'S FLIGHT? IT'S A...
WHAT'S THE WORD?
FUNICULAR. TAKES YOU UP BUNKER HILL. MY FOLKS USED TO BRING ME DOWN HERE ALL THE TIME WHEN I WAS LITTLE.
IT'S IN A DIFFERENT PLACE... I THOUGHT IT WAS FARTHER UP...
FRANK, THIS THING'S BEEN CLOSED SINCE... SHIT, FOREVER.
ANGEL'S FLIGHT
WHAT'RE YOU TALKIN' ABOUT? I RIDE IT ALL THE TIME-
OH. NO. RIGHT. THEY SHUT IT DOWN WHEN I WAS A KID. MADE ROOM FOR THE SKYSCRAPERS.
I'M OKAY. I JUST FORGOT. TOTALLY IN CONTROL.
NO BUNKER HILL, NO ANGEL'S FLIGHT.
I KNEW THAT.

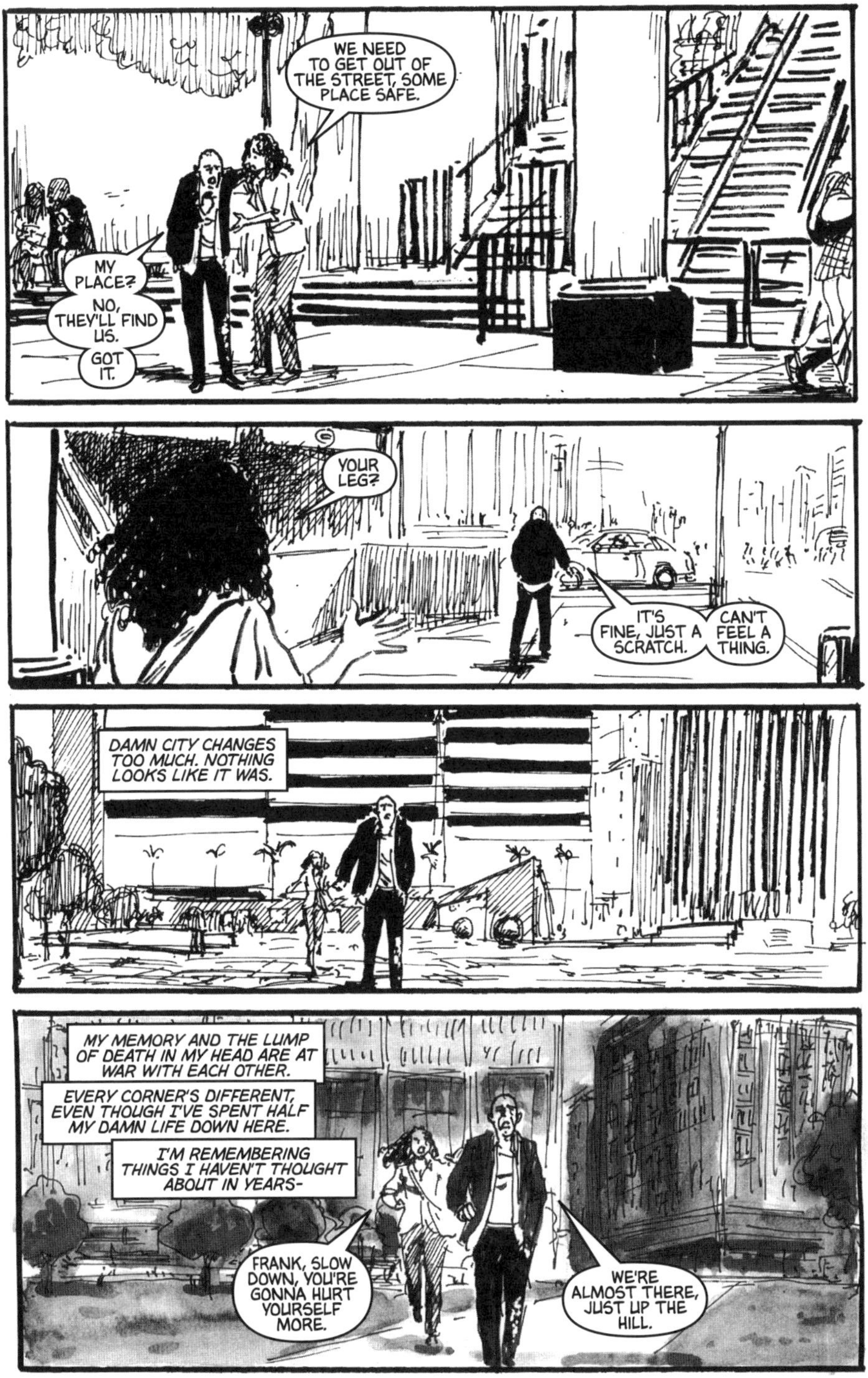
WE NEED TO GET OUT OF THE STREET, SOME PLACE SAFE.
MY PLACE?
NO, THEY'LL FIND US.
GOT IT.
YOUR LEG?
IT'S FINE, JUST A SCRATCH.
CAN'T FEEL A THING.
DAMN CITY CHANGES TOO MUCH. NOTHING LOOKS LIKE IT WAS.
MY MEMORY AND THE LUMP OF DEATH IN MY HEAD ARE AT WAR WITH EACH OTHER.
EVERY CORNER'S DIFFERENT, EVEN THOUGH I'VE SPENT HALF MY DAMN LIFE DOWN HERE.
I'M REMEMBERING THINGS I HAVEN'T THOUGHT ABOUT IN YEARS-
FRANK, SLOW DOWN, YOU'RE GONNA HURT YOURSELF MORE.
WE'RE ALMOST THERE, JUST UP THE HILL.

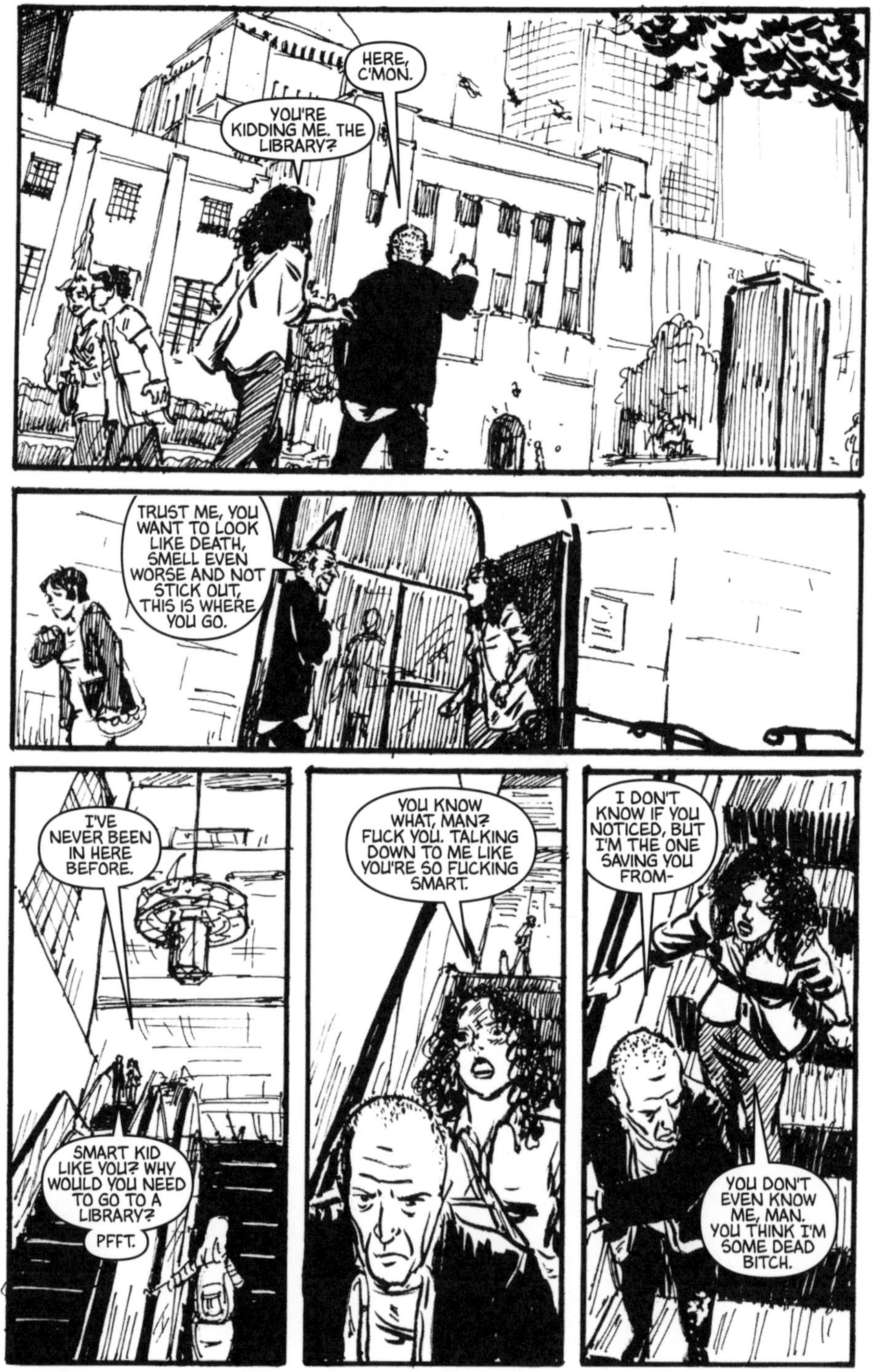
YOU'RE KIDDING ME. THE LIBRARY?
HERE, C'MON.
TRUST ME, YOU WANT TO LOOK LIKE DEATH, SMELL EVEN WORSE AND NOT STICK OUT, THIS IS WHERE YOU GO.
I'VE NEVER BEEN IN HERE BEFORE.
SMART KID LIKE YOU? WHY WOULD YOU NEED TO GO TO A LIBRARY?
PFFT.
YOU KNOW WHAT, MAN? FUCK YOU. TALKING DOWN TO ME LIKE YOU'RE SO FUCKING SMART.
I DON'T KNOW IF YOU NOTICED, BUT I'M THE ONE SAVING YOU FROM-
YOU DON'T EVEN KNOW ME, MAN. YOU THINK I'M SOME DEAD BITCH.

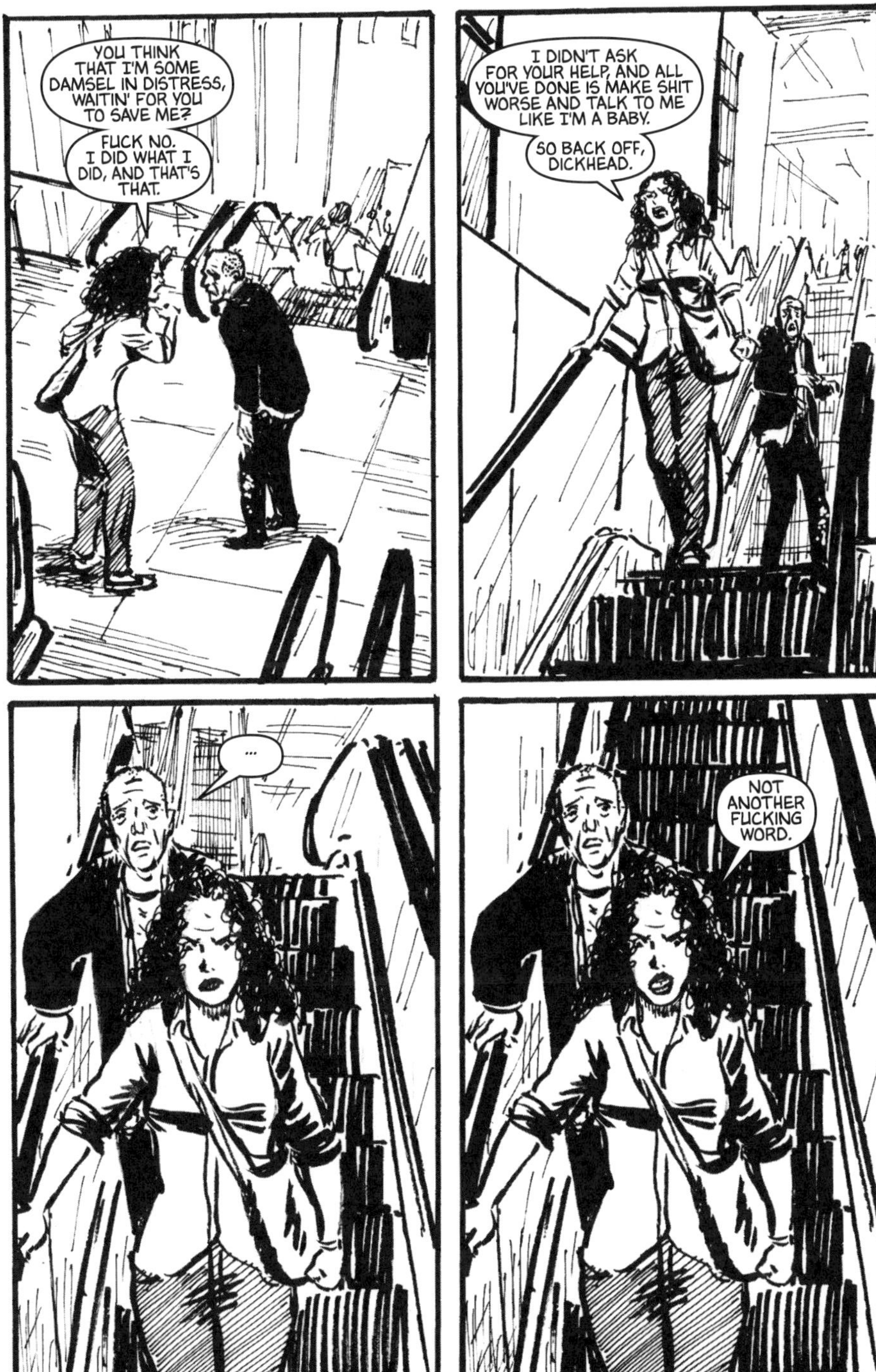
YOU THINK THAT I'M SOME DAMSEL IN DISTRESS, WAITIN' FOR YOU TO SAVE ME?
FUCK NO. I DID WHAT I DID, AND THAT'S THAT.
I DIDN'T ASK FOR YOUR HELP, AND ALL YOU'VE DONE IS MAKE SHIT WORSE AND TALK TO ME LIKE I'M A BABY.
SO BACK OFF, DICKHEAD.
...
NOT ANOTHER FUCKING WORD.

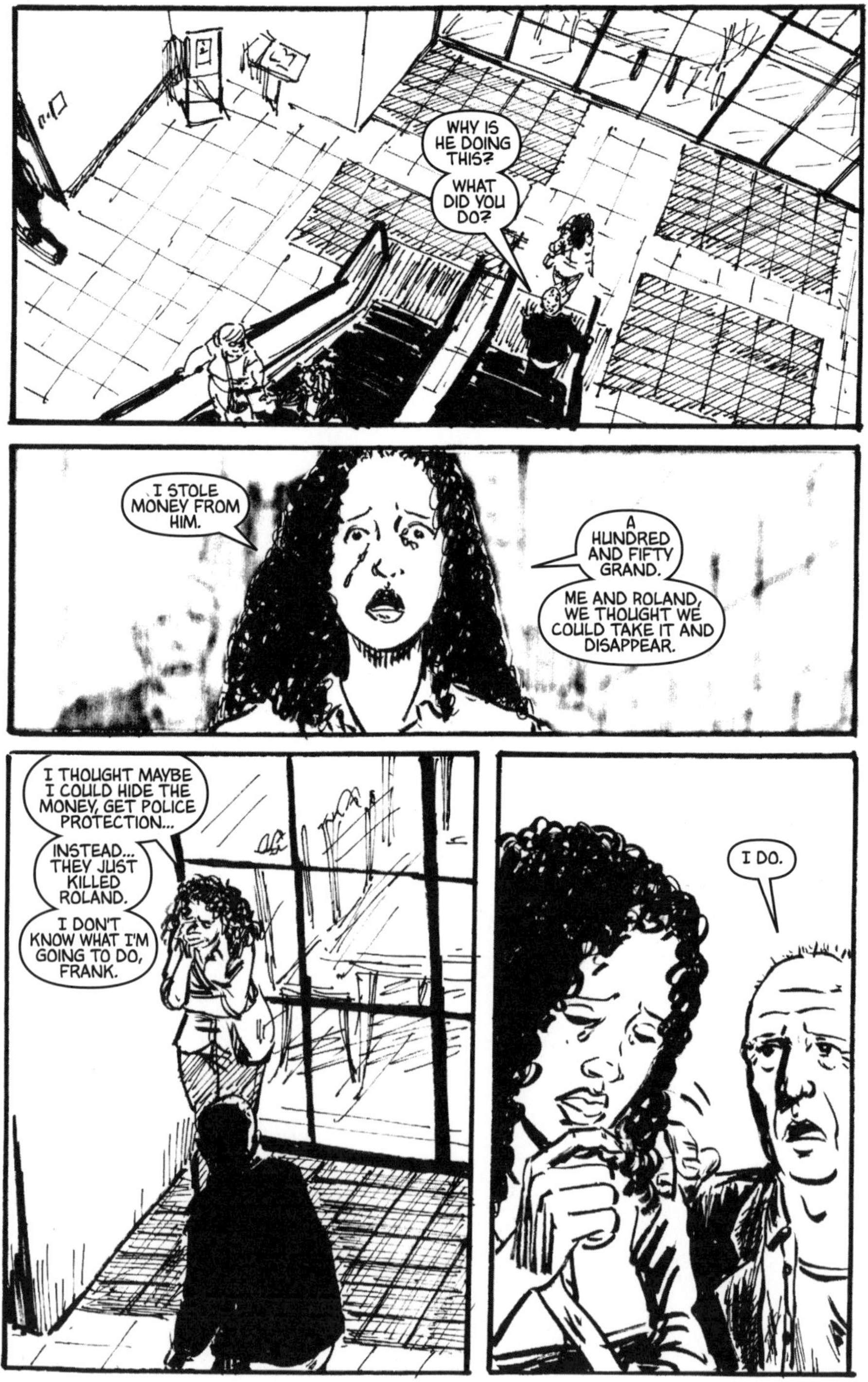
WHY IS HE DOING THIS?
WHAT DID YOU DO?
I STOLE MONEY FROM HIM.
A HUNDRED AND FIFTY GRAND.
ME AND ROLAND, WE THOUGHT WE COULD TAKE IT AND DISAPPEAR.
I THOUGHT MAYBE I COULD HIDE THE MONEY, GET POLICE PROTECTION...
INSTEAD... THEY JUST KILLED ROLAND.
I DON'T KNOW WHAT I'M GOING TO DO, FRANK.
I DO.

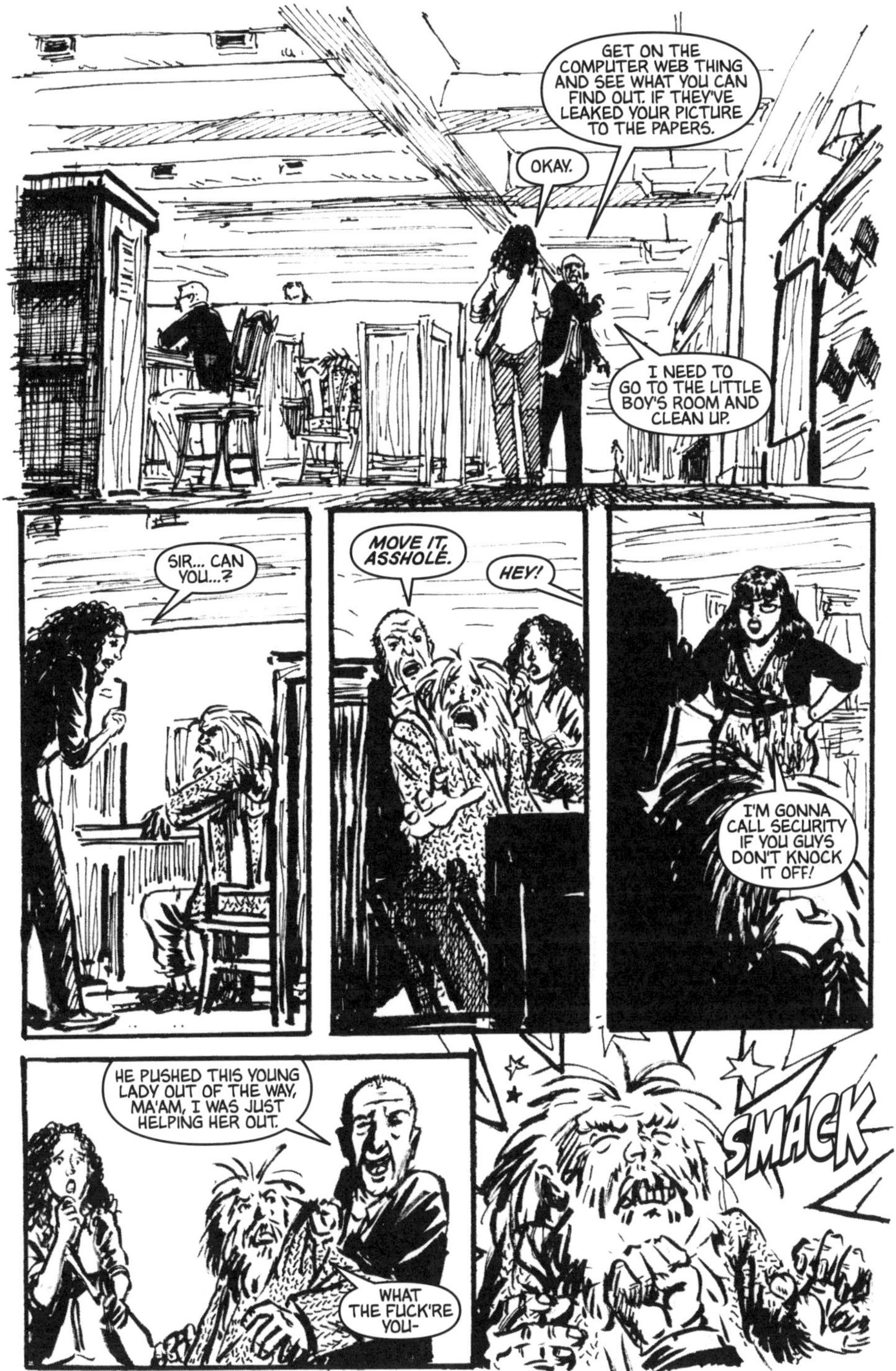
GET ON THE COMPUTER WEB THING AND SEE WHAT YOU CAN FIND OUT. IF THEY'VE LEAKED YOUR PICTURE TO THE PAPERS.
OKAY.
I NEED TO GO TO THE LITTLE BOY'S ROOM AND CLEAN UP.
SIR... CAN YOU...?
MOVE IT, ASSHOLE.
HEY!
I'M GONNA CALL SECURITY IF YOU GUYS DON'T KNOCK IT OFF!
HE PUSHED THIS YOUNG LADY OUT OF THE WAY, MA'AM, I WAS JUST HELPING HER OUT.
WHAT THE FUCK'RE YOU-
SMACK

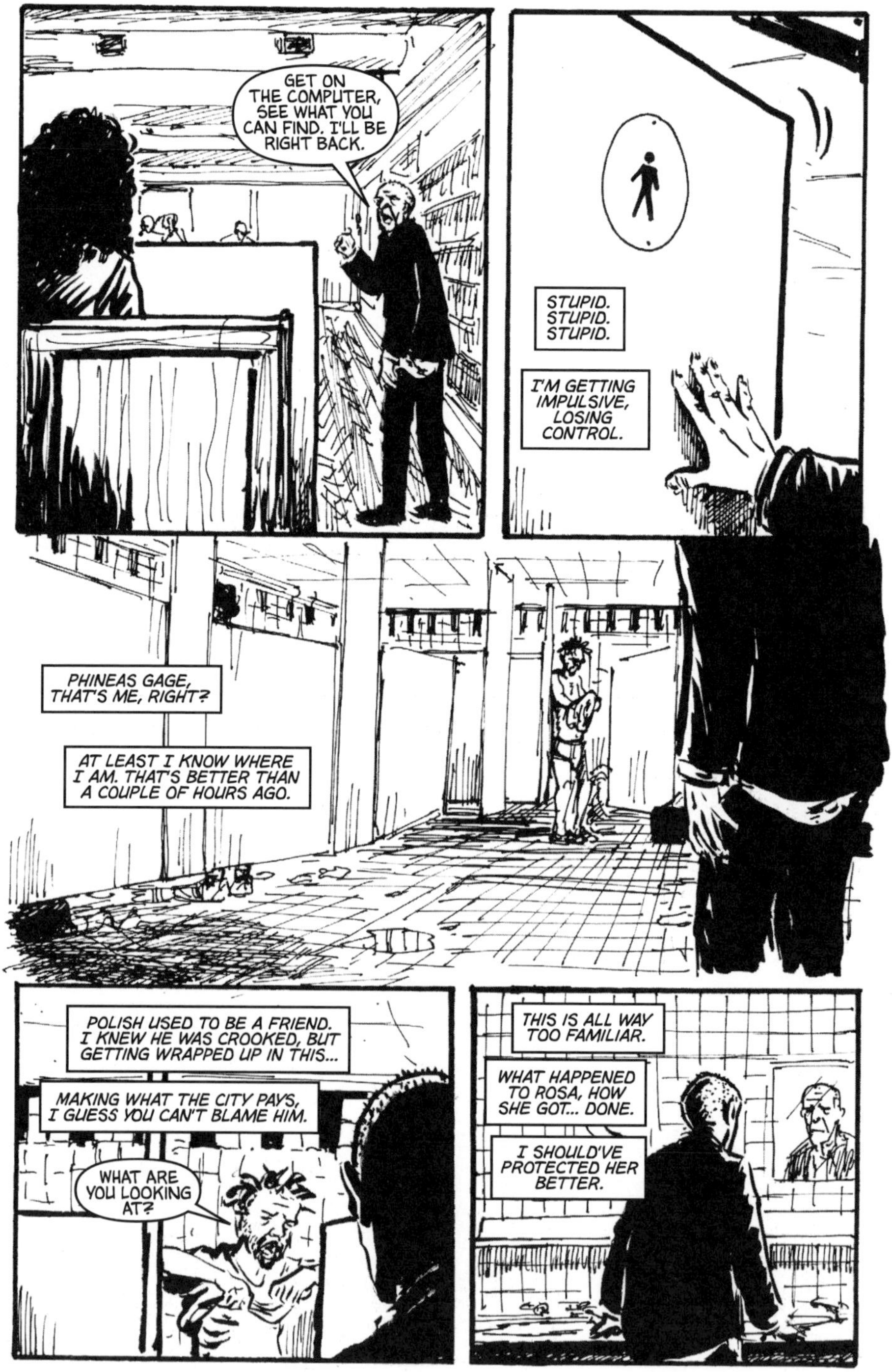
GET ON THE COMPUTER, SEE WHAT YOU CAN FIND. I'LL BE RIGHT BACK.
STUPID. STUPID. STUPID.
I'M GETTING IMPULSIVE, LOSING CONTROL.
PHINEAS GAGE, THAT'S ME, RIGHT?
AT LEAST I KNOW WHERE I AM. THAT'S BETTER THAN A COUPLE OF HOURS AGO.
POLISH USED TO BE A FRIEND. I KNEW HE WAS CROOKED, BUT GETTING WRAPPED UP IN THIS...
MAKING WHAT THE CITY PAYS, I GUESS YOU CAN'T BLAME HIM.
WHAT ARE YOU LOOKING AT?
THIS IS ALL WAY TOO FAMILIAR.
WHAT HAPPENED TO ROSA, HOW SHE GOT... DONE.
I SHOULD'VE PROTECTED HER BETTER.

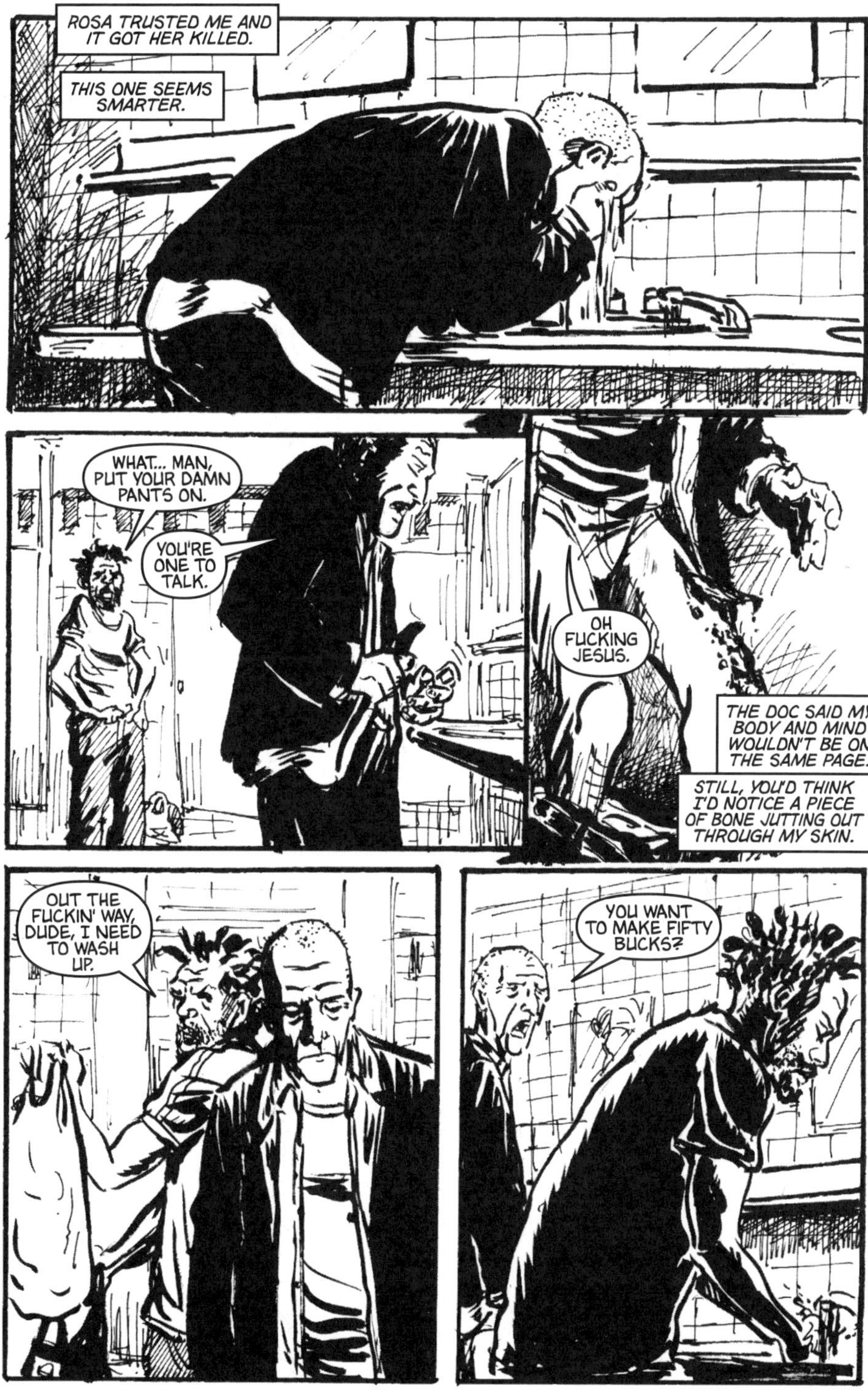

ROSA TRUSTED ME AND IT GOT HER KILLED.
THIS ONE SEEMS SMARTER.
WHAT... MAN, PUT YOUR DAMN PANTS ON.
YOU'RE ONE TO TALK.
OH FUCKING JESUS.
THE DOC SAID MY BODY AND MIND WOULDN'T BE ON THE SAME PAGE.
STILL, YOU'D THINK I'D NOTICE A PIECE OF BONE JUTTING OUT THROUGH MY SKIN.
OUT THE FUCKIN' WAY, DUDE, I NEED TO WASH UP.
YOU WANT TO MAKE FIFTY BUCKS?

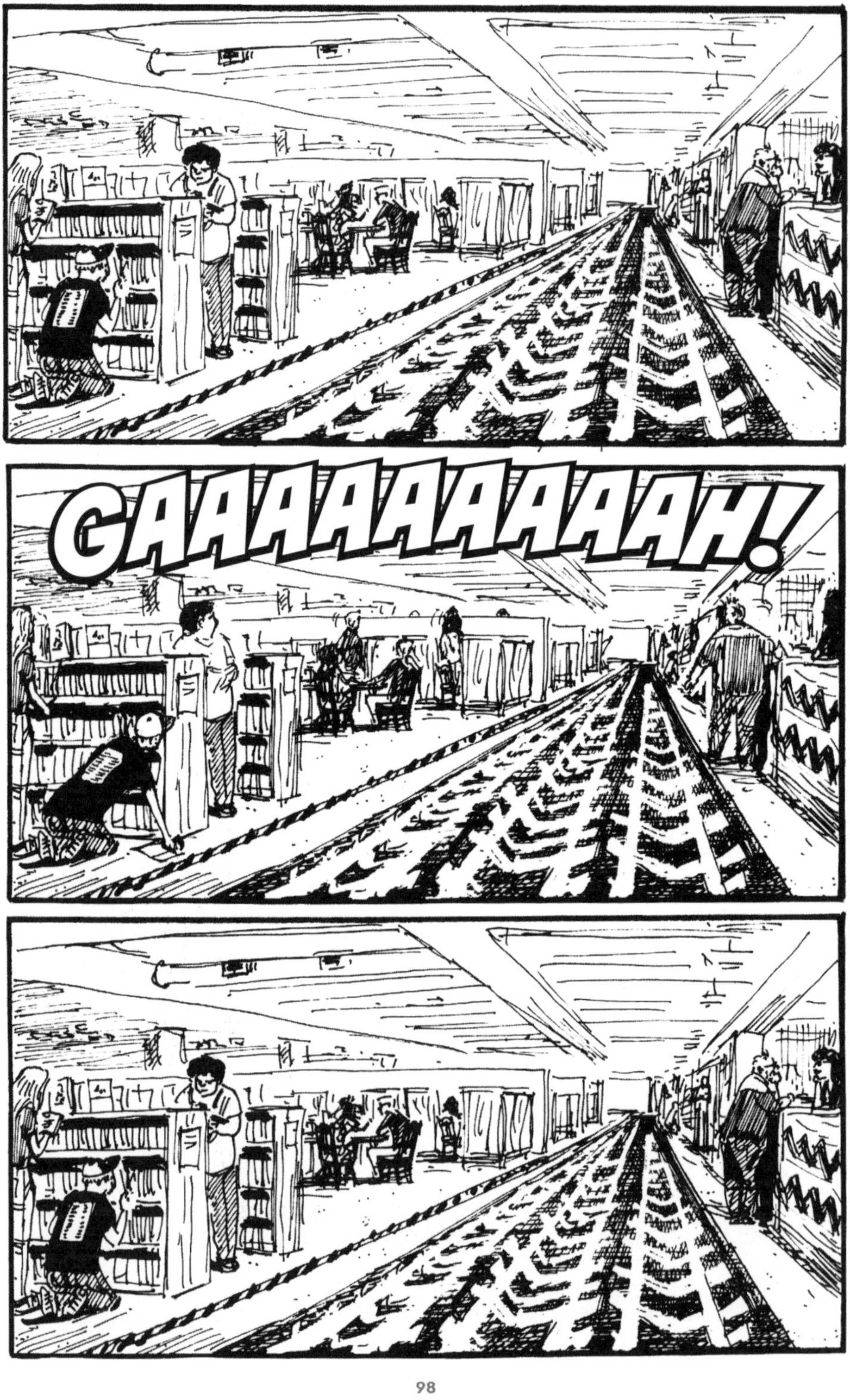
GAAAAAAAAAAH!

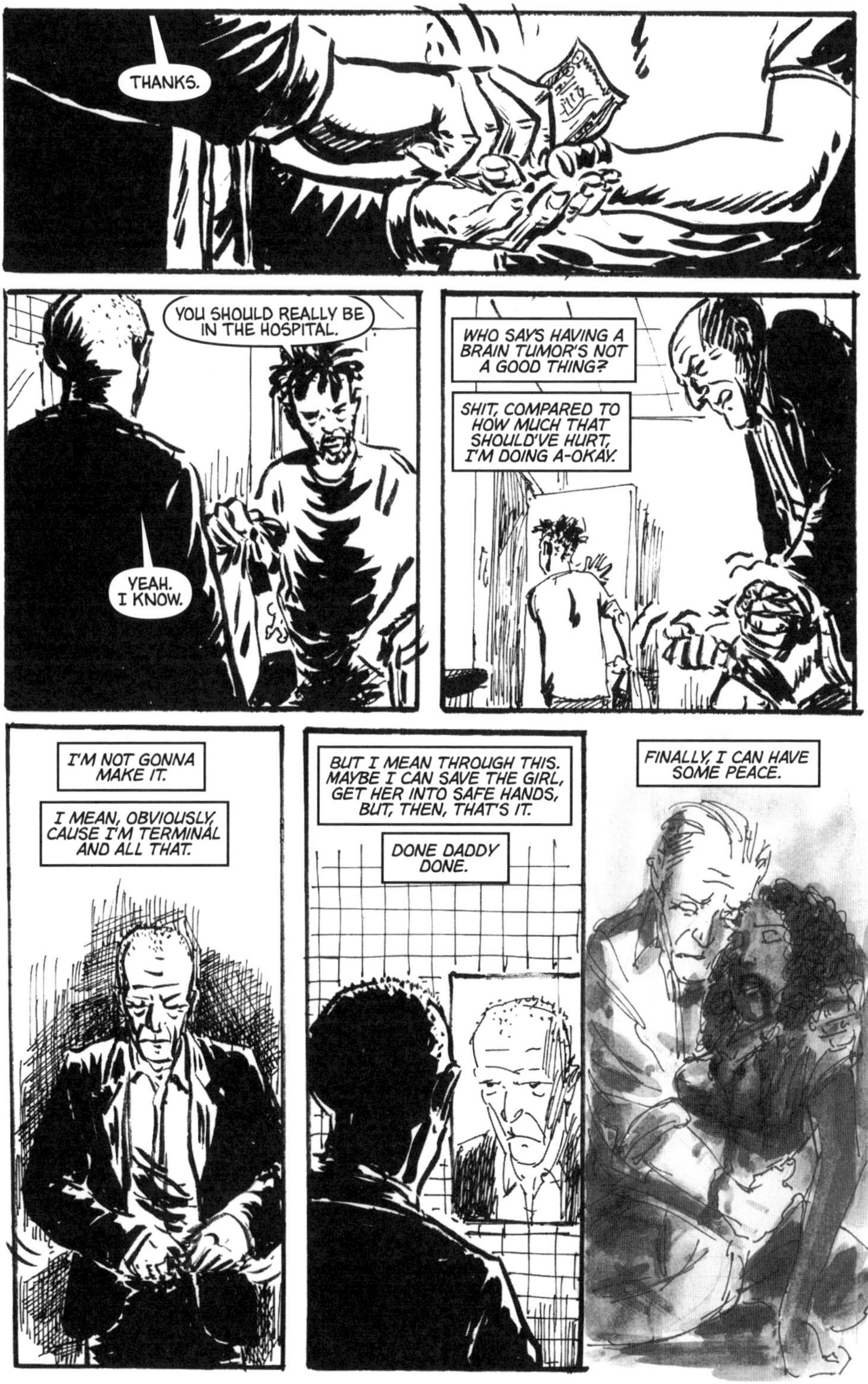
THANKS.
YOU SHOULD REALLY BE IN THE HOSPITAL.
YEAH. I KNOW.
WHO SAYS HAVING A BRAIN TUMOR'S NOT A GOOD THING?
SHIT, COMPARED TO HOW MUCH THAT SHOULD'VE HURT, I'M DOING A-OKAY.
I'M NOT GONNA MAKE IT.
I MEAN, OBVIOUSLY, CAUSE I'M TERMINAL AND ALL THAT.
BUT I MEAN THROUGH THIS. MAYBE I CAN SAVE THE GIRL, GET HER INTO SAFE HANDS, BUT, THEN, THAT'S IT.
DONE DADDY DONE.
FINALLY, I CAN HAVE SOME PEACE.

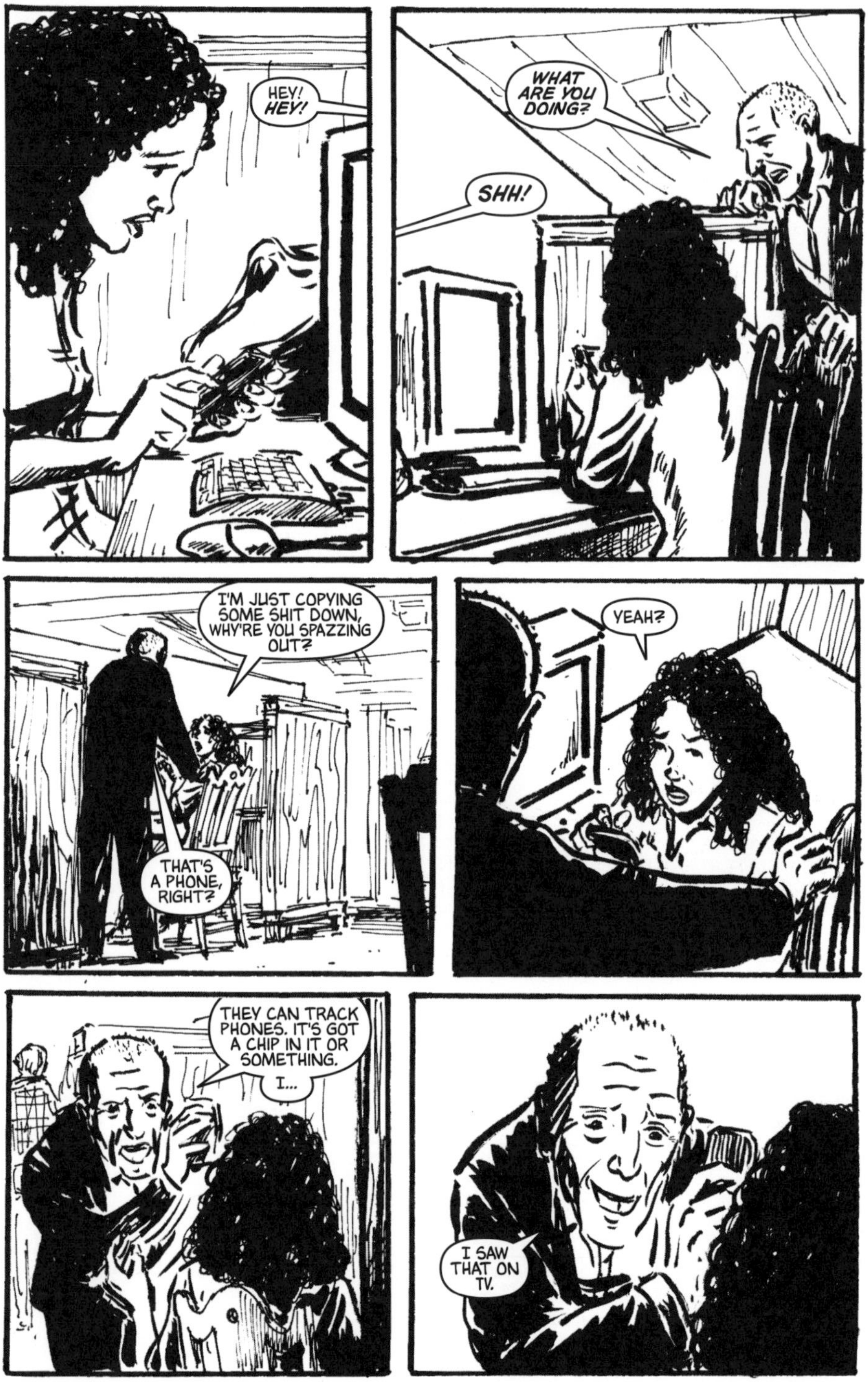
HEY!
HEY!
WHAT ARE YOU DOING?
SHH!
I'M JUST COPYING SOME SHIT DOWN, WHY'RE YOU SPAZZING OUT?
THAT'S A PHONE, RIGHT?
YEAH?
THEY CAN TRACK PHONES. IT'S GOT A CHIP IN IT OR SOMETHING.
I...
I SAW THAT ON TV.

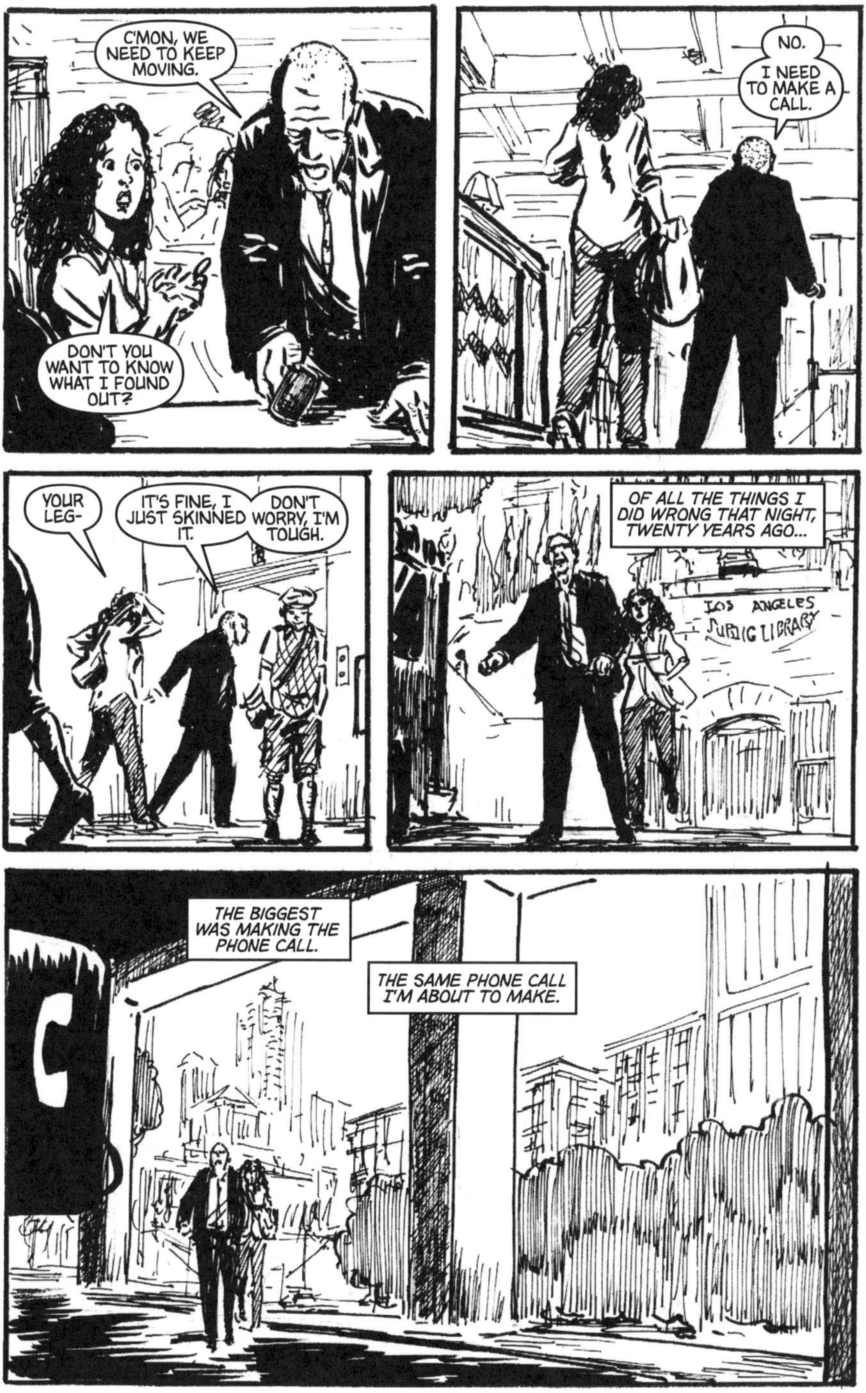
C'MON, WE NEED TO KEEP MOVING.
DON'T YOU WANT TO KNOW WHAT I FOUND OUT?
NO.
I NEED TO MAKE A CALL.
YOUR LEG-
IT'S FINE, I JUST SKINNED IT.
DON'T WORRY, I'M TOUGH.
OF ALL THE THINGS I DID WRONG THAT NIGHT, TWENTY YEARS AGO...
LOS ANGELES PUBLIC LIBRARY
THE BIGGEST WAS MAKING THE PHONE CALL.
THE SAME PHONE CALL I'M ABOUT TO MAKE.

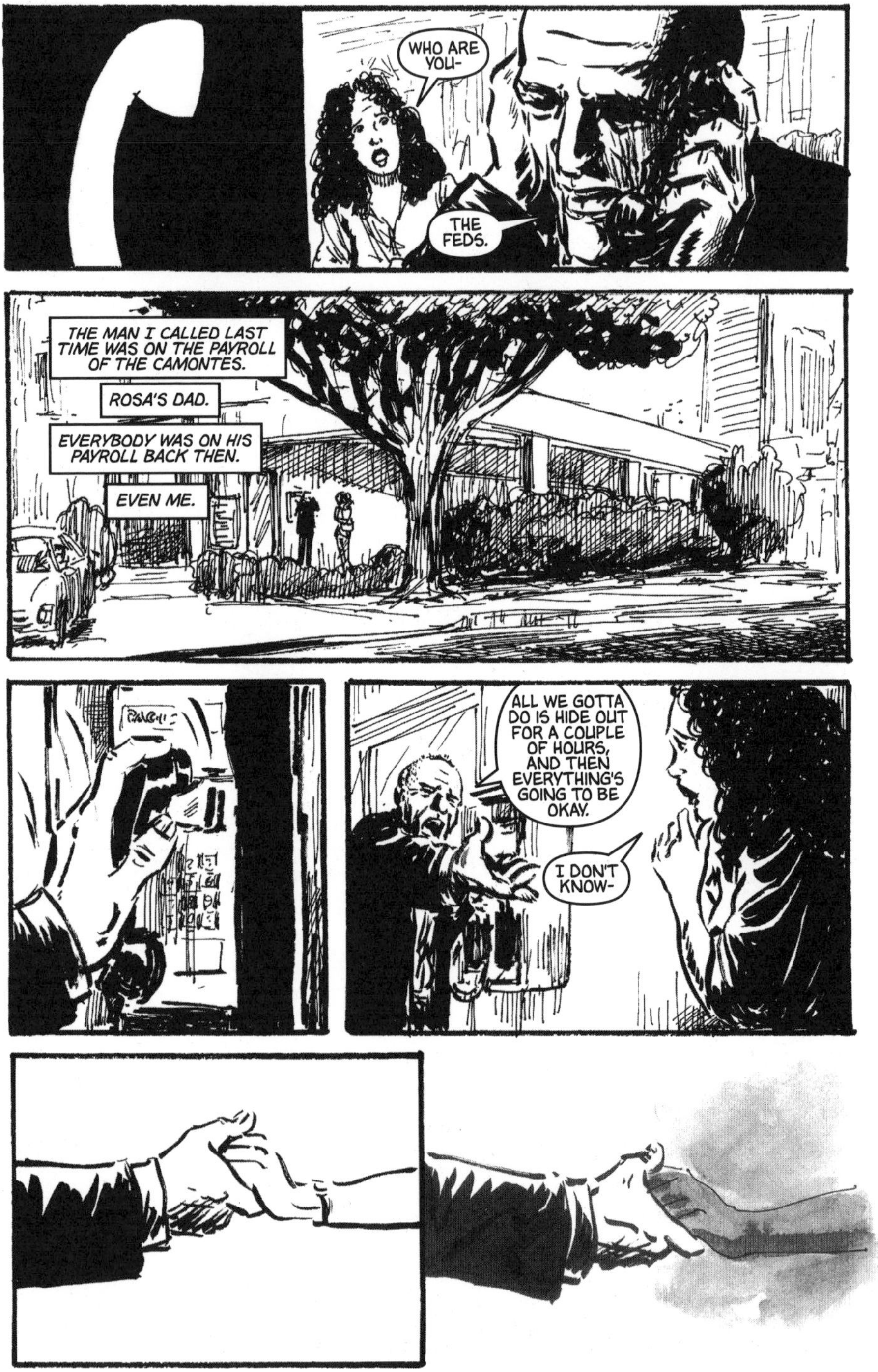
WHO ARE YOU-
THE FEDS.
THE MAN I CALLED LAST TIME WAS ON THE PAYROLL OF THE CAMONTES.
ROSA'S DAD.
EVERYBODY WAS ON HIS PAYROLL BACK THEN.
EVEN ME.
ALL WE GOTTA DO IS HIDE OUT FOR A COUPLE OF HOURS, AND THEN EVERYTHING'S GOING TO BE OKAY.
I DON'T KNOW-

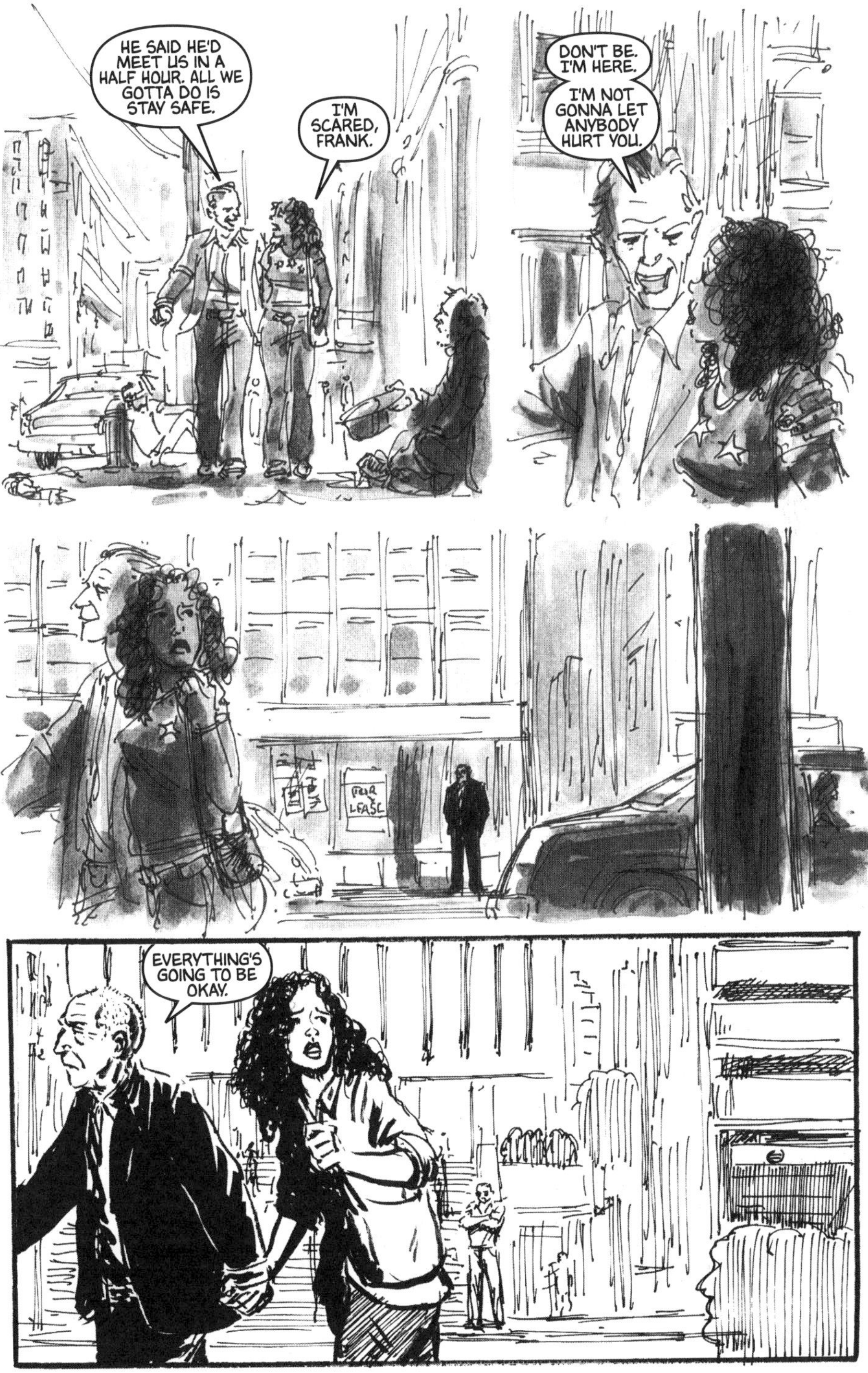
HE SAID HE'D MEET US IN A HALF HOUR. ALL WE GOTTA DO IS STAY SAFE.
I'M SCARED, FRANK.
DON'T BE. I'M HERE.
I'M NOT GONNA LET ANYBODY HURT YOU.
EVERYTHING'S GOING TO BE OKAY.

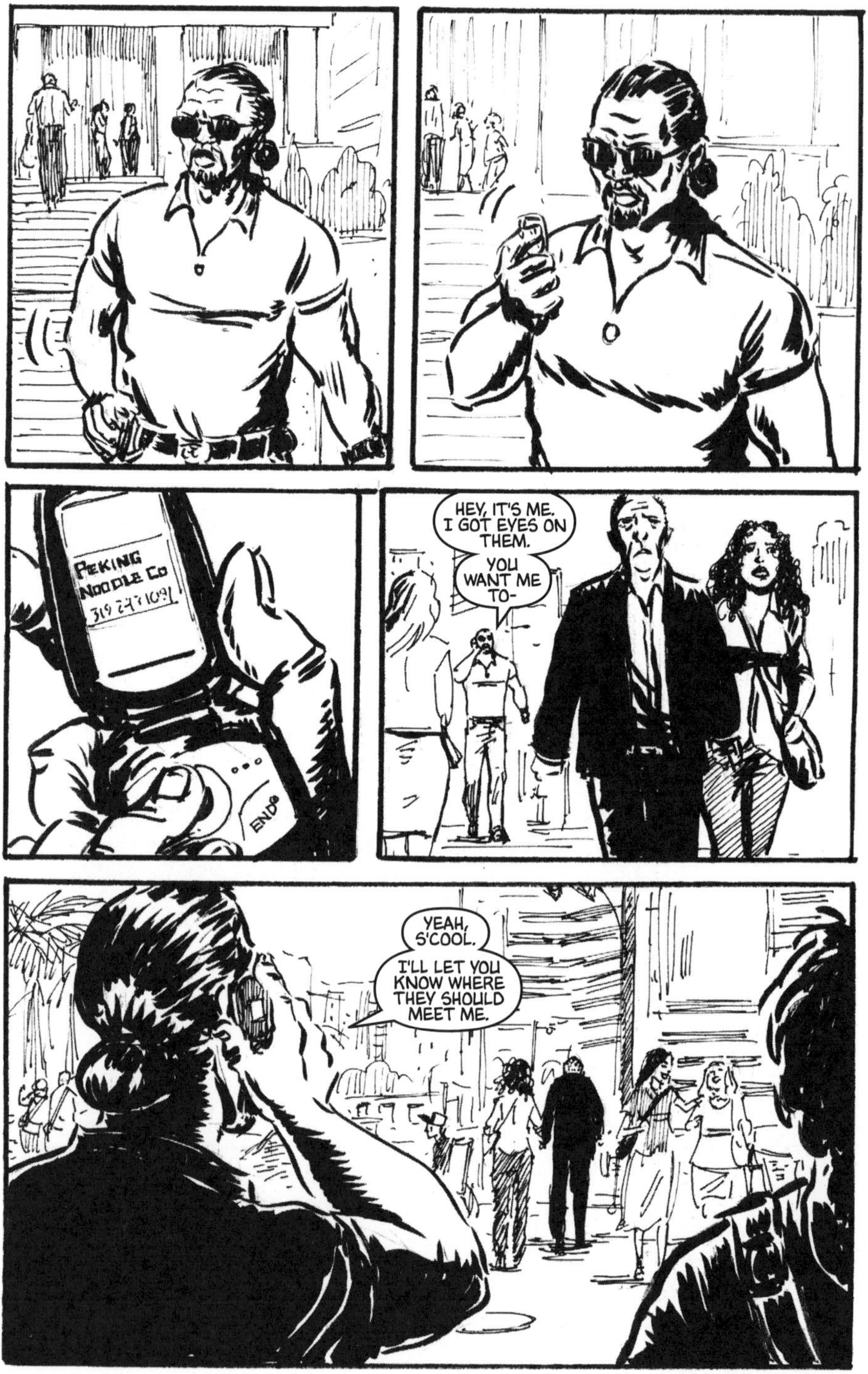
PEKING
NOODLE CO
END
HEY, IT'S ME. I GOT EYES ON THEM.
YOU WANT ME TO-
YEAH, S'COOL.
I'LL LET YOU KNOW WHERE THEY SHOULD MEET ME.

END CHAPTER 4

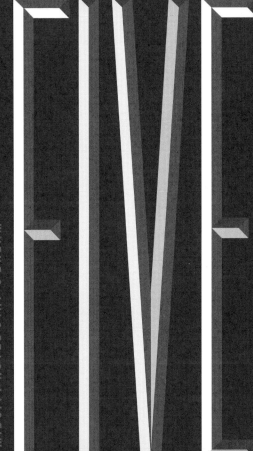

A MIDCITY HOTEL STAY'S DREAM

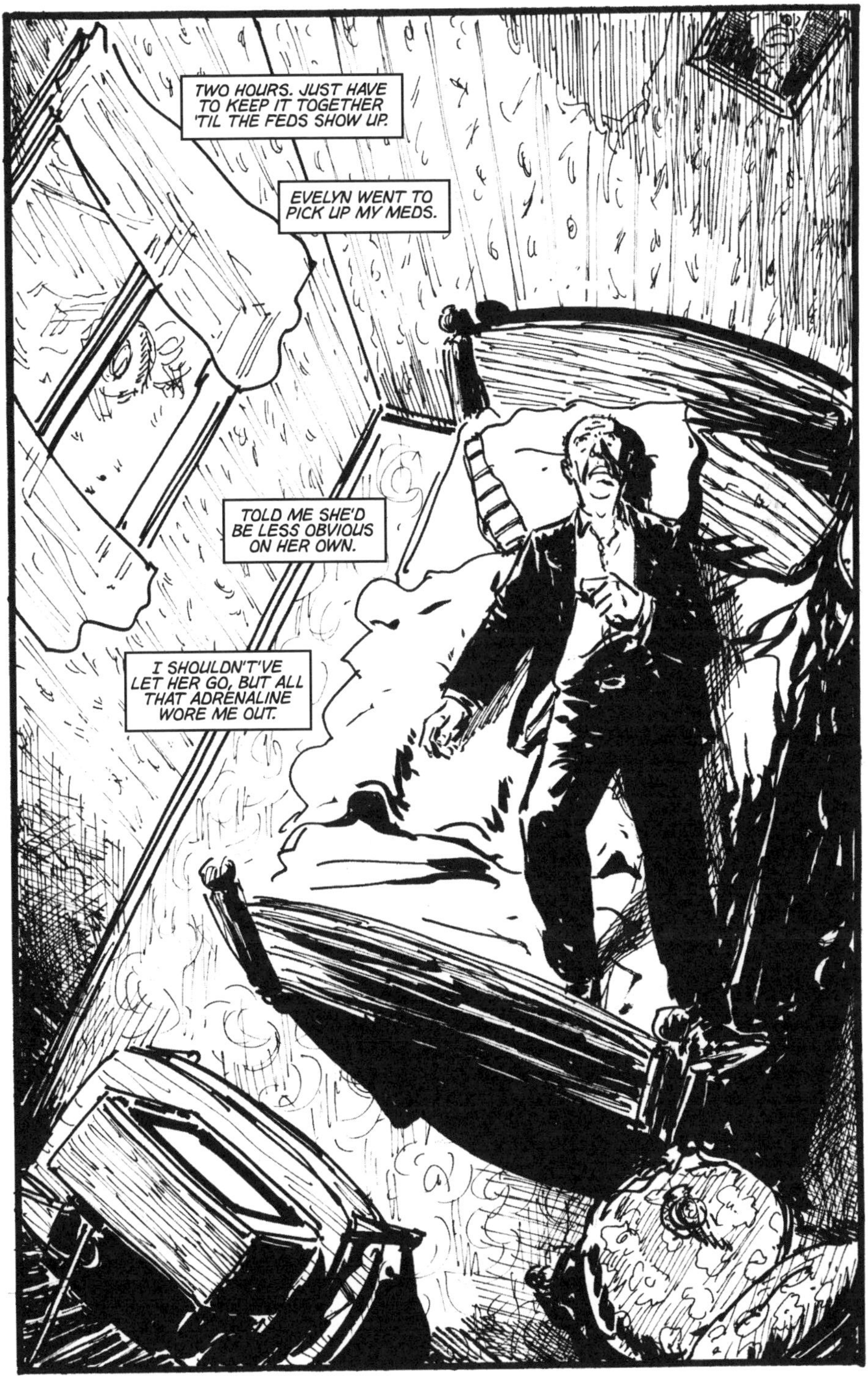
TWO HOURS. JUST HAVE TO KEEP IT TOGETHER 'TIL THE FEDS SHOW UP.
EVELYN WENT TO PICK UP MY MEDS.
TOLD ME SHE'D BE LESS OBVIOUS ON HER OWN.
I SHOULDN'T'VE LET HER GO, BUT ALL THAT ADRENALINE WORE ME OUT.

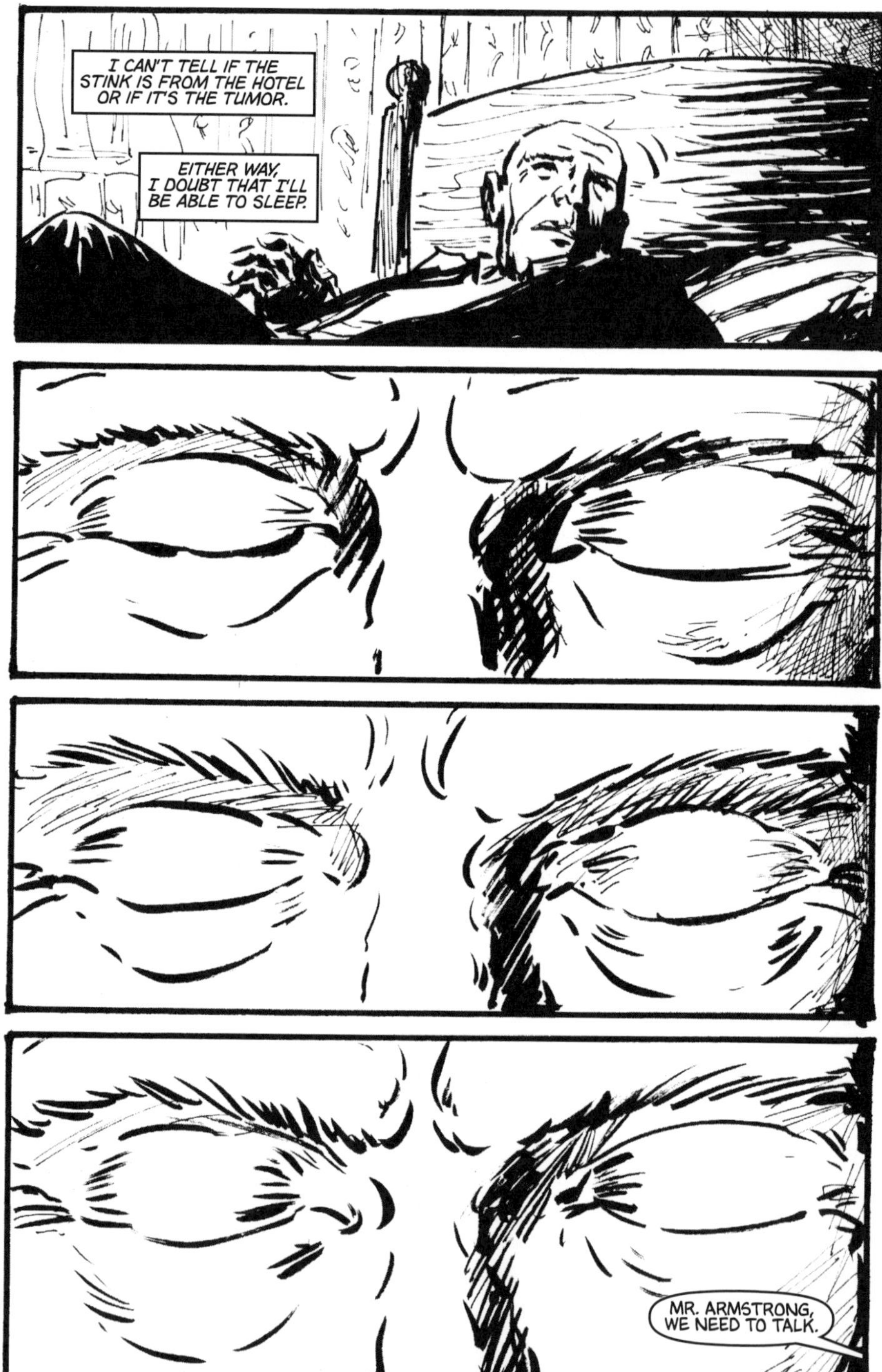

I CAN'T TELL IF THE STINK IS FROM THE HOTEL OR IF IT'S THE TUMOR.
EITHER WAY, I DOUBT THAT I'LL BE ABLE TO SLEEP.
MR. ARMSTRONG, WE NEED TO TALK.

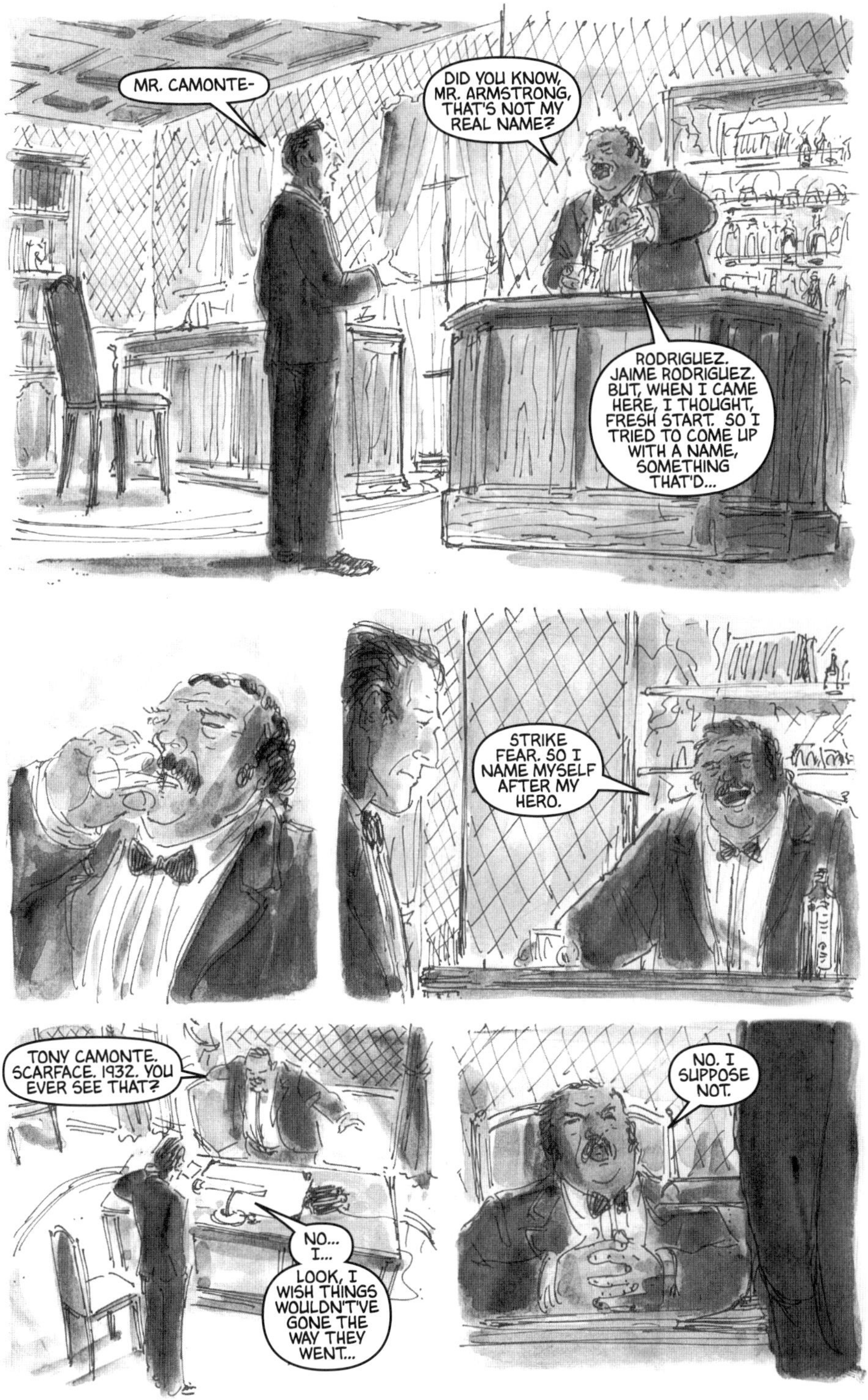
MR. CAMONTE-
DID YOU KNOW, MR. ARMSTRONG, THAT'S NOT MY REAL NAME?
RODRIGUEZ. JAIME RODRIGUEZ. BUT, WHEN I CAME HERE, I THOUGHT, FRESH START. SO I TRIED TO COME UP WITH A NAME, SOMETHING THAT'D...
STRIKE FEAR. SO I NAME MYSELF AFTER MY HERO.
TONY CAMONTE. SCARFACE. 1932. YOU EVER SEE THAT?
NO... I...
LOOK, I WISH THINGS WOULDN'T'VE GONE THE WAY THEY WENT...
NO. I SUPPOSE NOT.

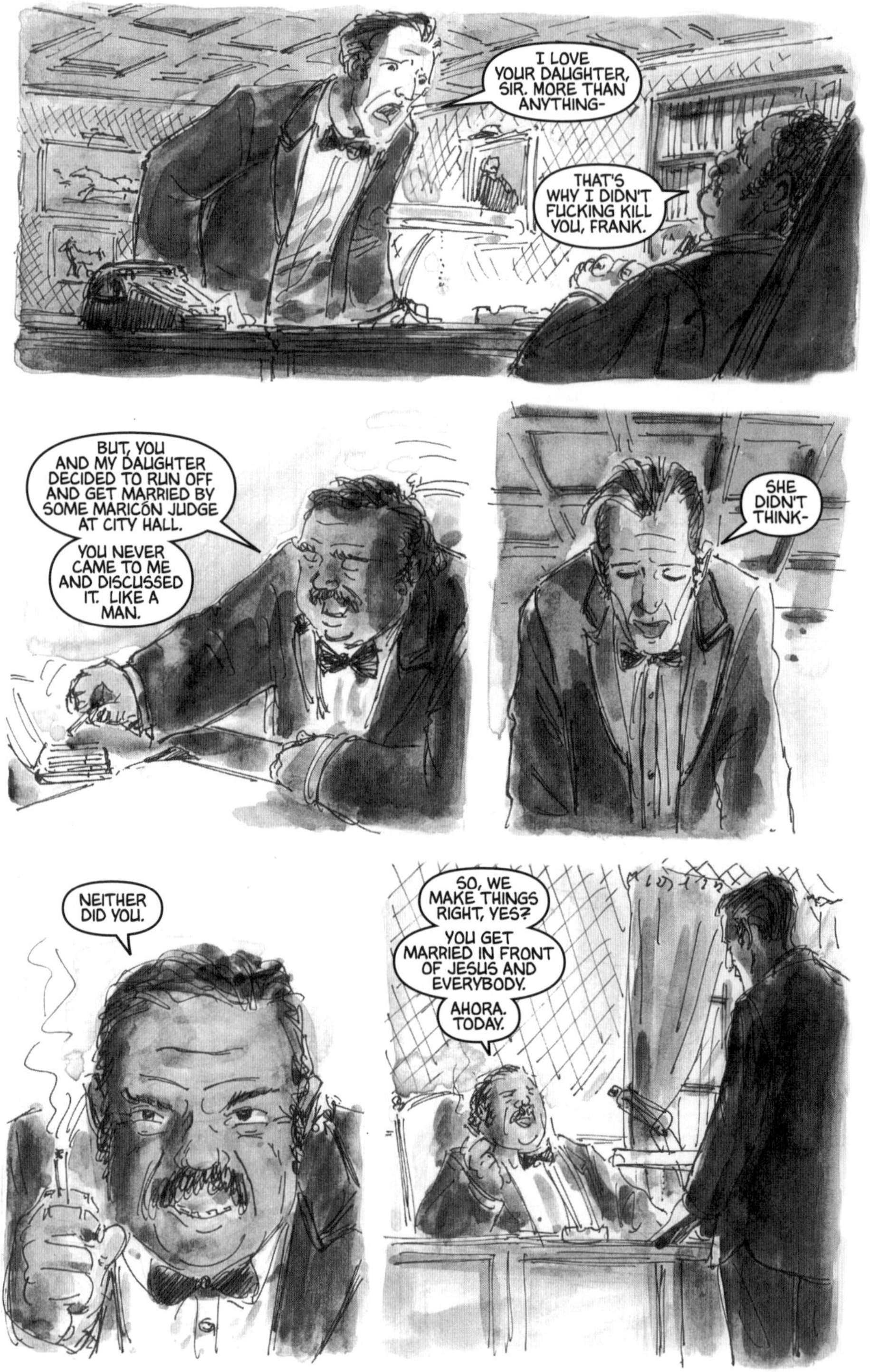
I LOVE YOUR DAUGHTER, SIR. MORE THAN ANYTHING-
THAT'S WHY I DIDN'T FUCKING KILL YOU, FRANK.
BUT, YOU AND MY DAUGHTER DECIDED TO RUN OFF AND GET MARRIED BY SOME MARICÓN JUDGE AT CITY HALL.
YOU NEVER CAME TO ME AND DISCUSSED IT. LIKE A MAN.
SHE DIDN'T THINK-
NEITHER DID YOU.
SO, WE MAKE THINGS RIGHT, YES?
YOU GET MARRIED IN FRONT OF JESUS AND EVERYBODY.
AHORA. TODAY.

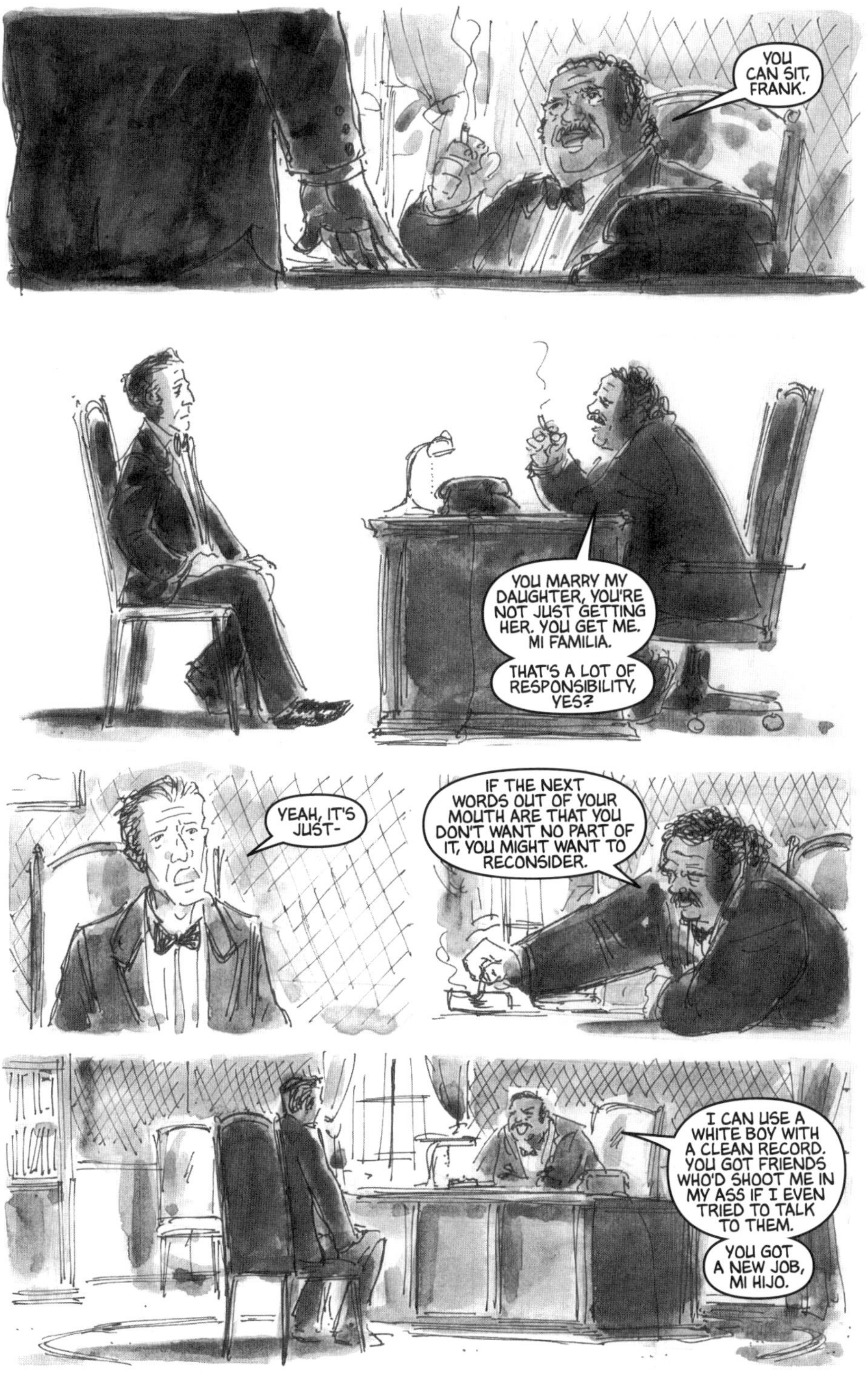
YOU CAN SIT, FRANK.
YOU MARRY MY DAUGHTER, YOU'RE NOT JUST GETTING HER. YOU GET ME. MI FAMILIA.
THAT'S A LOT OF RESPONSIBILITY, YES?
YEAH, IT'S JUST-
IF THE NEXT WORDS OUT OF YOUR MOUTH ARE THAT YOU DON'T WANT NO PART OF IT, YOU MIGHT WANT TO RECONSIDER.
I CAN USE A WHITE BOY WITH A CLEAN RECORD. YOU GOT FRIENDS WHO'D SHOOT ME IN MY ASS IF I EVEN TRIED TO TALK TO THEM.
YOU GOT A NEW JOB, MI HIJO.

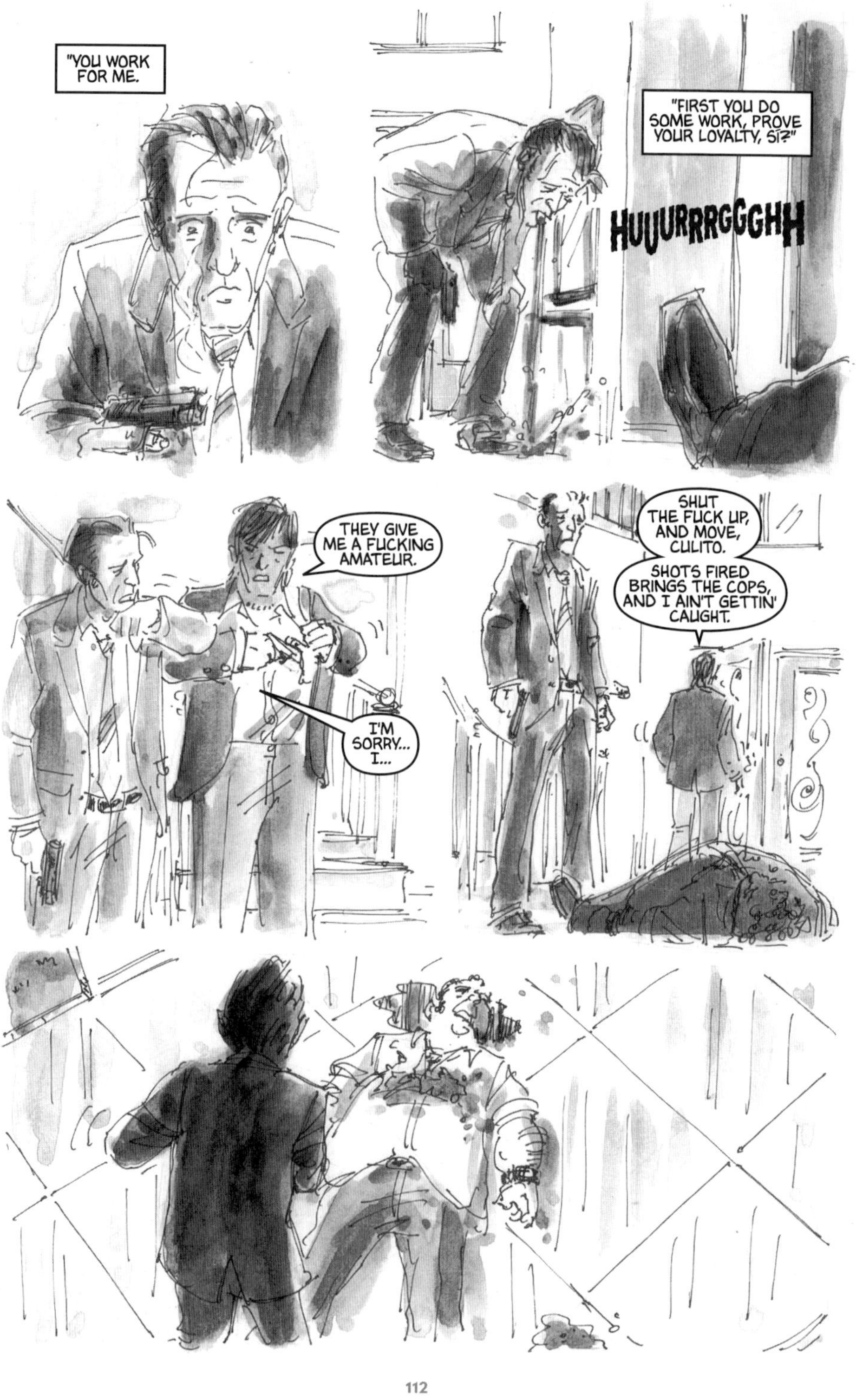
"YOU WORK FOR ME.
"FIRST YOU DO SOME WORK, PROVE YOUR LOYALTY, SÍ?"
HUUURRRGGGHH
THEY GIVE ME A FUCKING AMATEUR.
I'M SORRY... I...
SHUT THE FUCK UP, AND MOVE, CULITO.
SHOTS FIRED BRINGS THE COPS, AND I AIN'T GETTIN' CAUGHT.

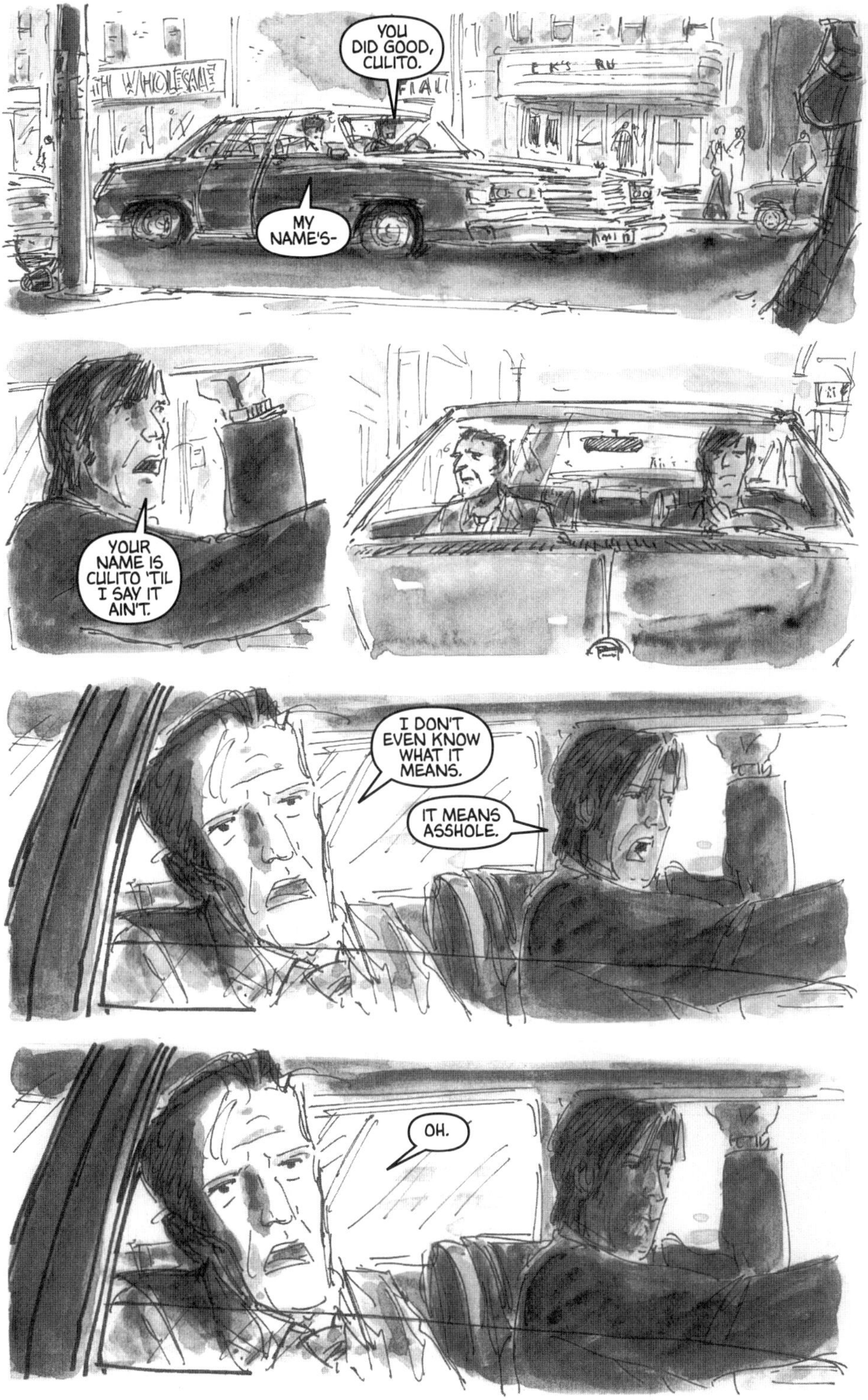
YOU DID GOOD, CULITO.
MY NAME'S-
YOUR NAME IS CULITO 'TIL I SAY IT AIN'T.
I DON'T EVEN KNOW WHAT IT MEANS.
IT MEANS ASSHOLE.
OH.

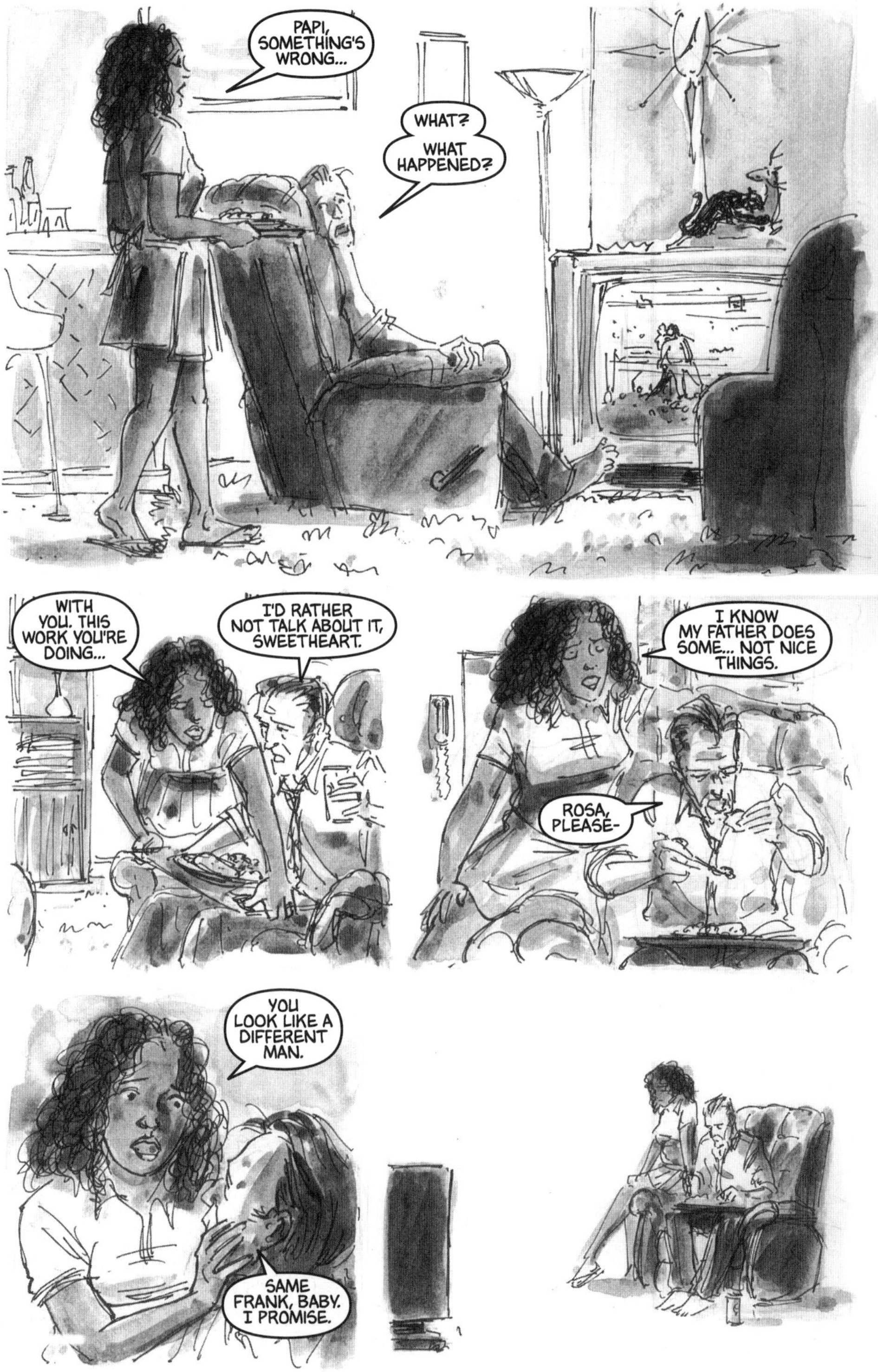
PAPI, SOMETHING'S WRONG...
WHAT? WHAT HAPPENED?
WITH YOU. THIS WORK YOU'RE DOING...
I'D RATHER NOT TALK ABOUT IT, SWEETHEART.
I KNOW MY FATHER DOES SOME... NOT NICE THINGS.
ROSA, PLEASE-
YOU LOOK LIKE A DIFFERENT MAN.
SAME FRANK, BABY. I PROMISE.

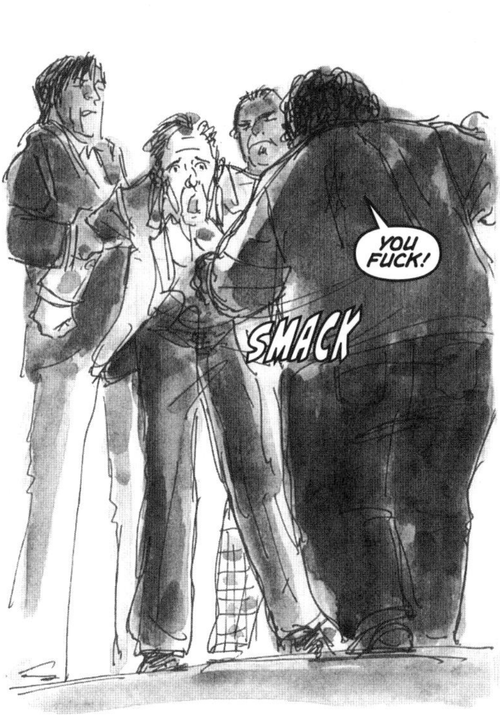
YOU FUCK!
SMACK

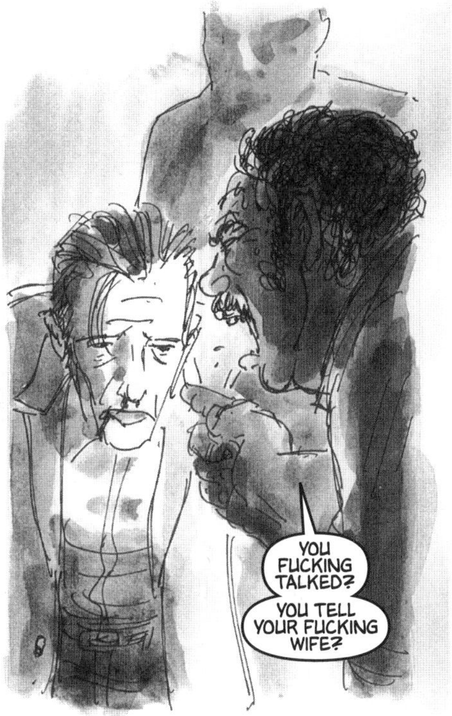
YOU FUCKING TALKED?
YOU TELL YOUR FUCKING WIFE?

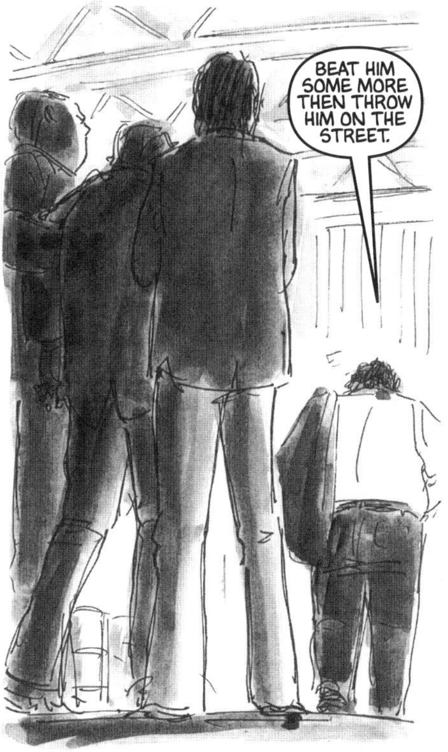
BEAT HIM SOME MORE THEN THROW HIM ON THE STREET.

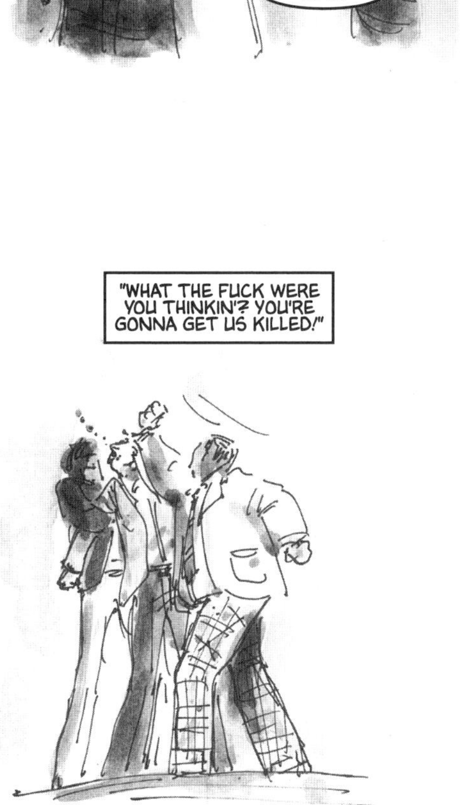
"WHAT THE FUCK WERE YOU THINKIN'? YOU'RE GONNA GET US KILLED!"

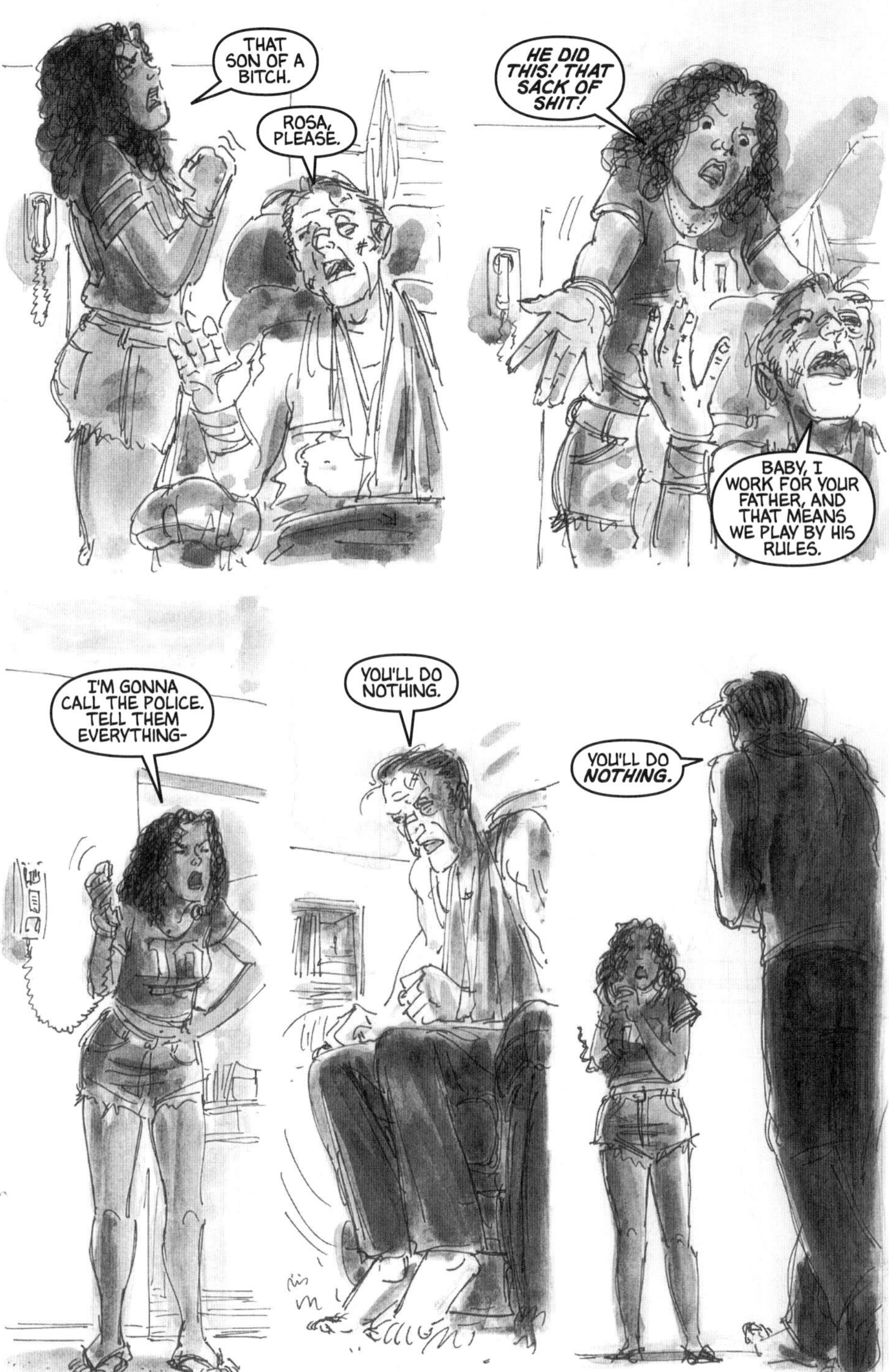
THAT SON OF A BITCH.
ROSA, PLEASE.
HE DID THIS! THAT SACK OF SHIT!
BABY, I WORK FOR YOUR FATHER, AND THAT MEANS WE PLAY BY HIS RULES.
I'M GONNA CALL THE POLICE. TELL THEM EVERYTHING-
YOU'LL DO NOTHING.
YOU'LL DO *NOTHING.*

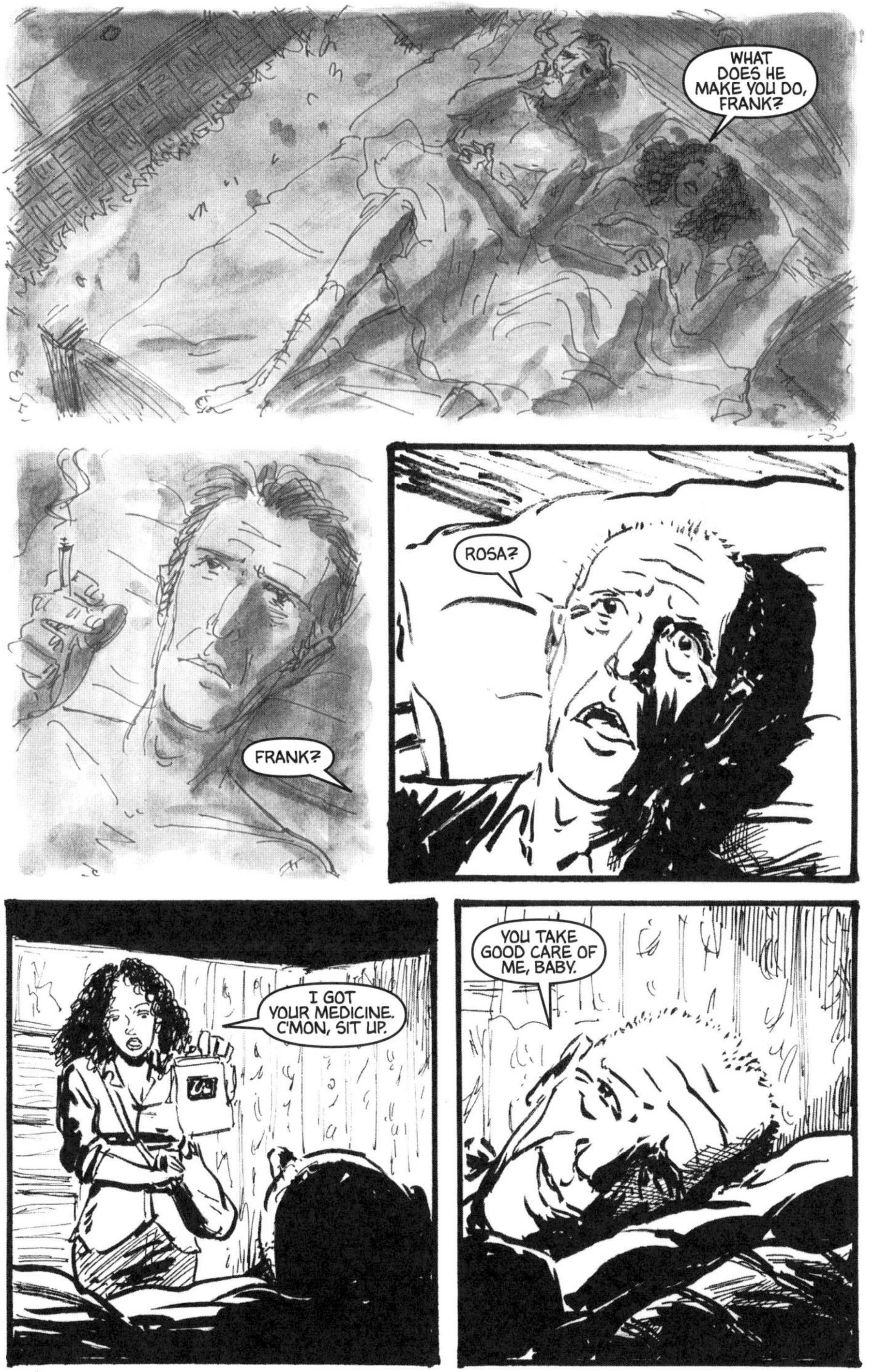
WHAT DOES HE MAKE YOU DO, FRANK?
FRANK?
ROSA?
I GOT YOUR MEDICINE. C'MON, SIT UP.
YOU TAKE GOOD CARE OF ME, BABY.

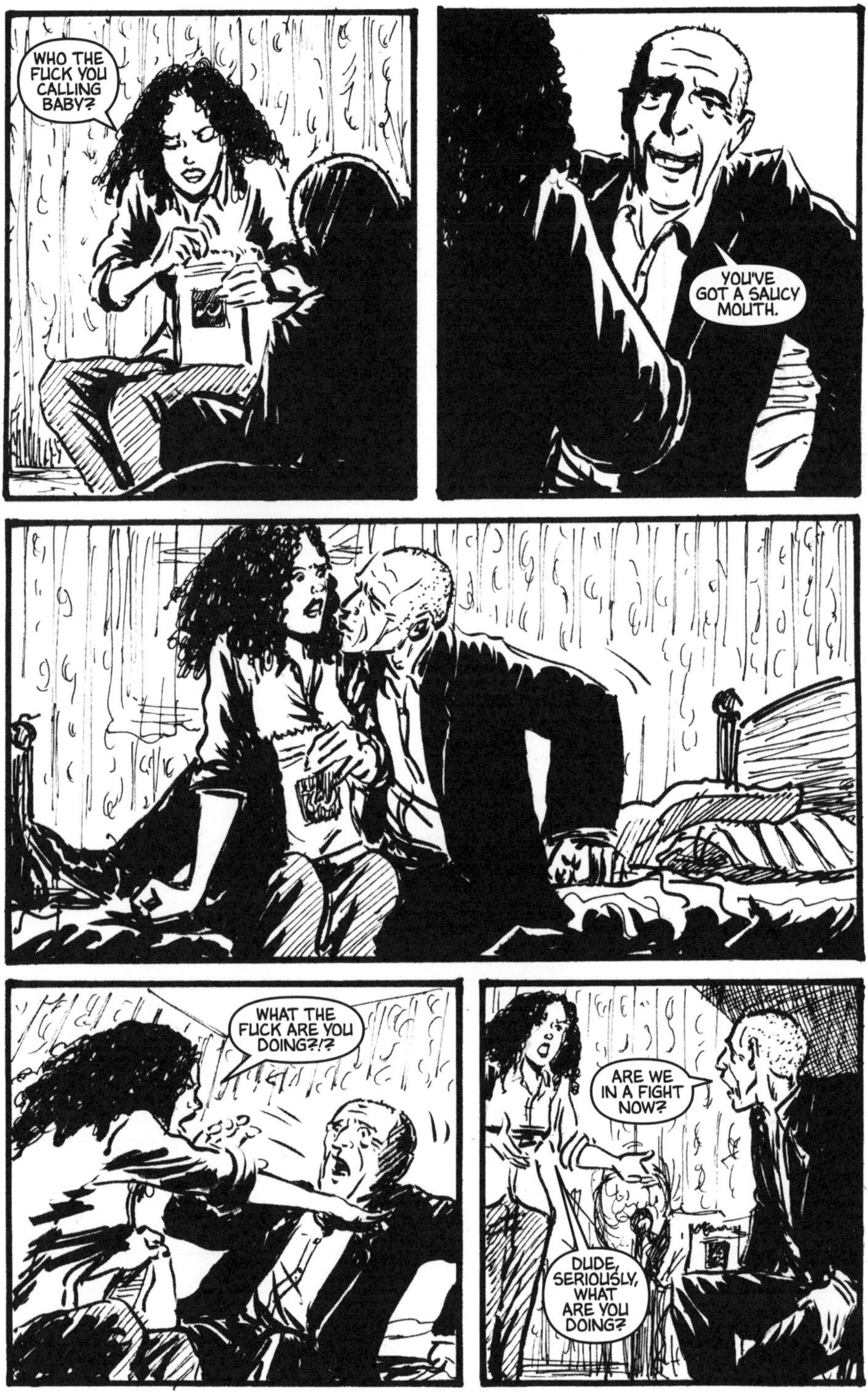
WHO THE FUCK YOU CALLING BABY?
YOU'VE GOT A SAUCY MOUTH.
WHAT THE FUCK ARE YOU DOING?!?
ARE WE IN A FIGHT NOW?
DUDE, SERIOUSLY, WHAT ARE YOU DOING?

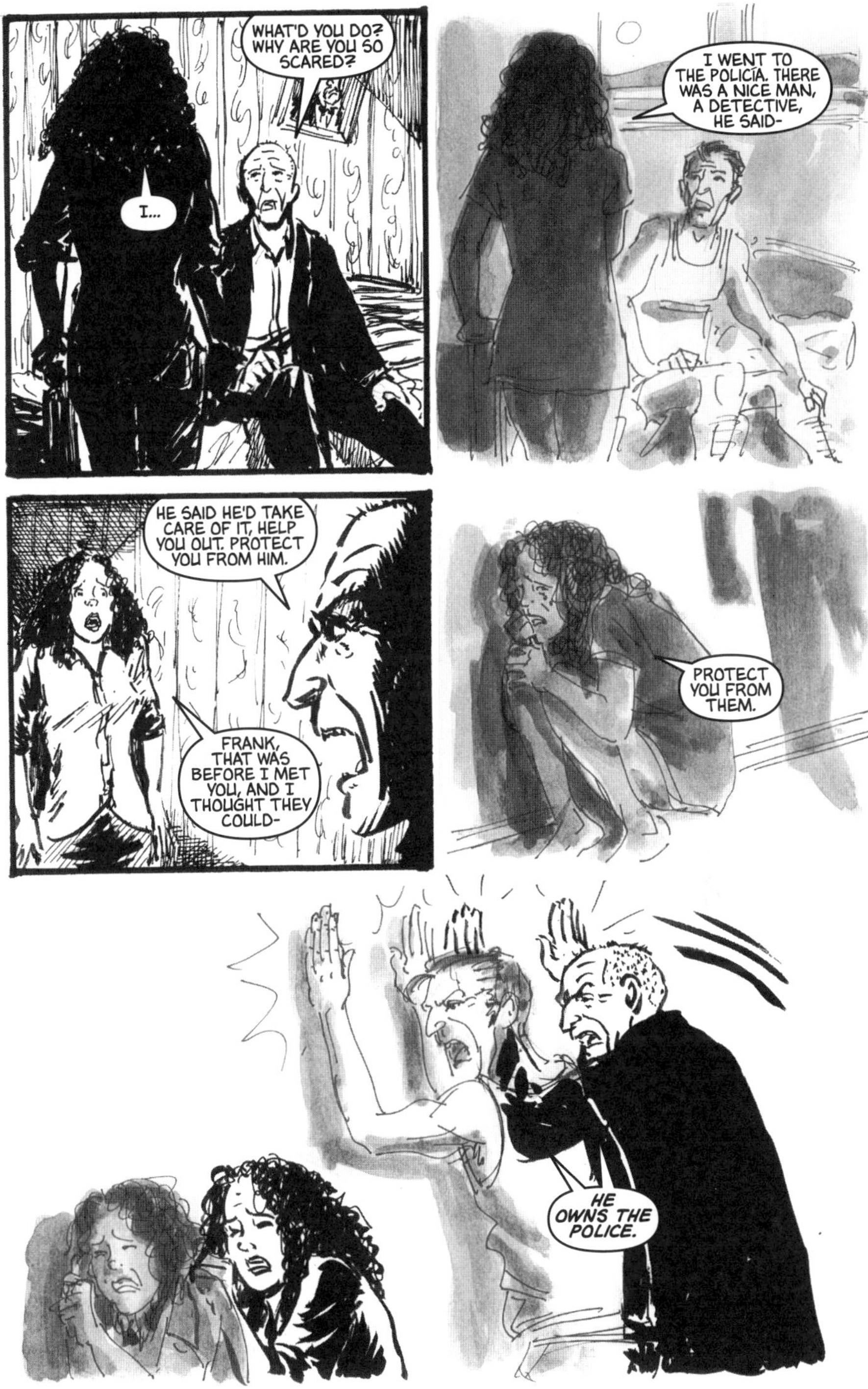
WHAT'D YOU DO? WHY ARE YOU SO SCARED?
I...
I WENT TO THE POLICÍA. THERE WAS A NICE MAN, A DETECTIVE, HE SAID-
HE SAID HE'D TAKE CARE OF IT, HELP YOU OUT. PROTECT YOU FROM HIM.
FRANK, THAT WAS BEFORE I MET YOU, AND I THOUGHT THEY COULD-
PROTECT YOU FROM THEM.
HE OWNS THE POLICE.

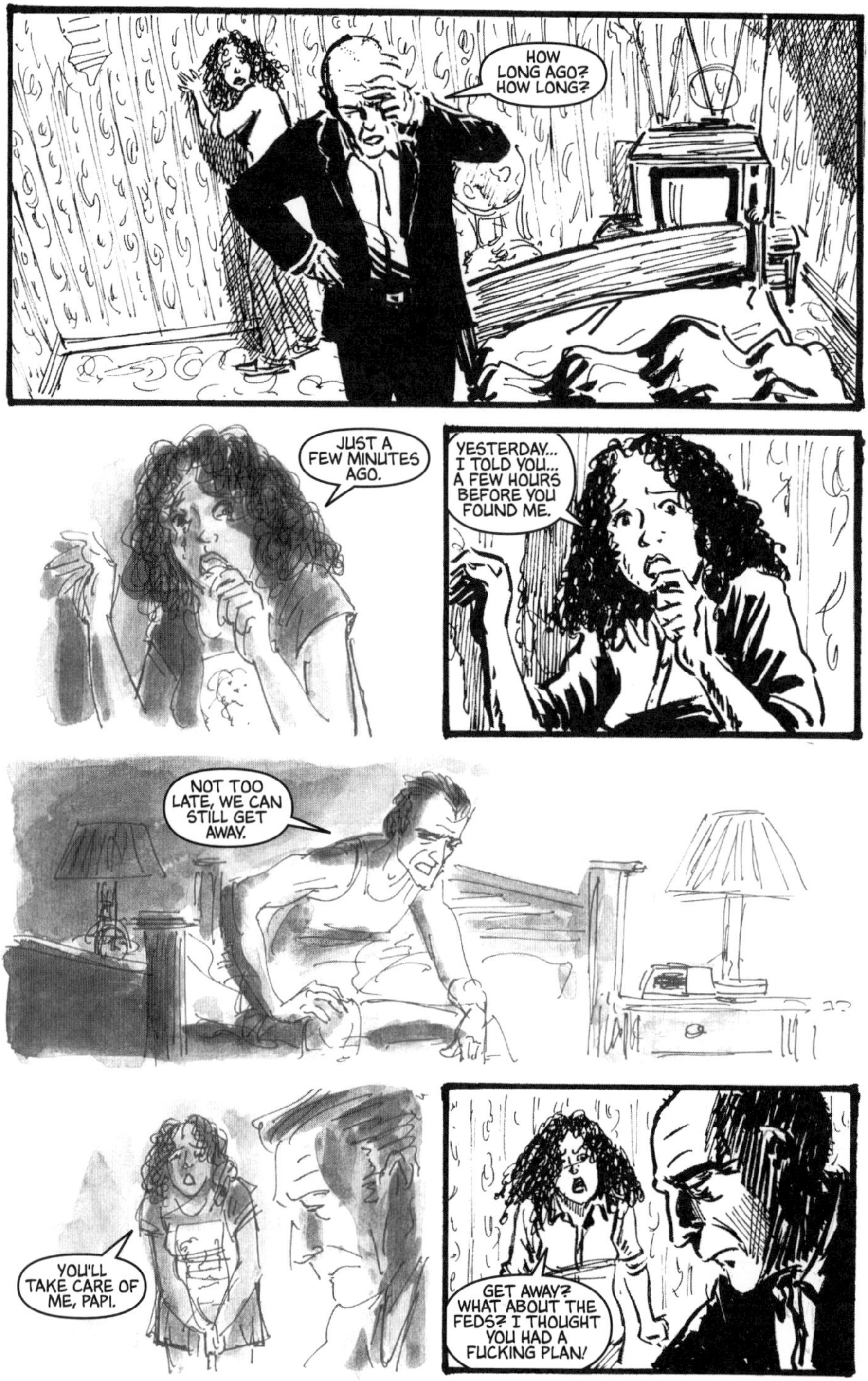
HOW LONG AGO? HOW LONG?
JUST A FEW MINUTES AGO.
YESTERDAY... I TOLD YOU... A FEW HOURS BEFORE YOU FOUND ME.
NOT TOO LATE, WE CAN STILL GET AWAY.
YOU'LL TAKE CARE OF ME, PAPI.
GET AWAY? WHAT ABOUT THE FEDS? I THOUGHT YOU HAD A FUCKING PLAN!

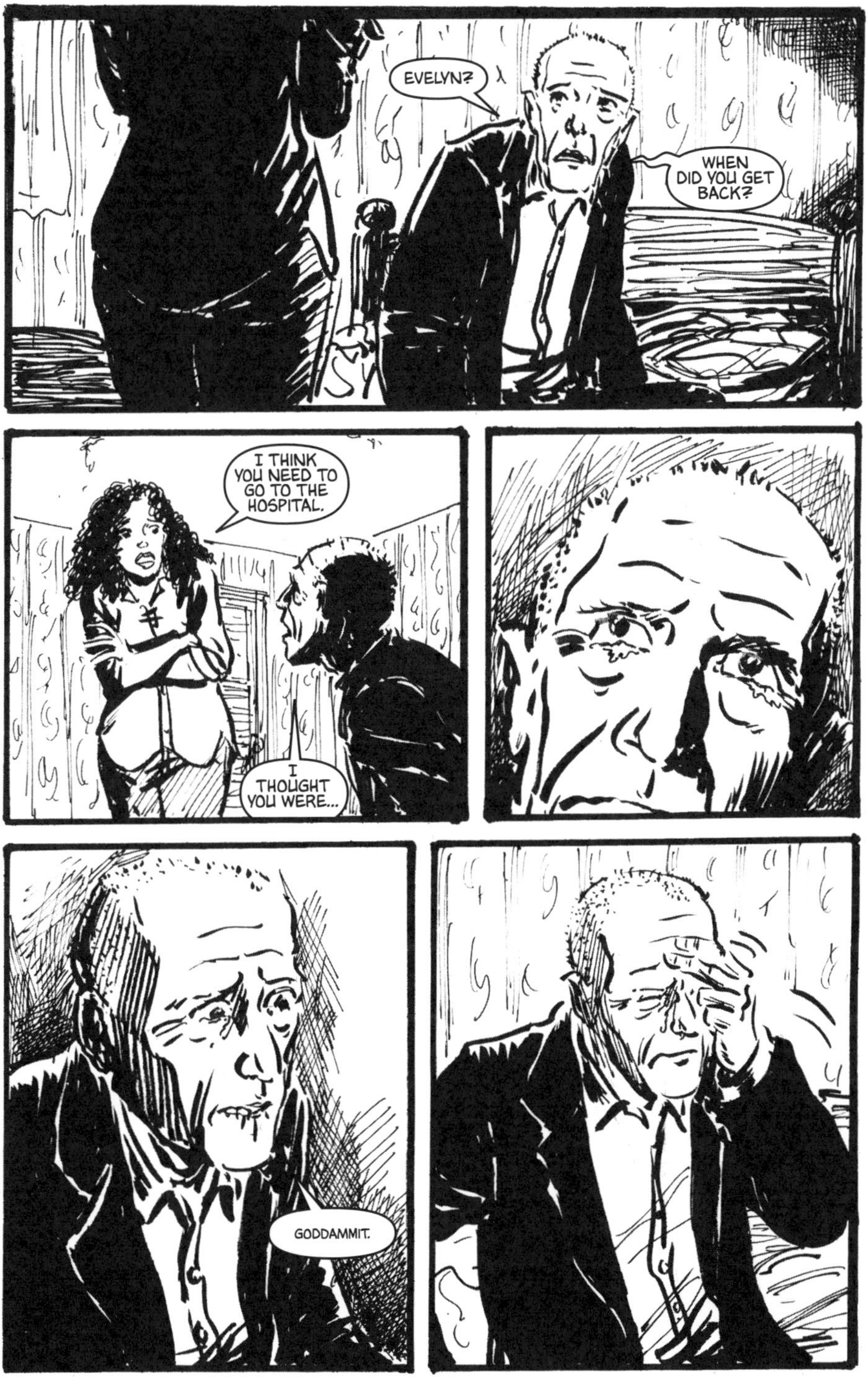
EVELYN?
WHEN DID YOU GET BACK?
I THINK YOU NEED TO GO TO THE HOSPITAL.
I THOUGHT YOU WERE...
GODDAMMIT.

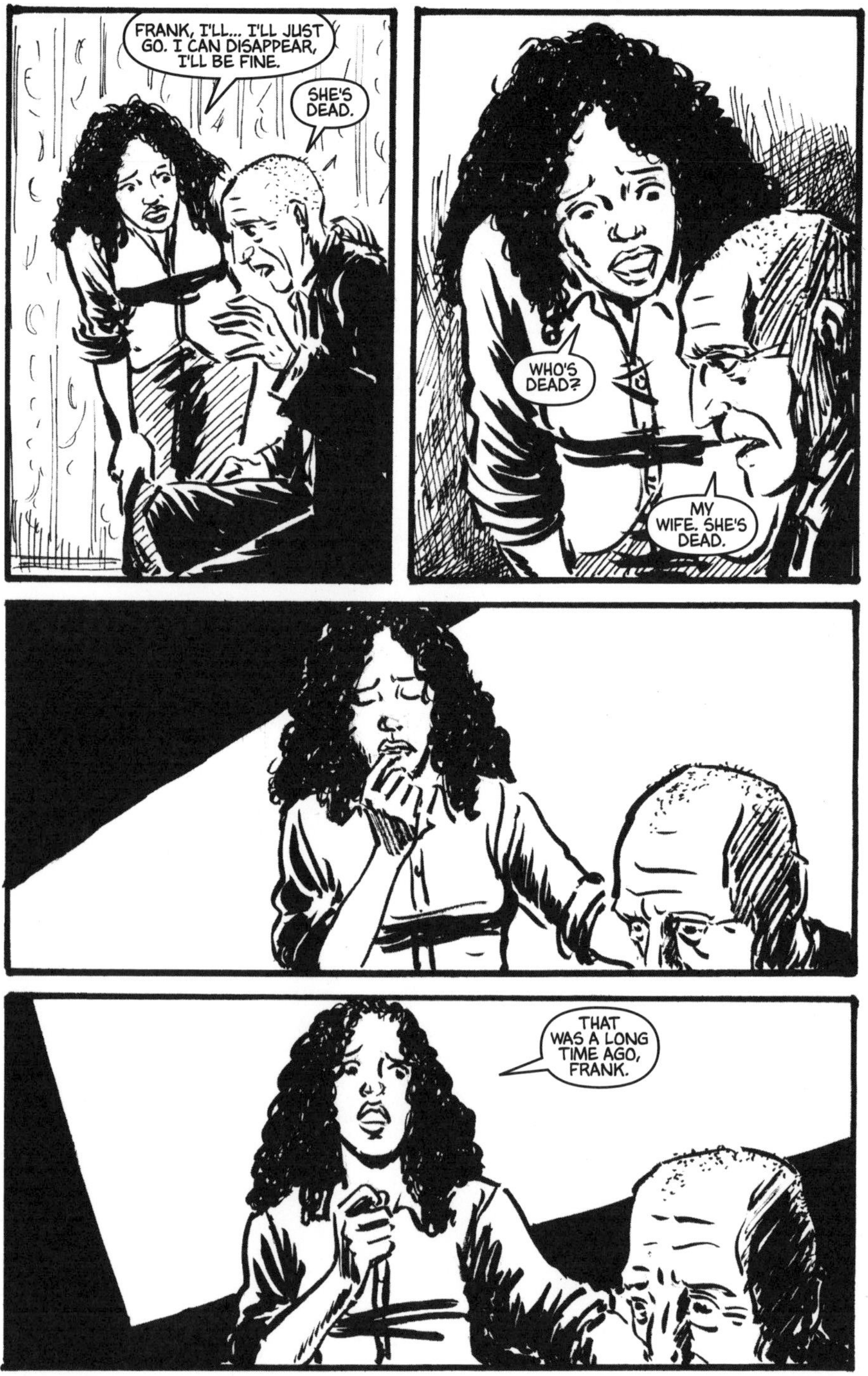
FRANK, I'LL... I'LL JUST GO. I CAN DISAPPEAR, I'LL BE FINE.
SHE'S DEAD.
WHO'S DEAD?
MY WIFE. SHE'S DEAD.
THAT WAS A LONG TIME AGO, FRANK.

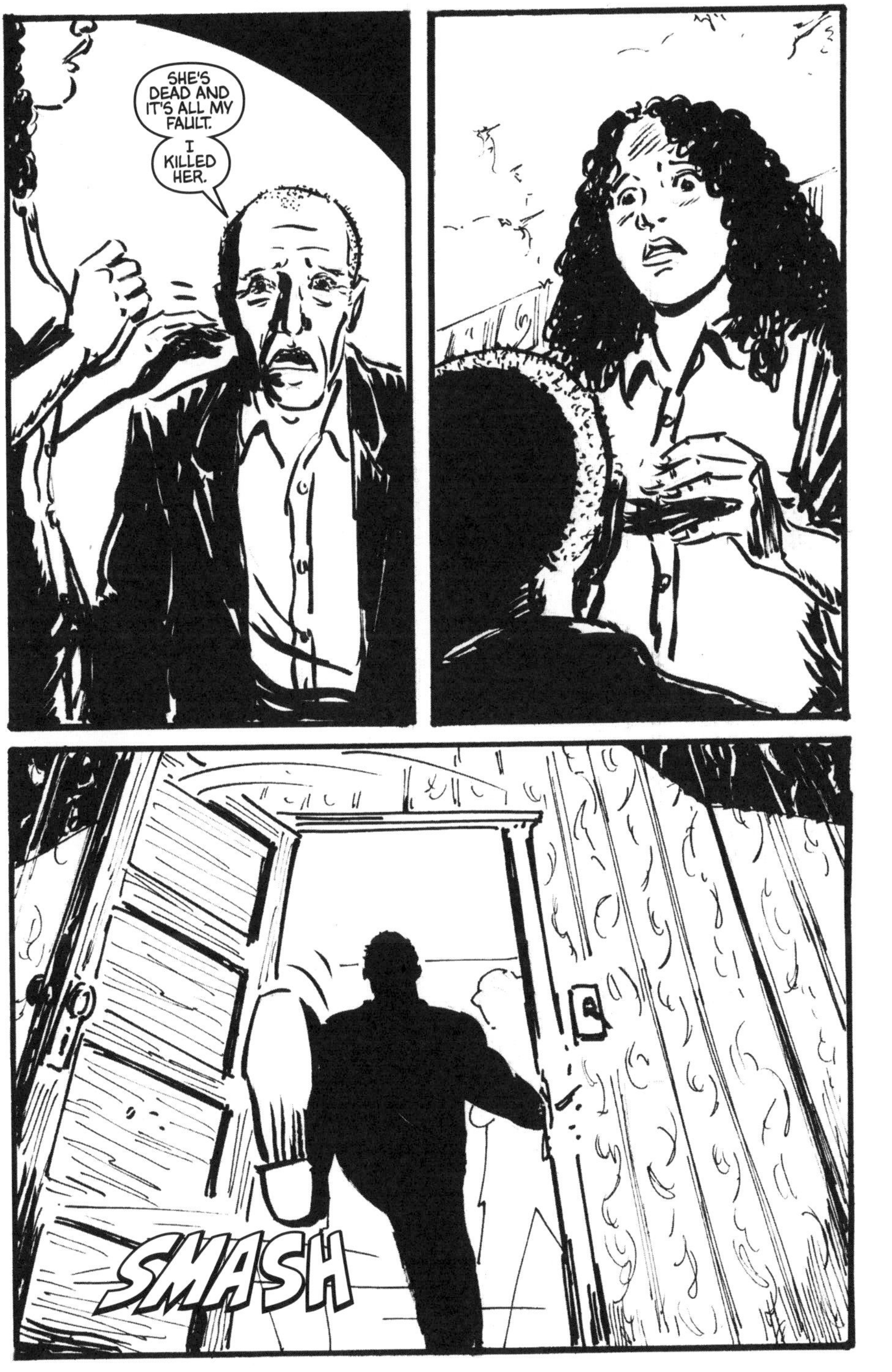
SHE'S DEAD AND IT'S ALL MY FAULT.
I KILLED HER.
SMASH

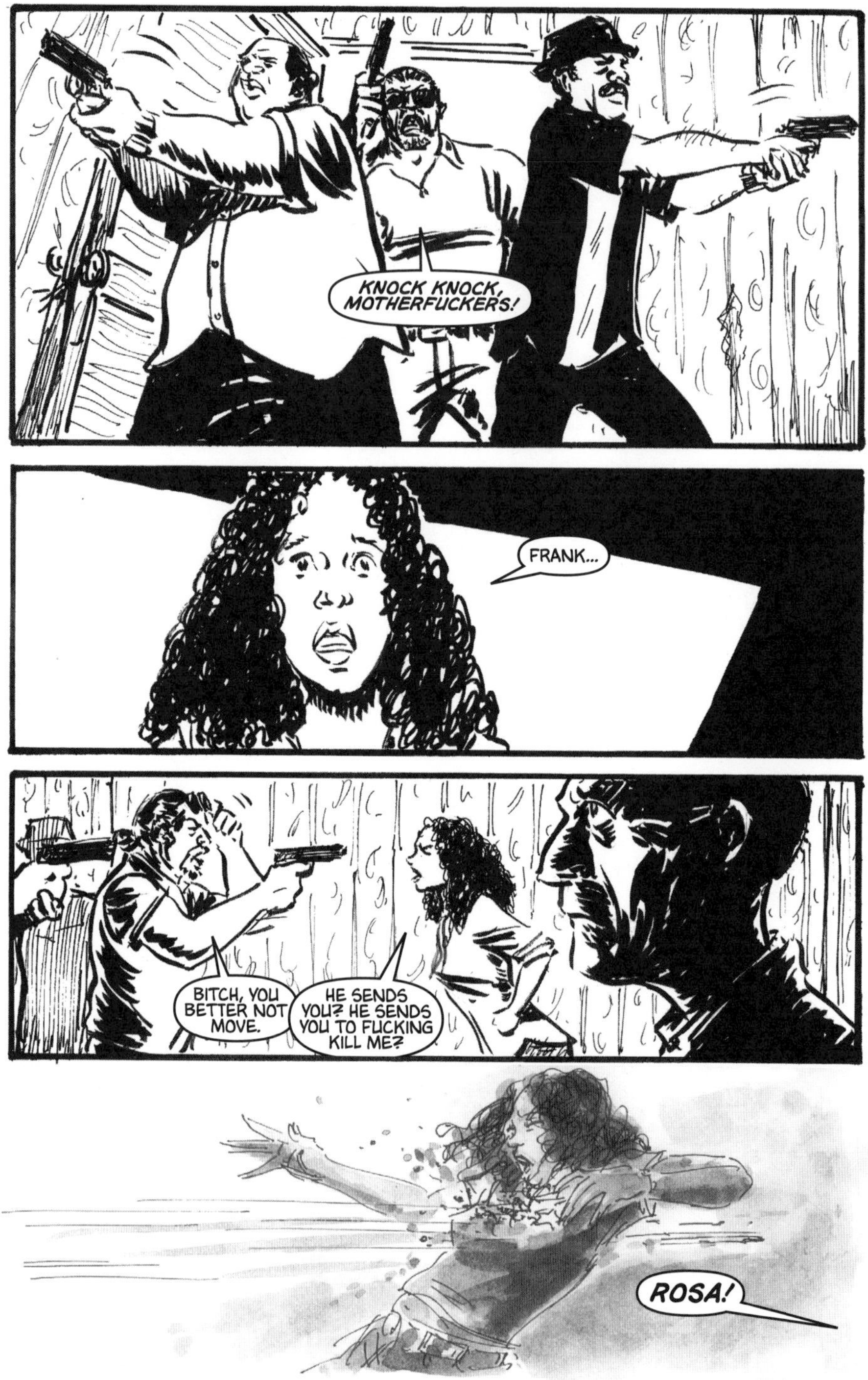
KNOCK KNOCK, MOTHERFUCKERS!
FRANK...
BITCH, YOU BETTER NOT MOVE.
HE SENDS YOU? HE SENDS YOU TO FUCKING KILL ME?
ROSA!

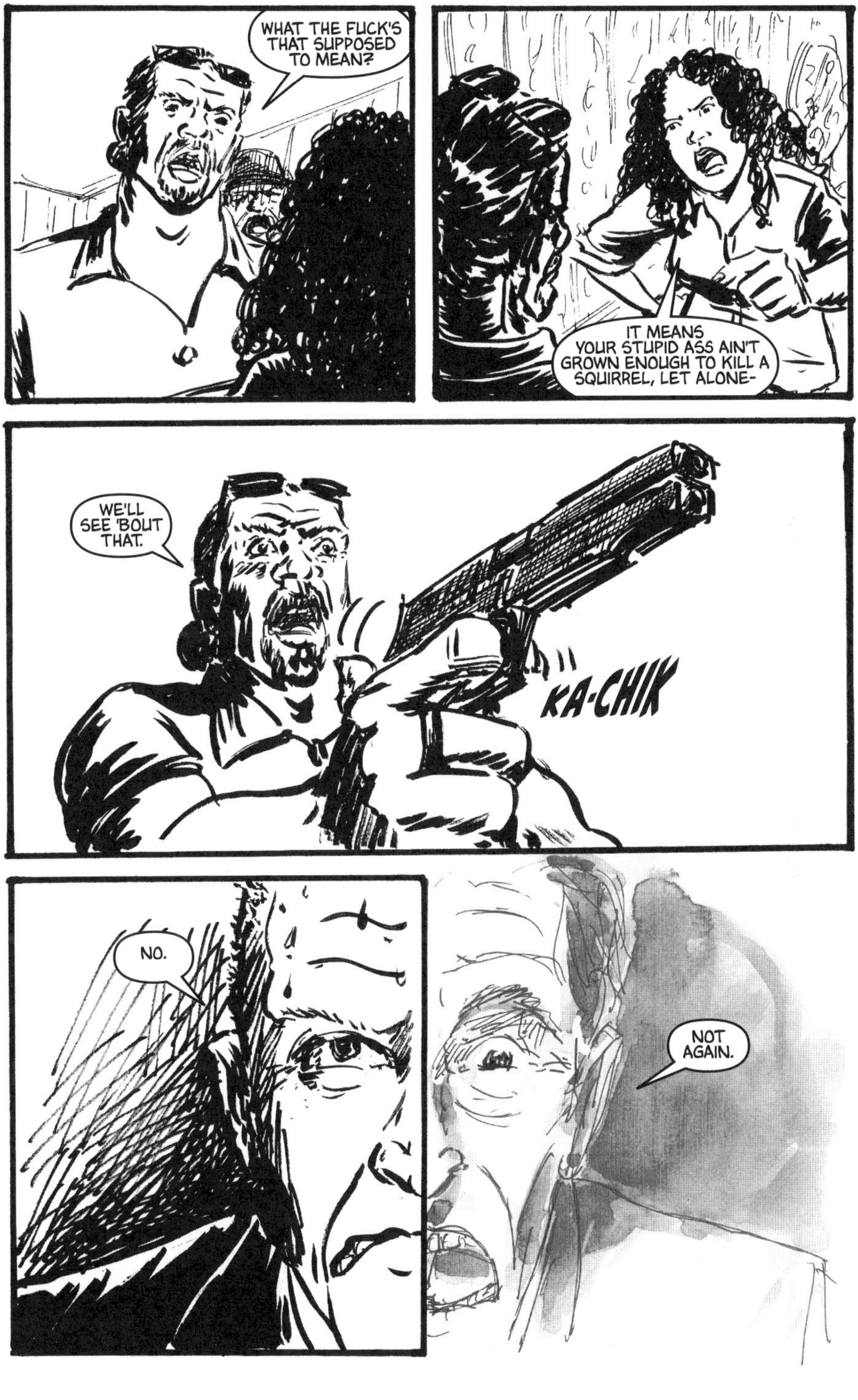
WHAT THE FUCK'S THAT SUPPOSED TO MEAN?
IT MEANS YOUR STUPID ASS AIN'T GROWN ENOUGH TO KILL A SQUIRREL, LET ALONE-
WE'LL SEE 'BOUT THAT.
KA-CHIK
NO.
NOT AGAIN.

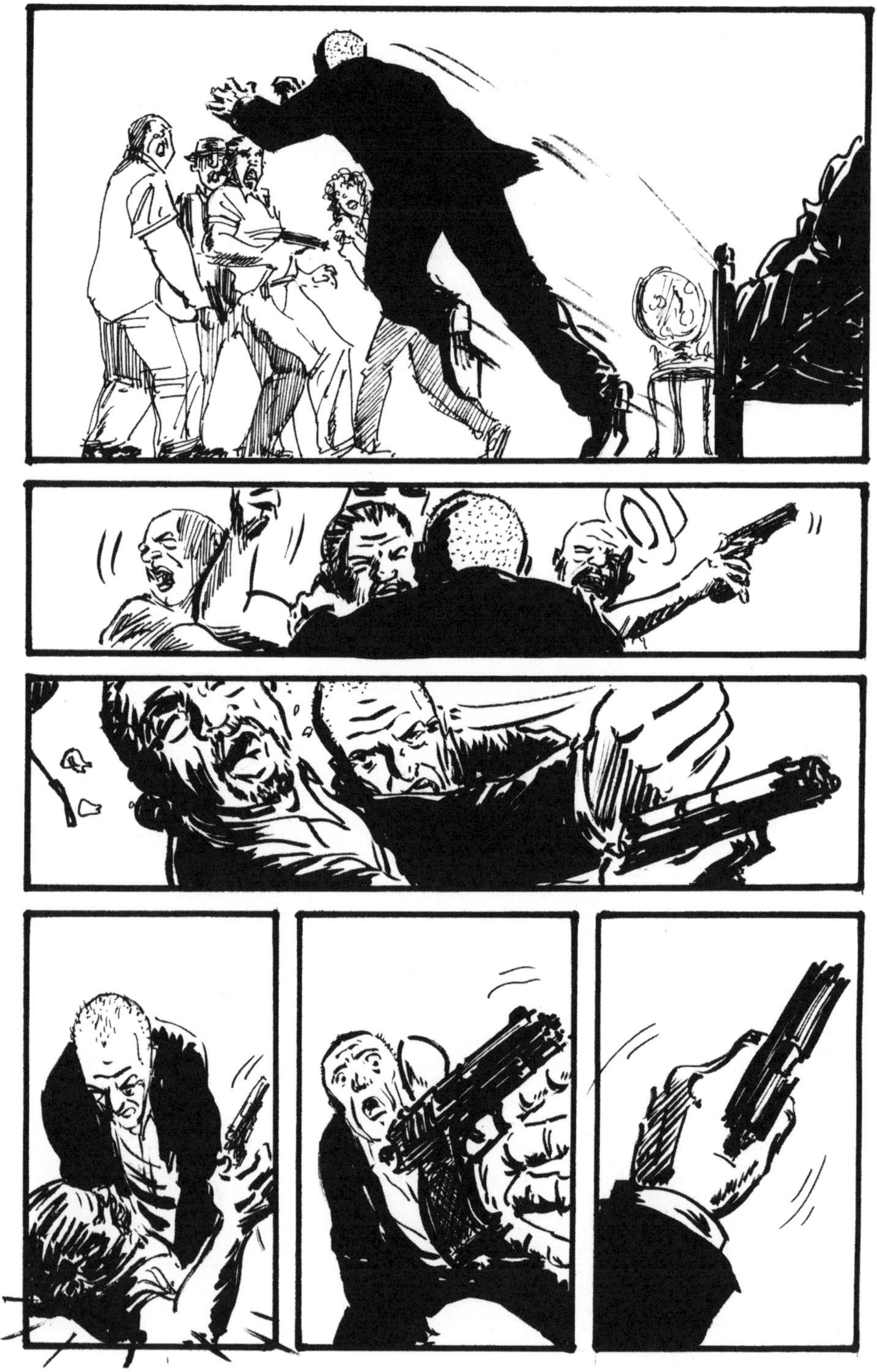

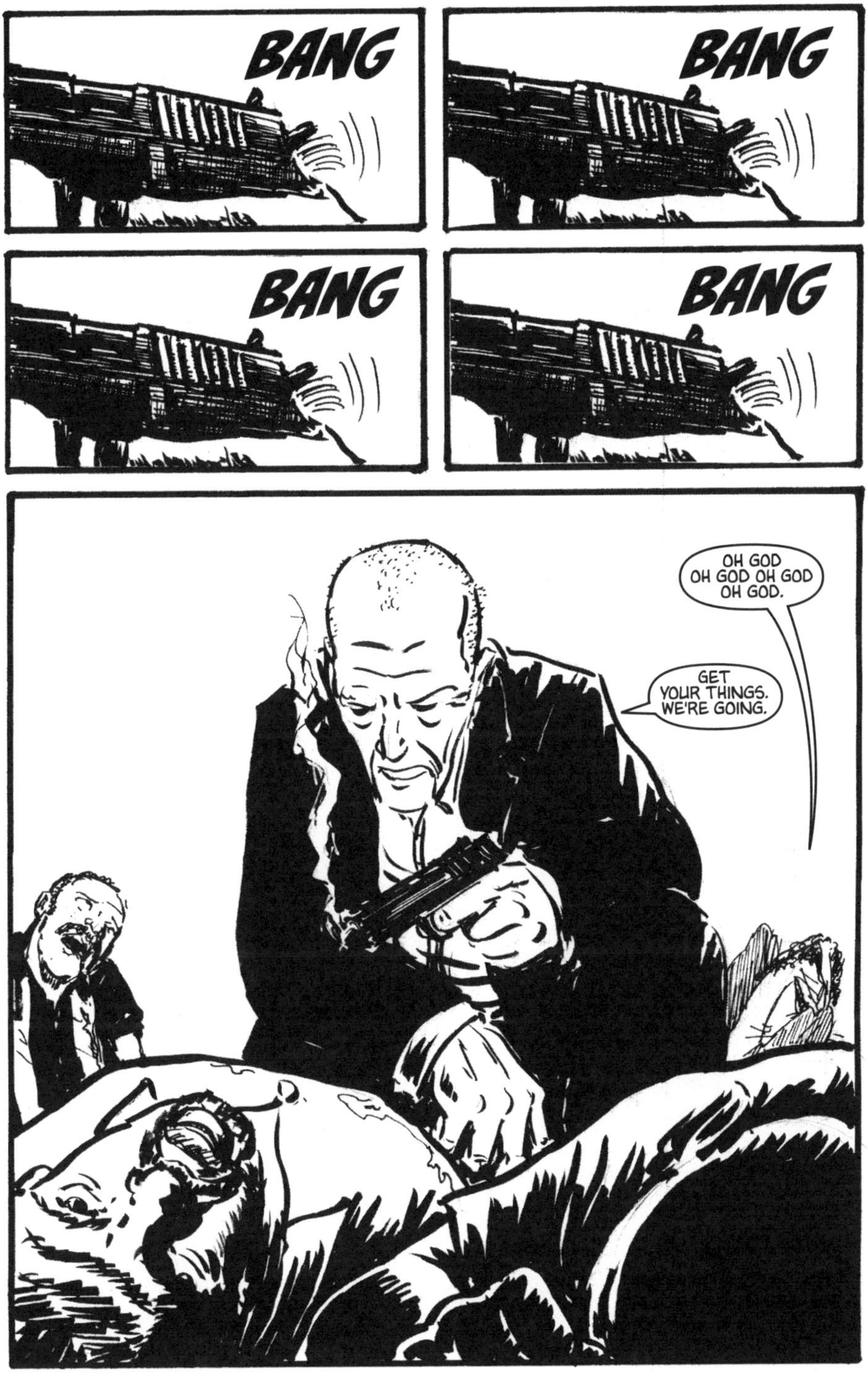
BANG
BANG
BANG
BANG
OH GOD OH GOD OH GOD OH GOD.
GET YOUR THINGS. WE'RE GOING.

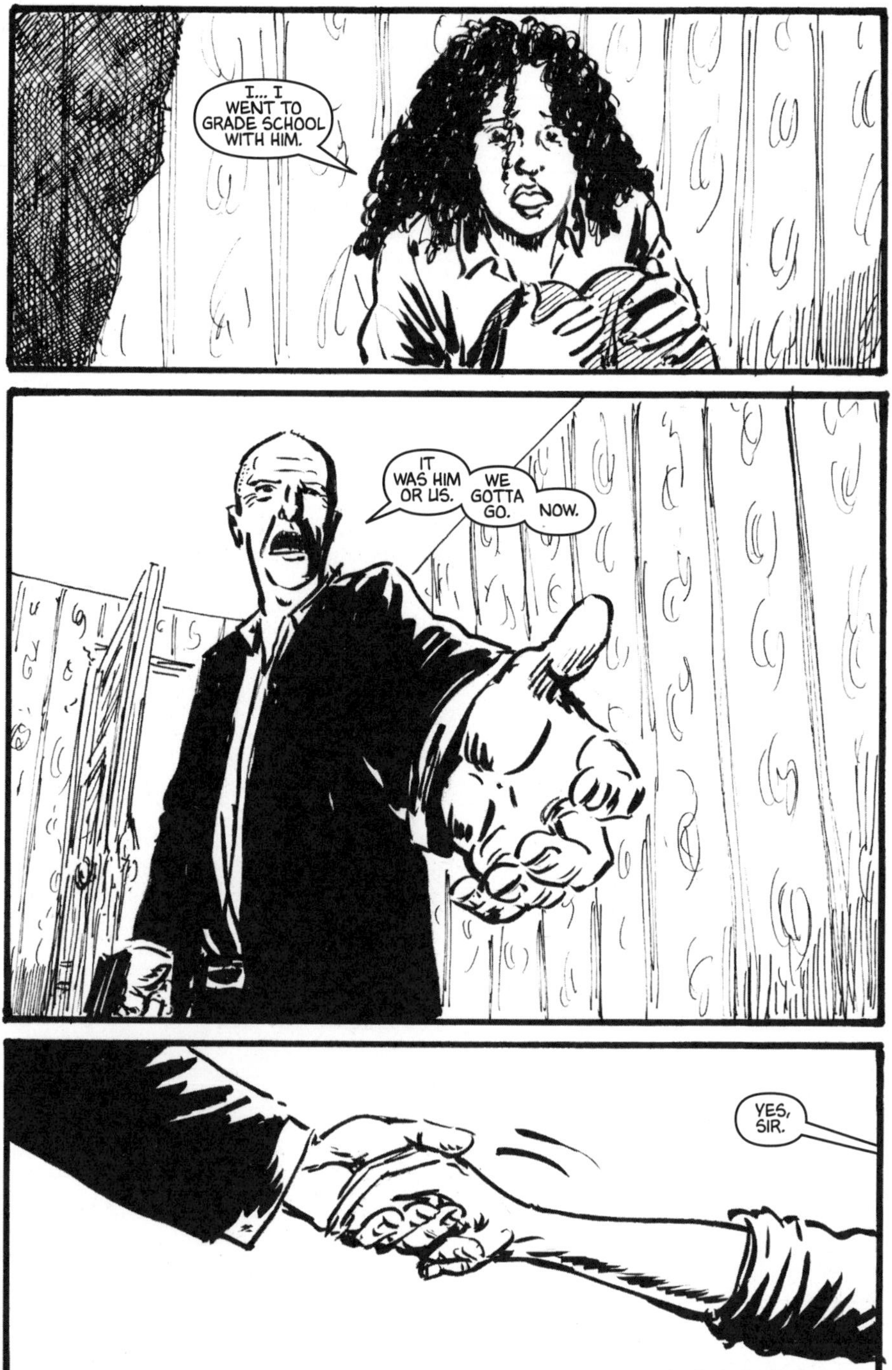
I... I WENT TO GRADE SCHOOL WITH HIM.
IT WAS HIM OR US.
WE GOTTA GO.
NOW.
YES, SIR.
END CHAPTER 5

SIX

MISTAKES WERE MADE

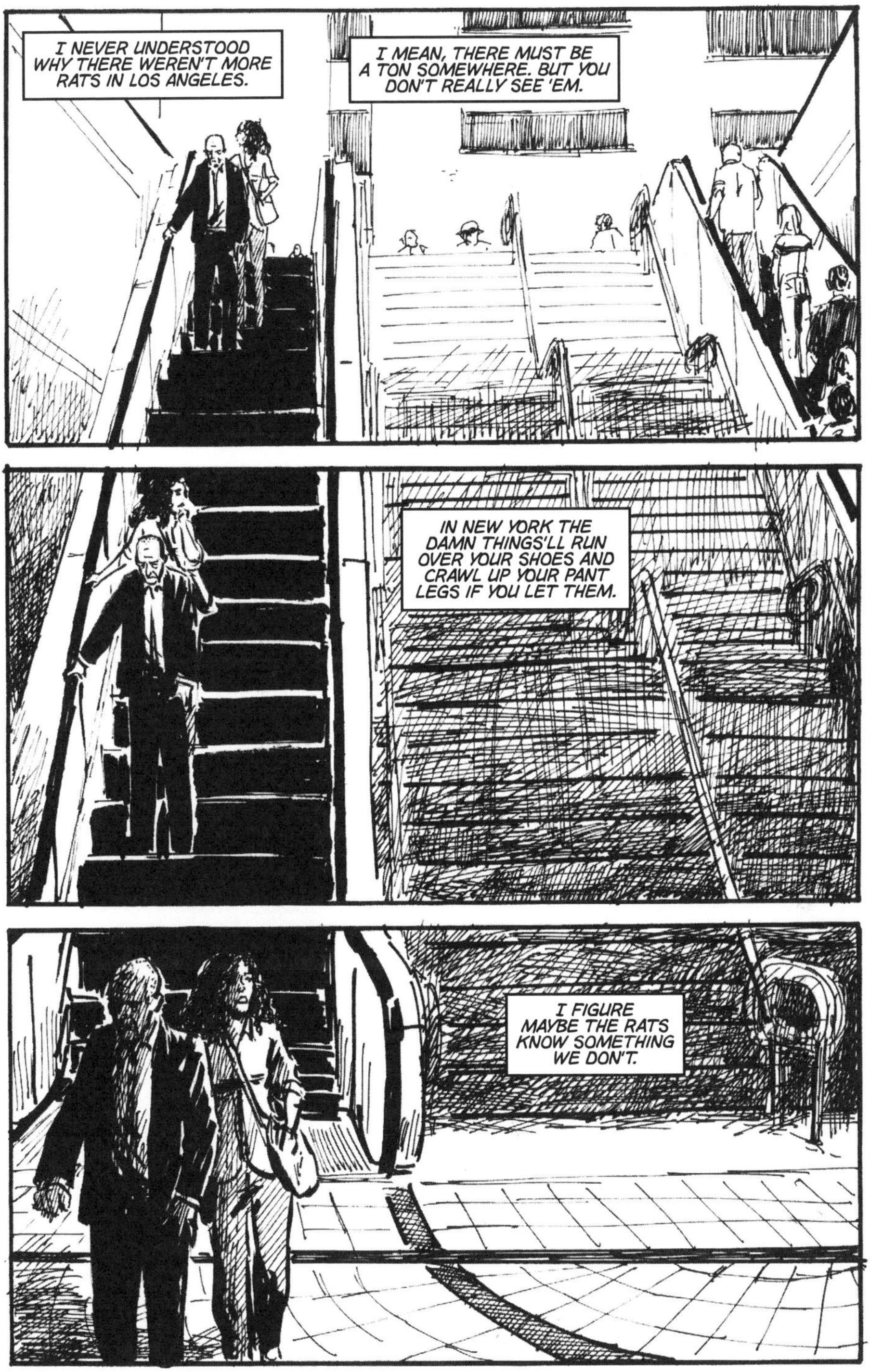
I NEVER UNDERSTOOD WHY THERE WEREN'T MORE RATS IN LOS ANGELES.
I MEAN, THERE MUST BE A TON SOMEWHERE. BUT YOU DON'T REALLY SEE 'EM.
IN NEW YORK THE DAMN THINGS'LL RUN OVER YOUR SHOES AND CRAWL UP YOUR PANT LEGS IF YOU LET THEM.
I FIGURE MAYBE THE RATS KNOW SOMETHING WE DON'T.

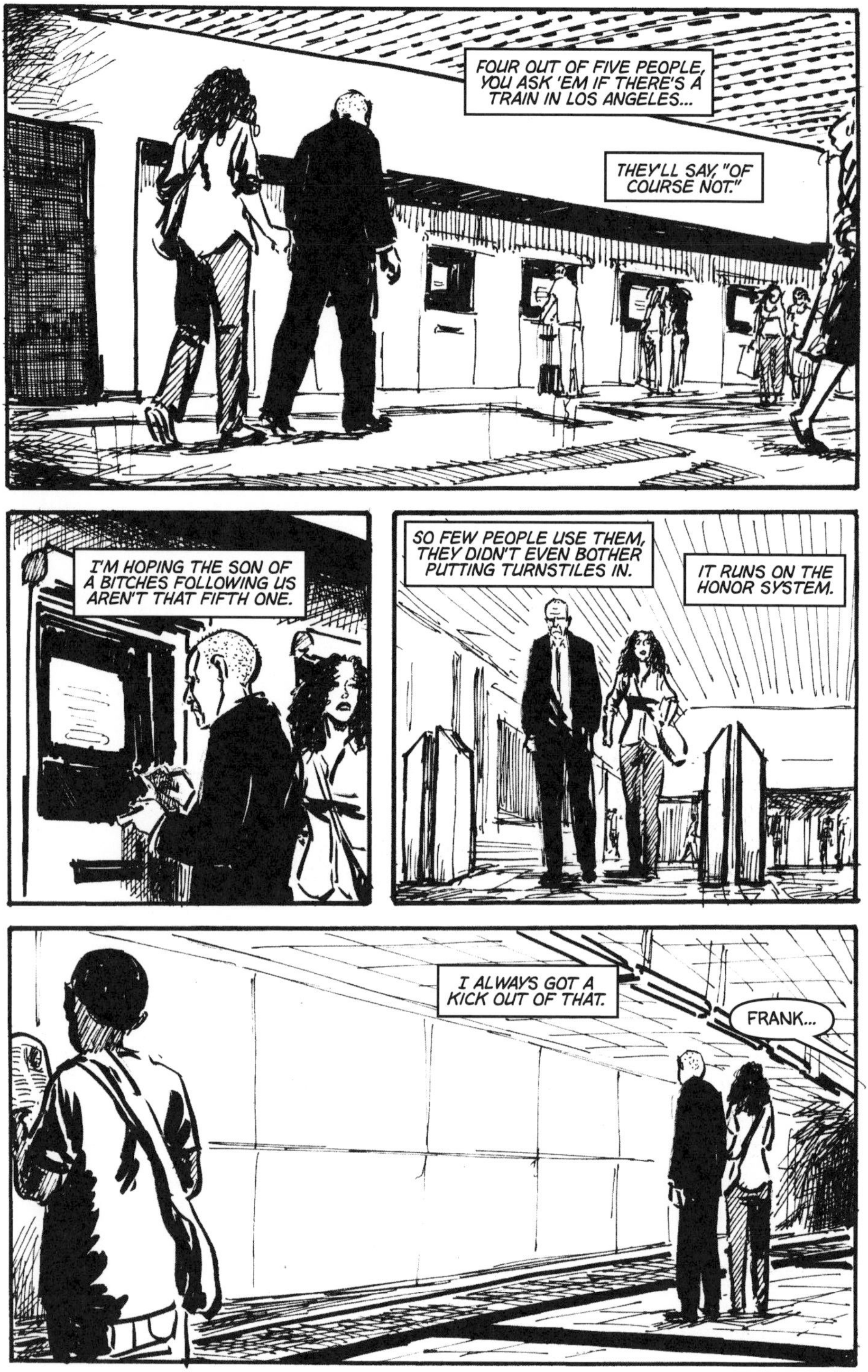
FOUR OUT OF FIVE PEOPLE, YOU ASK 'EM IF THERE'S A TRAIN IN LOS ANGELES...
THEY'LL SAY, "OF COURSE NOT."
I'M HOPING THE SON OF A BITCHES FOLLOWING US AREN'T THAT FIFTH ONE.
SO FEW PEOPLE USE THEM, THEY DIDN'T EVEN BOTHER PUTTING TURNSTILES IN.
IT RUNS ON THE HONOR SYSTEM.
I ALWAYS GOT A KICK OUT OF THAT.
FRANK...

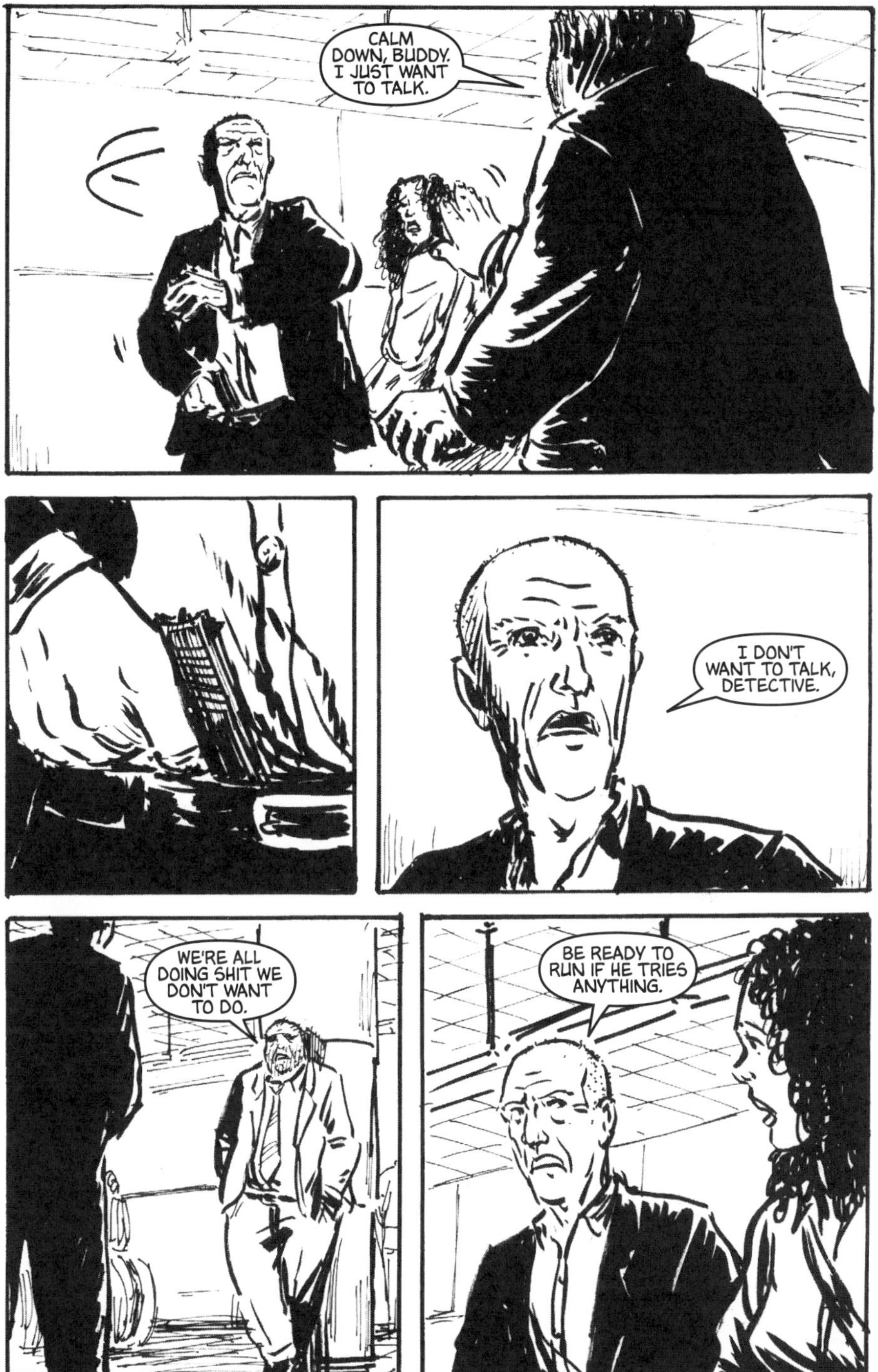
CALM DOWN, BUDDY. I JUST WANT TO TALK.
I DON'T WANT TO TALK, DETECTIVE.
WE'RE ALL DOING SHIT WE DON'T WANT TO DO.
BE READY TO RUN IF HE TRIES ANYTHING.

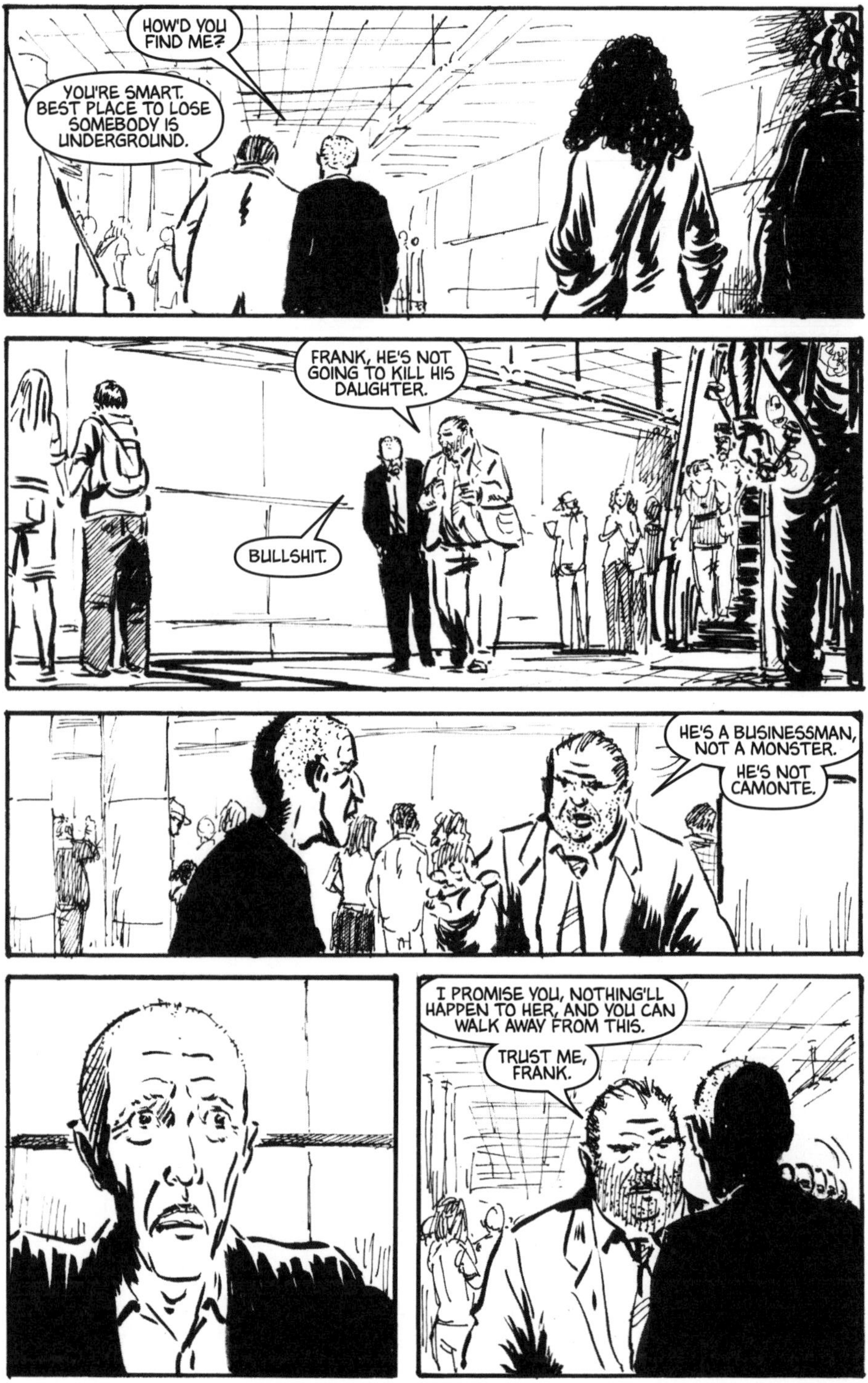
HOW'D YOU FIND ME?
YOU'RE SMART. BEST PLACE TO LOSE SOMEBODY IS UNDERGROUND.
FRANK, HE'S NOT GOING TO KILL HIS DAUGHTER.
BULLSHIT.
HE'S A BUSINESSMAN, NOT A MONSTER.
HE'S NOT CAMONTE.
I PROMISE YOU, NOTHING'LL HAPPEN TO HER, AND YOU CAN WALK AWAY FROM THIS.
TRUST ME, FRANK.

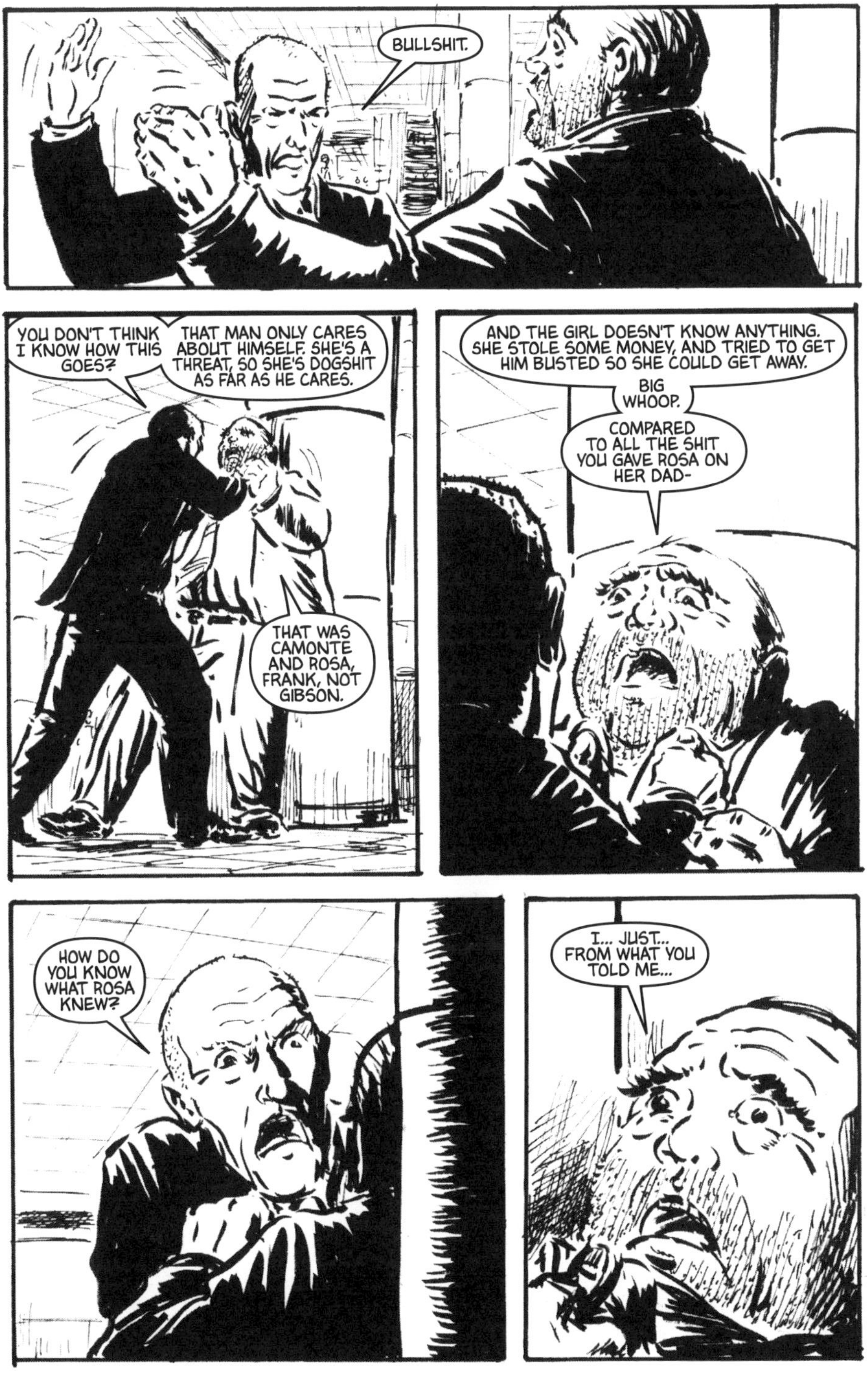
BULLSHIT.
YOU DON'T THINK I KNOW HOW THIS GOES?
THAT MAN ONLY CARES ABOUT HIMSELF. SHE'S A THREAT, SO SHE'S DOGSHIT AS FAR AS HE CARES.
THAT WAS CAMONTE AND ROSA, FRANK, NOT GIBSON.
AND THE GIRL DOESN'T KNOW ANYTHING. SHE STOLE SOME MONEY, AND TRIED TO GET HIM BUSTED SO SHE COULD GET AWAY.
BIG WHOOP.
COMPARED TO ALL THE SHIT YOU GAVE ROSA ON HER DAD-
HOW DO YOU KNOW WHAT ROSA KNEW?
I... JUST... FROM WHAT YOU TOLD ME...

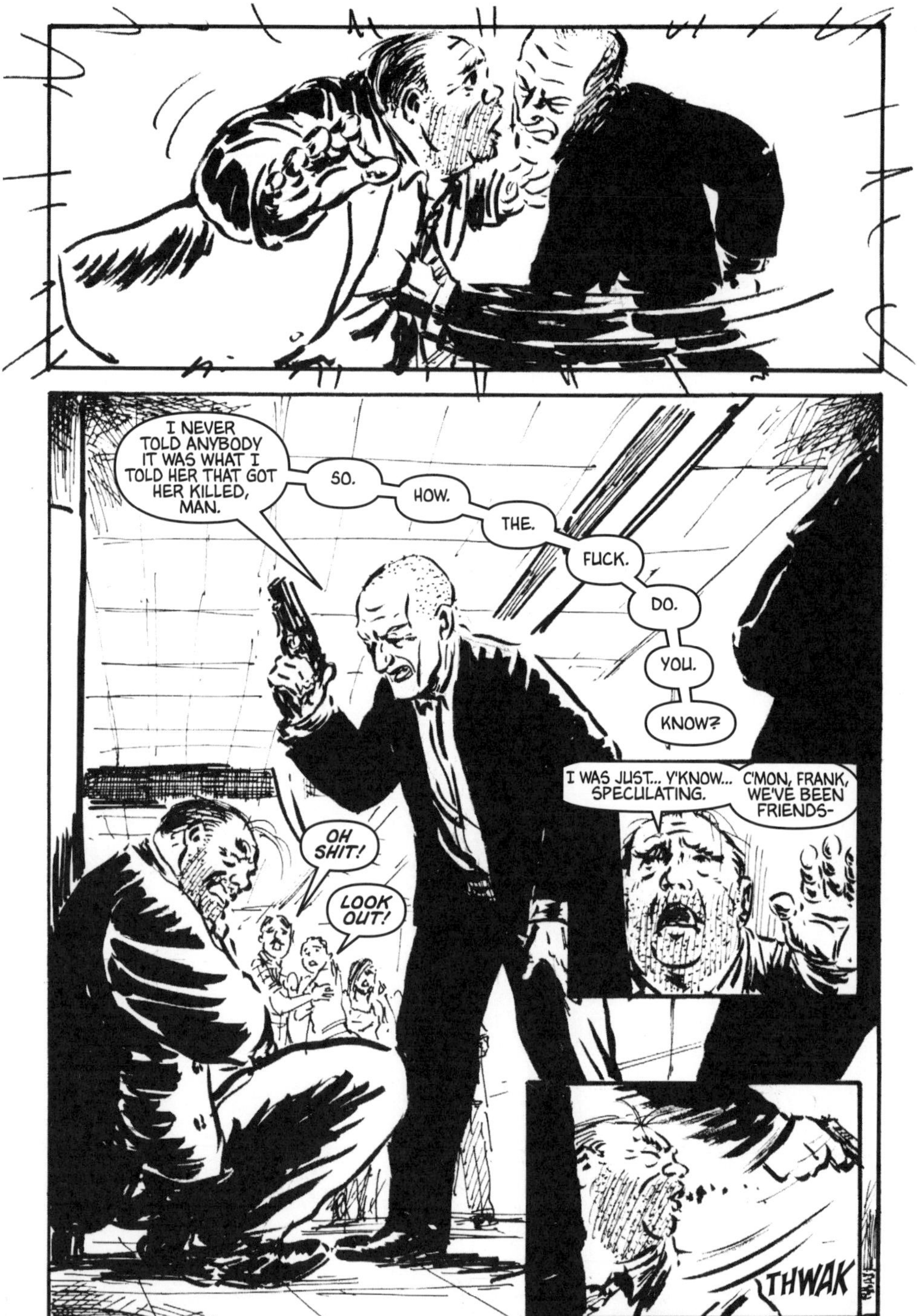

I NEVER TOLD ANYBODY IT WAS WHAT I TOLD HER THAT GOT HER KILLED, MAN.
SO.
HOW.
THE.
FUCK.
DO.
YOU.
KNOW?
I WAS JUST... Y'KNOW... SPECULATING.
C'MON, FRANK, WE'VE BEEN FRIENDS-
OH SHIT!
LOOK OUT!
THWAK

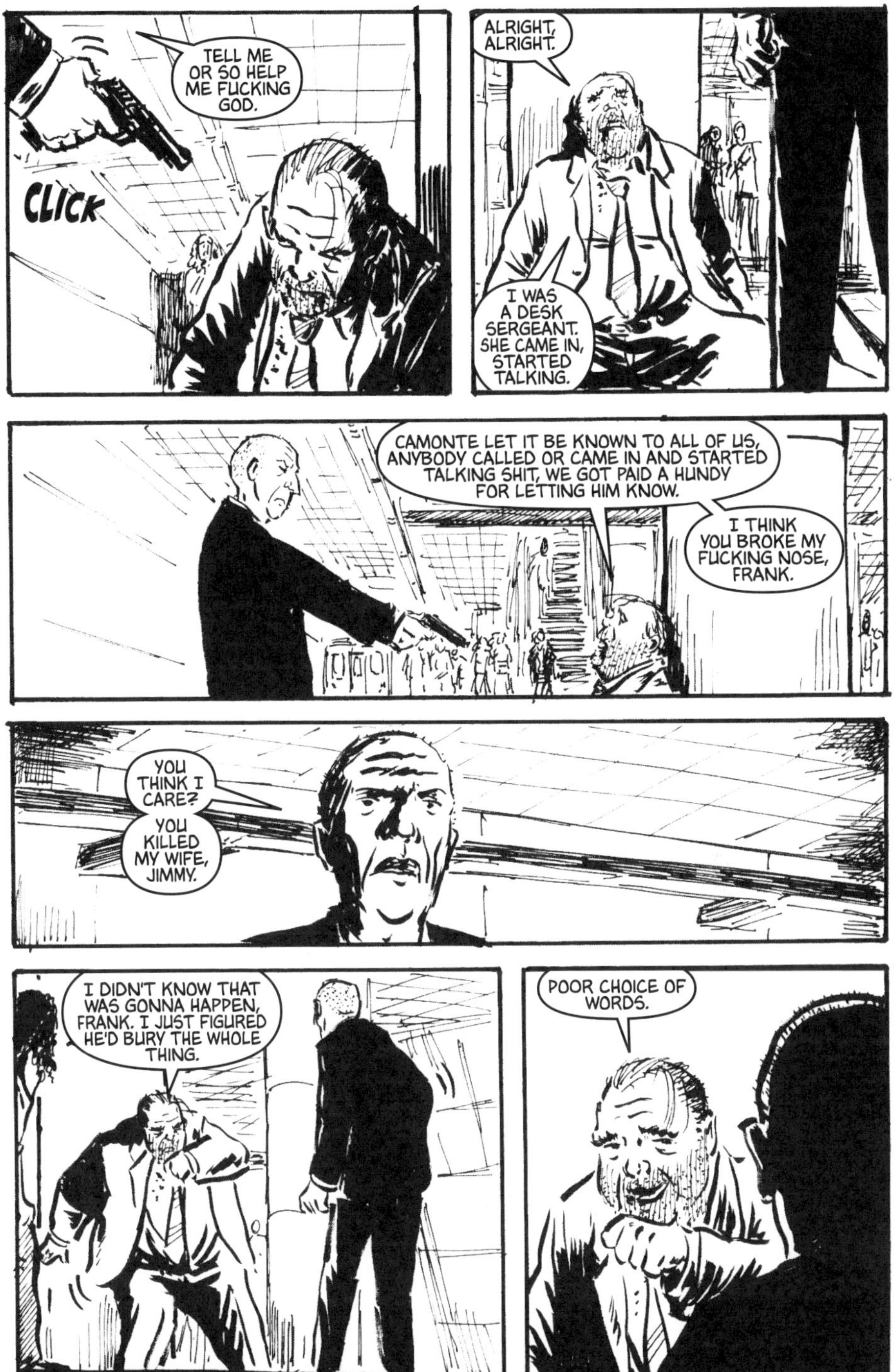
TELL ME OR SO HELP ME FUCKING GOD.
CLICK
ALRIGHT, ALRIGHT.
I WAS A DESK SERGEANT. SHE CAME IN, STARTED TALKING.
CAMONTE LET IT BE KNOWN TO ALL OF US, ANYBODY CALLED OR CAME IN AND STARTED TALKING SHIT, WE GOT PAID A HUNDY FOR LETTING HIM KNOW.
I THINK YOU BROKE MY FUCKING NOSE, FRANK.
YOU THINK I CARE?
YOU KILLED MY WIFE, JIMMY.
I DIDN'T KNOW THAT WAS GONNA HAPPEN, FRANK. I JUST FIGURED HE'D BURY THE WHOLE THING.
POOR CHOICE OF WORDS.

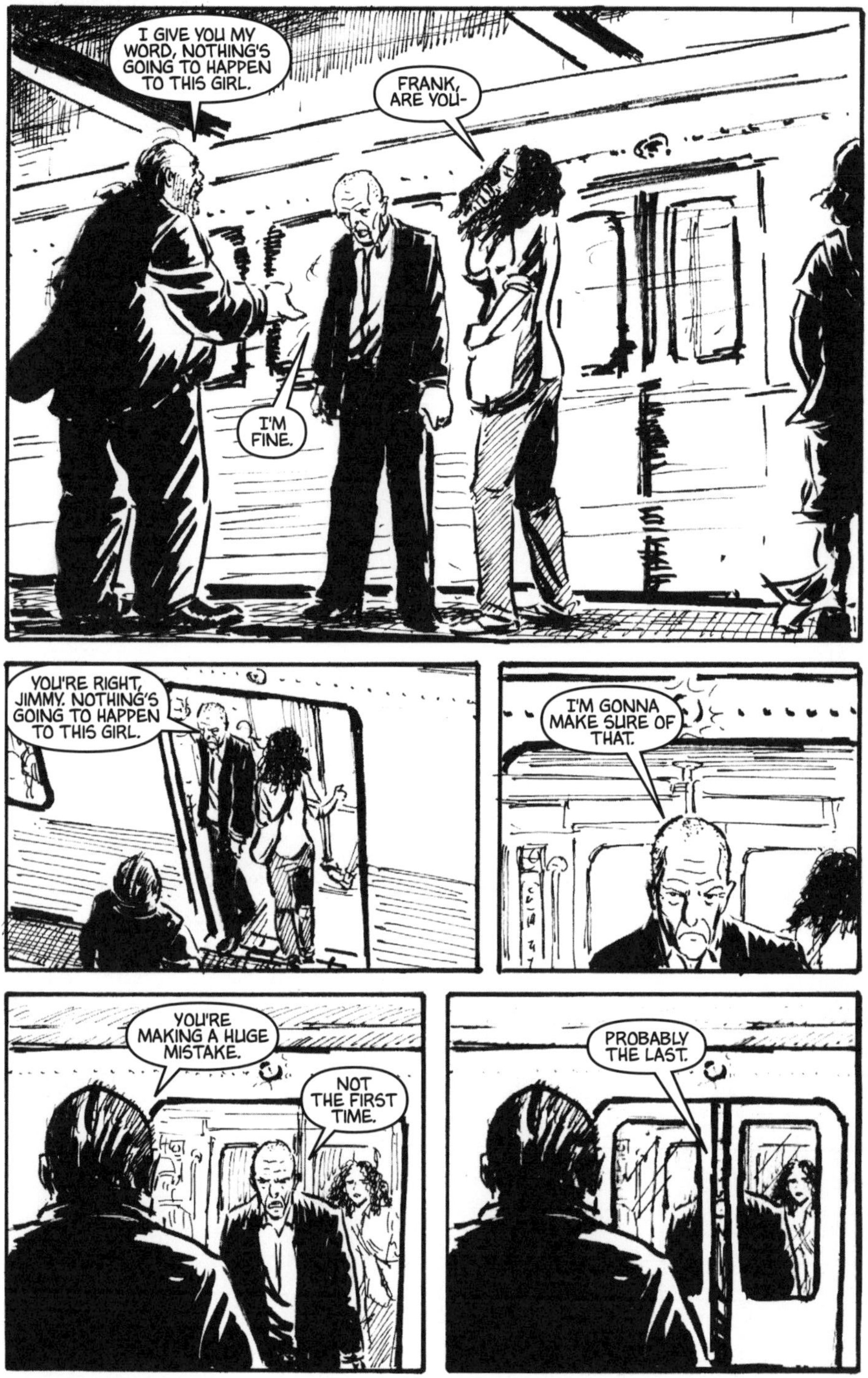
I GIVE YOU MY WORD, NOTHING'S GOING TO HAPPEN TO THIS GIRL.
FRANK, ARE YOU-
I'M FINE.
YOU'RE RIGHT, JIMMY. NOTHING'S GOING TO HAPPEN TO THIS GIRL.
I'M GONNA MAKE SURE OF THAT.
YOU'RE MAKING A HUGE MISTAKE.
NOT THE FIRST TIME.
PROBABLY THE LAST.

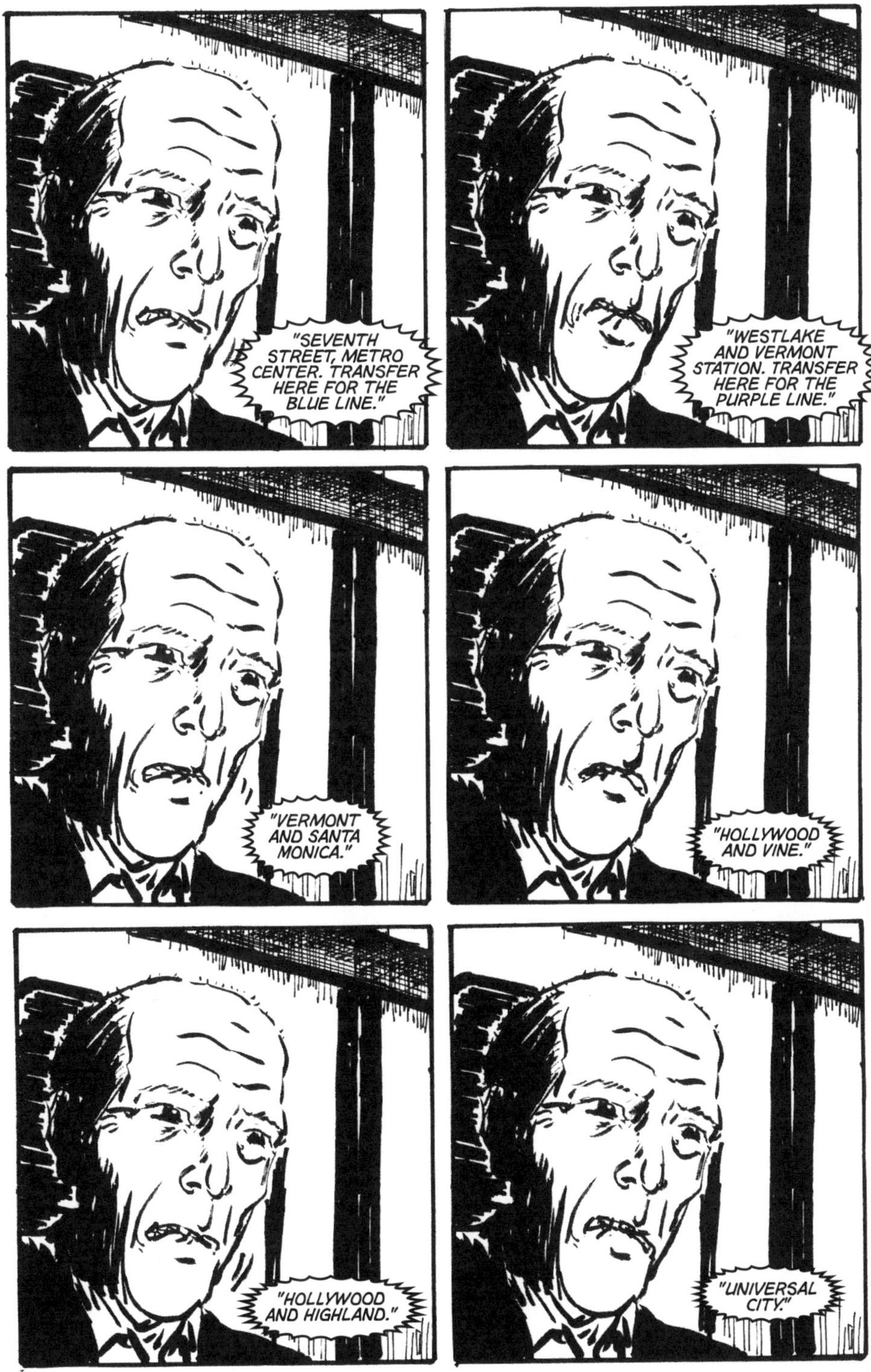
"SEVENTH STREET, METRO CENTER. TRANSFER HERE FOR THE BLUE LINE."
"WESTLAKE AND VERMONT STATION. TRANSFER HERE FOR THE PURPLE LINE."
"VERMONT AND SANTA MONICA."
"HOLLYWOOD AND VINE."
"HOLLYWOOD AND HIGHLAND."
"UNIVERSAL CITY."

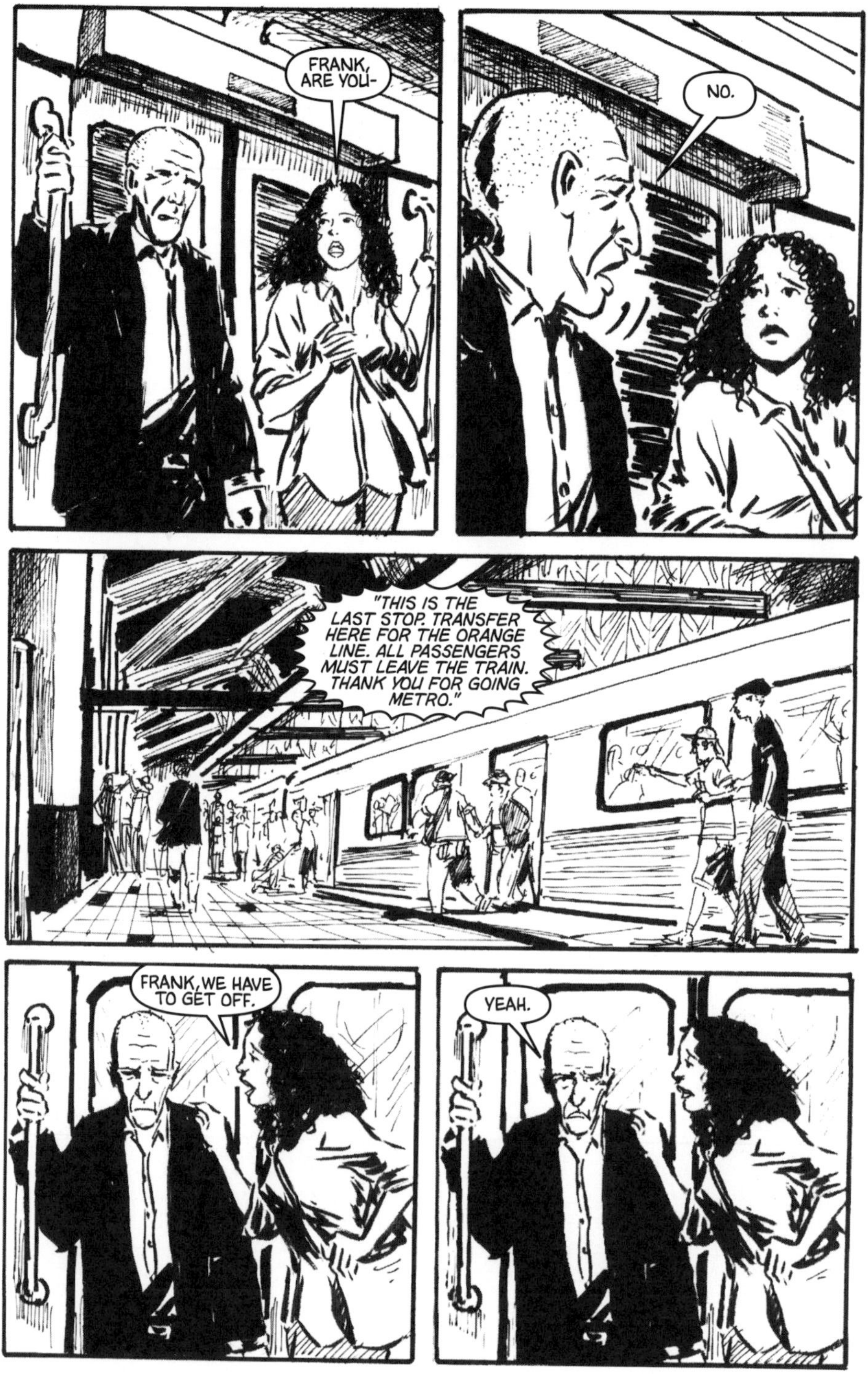
FRANK, ARE YOU-
NO.
"THIS IS THE LAST STOP. TRANSFER HERE FOR THE ORANGE LINE. ALL PASSENGERS MUST LEAVE THE TRAIN. THANK YOU FOR GOING METRO."
FRANK, WE HAVE TO GET OFF.
YEAH.

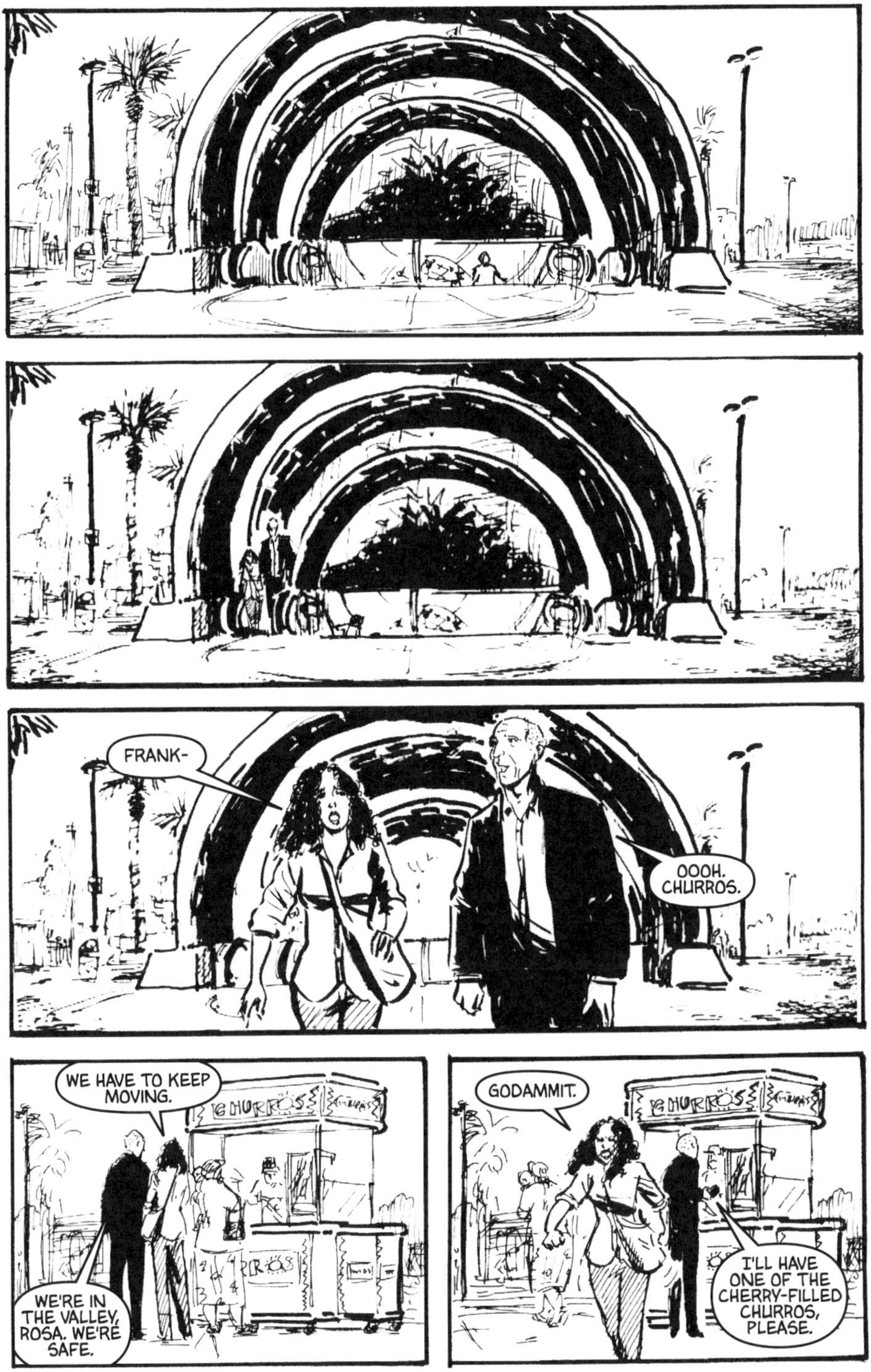
FRANK-
OOOH. CHURROS.
WE HAVE TO KEEP MOVING.
WE'RE IN THE VALLEY, ROSA. WE'RE SAFE.
CHURROS
GODAMMIT.
I'LL HAVE ONE OF THE CHERRY-FILLED CHURROS, PLEASE.

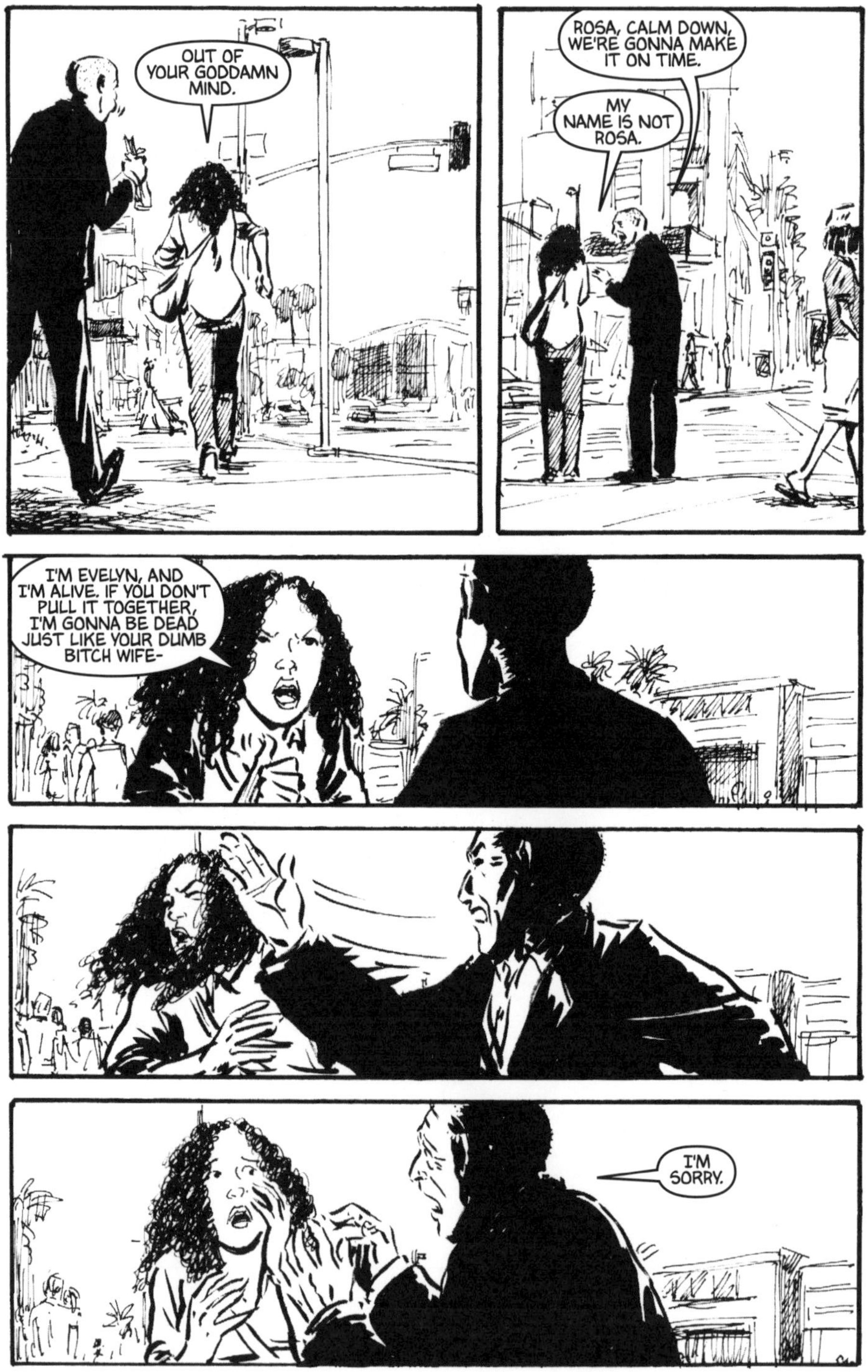
OUT OF YOUR GODDAMN MIND.
ROSA, CALM DOWN, WE'RE GONNA MAKE IT ON TIME.
MY NAME IS NOT ROSA.
I'M EVELYN, AND I'M ALIVE. IF YOU DON'T PULL IT TOGETHER, I'M GONNA BE DEAD JUST LIKE YOUR DUMB BITCH WIFE-
I'M SORRY.

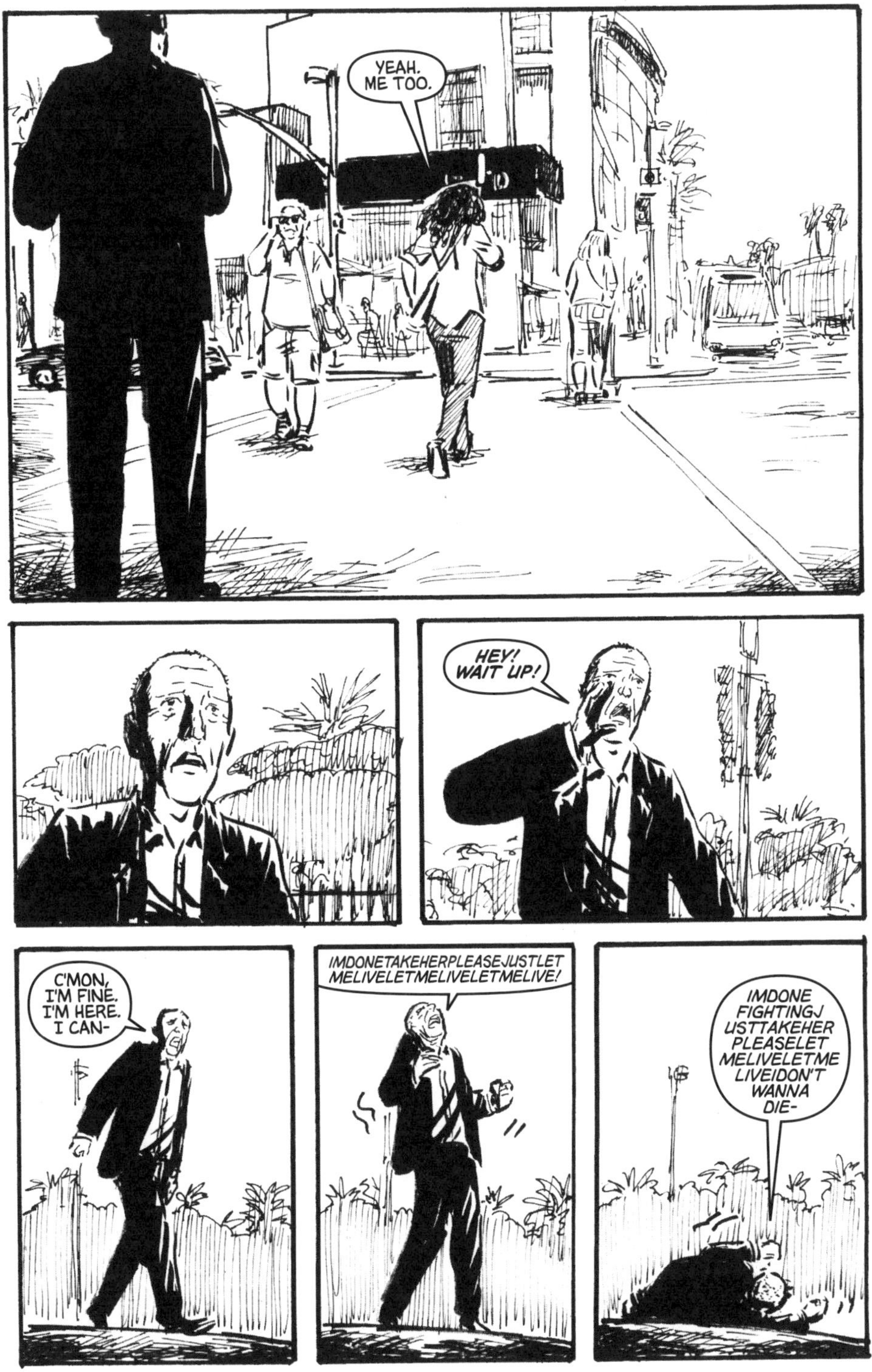
YEAH. ME TOO.
HEY! WAIT UP!
C'MON, I'M FINE. I'M HERE. I CAN-
IMDONETAKEHERPLEASEJUSTLET MELIVELETMELIVELETMELIVE!
IMDONE FIGHTINGJ USTTAKEHER PLEASELET MELIVELETME LIVEIDON'T WANNA DIE-

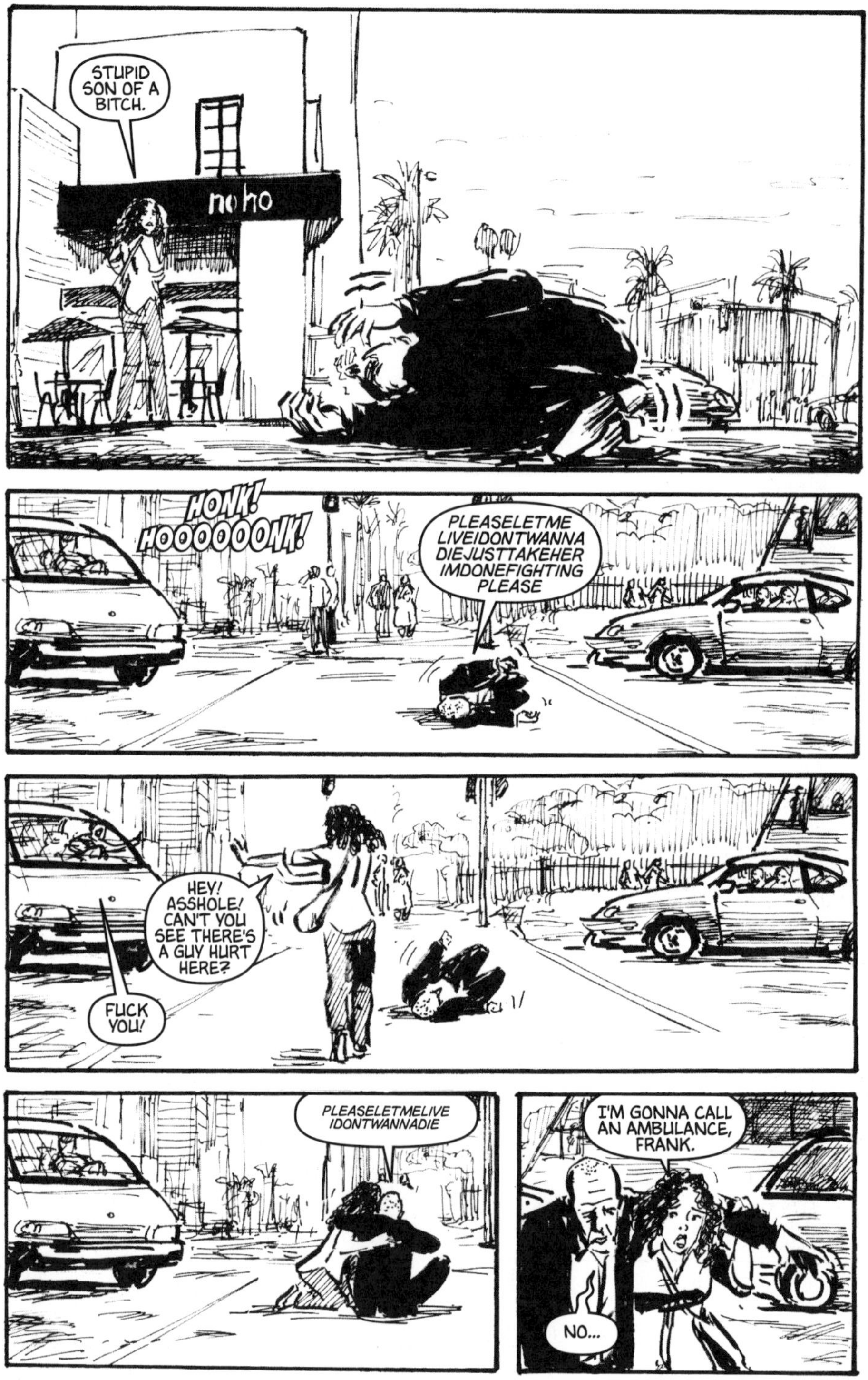
STUPID SON OF A BITCH.
noho
HONK! HOOOOOOONK!
PLEASELETME LIVEIDONTWANNA DIEJUSTTAKEHER IMDONEFIGHTING PLEASE
HEY! ASSHOLE! CAN'T YOU SEE THERE'S A GUY HURT HERE?
FUCK YOU!
PLEASELETMELIVE IDONTWANNADIE
I'M GONNA CALL AN AMBULANCE, FRANK.
NO...

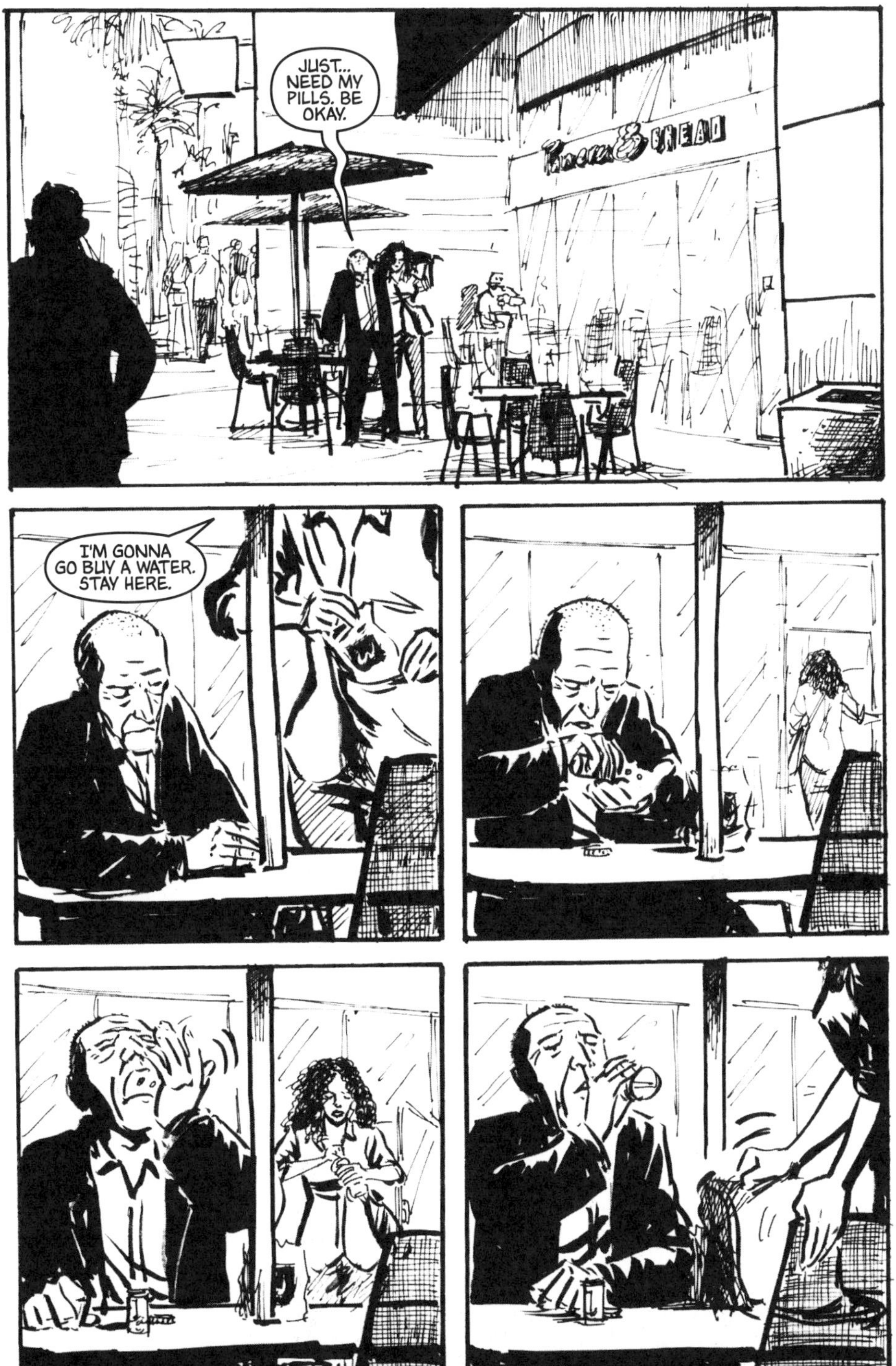
JUST... NEED MY PILLS. BE OKAY.
I'M GONNA GO BUY A WATER. STAY HERE.

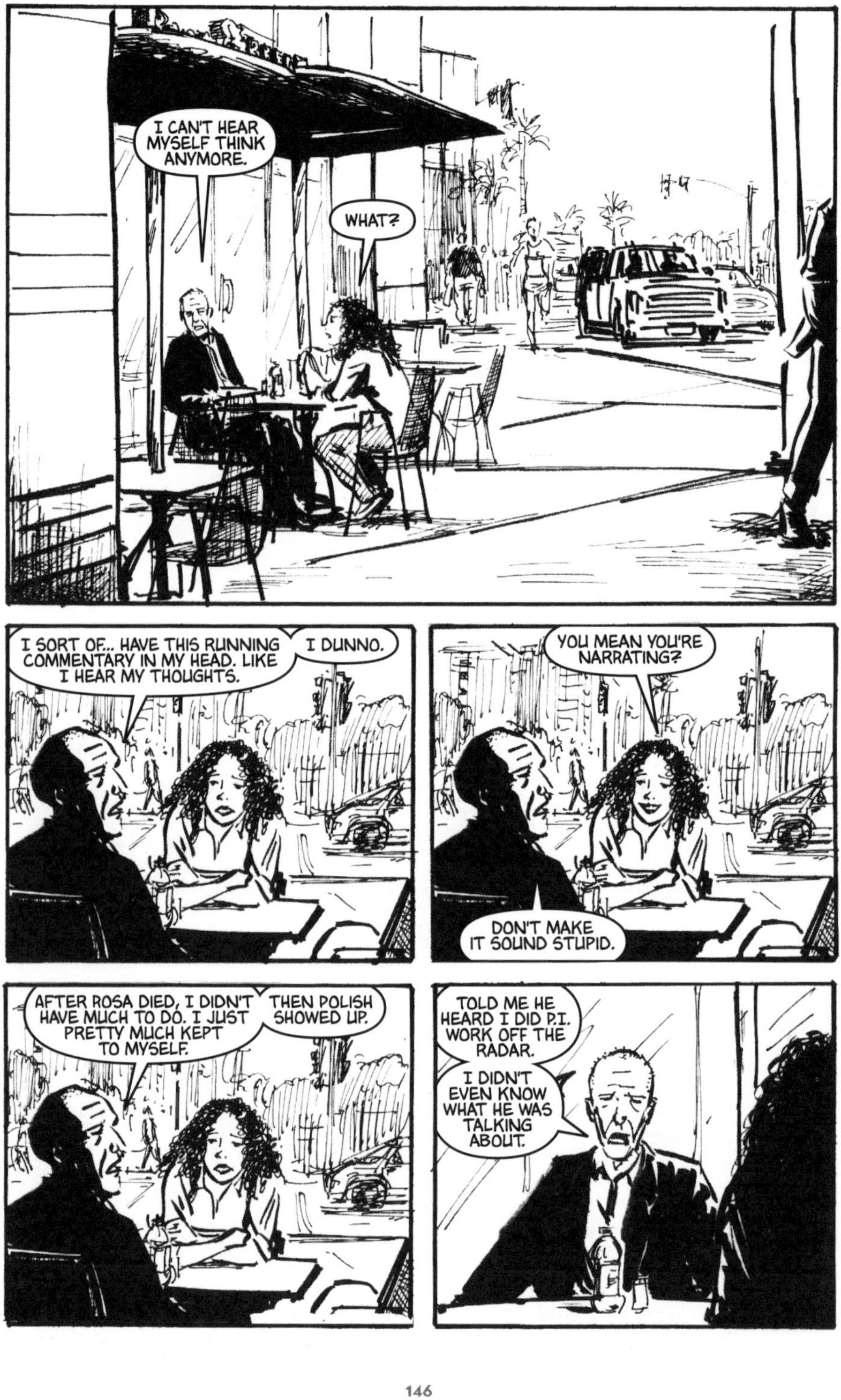
I CAN'T HEAR MYSELF THINK ANYMORE.
WHAT?
I SORT OF... HAVE THIS RUNNING COMMENTARY IN MY HEAD. LIKE I HEAR MY THOUGHTS.
I DUNNO.
YOU MEAN YOU'RE NARRATING?
DON'T MAKE IT SOUND STUPID.
AFTER ROSA DIED, I DIDN'T HAVE MUCH TO DO. I JUST PRETTY MUCH KEPT TO MYSELF.
THEN POLISH SHOWED UP.
TOLD ME HE HEARD I DID P.I. WORK OFF THE RADAR.
I DIDN'T EVEN KNOW WHAT HE WAS TALKING ABOUT.

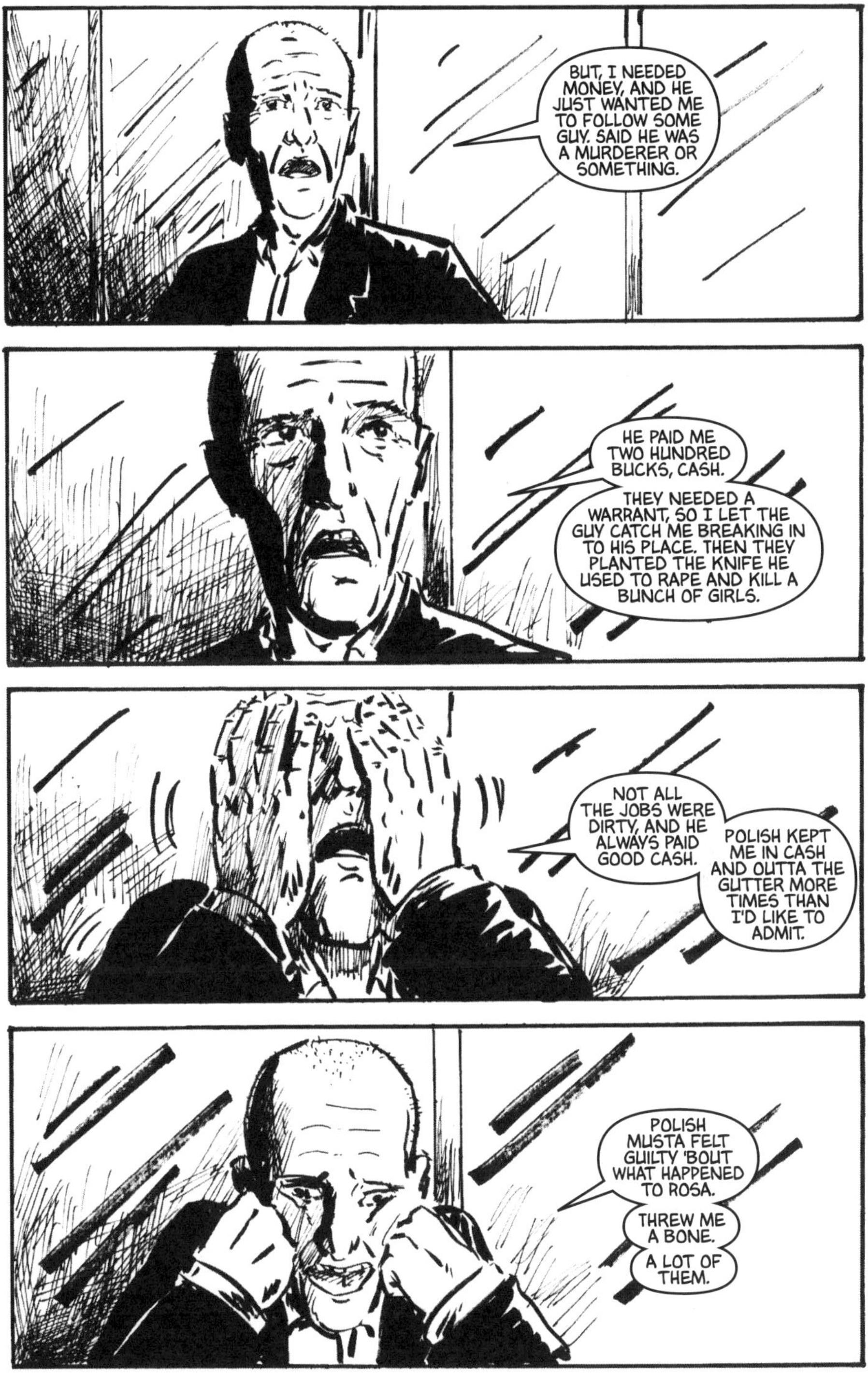
BUT, I NEEDED MONEY, AND HE JUST WANTED ME TO FOLLOW SOME GUY. SAID HE WAS A MURDERER OR SOMETHING.
HE PAID ME TWO HUNDRED BUCKS, CASH.
THEY NEEDED A WARRANT, SO I LET THE GUY CATCH ME BREAKING IN TO HIS PLACE. THEN THEY PLANTED THE KNIFE HE USED TO RAPE AND KILL A BUNCH OF GIRLS.
NOT ALL THE JOBS WERE DIRTY, AND HE ALWAYS PAID GOOD CASH.
POLISH KEPT ME IN CASH AND OUTTA THE GUTTER MORE TIMES THAN I'D LIKE TO ADMIT.
POLISH MUSTA FELT GUILTY 'BOUT WHAT HAPPENED TO ROSA.
THREW ME A BONE.
A LOT OF THEM.

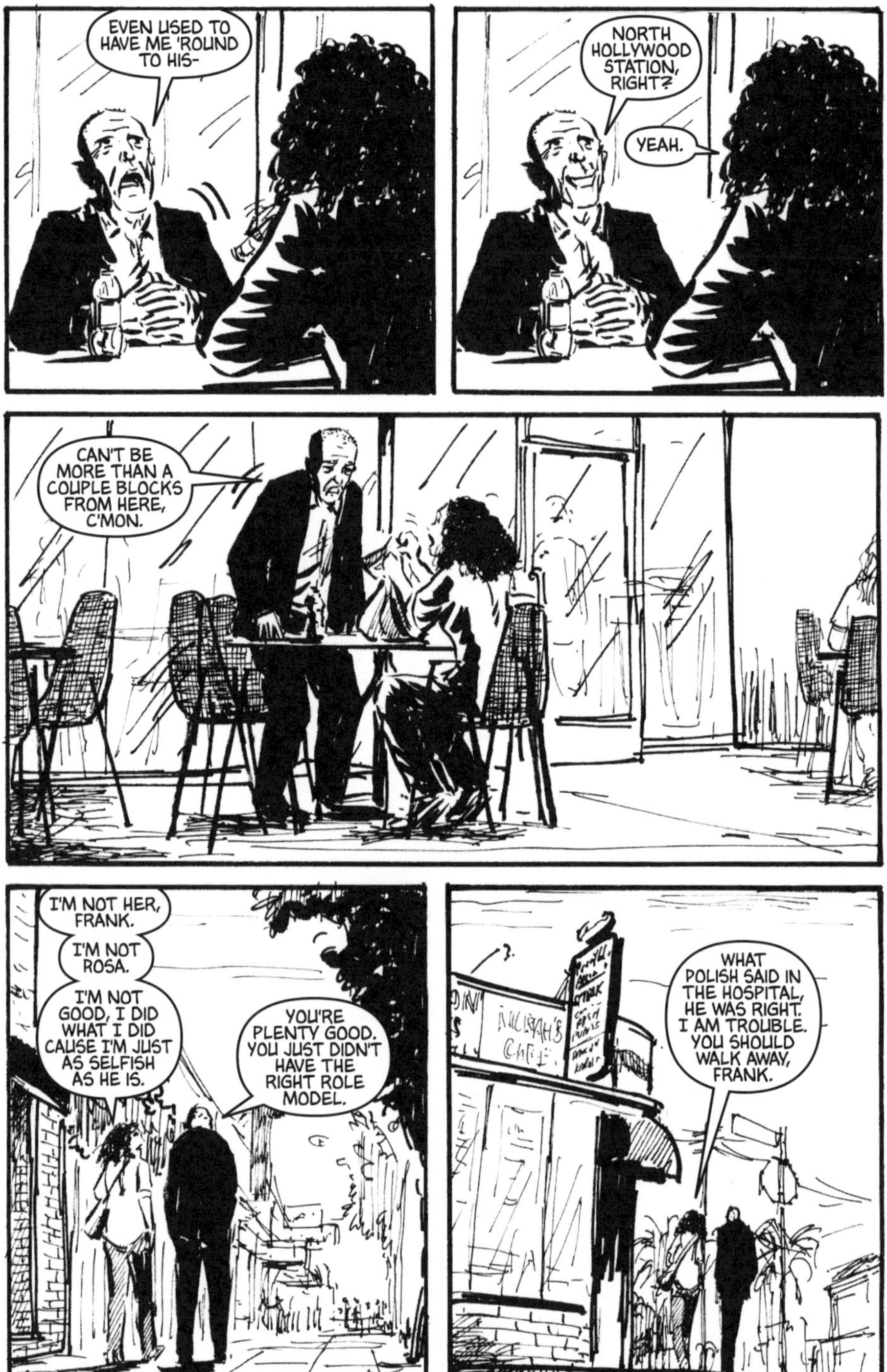
EVEN USED TO HAVE ME 'ROUND TO HIS-
NORTH HOLLYWOOD STATION, RIGHT?
YEAH.
CAN'T BE MORE THAN A COUPLE BLOCKS FROM HERE, C'MON.
I'M NOT HER, FRANK.
I'M NOT ROSA.
I'M NOT GOOD, I DID WHAT I DID CAUSE I'M JUST AS SELFISH AS HE IS.
YOU'RE PLENTY GOOD. YOU JUST DIDN'T HAVE THE RIGHT ROLE MODEL.
WHAT POLISH SAID IN THE HOSPITAL, HE WAS RIGHT. I AM TROUBLE. YOU SHOULD WALK AWAY, FRANK.

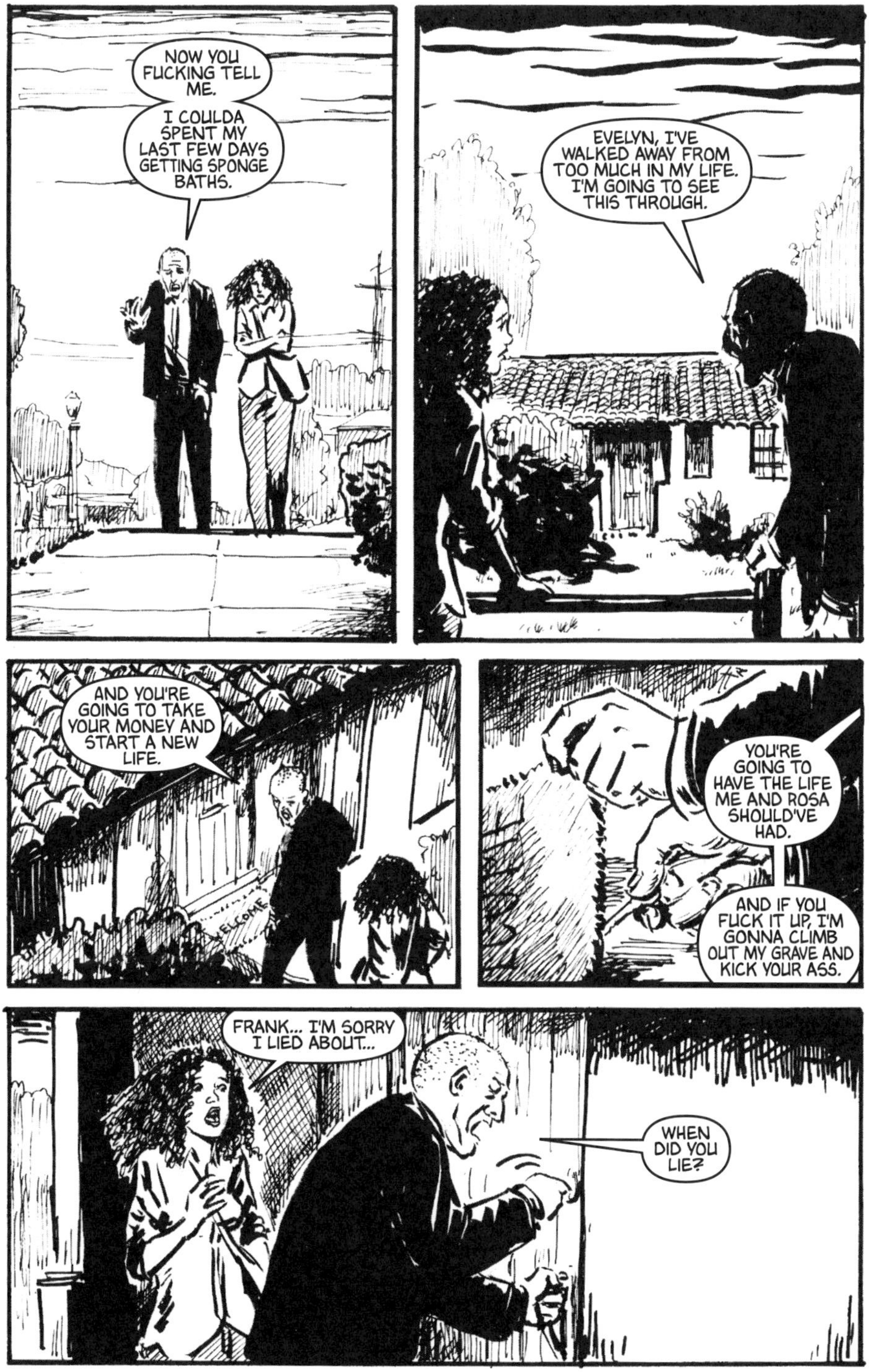
NOW YOU FUCKING TELL ME.
I COULDA SPENT MY LAST FEW DAYS GETTING SPONGE BATHS.
EVELYN, I'VE WALKED AWAY FROM TOO MUCH IN MY LIFE. I'M GOING TO SEE THIS THROUGH.
AND YOU'RE GOING TO TAKE YOUR MONEY AND START A NEW LIFE.
WELCOME
YOU'RE GOING TO HAVE THE LIFE ME AND ROSA SHOULD'VE HAD.
AND IF YOU FUCK IT UP, I'M GONNA CLIMB OUT MY GRAVE AND KICK YOUR ASS.
FRANK... I'M SORRY I LIED ABOUT...
WHEN DID YOU LIE?

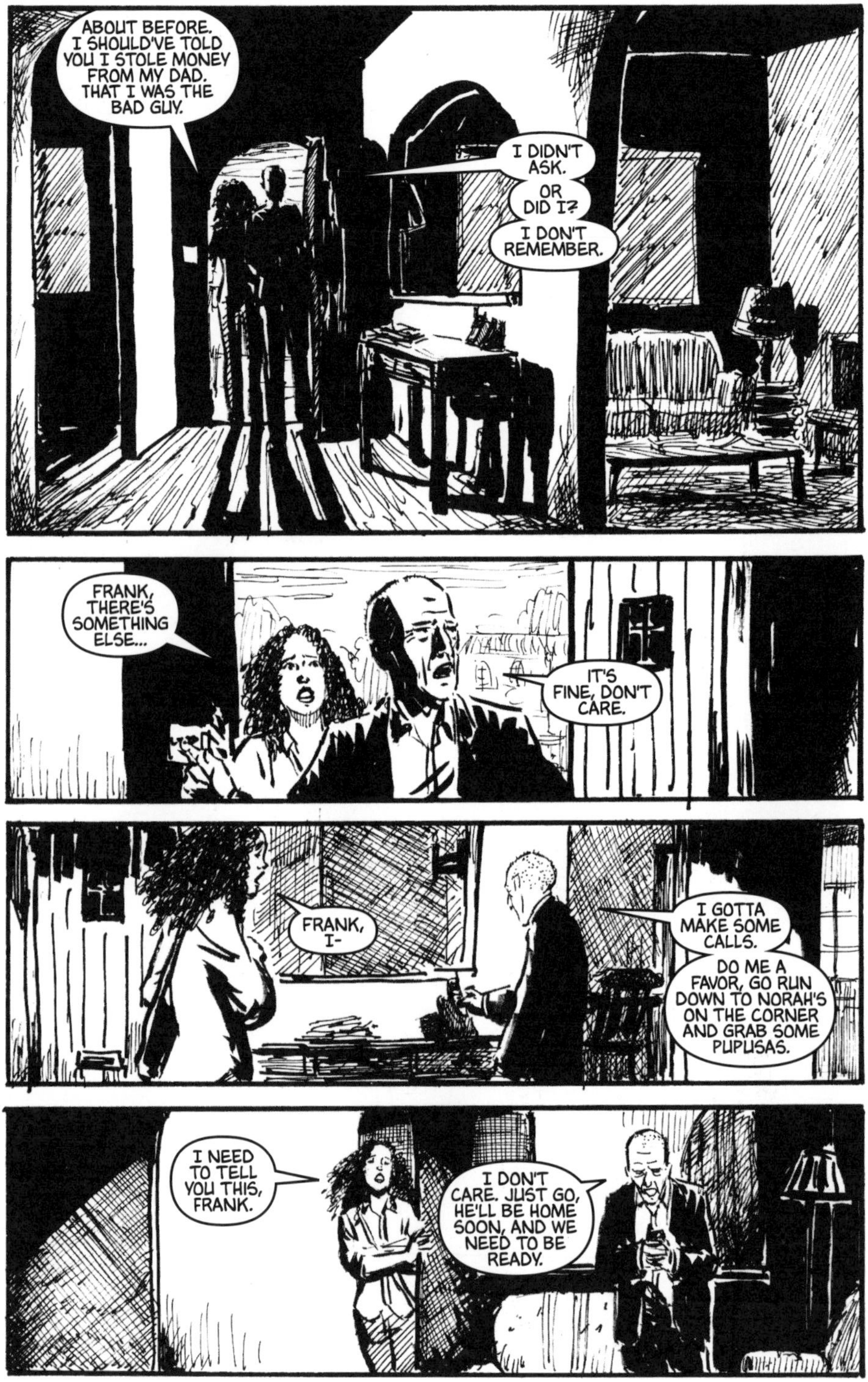
ABOUT BEFORE. I SHOULD'VE TOLD YOU I STOLE MONEY FROM MY DAD. THAT I WAS THE BAD GUY.
I DIDN'T ASK.
OR DID I?
I DON'T REMEMBER.
FRANK, THERE'S SOMETHING ELSE...
IT'S FINE, DON'T CARE.
FRANK, I-
I GOTTA MAKE SOME CALLS.
DO ME A FAVOR, GO RUN DOWN TO NORAH'S ON THE CORNER AND GRAB SOME PUPUSAS.
I NEED TO TELL YOU THIS, FRANK.
I DON'T CARE. JUST GO, HE'LL BE HOME SOON, AND WE NEED TO BE READY.

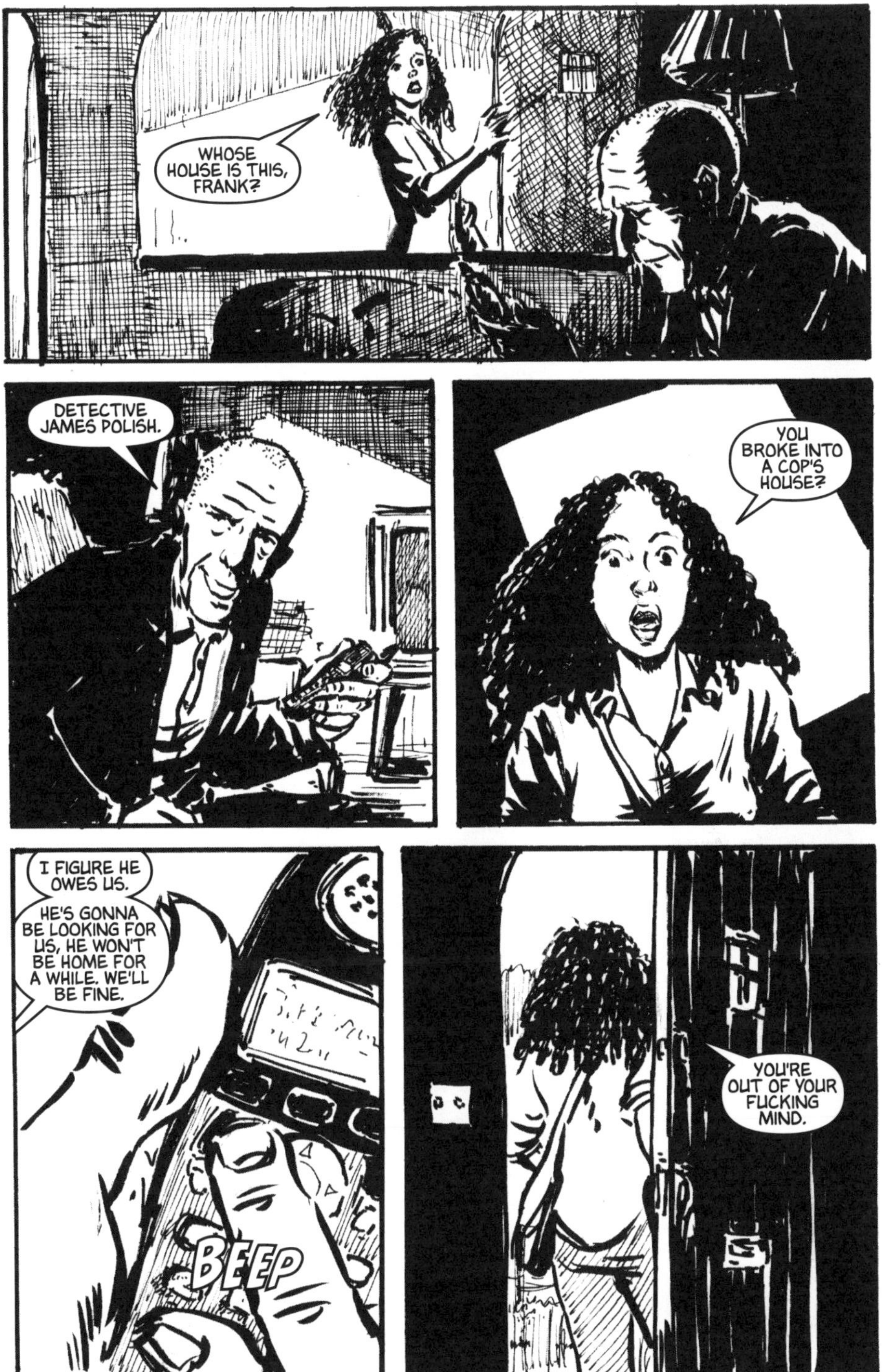
WHOSE HOUSE IS THIS, FRANK?
DETECTIVE JAMES POLISH.
YOU BROKE INTO A COP'S HOUSE?
I FIGURE HE OWES US.
HE'S GONNA BE LOOKING FOR US, HE WON'T BE HOME FOR A WHILE. WE'LL BE FINE.
BEEP
YOU'RE OUT OF YOUR FUCKING MIND.

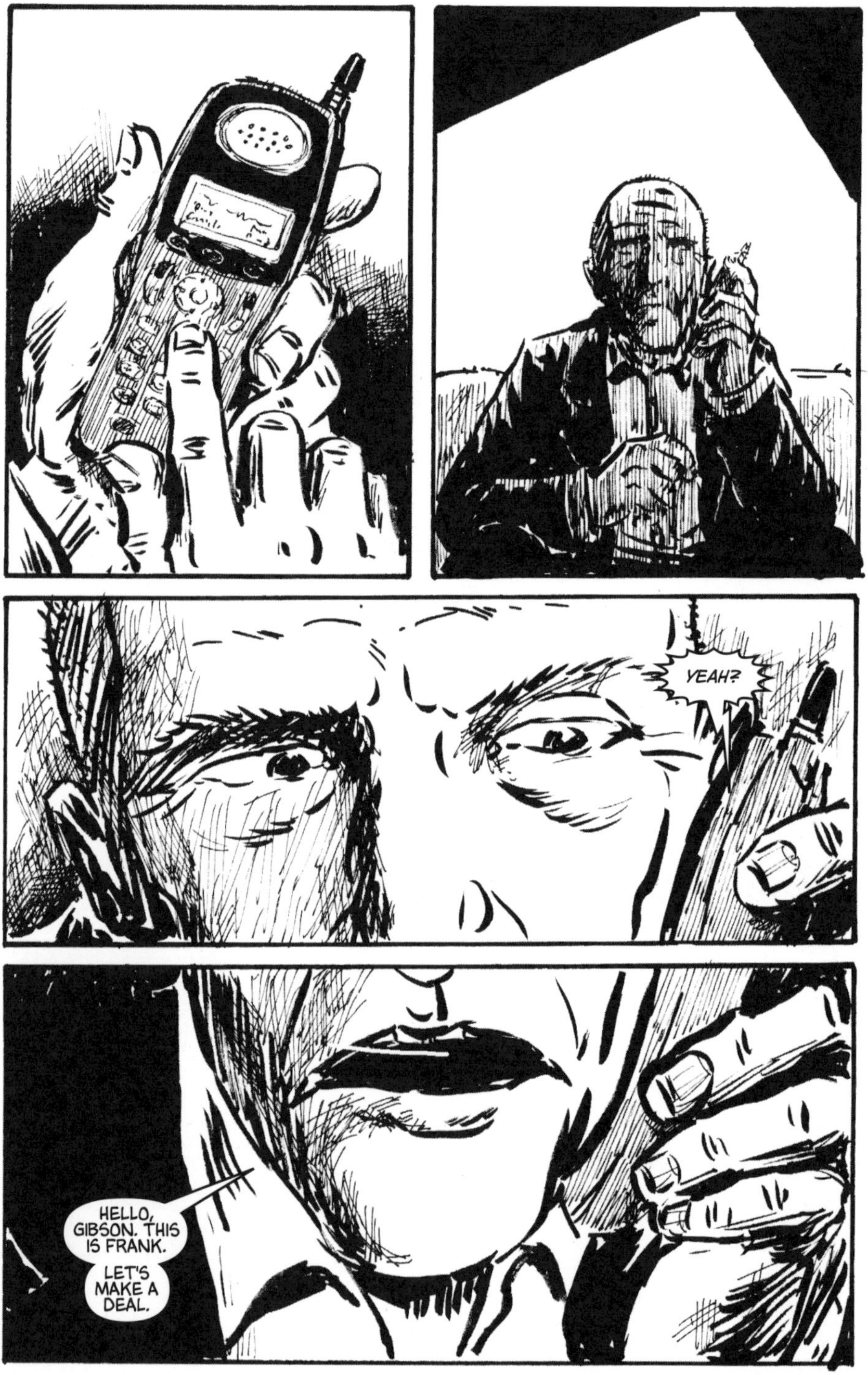
YEAH?
HELLO, GIBSON. THIS IS FRANK.
LET'S MAKE A DEAL.

END CHAPTER 6

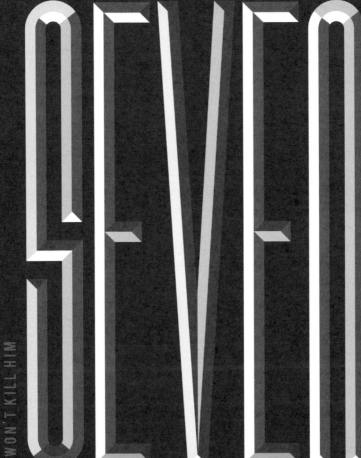

SEVEN

I WON'T KILL HIM

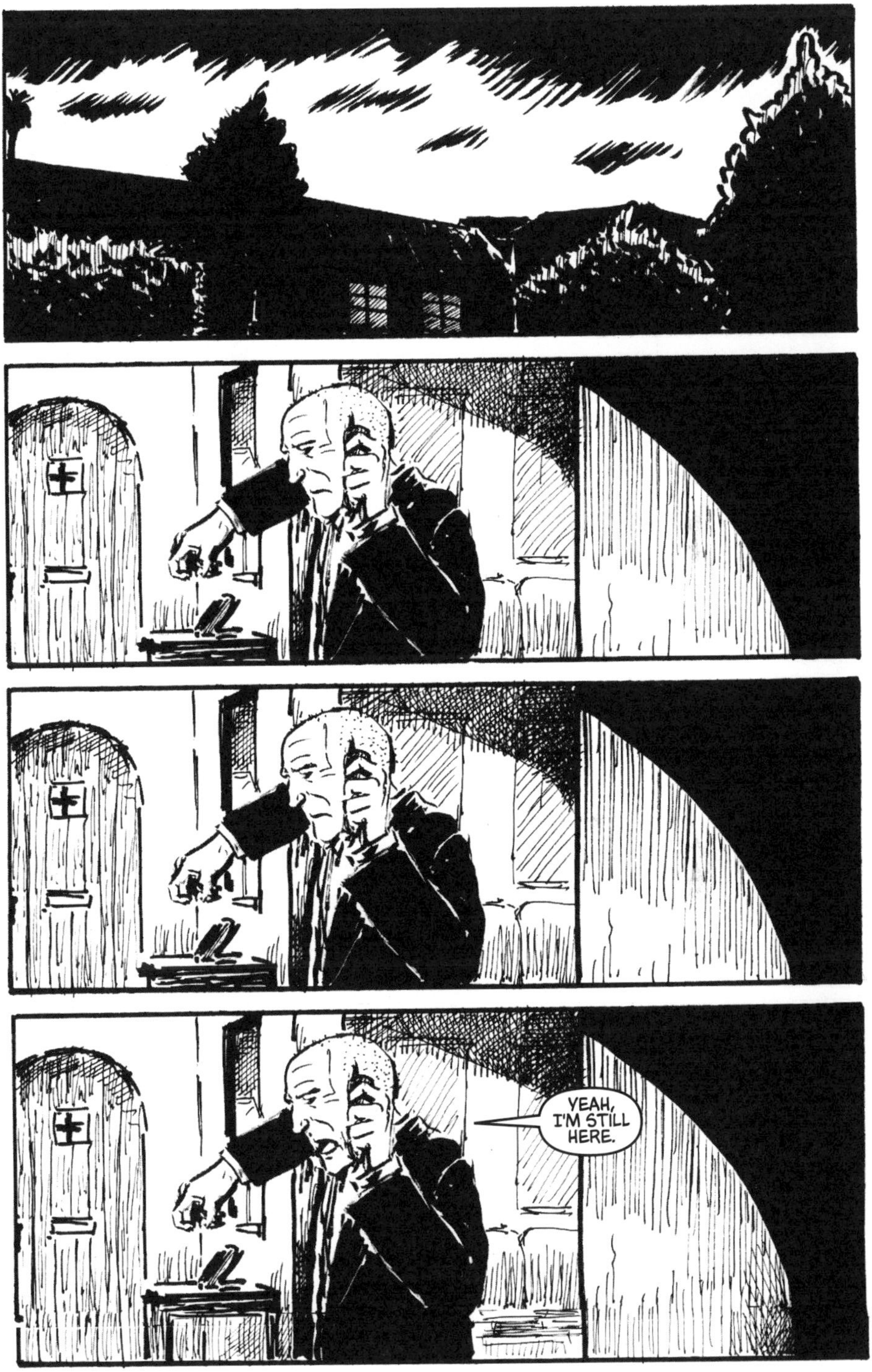
YEAH, I'M STILL HERE.

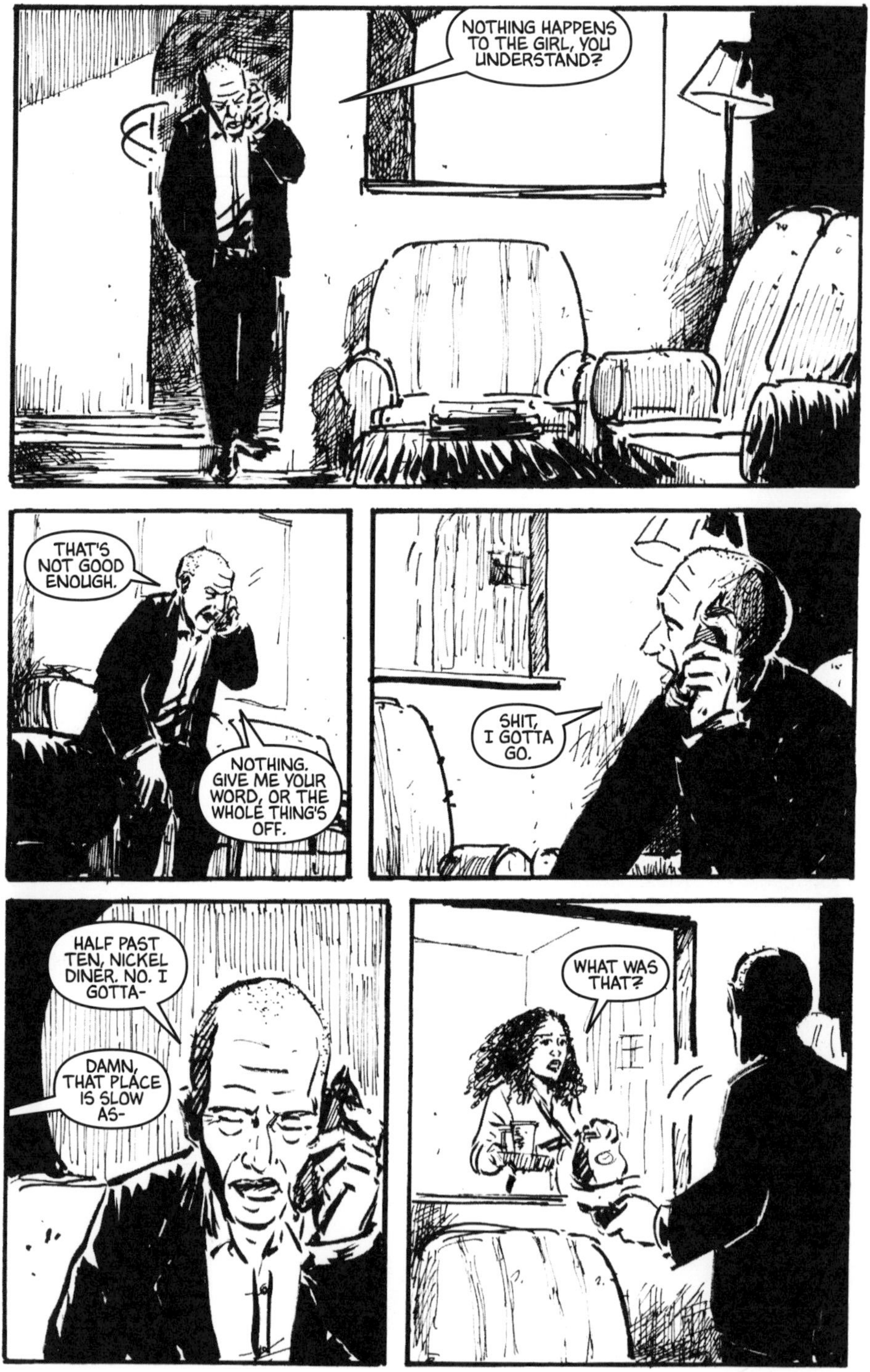
NOTHING HAPPENS TO THE GIRL, YOU UNDERSTAND?
THAT'S NOT GOOD ENOUGH.
NOTHING. GIVE ME YOUR WORD, OR THE WHOLE THING'S OFF.
SHIT, I GOTTA GO.
HALF PAST TEN, NICKEL DINER. NO. I GOTTA-
DAMN, THAT PLACE IS SLOW AS-
WHAT WAS THAT?

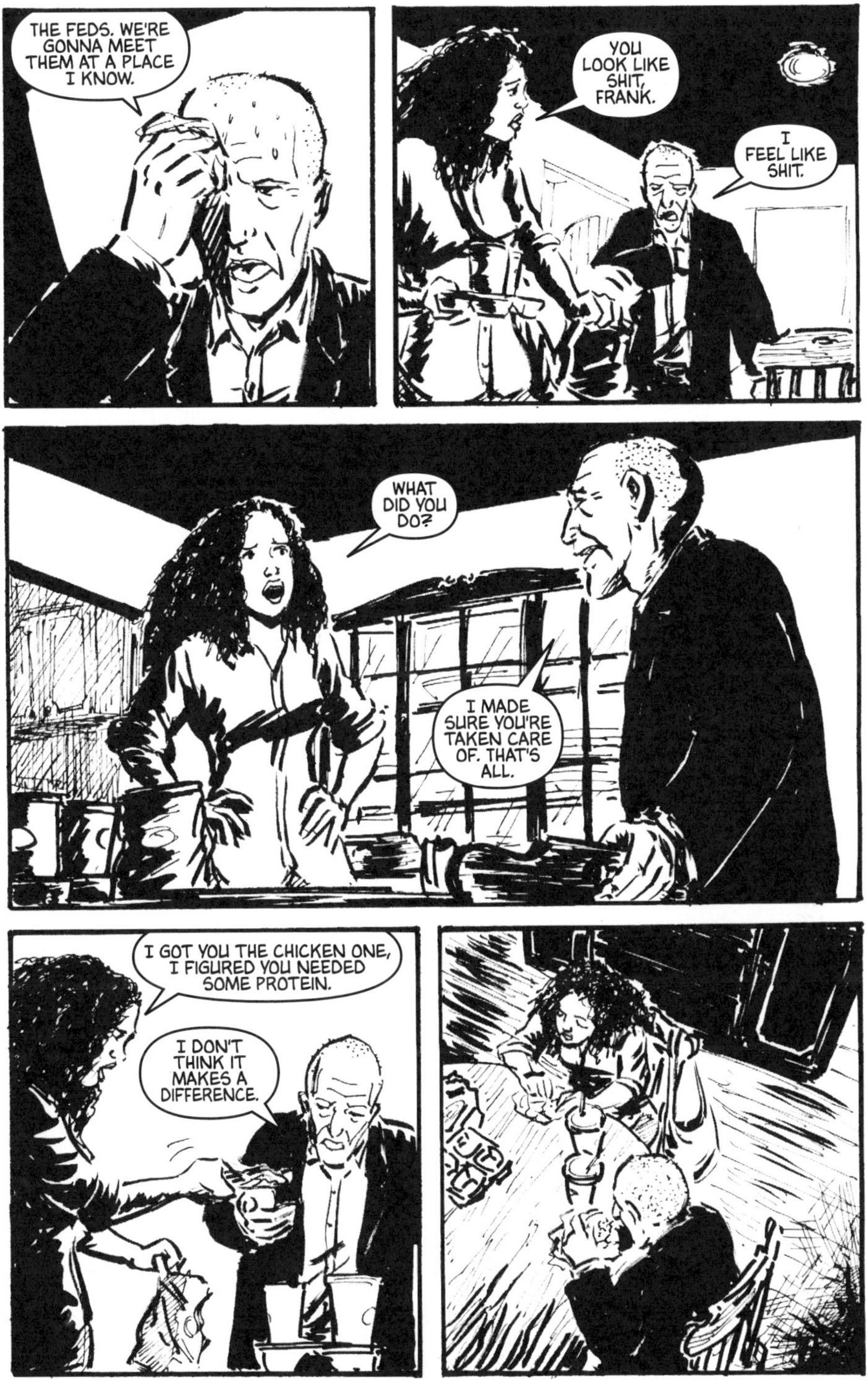
THE FEDS. WE'RE GONNA MEET THEM AT A PLACE I KNOW.
YOU LOOK LIKE SHIT, FRANK.
I FEEL LIKE SHIT.
WHAT DID YOU DO?
I MADE SURE YOU'RE TAKEN CARE OF. THAT'S ALL.
I GOT YOU THE CHICKEN ONE, I FIGURED YOU NEEDED SOME PROTEIN.
I DON'T THINK IT MAKES A DIFFERENCE.

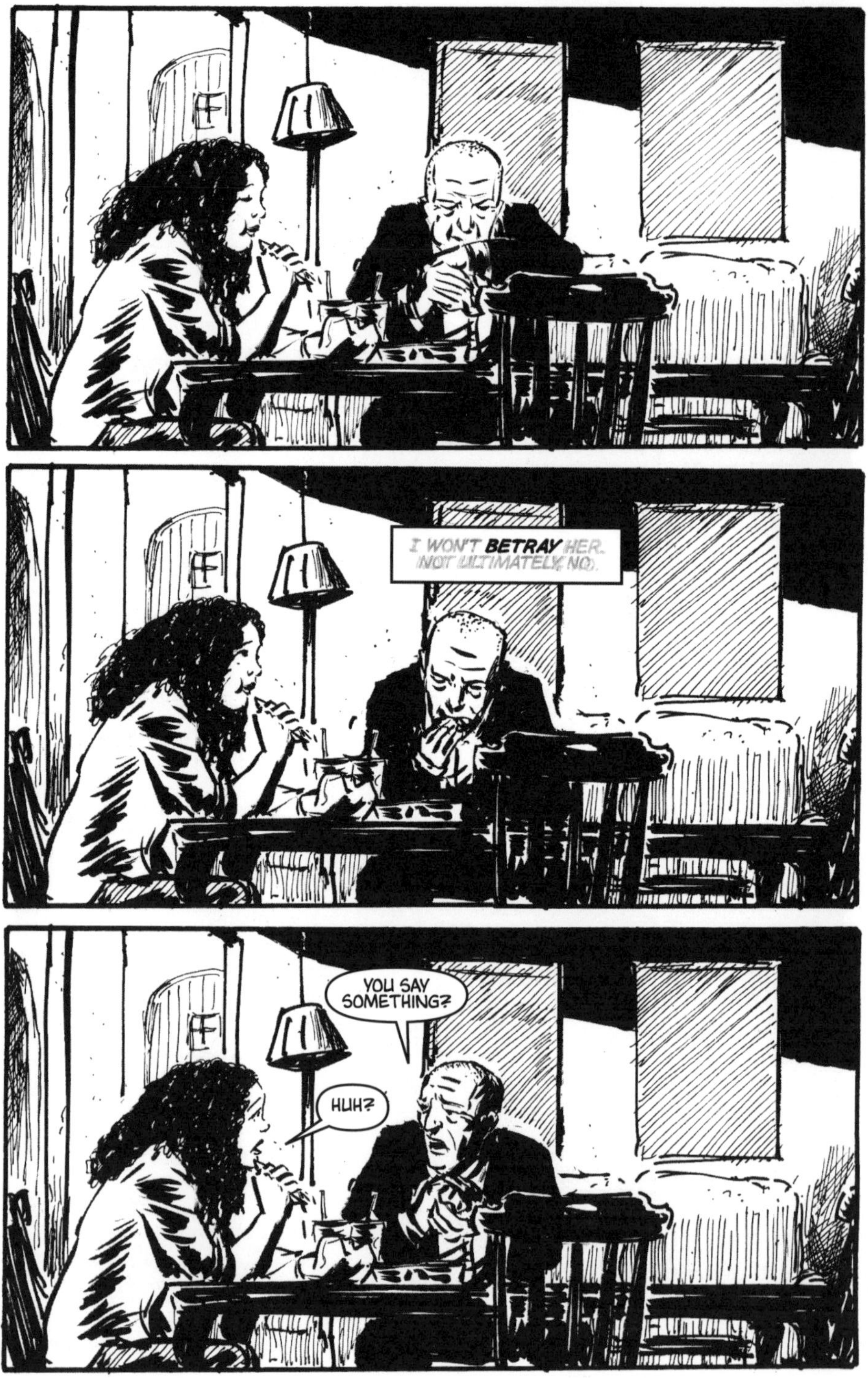
I WON'T BETRAY HER. NOT ULTIMATELY, NO.
YOU SAY SOMETHING?
HUH?

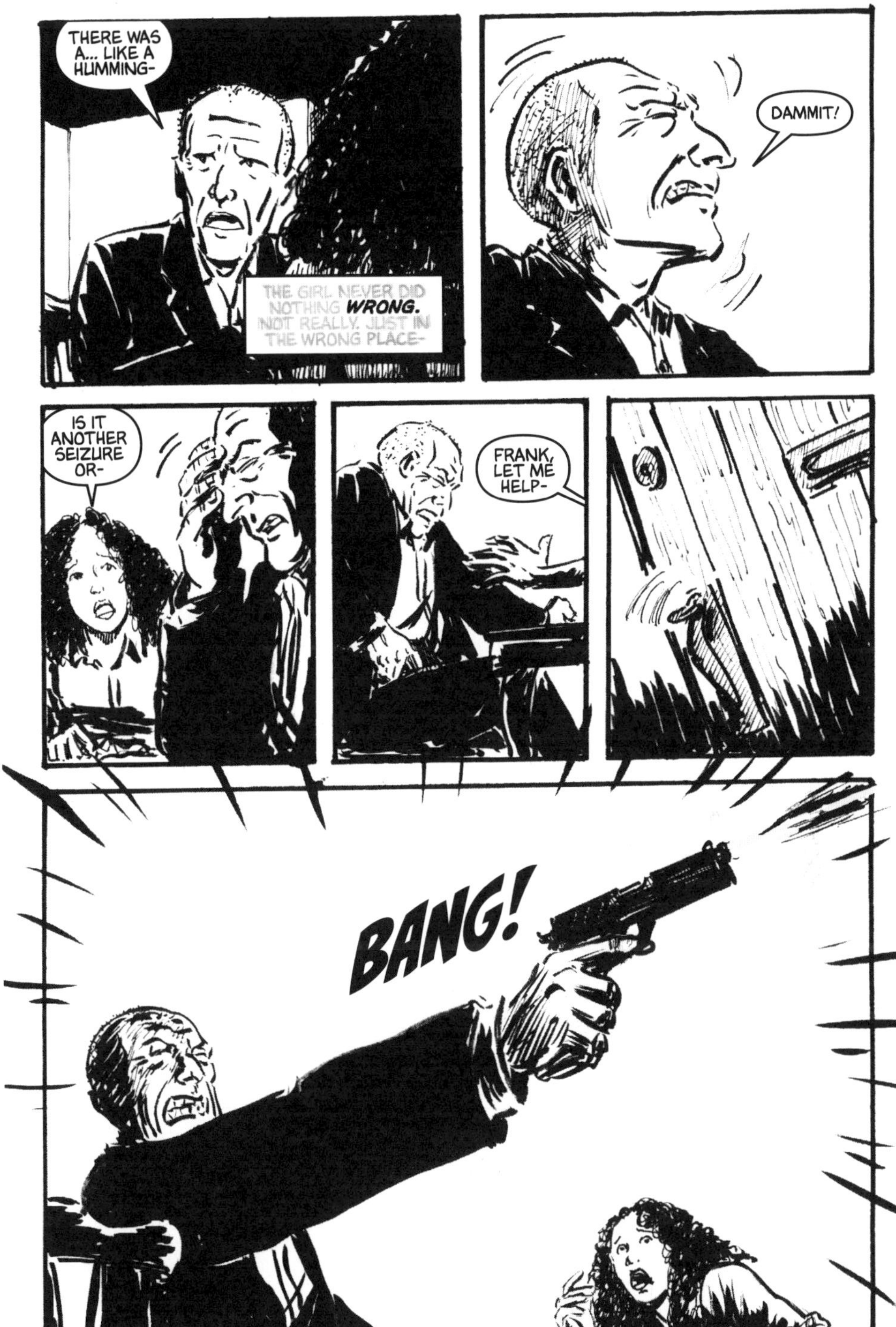
THERE WAS A... LIKE A HUMMING-
THE GIRL NEVER DID NOTHING WRONG. NOT REALLY. JUST IN THE WRONG PLACE-
DAMMIT!
IS IT ANOTHER SEIZURE OR-
FRANK, LET ME HELP-
BANG!

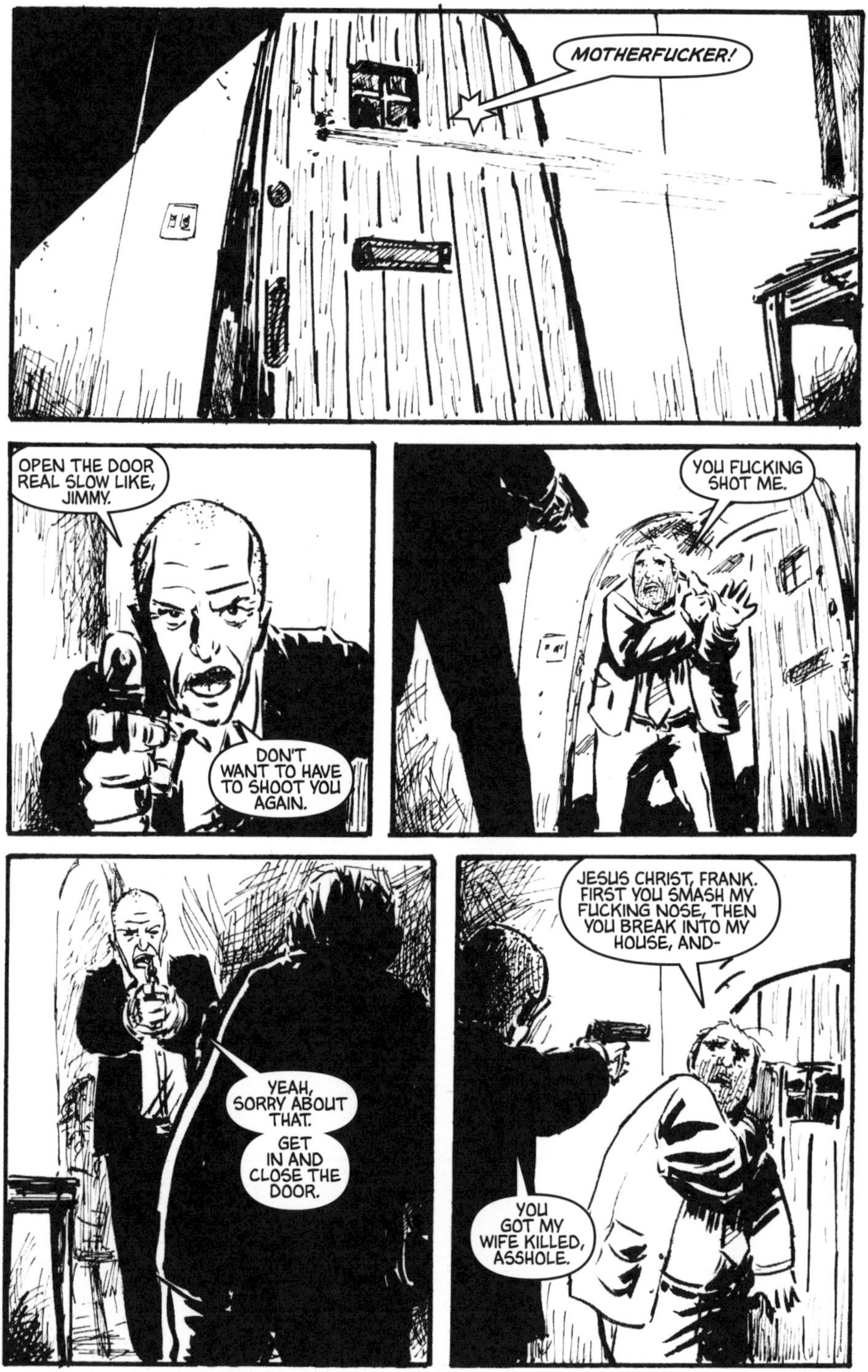
MOTHERFUCKER!
OPEN THE DOOR REAL SLOW LIKE, JIMMY.
DON'T WANT TO HAVE TO SHOOT YOU AGAIN.
YOU FUCKING SHOT ME.
YEAH, SORRY ABOUT THAT.
GET IN AND CLOSE THE DOOR.
JESUS CHRIST, FRANK. FIRST YOU SMASH MY FUCKING NOSE, THEN YOU BREAK INTO MY HOUSE, AND-
YOU GOT MY WIFE KILLED, ASSHOLE.

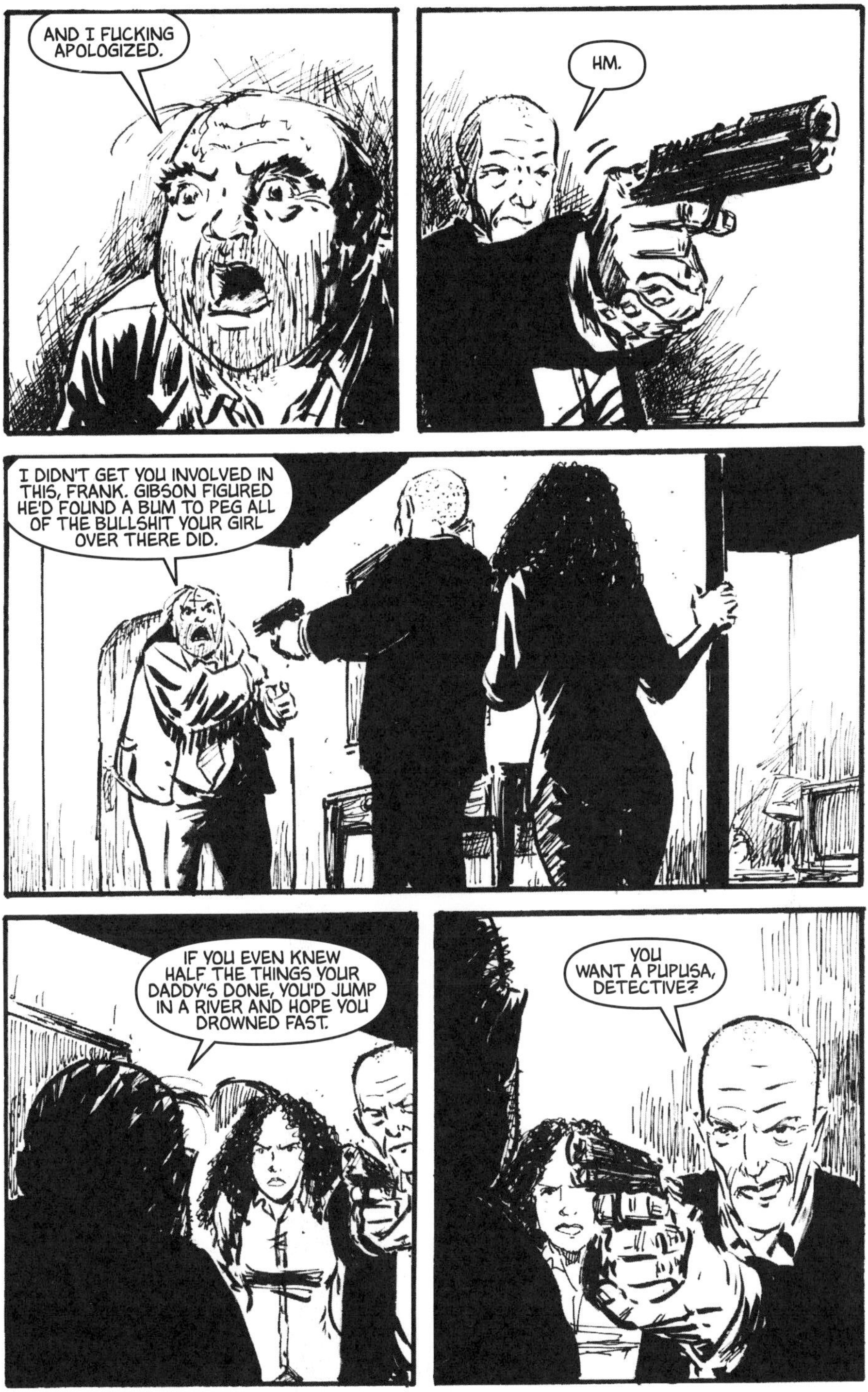
AND I FUCKING APOLOGIZED.
HM.
I DIDN'T GET YOU INVOLVED IN THIS, FRANK. GIBSON FIGURED HE'D FOUND A BUM TO PEG ALL OF THE BULLSHIT YOUR GIRL OVER THERE DID.
IF YOU EVEN KNEW HALF THE THINGS YOUR DADDY'S DONE, YOU'D JUMP IN A RIVER AND HOPE YOU DROWNED FAST.
YOU WANT A PUPUSA, DETECTIVE?

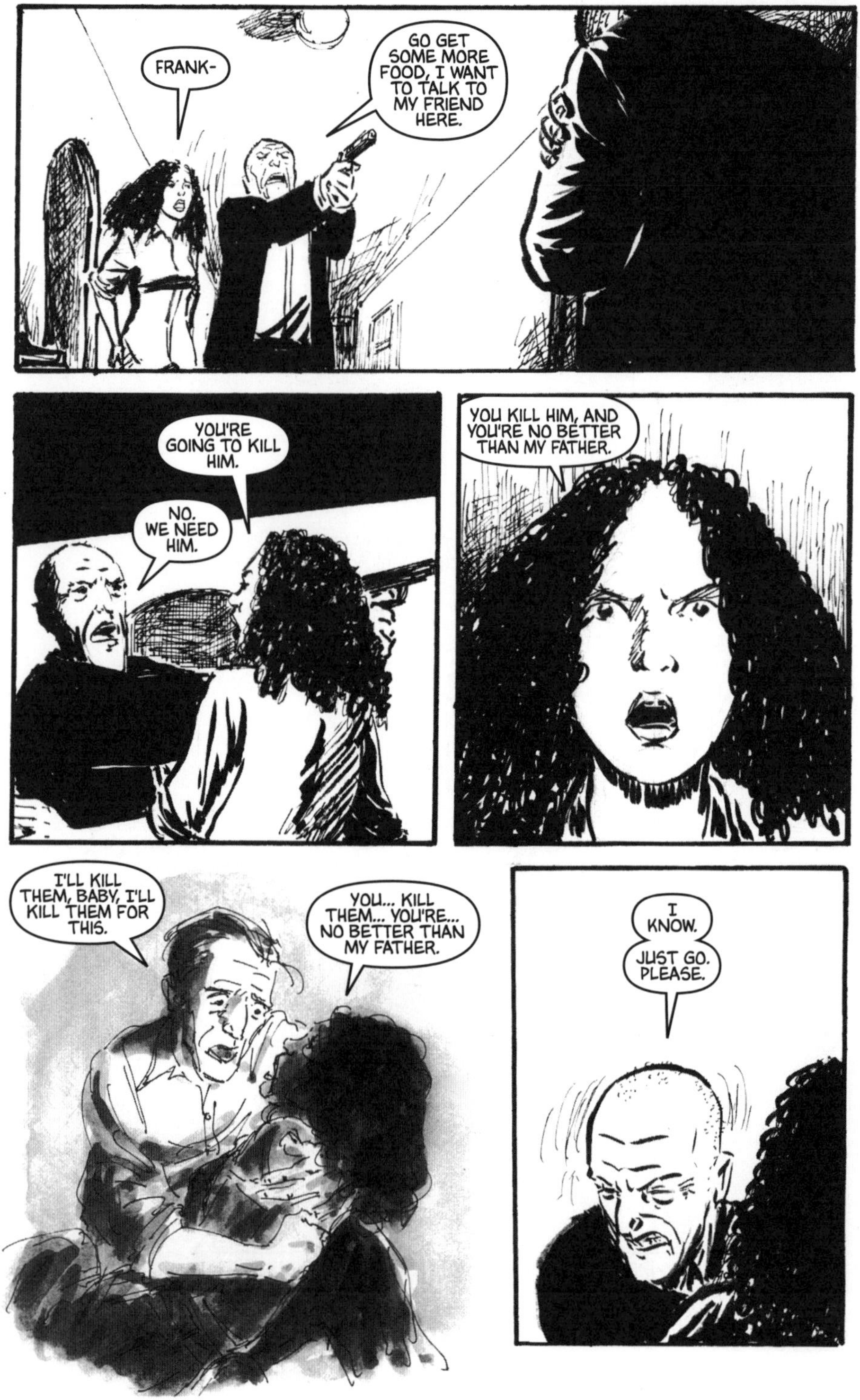
FRANK-
GO GET SOME MORE FOOD, I WANT TO TALK TO MY FRIEND HERE.
YOU'RE GOING TO KILL HIM.
NO. WE NEED HIM.
YOU KILL HIM, AND YOU'RE NO BETTER THAN MY FATHER.
I'LL KILL THEM, BABY, I'LL KILL THEM FOR THIS.
YOU... KILL THEM... YOU'RE... NO BETTER THAN MY FATHER.
I KNOW.
JUST GO. PLEASE.

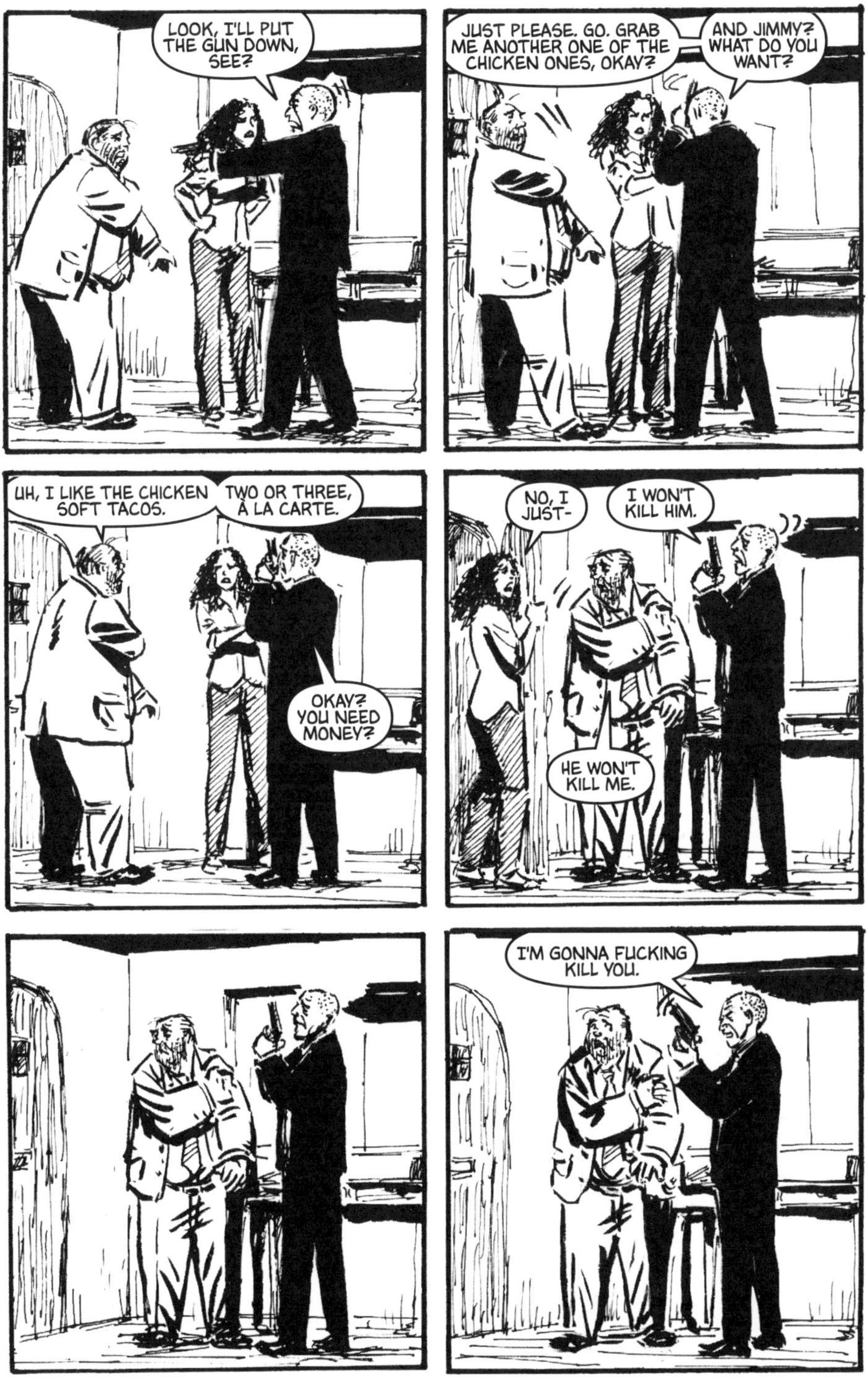
LOOK, I'LL PUT THE GUN DOWN, SEE?
JUST PLEASE. GO. GRAB ME ANOTHER ONE OF THE CHICKEN ONES, OKAY?
AND JIMMY? WHAT DO YOU WANT?
UH, I LIKE THE CHICKEN SOFT TACOS.
TWO OR THREE, À LA CARTE.
OKAY? YOU NEED MONEY?
NO, I JUST-
I WON'T KILL HIM.
HE WON'T KILL ME.
I'M GONNA FUCKING KILL YOU.

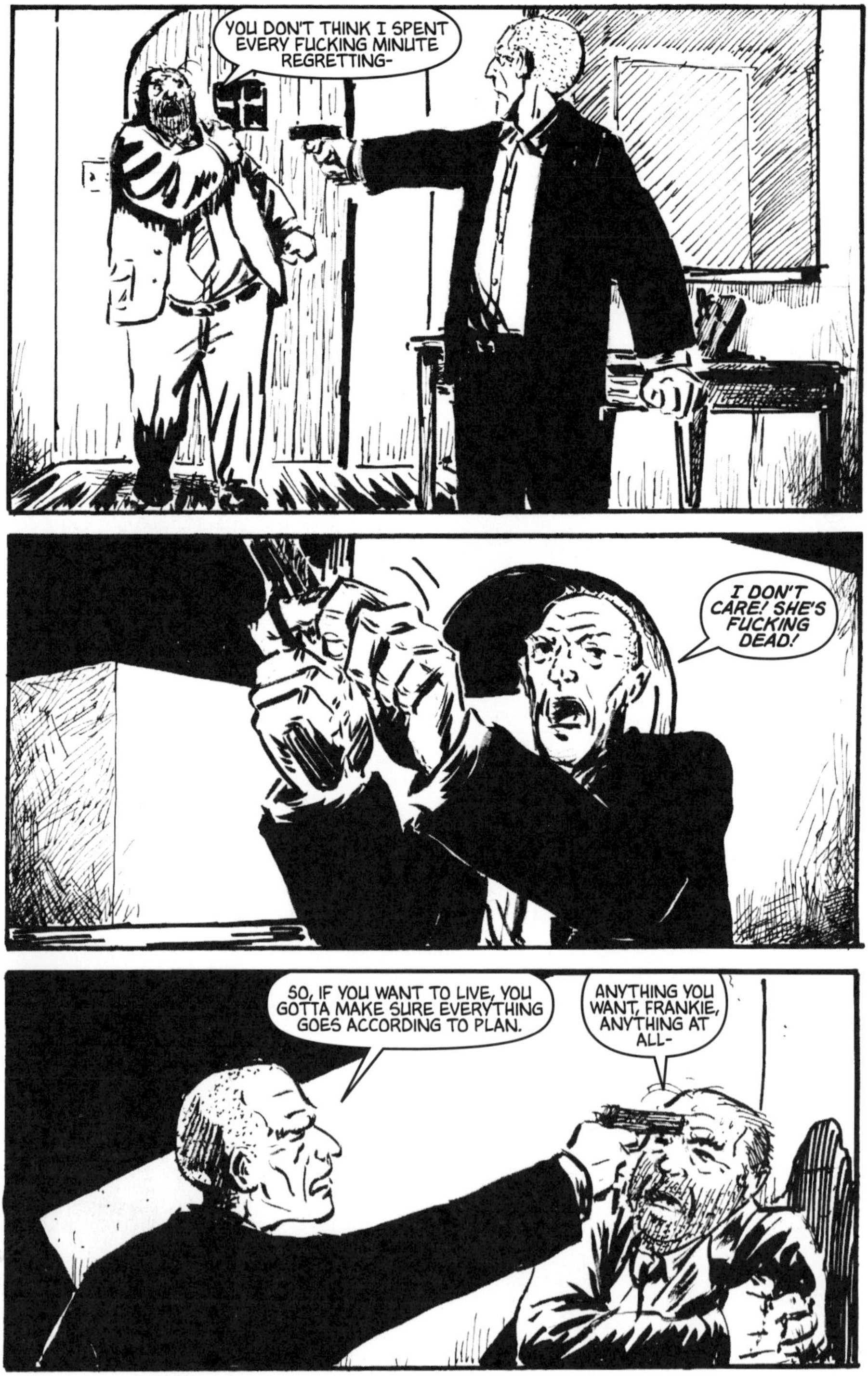
YOU DON'T THINK I SPENT EVERY FUCKING MINUTE REGRETTING-
I DON'T CARE! SHE'S FUCKING DEAD!
SO, IF YOU WANT TO LIVE, YOU GOTTA MAKE SURE EVERYTHING GOES ACCORDING TO PLAN.
ANYTHING YOU WANT, FRANKIE, ANYTHING AT ALL-

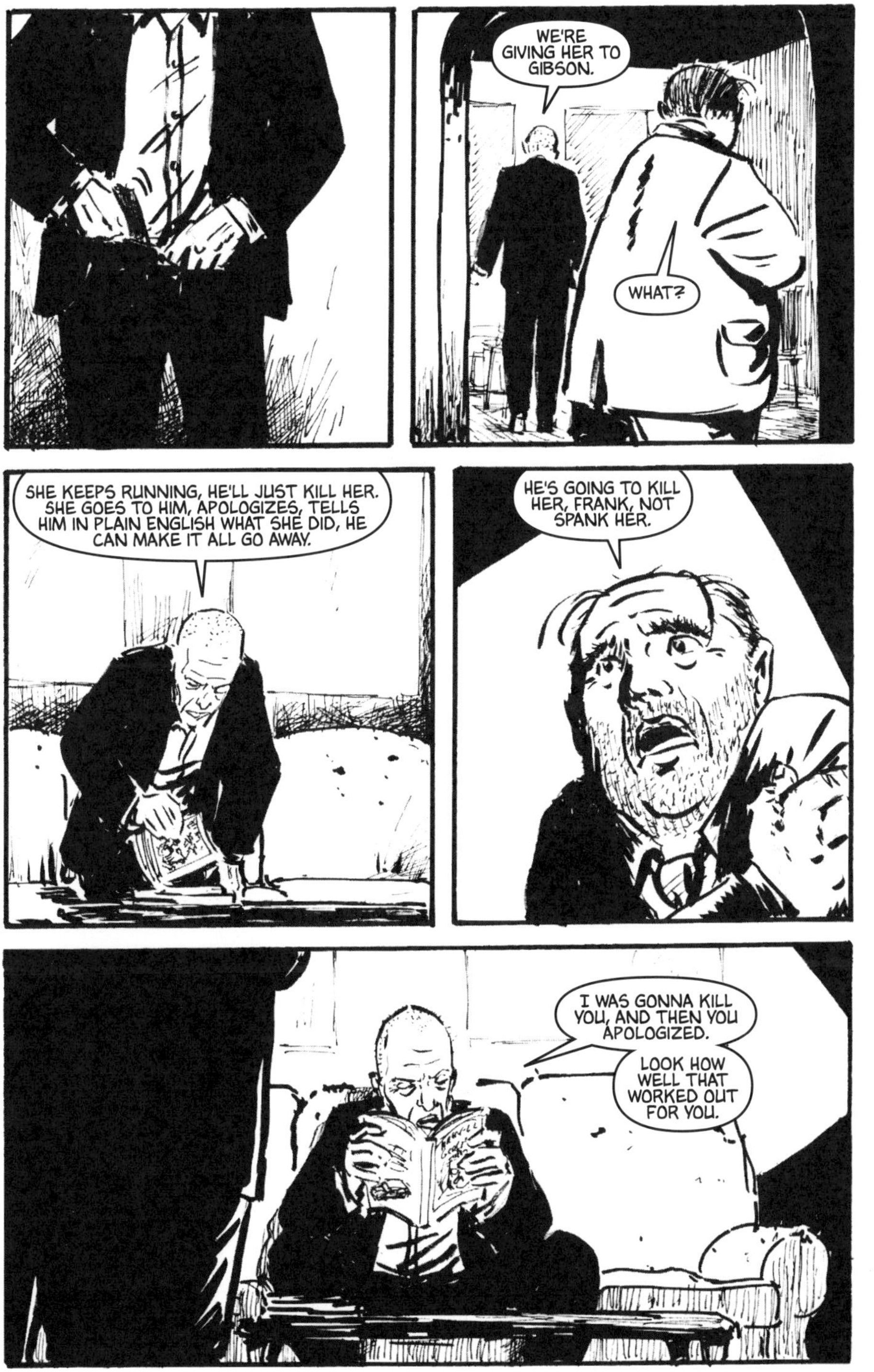
WE'RE GIVING HER TO GIBSON.
WHAT?
SHE KEEPS RUNNING, HE'LL JUST KILL HER. SHE GOES TO HIM, APOLOGIZES, TELLS HIM IN PLAIN ENGLISH WHAT SHE DID, HE CAN MAKE IT ALL GO AWAY.
HE'S GOING TO KILL HER, FRANK, NOT SPANK HER.
I WAS GONNA KILL YOU, AND THEN YOU APOLOGIZED.
LOOK HOW WELL THAT WORKED OUT FOR YOU.

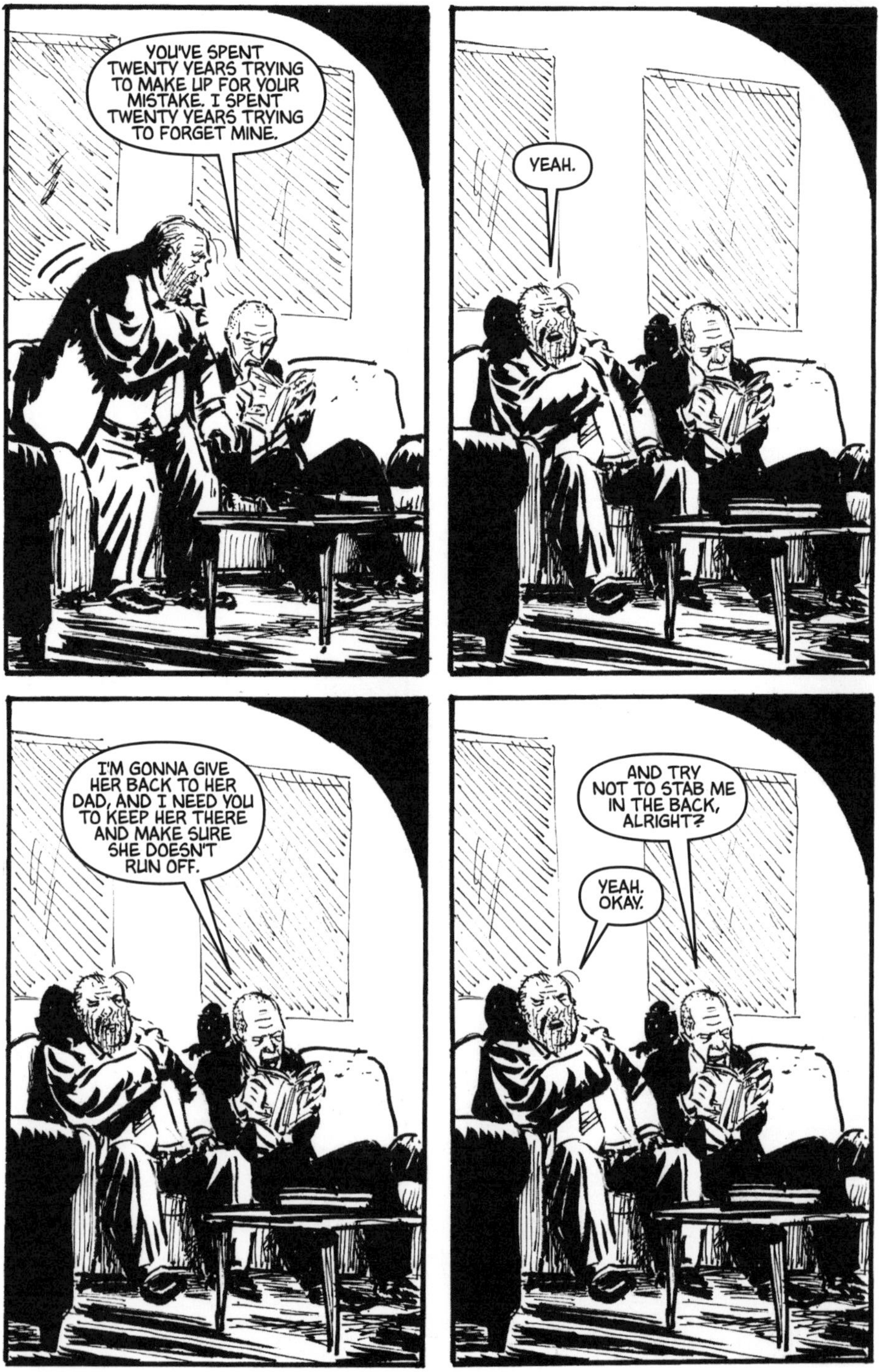
YOU'VE SPENT TWENTY YEARS TRYING TO MAKE UP FOR YOUR MISTAKE. I SPENT TWENTY YEARS TRYING TO FORGET MINE.
YEAH.
I'M GONNA GIVE HER BACK TO HER DAD, AND I NEED YOU TO KEEP HER THERE AND MAKE SURE SHE DOESN'T RUN OFF.
AND TRY NOT TO STAB ME IN THE BACK, ALRIGHT?
YEAH. OKAY.

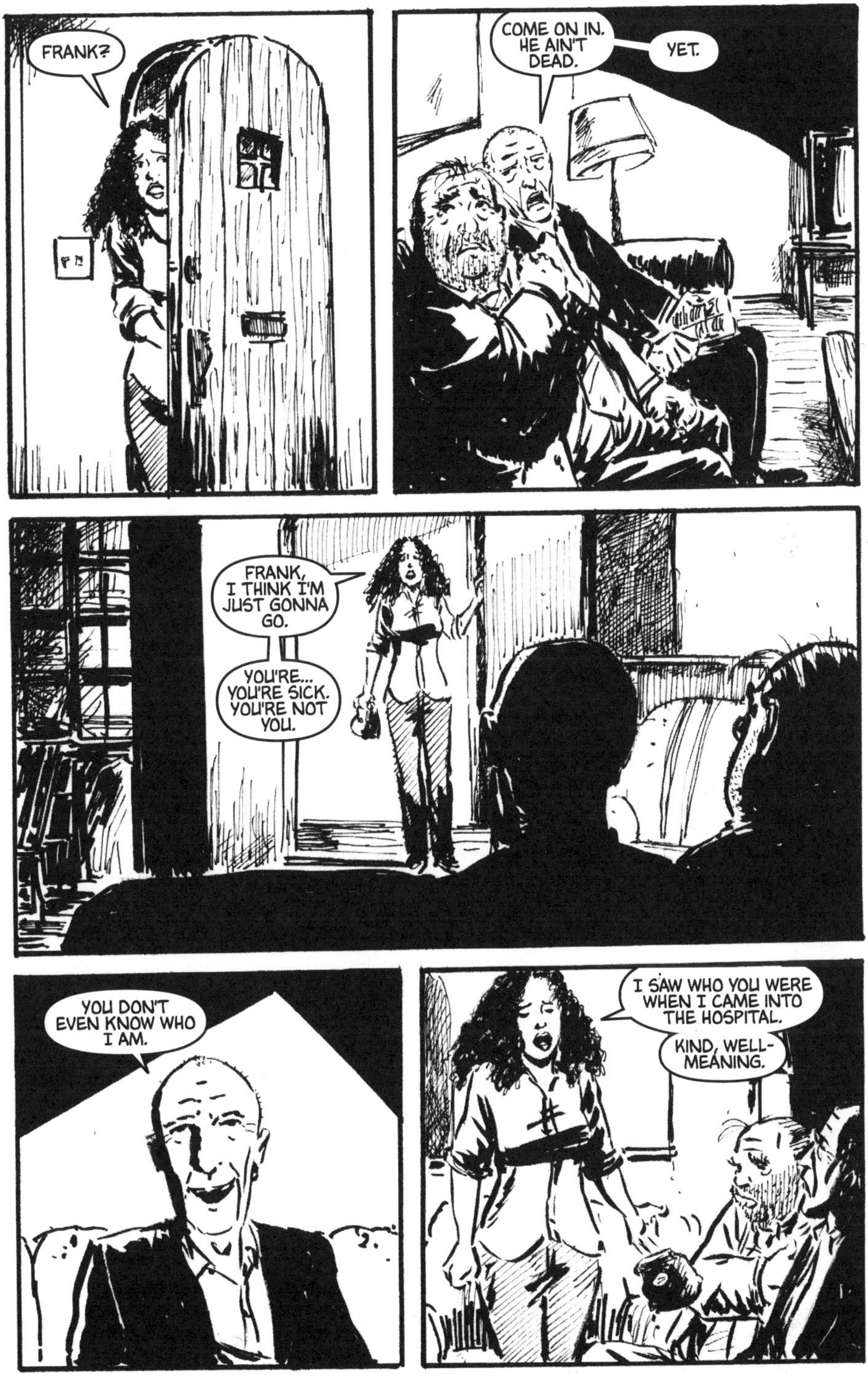
FRANK?
COME ON IN. HE AIN'T DEAD.
YET.
FRANK, I THINK I'M JUST GONNA GO.
YOU'RE... YOU'RE SICK. YOU'RE NOT YOU.
YOU DON'T EVEN KNOW WHO I AM.
I SAW WHO YOU WERE WHEN I CAME INTO THE HOSPITAL.
KIND, WELL-MEANING.

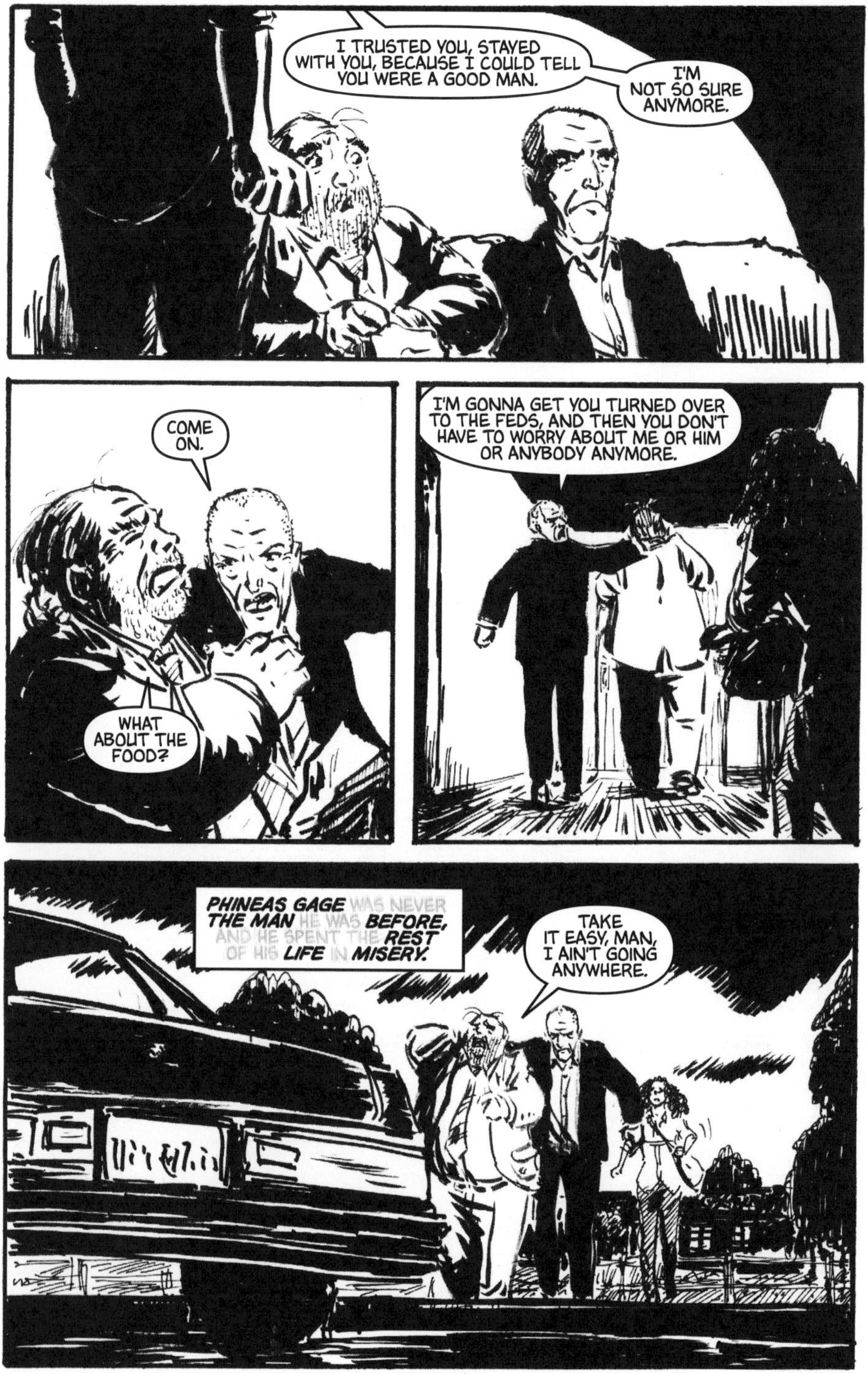
I TRUSTED YOU, STAYED WITH YOU, BECAUSE I COULD TELL YOU WERE A GOOD MAN.
I'M NOT SO SURE ANYMORE.
COME ON.
WHAT ABOUT THE FOOD?
I'M GONNA GET YOU TURNED OVER TO THE FEDS, AND THEN YOU DON'T HAVE TO WORRY ABOUT ME OR HIM OR ANYBODY ANYMORE.
PHINEAS GAGE WAS NEVER THE MAN HE WAS BEFORE, AND HE SPENT THE REST OF HIS LIFE IN MISERY.
TAKE IT EASY, MAN, I AIN'T GOING ANYWHERE.

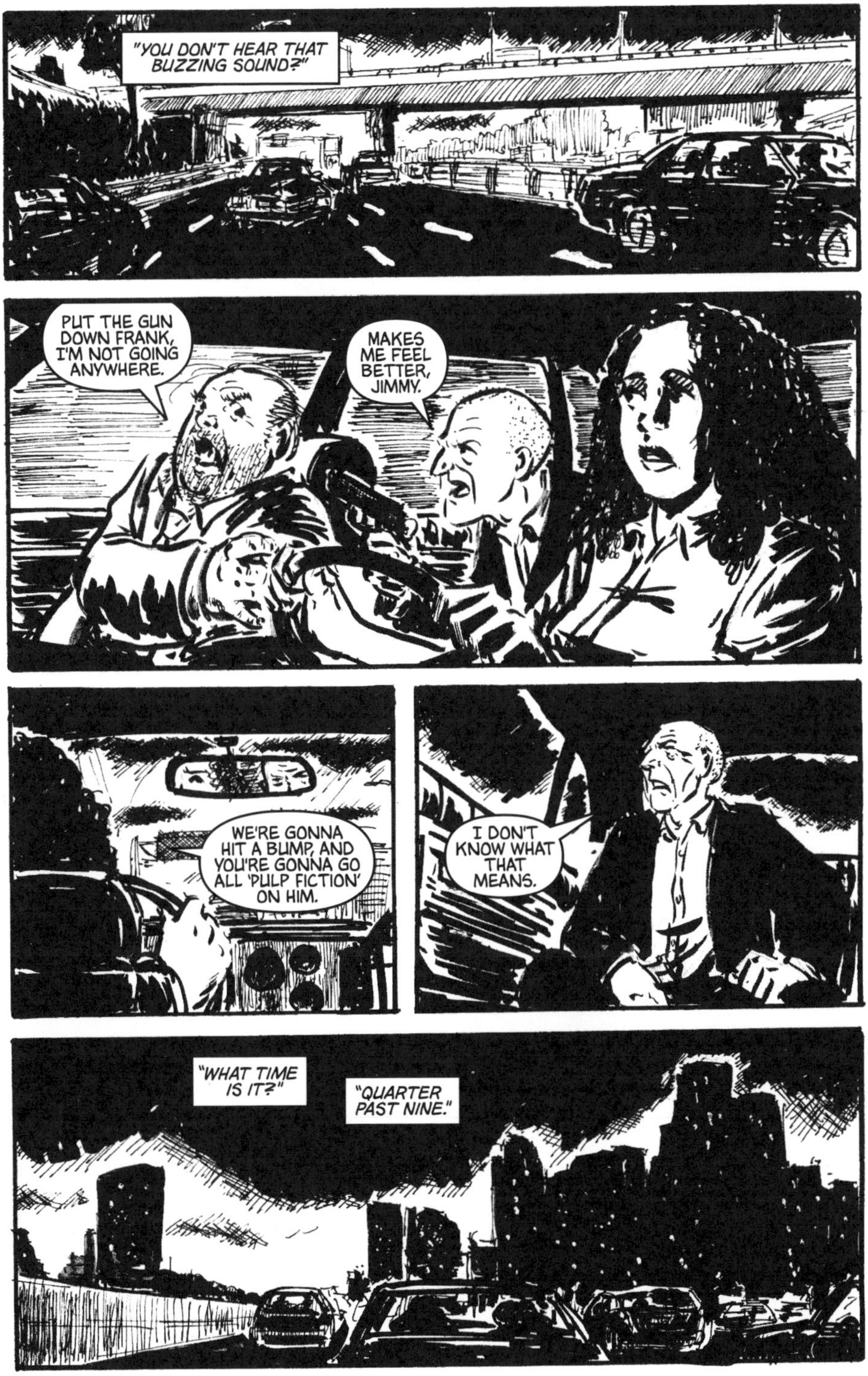
"YOU DON'T HEAR THAT BUZZING SOUND?"
PUT THE GUN DOWN FRANK, I'M NOT GOING ANYWHERE.
MAKES ME FEEL BETTER, JIMMY.
WE'RE GONNA HIT A BUMP, AND YOU'RE GONNA GO ALL 'PULP FICTION' ON HIM.
I DON'T KNOW WHAT THAT MEANS.
"WHAT TIME IS IT?"
"QUARTER PAST NINE."

ZZZZZZAP

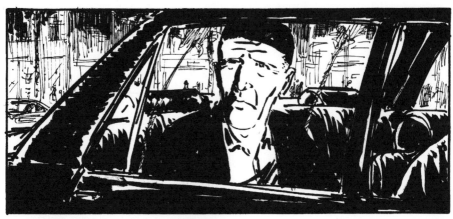

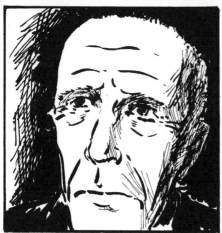

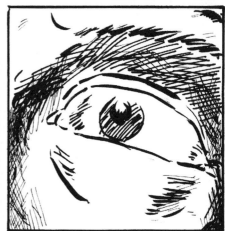

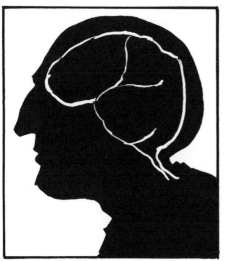

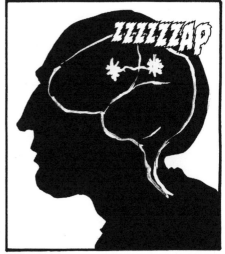

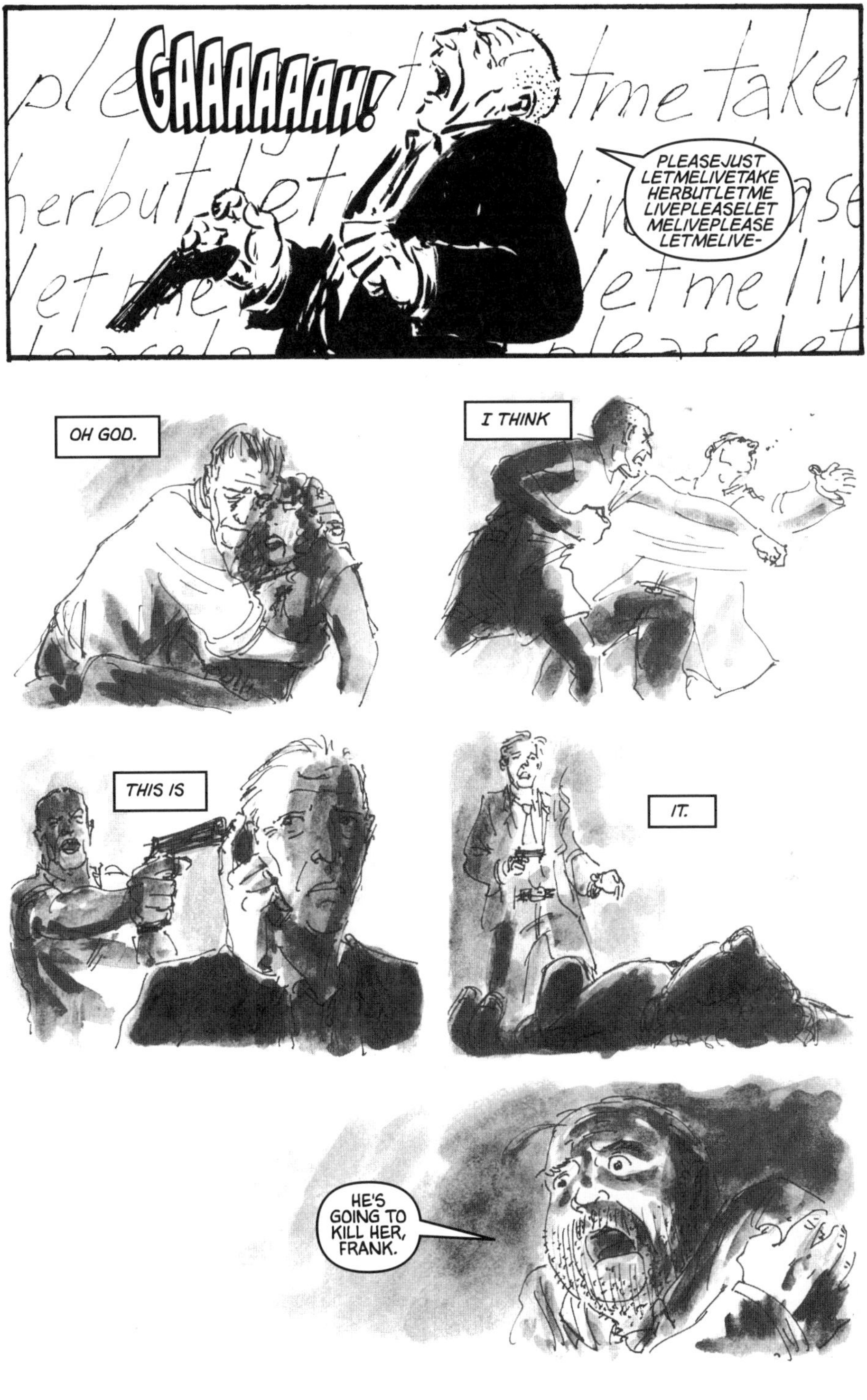

GAAAAAAH!
PLEASEJUST LETMELIVETAKE HERBUTLETME LIVEPLEASELET MELIVEPLEASE LETMELIVE-
OH GOD.
I THINK
THIS IS
IT.
HE'S GOING TO KILL HER, FRANK.

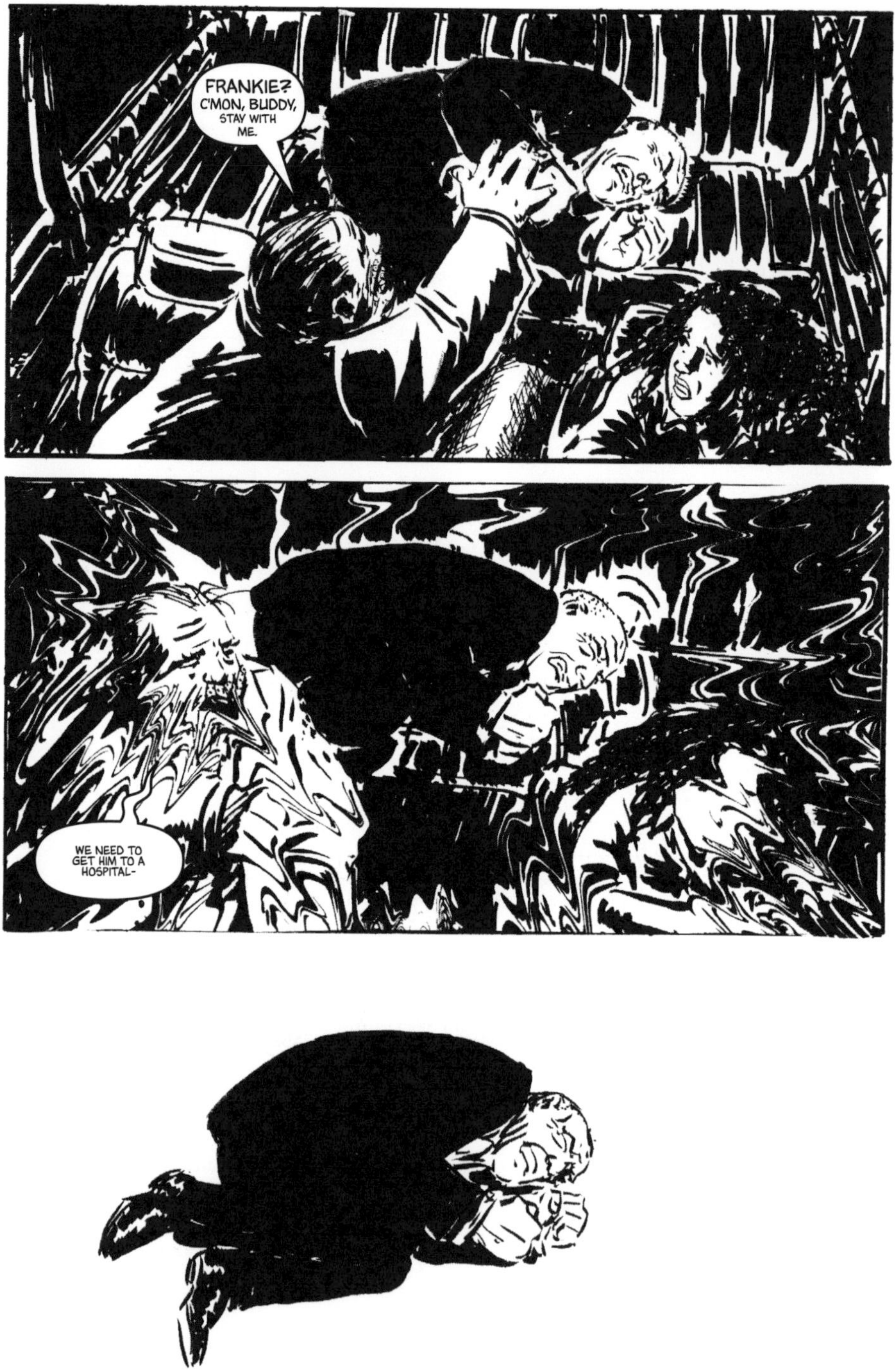
FRANKIE? C'MON, BUDDY, STAY WITH ME.
WE NEED TO GET HIM TO A HOSPITAL-

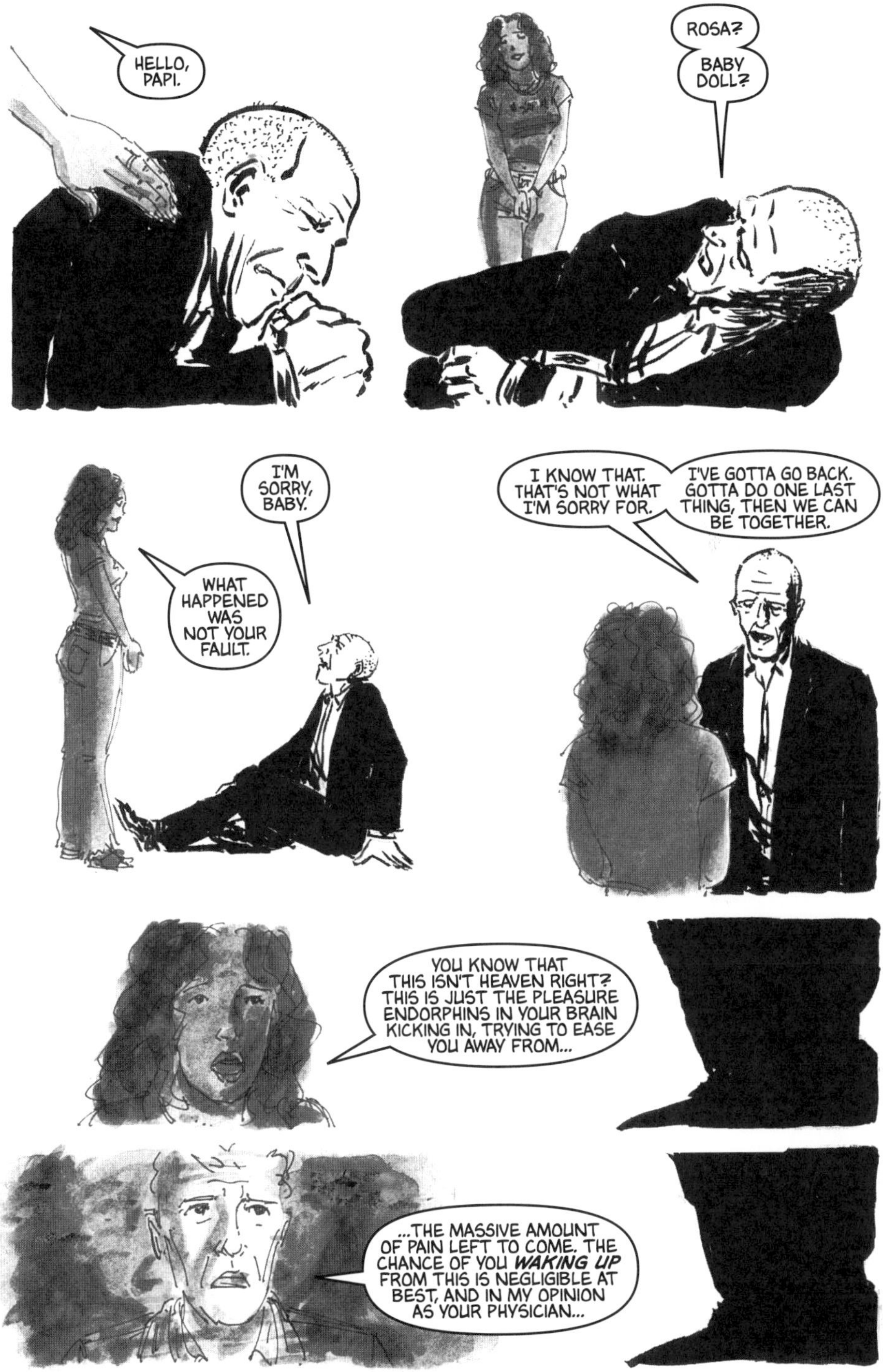

HELLO, PAPI.
ROSA?
BABY DOLL?
I'M SORRY, BABY.
WHAT HAPPENED WAS NOT YOUR FAULT.
I KNOW THAT. THAT'S NOT WHAT I'M SORRY FOR.
I'VE GOTTA GO BACK. GOTTA DO ONE LAST THING, THEN WE CAN BE TOGETHER.
YOU KNOW THAT THIS ISN'T HEAVEN RIGHT? THIS IS JUST THE PLEASURE ENDORPHINS IN YOUR BRAIN KICKING IN, TRYING TO EASE YOU AWAY FROM...
...THE MASSIVE AMOUNT OF PAIN LEFT TO COME. THE CHANCE OF YOU *WAKING UP* FROM THIS IS NEGLIGIBLE AT BEST, AND IN MY OPINION AS YOUR PHYSICIAN...

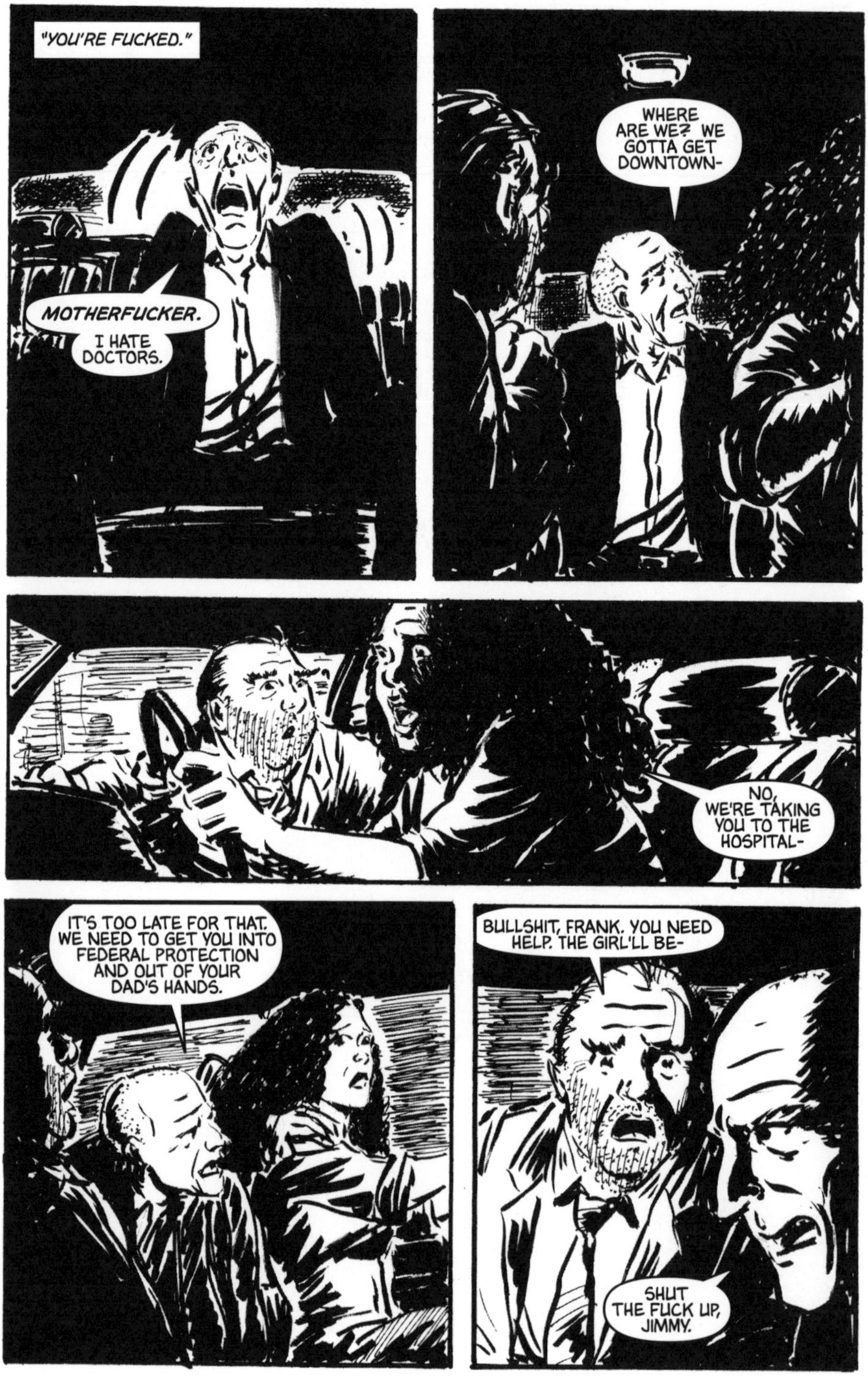
"YOU'RE FUCKED."
MOTHERFUCKER. I HATE DOCTORS.
WHERE ARE WE? WE GOTTA GET DOWNTOWN-
NO, WE'RE TAKING YOU TO THE HOSPITAL-
IT'S TOO LATE FOR THAT. WE NEED TO GET YOU INTO FEDERAL PROTECTION AND OUT OF YOUR DAD'S HANDS.
BULLSHIT, FRANK. YOU NEED HELP. THE GIRL'LL BE-
SHUT THE FUCK UP, JIMMY.

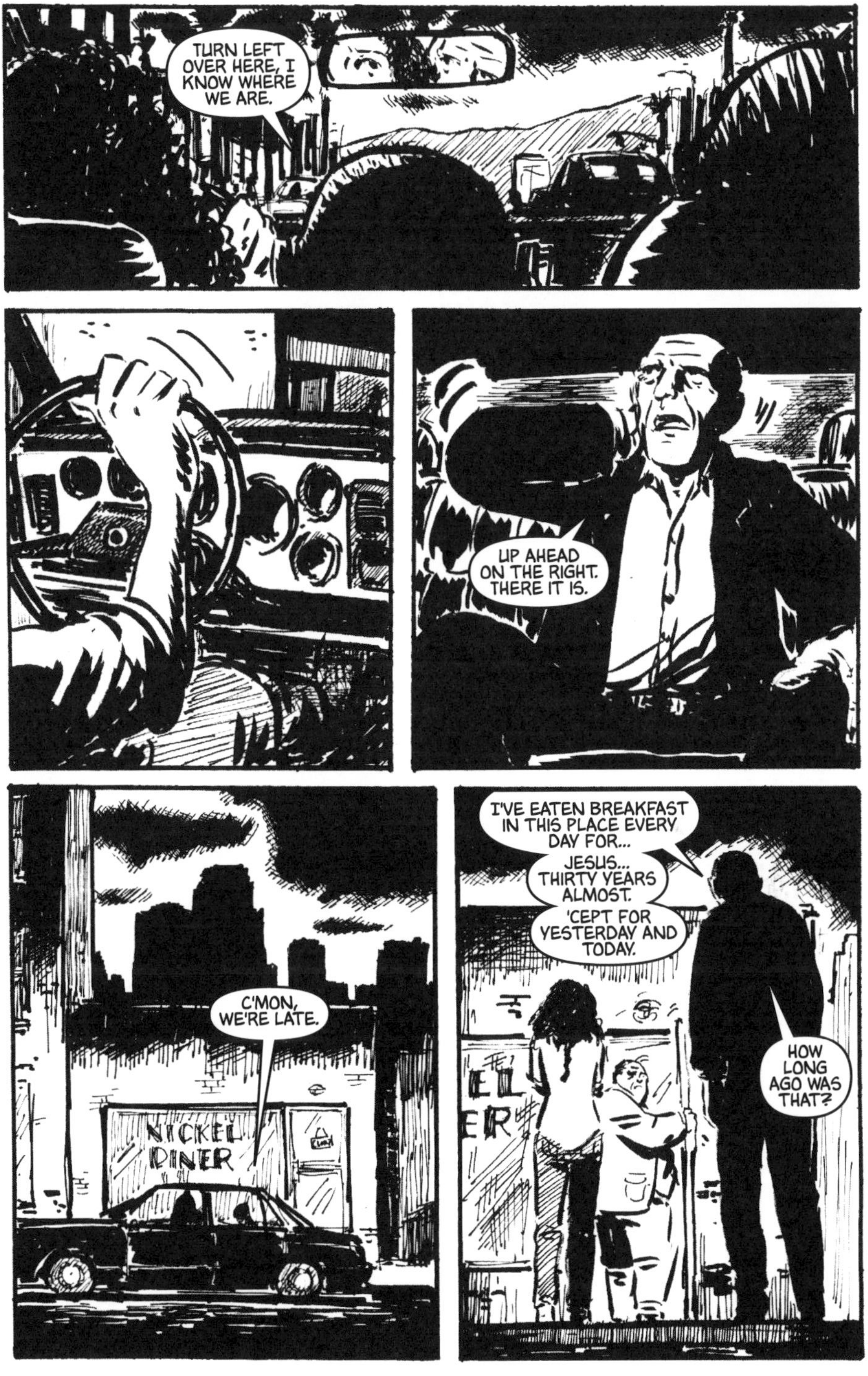
TURN LEFT OVER HERE, I KNOW WHERE WE ARE.
UP AHEAD ON THE RIGHT. THERE IT IS.
C'MON, WE'RE LATE.
NICKEL DINER
I'VE EATEN BREAKFAST IN THIS PLACE EVERY DAY FOR...
JESUS... THIRTY YEARS ALMOST.
'CEPT FOR YESTERDAY AND TODAY.
HOW LONG AGO WAS THAT?

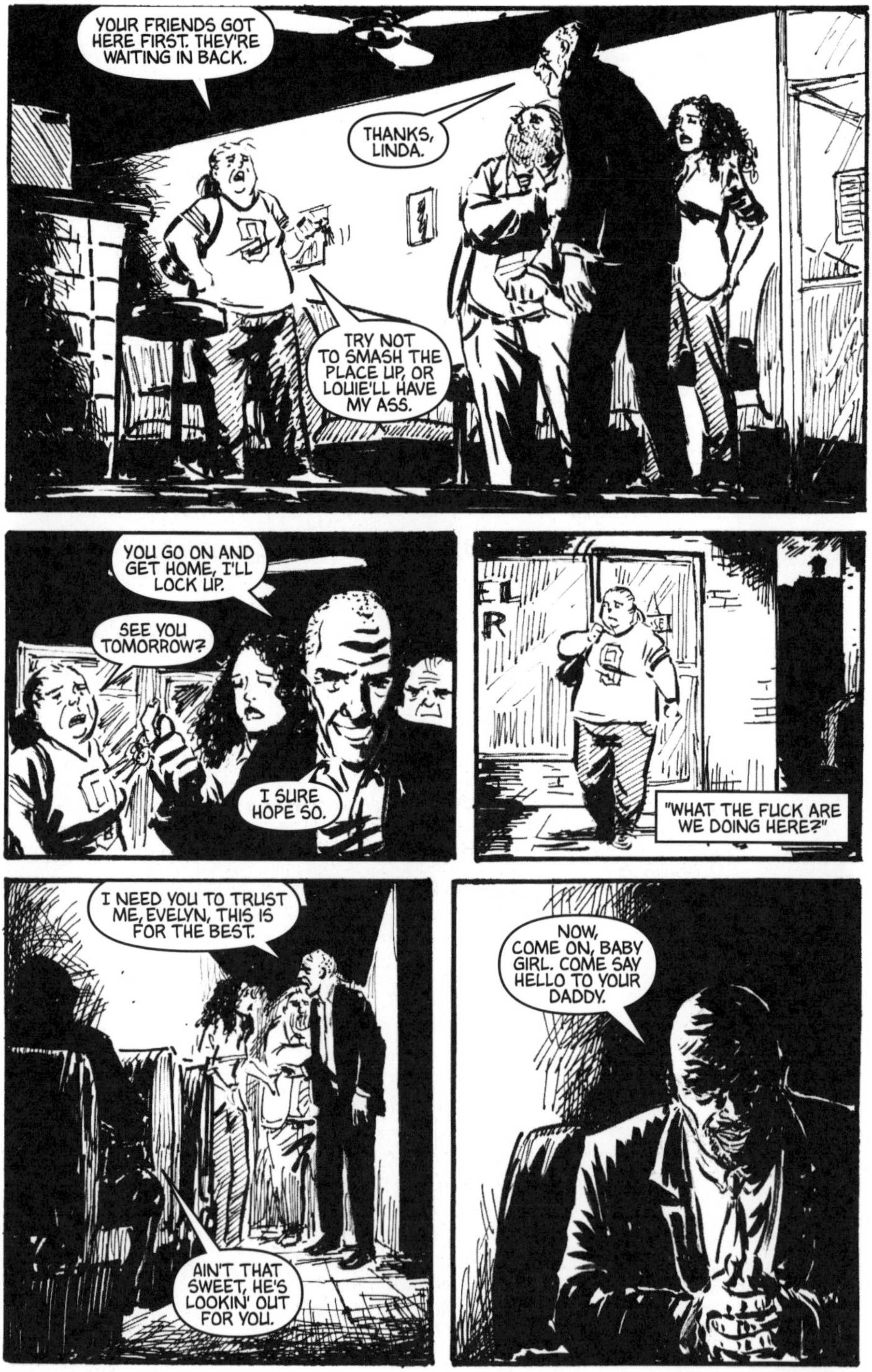
YOUR FRIENDS GOT HERE FIRST. THEY'RE WAITING IN BACK.
THANKS, LINDA.
TRY NOT TO SMASH THE PLACE UP, OR LOUIE'LL HAVE MY ASS.
YOU GO ON AND GET HOME, I'LL LOCK UP.
SEE YOU TOMORROW?
I SURE HOPE SO.
"WHAT THE FUCK ARE WE DOING HERE?"
I NEED YOU TO TRUST ME, EVELYN, THIS IS FOR THE BEST.
AIN'T THAT SWEET, HE'S LOOKIN' OUT FOR YOU.
NOW, COME ON, BABY GIRL. COME SAY HELLO TO YOUR DADDY.

END CHAPTER 7

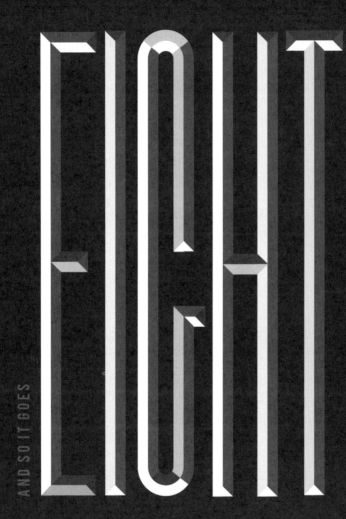

EIGHT

AND SO IT GOES

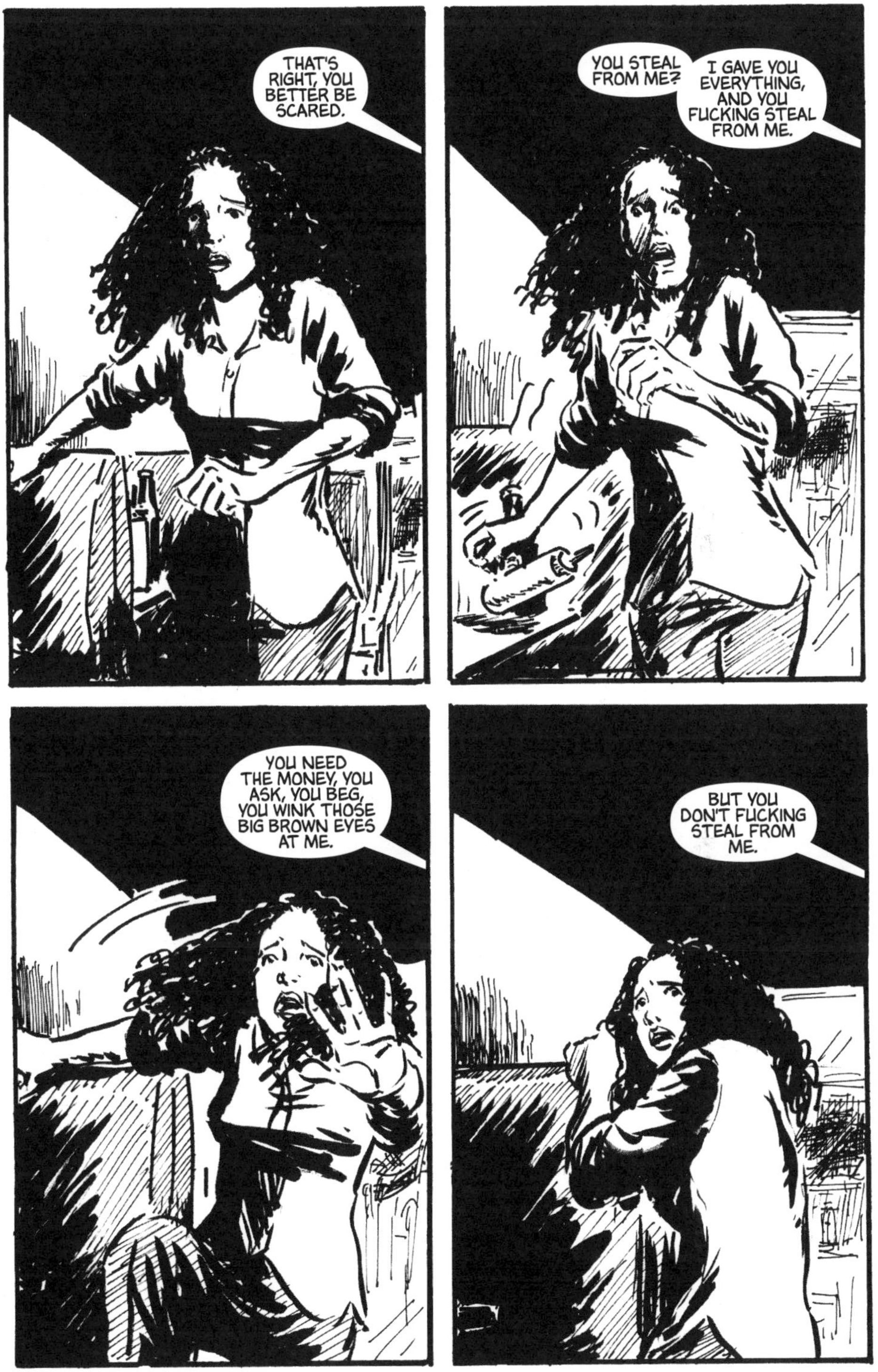
THAT'S RIGHT, YOU BETTER BE SCARED.
YOU STEAL FROM ME?
I GAVE YOU EVERYTHING, AND YOU FUCKING STEAL FROM ME.
YOU NEED THE MONEY, YOU ASK, YOU BEG, YOU WINK THOSE BIG BROWN EYES AT ME.
BUT YOU DON'T FUCKING STEAL FROM ME.

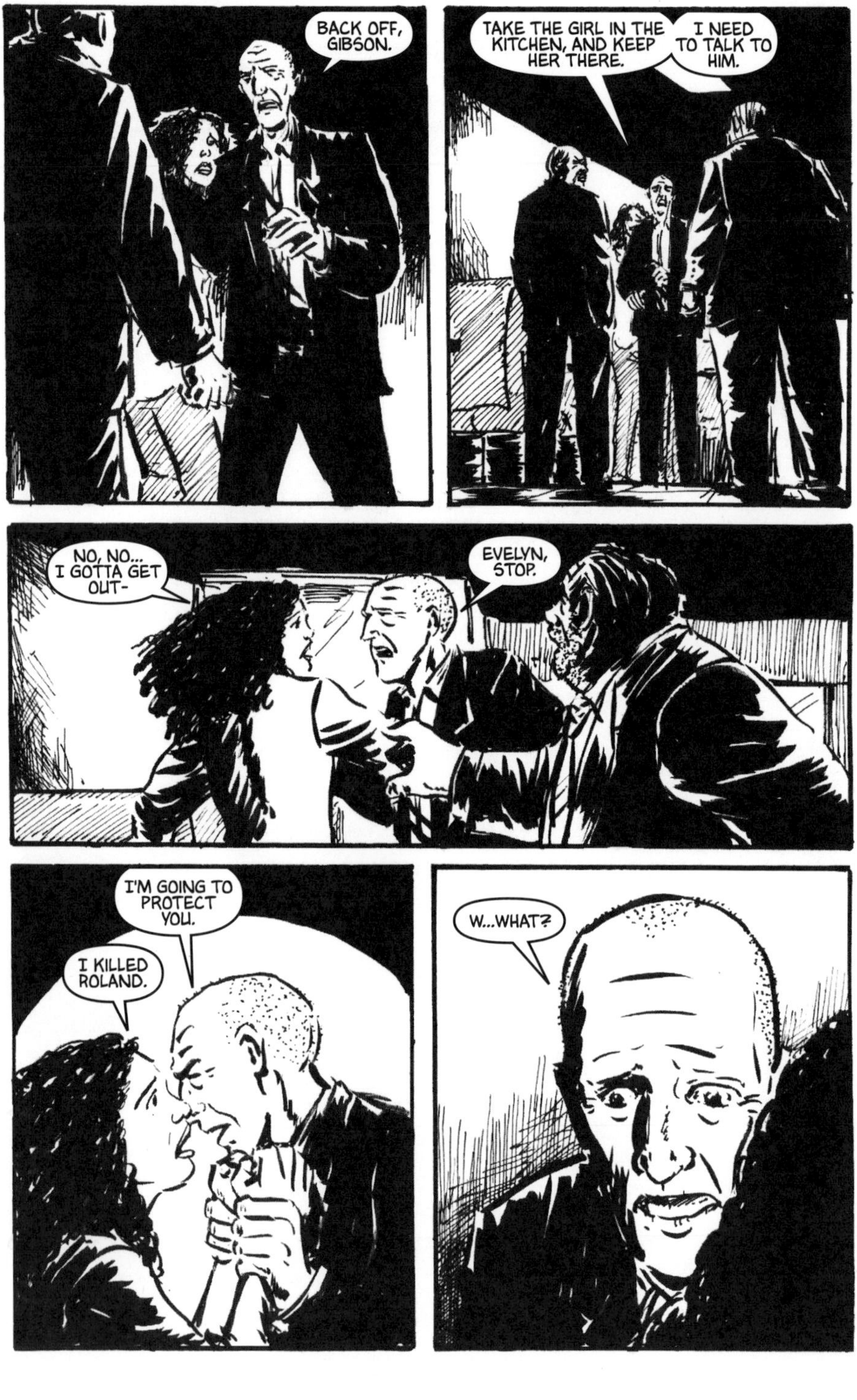
BACK OFF, GIBSON.
TAKE THE GIRL IN THE KITCHEN, AND KEEP HER THERE.
I NEED TO TALK TO HIM.
NO, NO... I GOTTA GET OUT-
EVELYN, STOP.
I'M GOING TO PROTECT YOU.
I KILLED ROLAND.
W...WHAT?

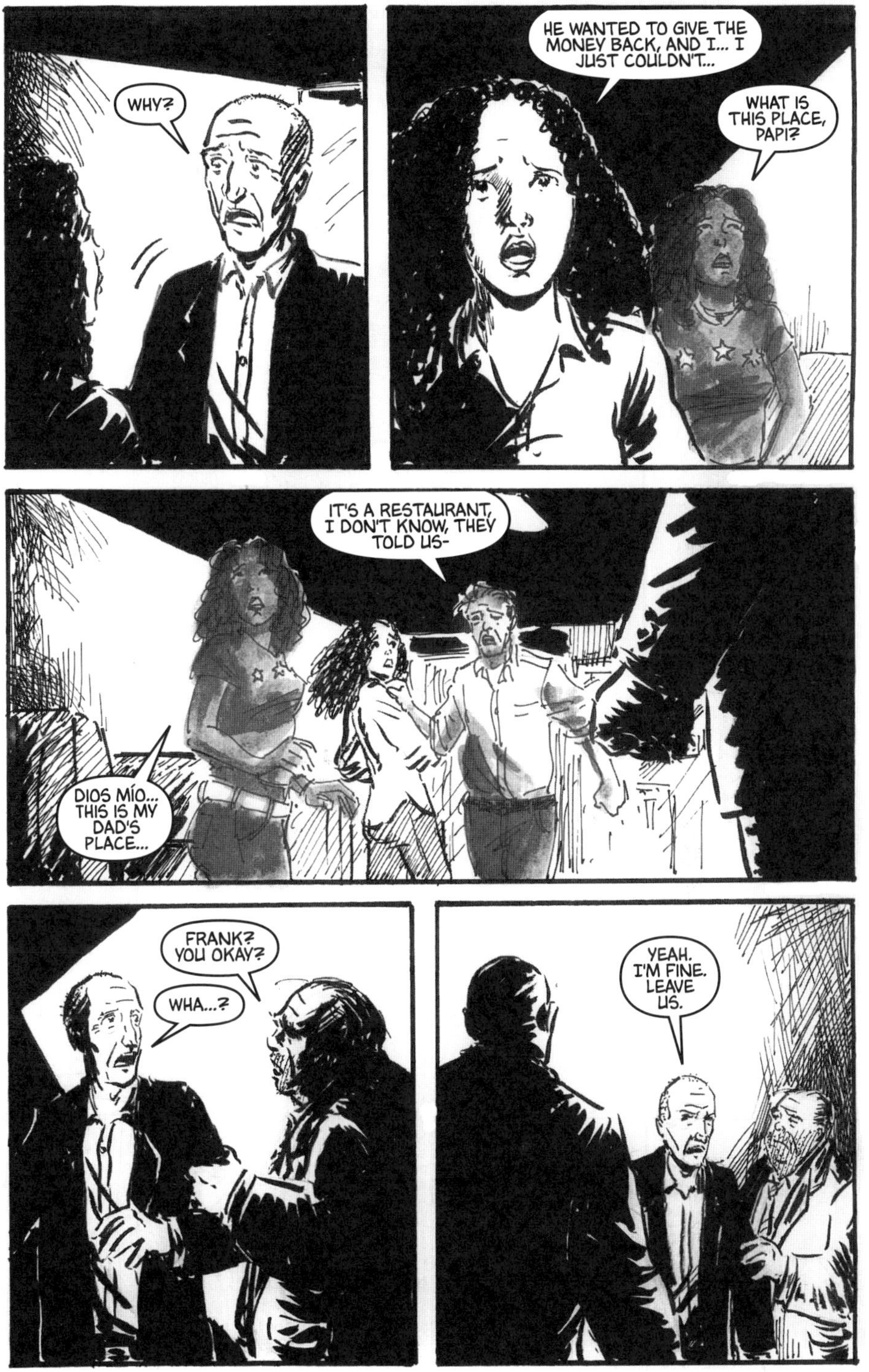
WHY?
HE WANTED TO GIVE THE MONEY BACK, AND I... I JUST COULDN'T...
WHAT IS THIS PLACE, PAPI?
IT'S A RESTAURANT, I DON'T KNOW, THEY TOLD US-
DIOS MÍO... THIS IS MY DAD'S PLACE...
FRANK? YOU OKAY?
WHA...?
YEAH. I'M FINE. LEAVE US.

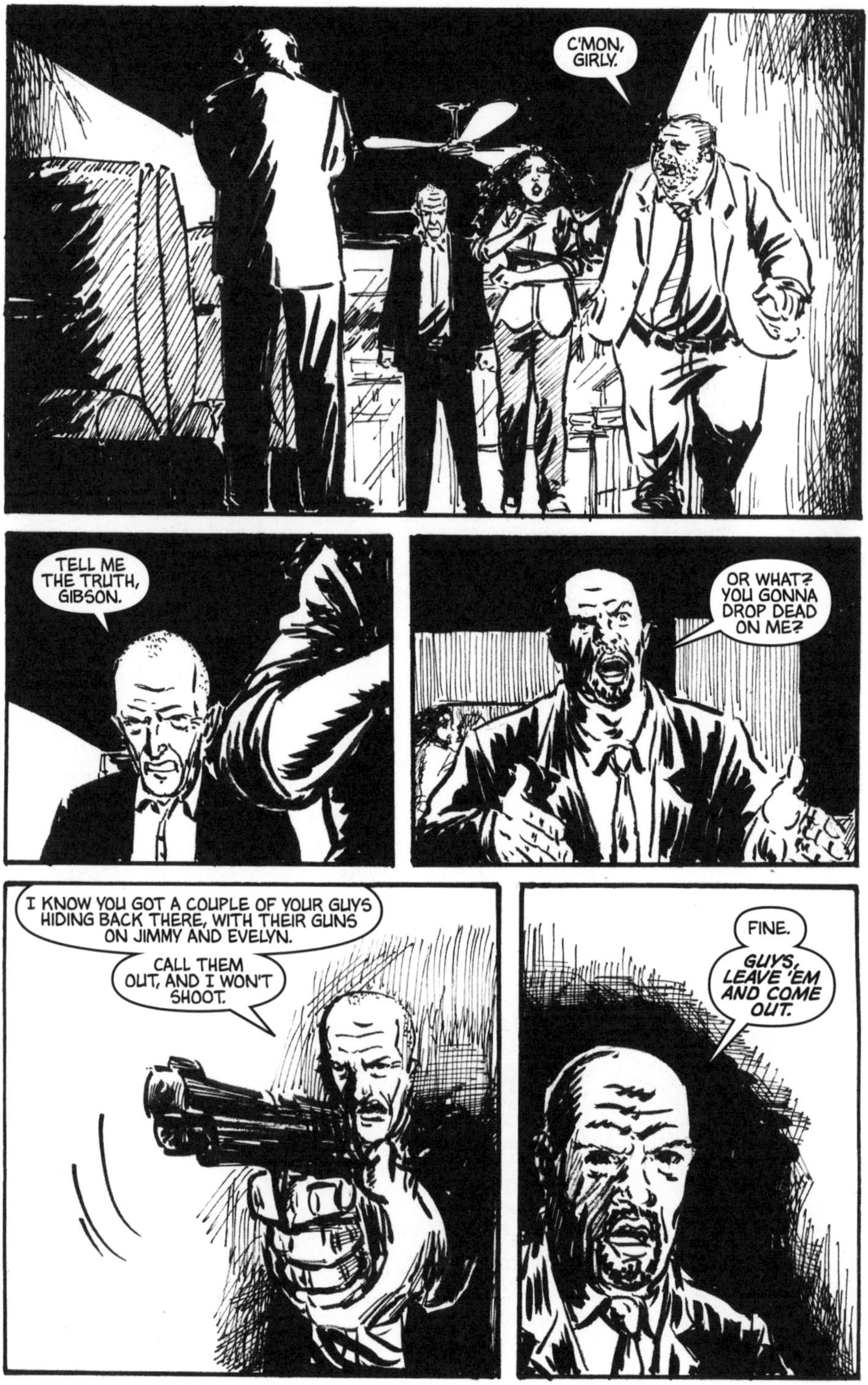
C'MON, GIRLY.
TELL ME THE TRUTH, GIBSON.
OR WHAT? YOU GONNA DROP DEAD ON ME?
I KNOW YOU GOT A COUPLE OF YOUR GUYS HIDING BACK THERE, WITH THEIR GUNS ON JIMMY AND EVELYN.
CALL THEM OUT, AND I WON'T SHOOT.
FINE.
GUYS, LEAVE 'EM AND COME OUT.

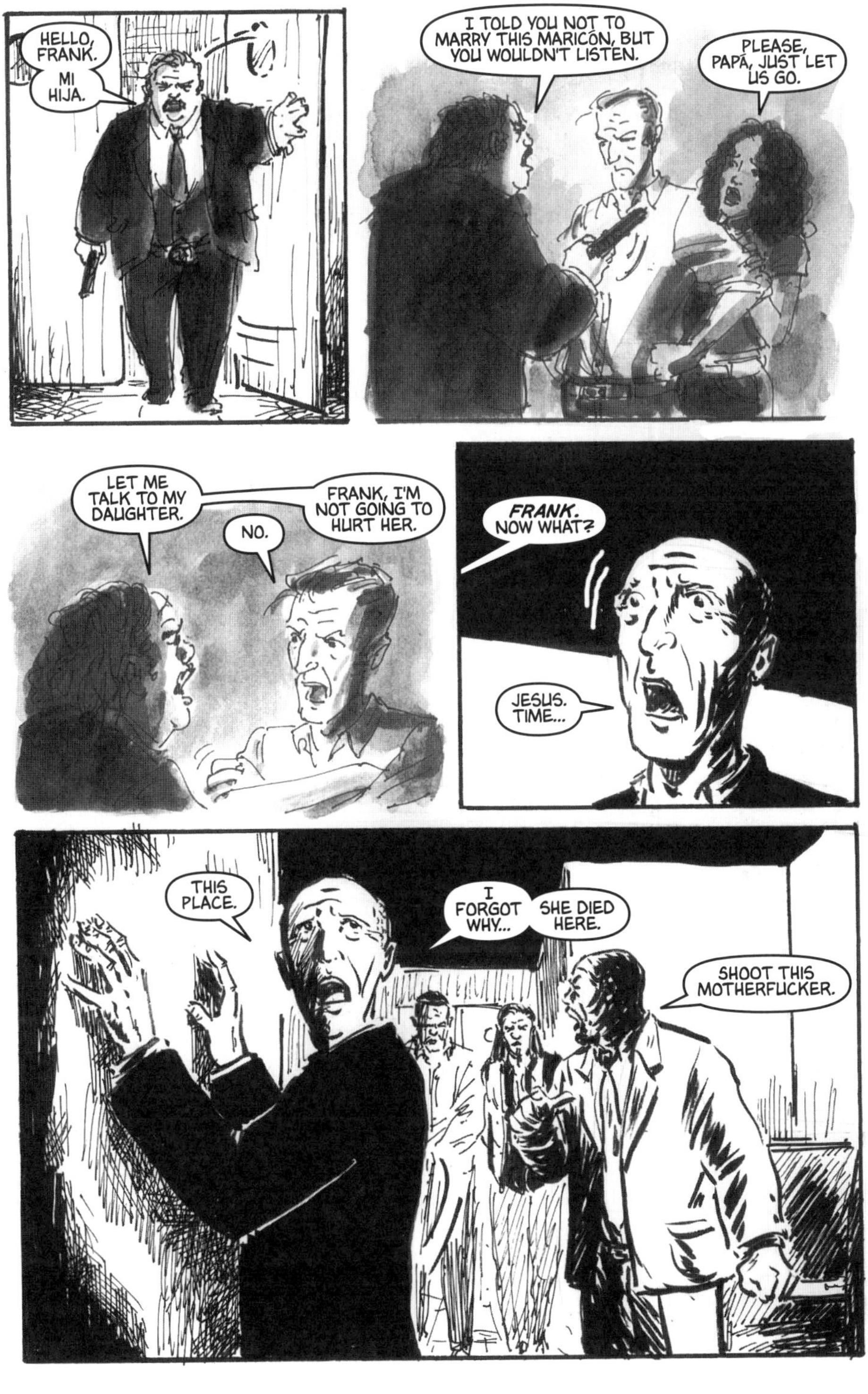
HELLO, FRANK.
MI HIJA.
I TOLD YOU NOT TO MARRY THIS MARICÓN, BUT YOU WOULDN'T LISTEN.
PLEASE, PAPÁ, JUST LET US GO.
LET ME TALK TO MY DAUGHTER.
NO.
FRANK, I'M NOT GOING TO HURT HER.
FRANK. NOW WHAT?
JESUS. TIME...
THIS PLACE.
I FORGOT WHY...
SHE DIED HERE.
SHOOT THIS MOTHERFUCKER.

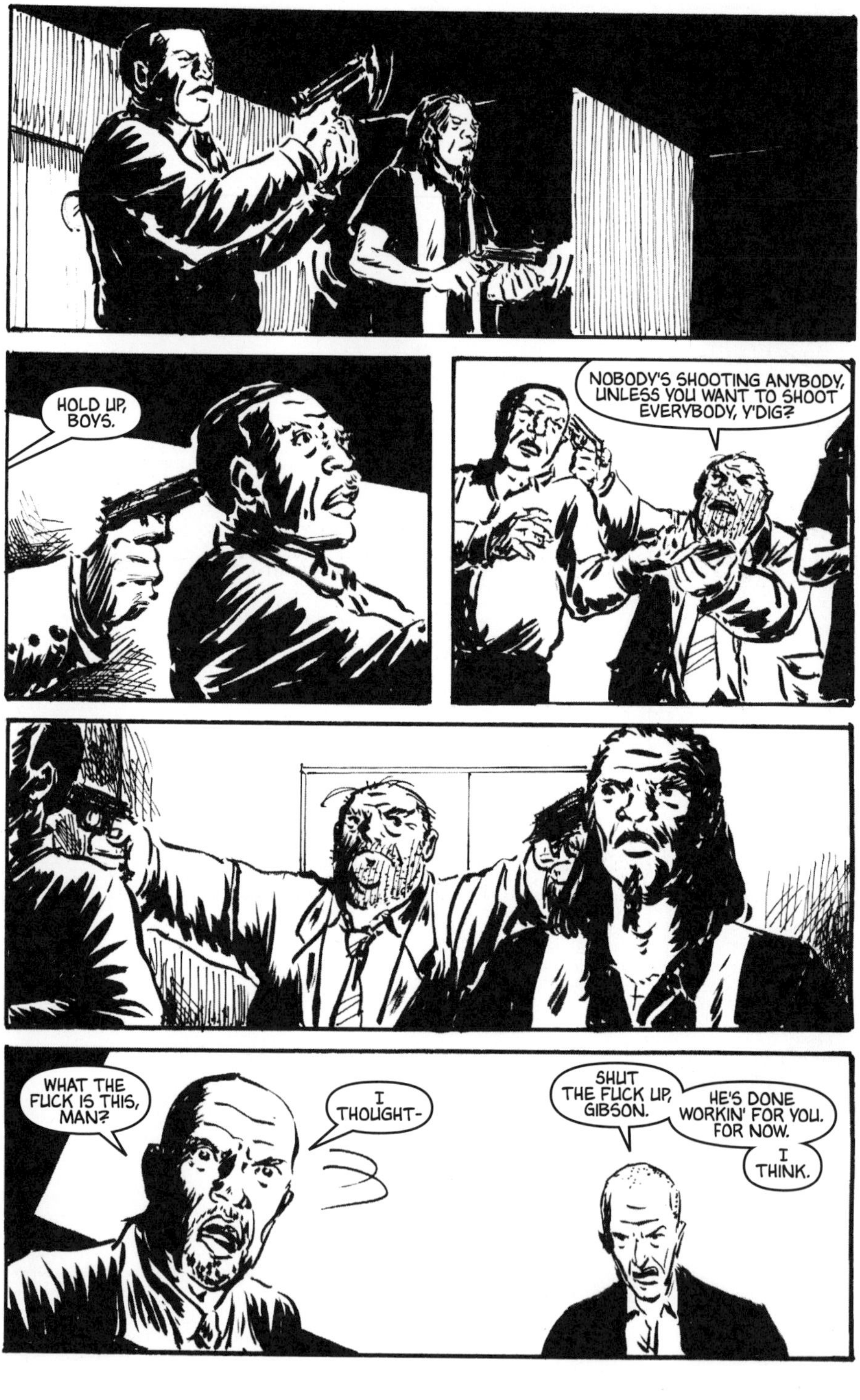
HOLD UP, BOYS.
NOBODY'S SHOOTING ANYBODY, UNLESS YOU WANT TO SHOOT EVERYBODY, Y'DIG?
WHAT THE FUCK IS THIS, MAN?
I THOUGHT-
SHUT THE FUCK UP, GIBSON.
HE'S DONE WORKIN' FOR YOU. FOR NOW.
I THINK.

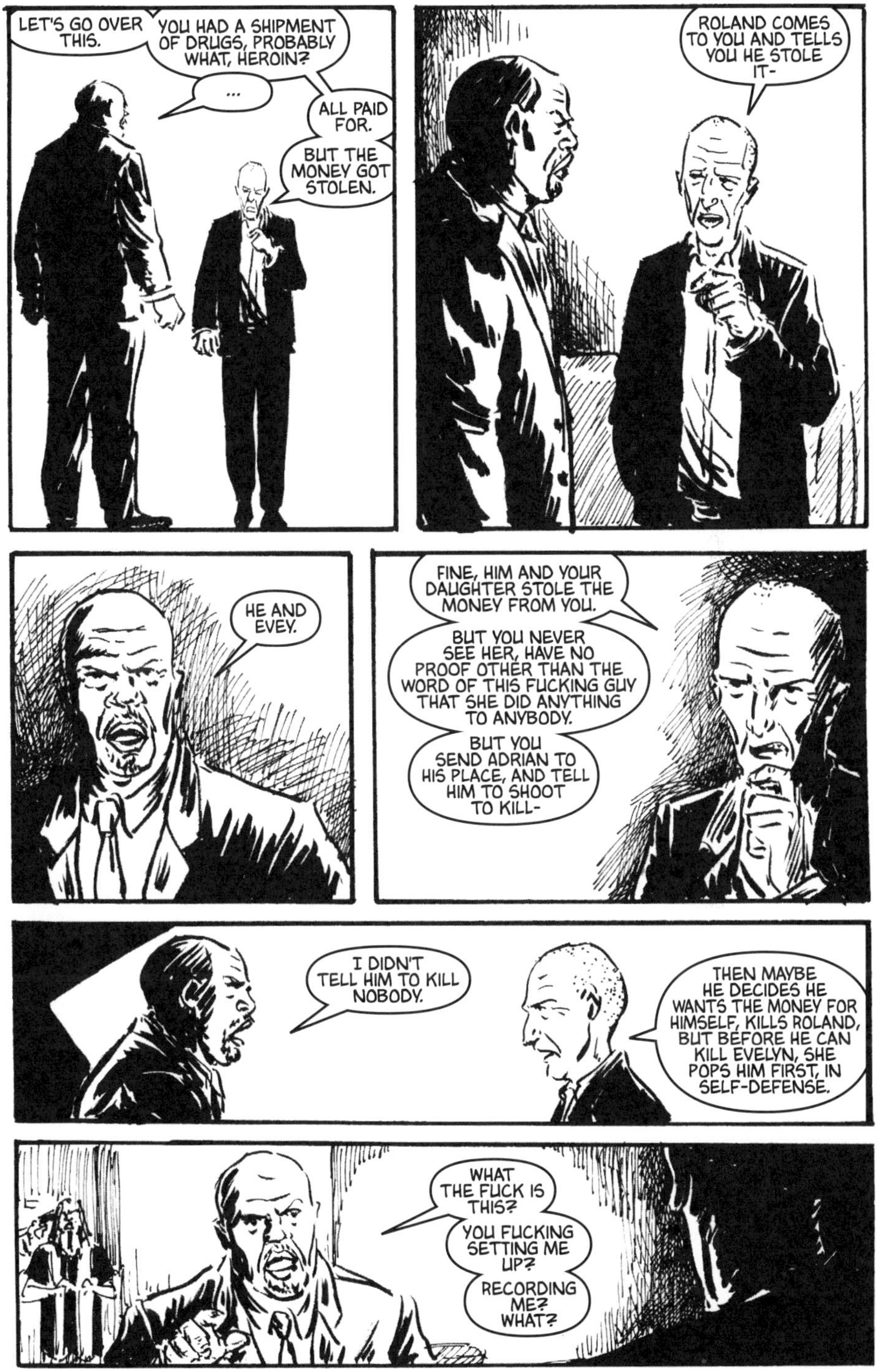
LET'S GO OVER THIS.
YOU HAD A SHIPMENT OF DRUGS, PROBABLY WHAT, HEROIN?
...
ALL PAID FOR.
BUT THE MONEY GOT STOLEN.
ROLAND COMES TO YOU AND TELLS YOU HE STOLE IT-
HE AND EVEY.
FINE, HIM AND YOUR DAUGHTER STOLE THE MONEY FROM YOU.
BUT YOU NEVER SEE HER, HAVE NO PROOF OTHER THAN THE WORD OF THIS FUCKING GUY THAT SHE DID ANYTHING TO ANYBODY.
BUT YOU SEND ADRIAN TO HIS PLACE, AND TELL HIM TO SHOOT TO KILL-
I DIDN'T TELL HIM TO KILL NOBODY.
THEN MAYBE HE DECIDES HE WANTS THE MONEY FOR HIMSELF, KILLS ROLAND, BUT BEFORE HE CAN KILL EVELYN, SHE POPS HIM FIRST, IN SELF-DEFENSE.
WHAT THE FUCK IS THIS?
YOU FUCKING SETTING ME UP?
RECORDING ME? WHAT?

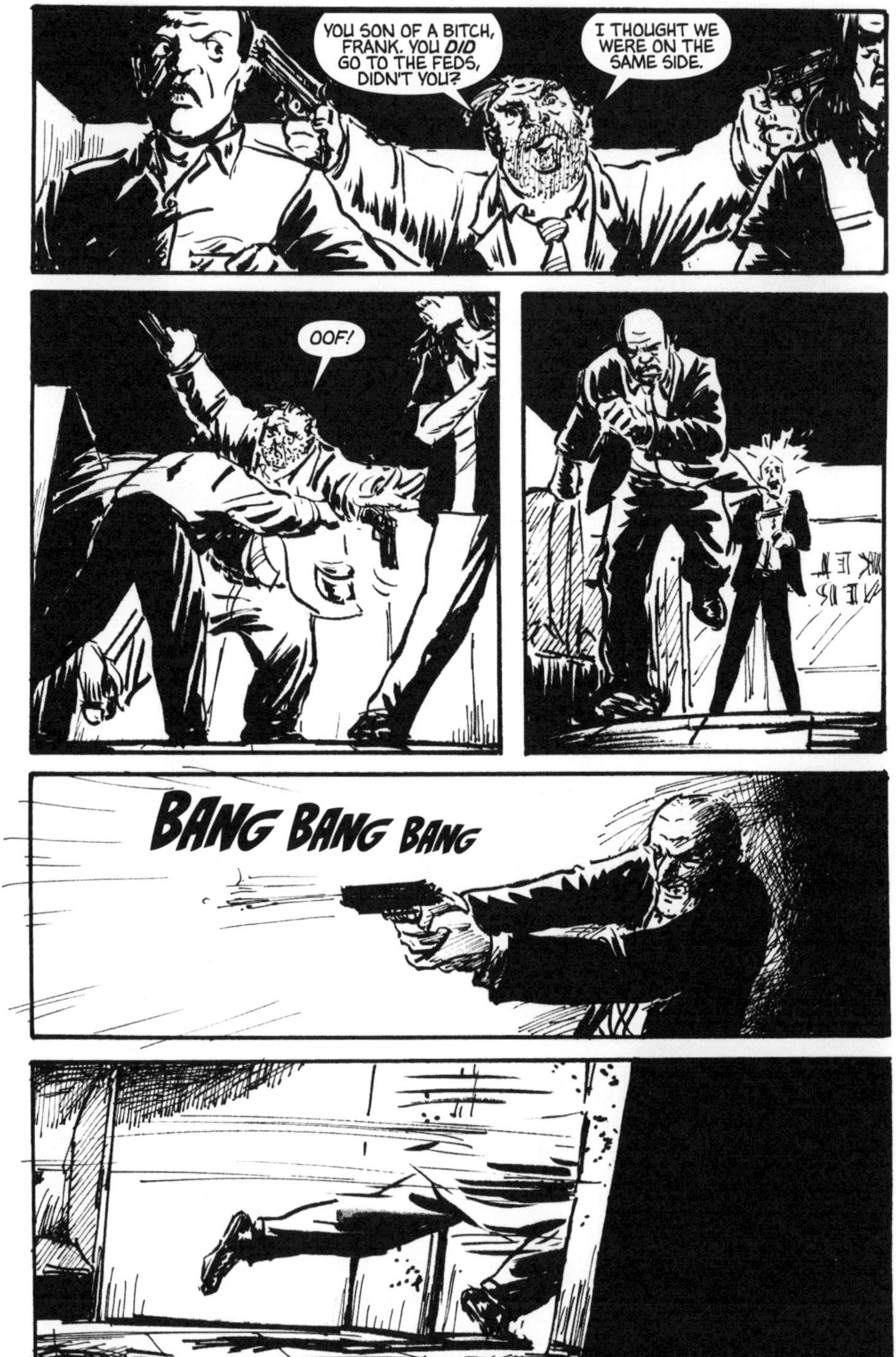
YOU SON OF A BITCH, FRANK. YOU DID GO TO THE FEDS, DIDN'T YOU?
I THOUGHT WE WERE ON THE SAME SIDE.
OOF!
BANG BANG BANG

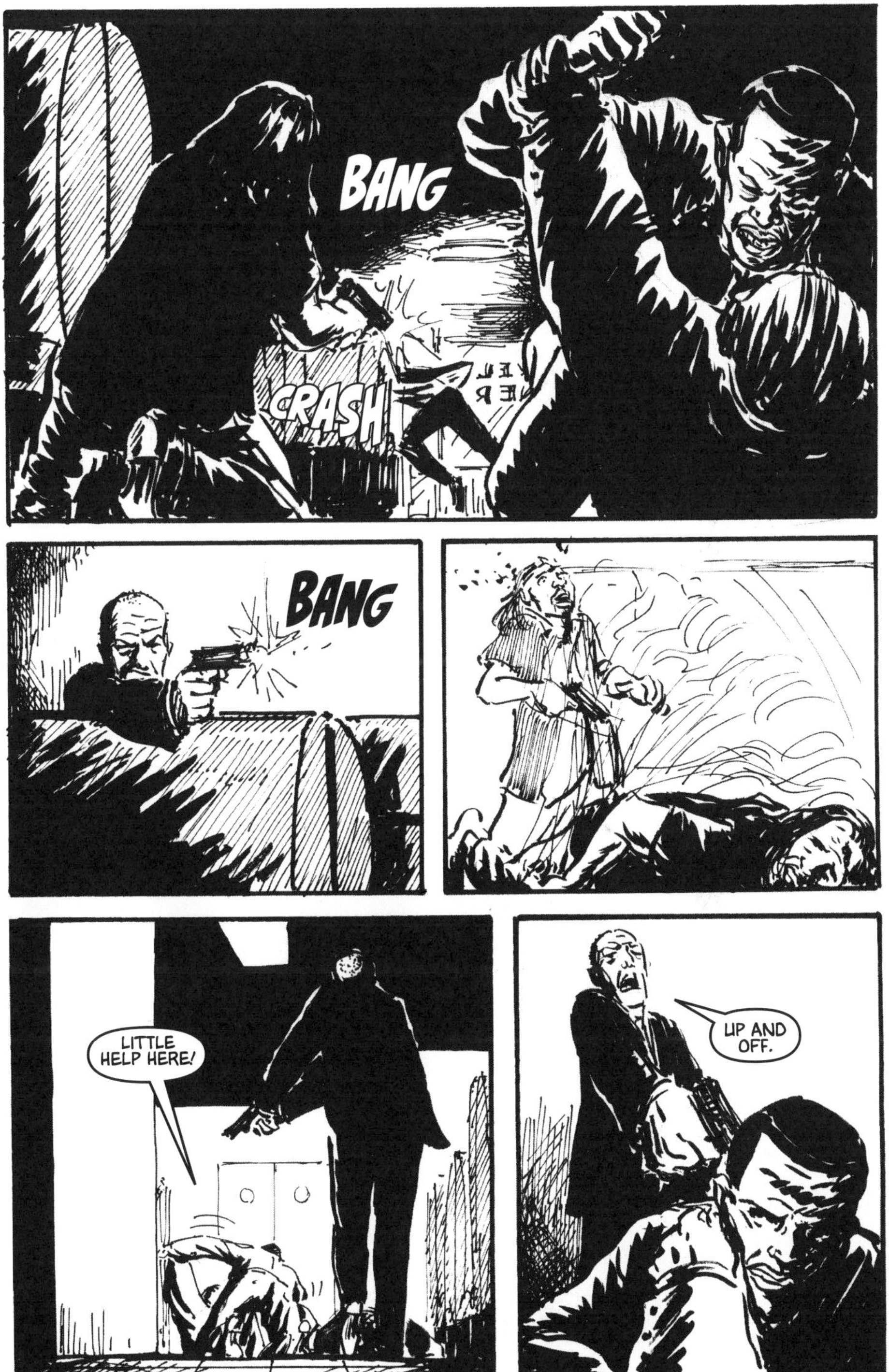
BANG
CRASH
BANG
LITTLE HELP HERE!
UP AND OFF.

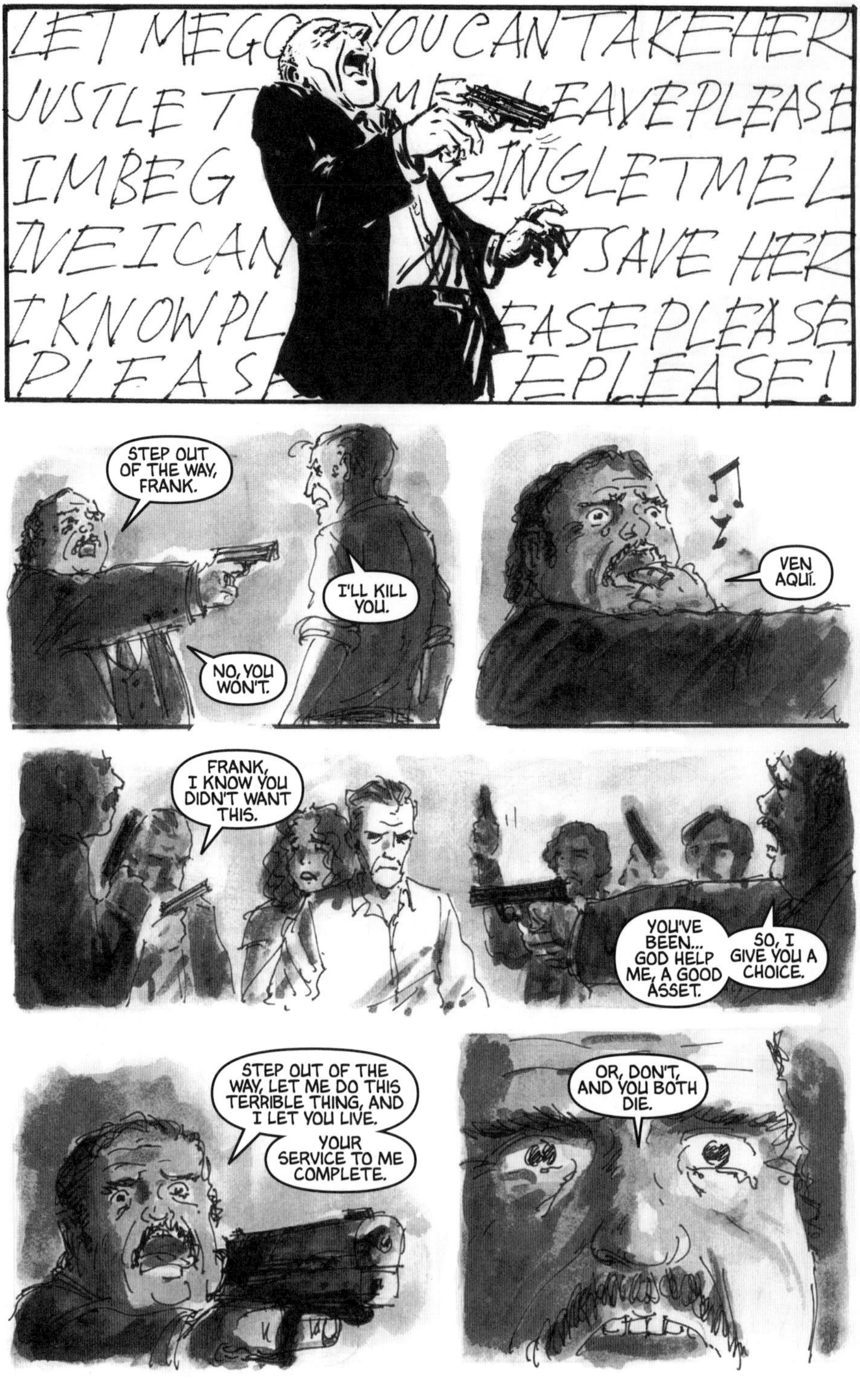

LET ME GO YOU CAN TAKE HER
JUSTLET T ME LEAVE PLEASE
IMBEG INGLETME L
IVE I CAN TSAVE HER
I KNOW PL EASE PLEASE
PLEAS EPLEASE!
STEP OUT OF THE WAY, FRANK.
I'LL KILL YOU.
NO, YOU WON'T.
VEN AQUÍ.
FRANK, I KNOW YOU DIDN'T WANT THIS.
SO, I GIVE YOU A CHOICE.
YOU'VE BEEN... GOD HELP ME, A GOOD ASSET.
STEP OUT OF THE WAY, LET ME DO THIS TERRIBLE THING, AND I LET YOU LIVE.
YOUR SERVICE TO ME COMPLETE.
OR, DON'T, AND YOU BOTH DIE.

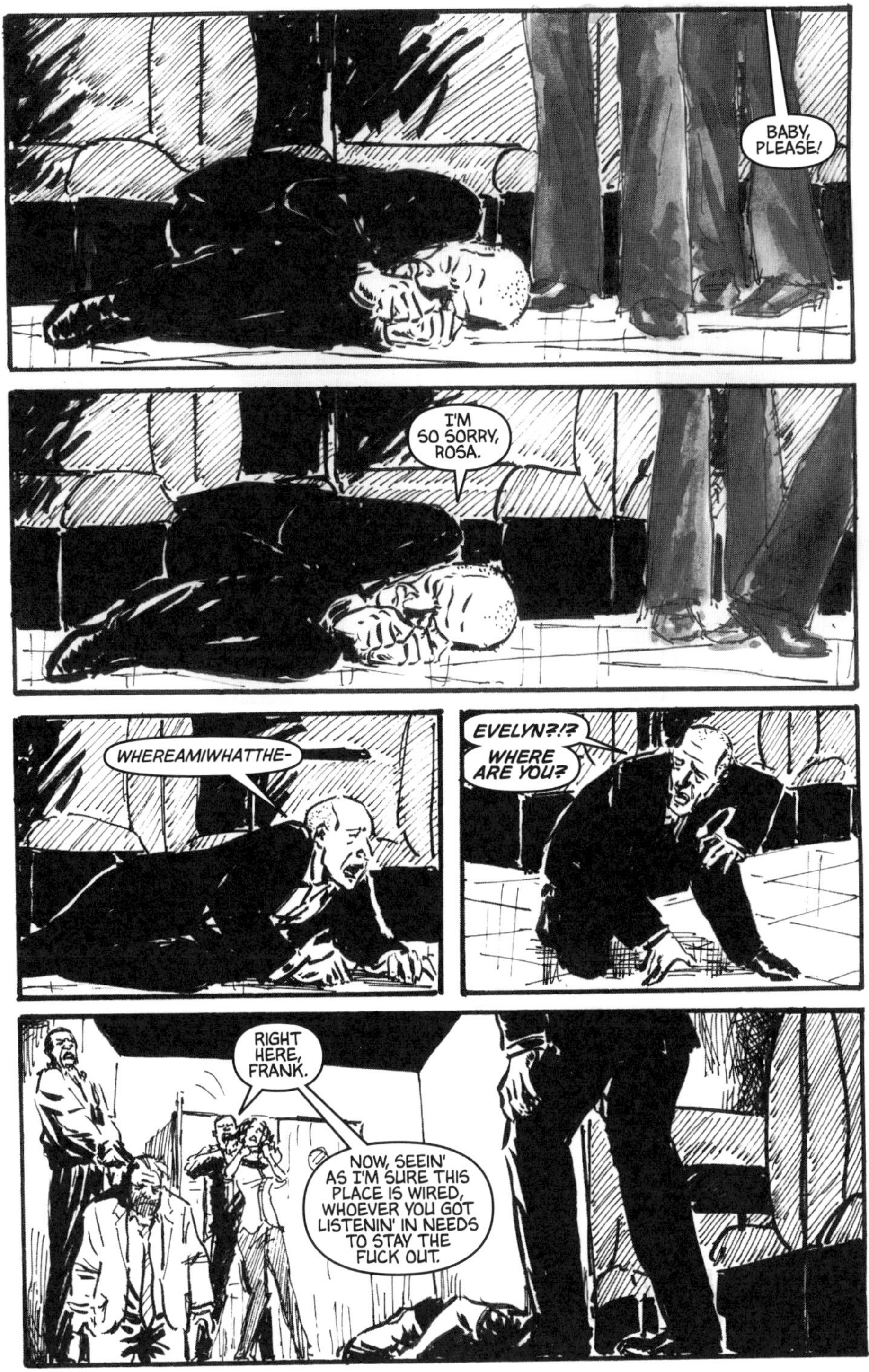
BABY, PLEASE!
I'M SO SORRY, ROSA.
WHEREAMIWHATTHE-
EVELYN?!? WHERE ARE YOU?
RIGHT HERE, FRANK.
NOW, SEEIN' AS I'M SURE THIS PLACE IS WIRED, WHOEVER YOU GOT LISTENIN' IN NEEDS TO STAY THE FUCK OUT.

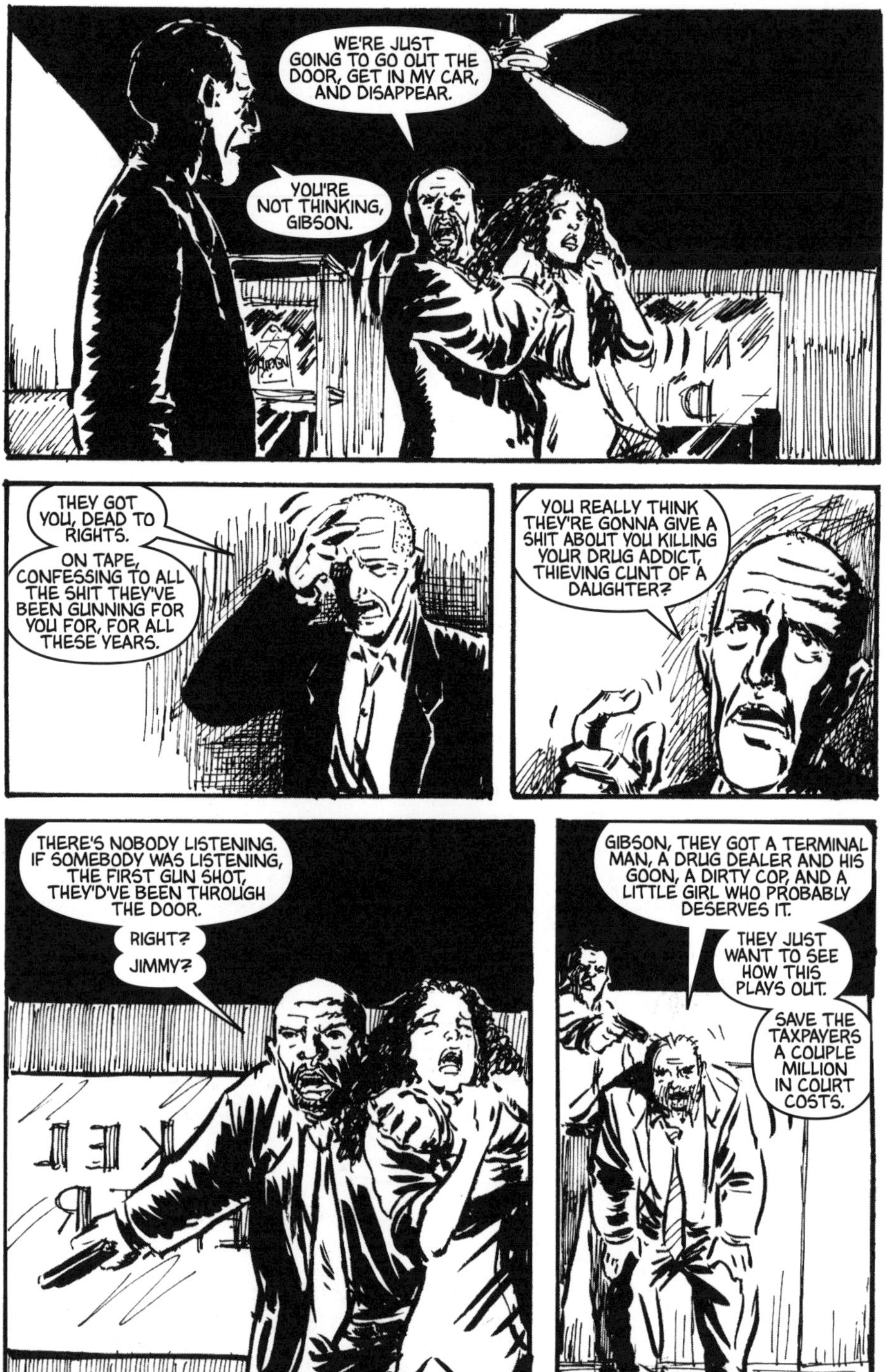
WE'RE JUST GOING TO GO OUT THE DOOR, GET IN MY CAR, AND DISAPPEAR.
YOU'RE NOT THINKING, GIBSON.
THEY GOT YOU, DEAD TO RIGHTS.
ON TAPE, CONFESSING TO ALL THE SHIT THEY'VE BEEN GUNNING FOR YOU FOR, FOR ALL THESE YEARS.
YOU REALLY THINK THEY'RE GONNA GIVE A SHIT ABOUT YOU KILLING YOUR DRUG ADDICT, THIEVING CUNT OF A DAUGHTER?
THERE'S NOBODY LISTENING. IF SOMEBODY WAS LISTENING, THE FIRST GUN SHOT, THEY'D'VE BEEN THROUGH THE DOOR.
RIGHT?
JIMMY?
GIBSON, THEY GOT A TERMINAL MAN, A DRUG DEALER AND HIS GOON, A DIRTY COP, AND A LITTLE GIRL WHO PROBABLY DESERVES IT.
THEY JUST WANT TO SEE HOW THIS PLAYS OUT.
SAVE THE TAXPAYERS A COUPLE MILLION IN COURT COSTS.

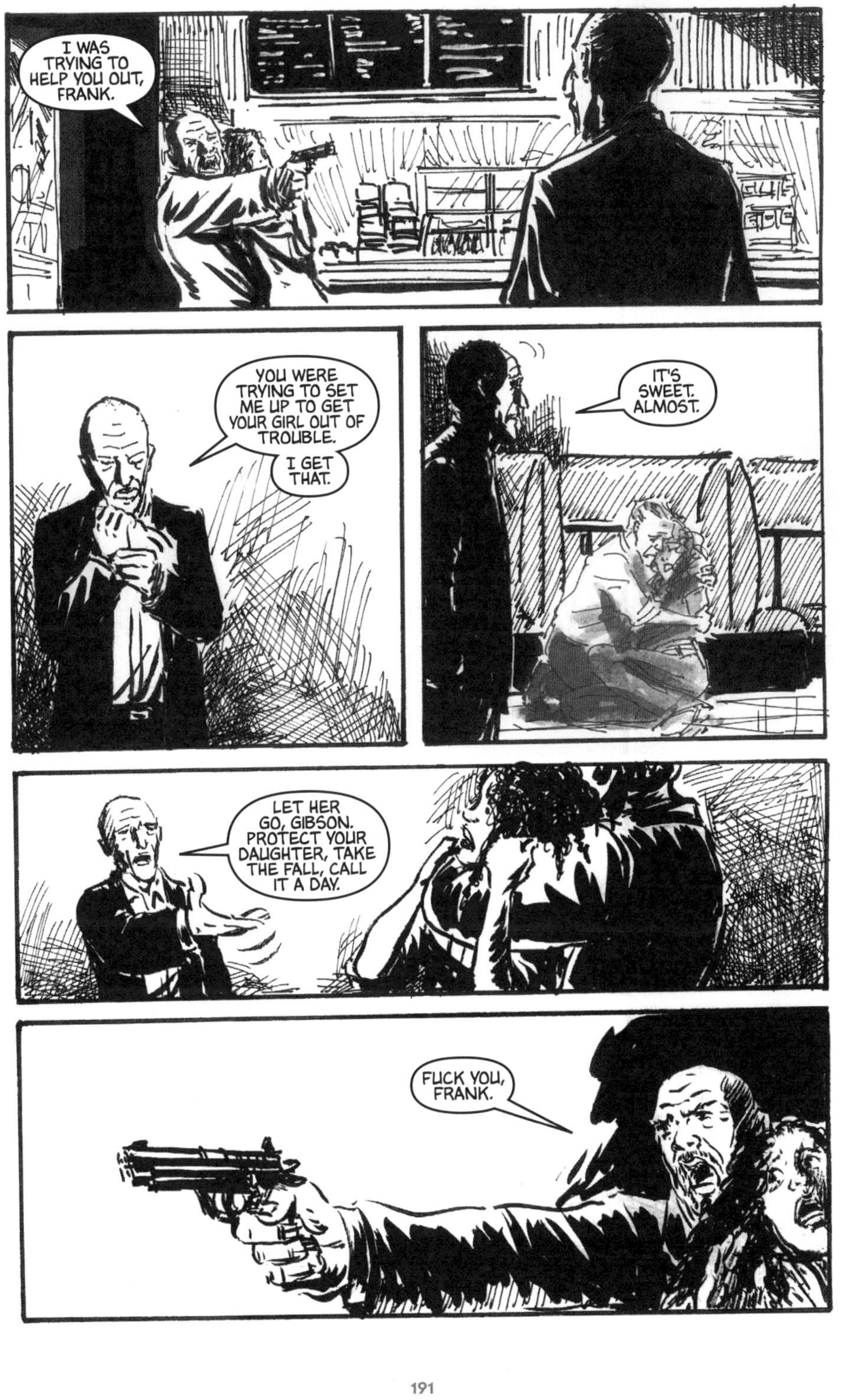
I WAS TRYING TO HELP YOU OUT, FRANK.
YOU WERE TRYING TO SET ME UP TO GET YOUR GIRL OUT OF TROUBLE.
I GET THAT.
IT'S SWEET. ALMOST.
LET HER GO, GIBSON. PROTECT YOUR DAUGHTER, TAKE THE FALL, CALL IT A DAY.
FUCK YOU, FRANK.

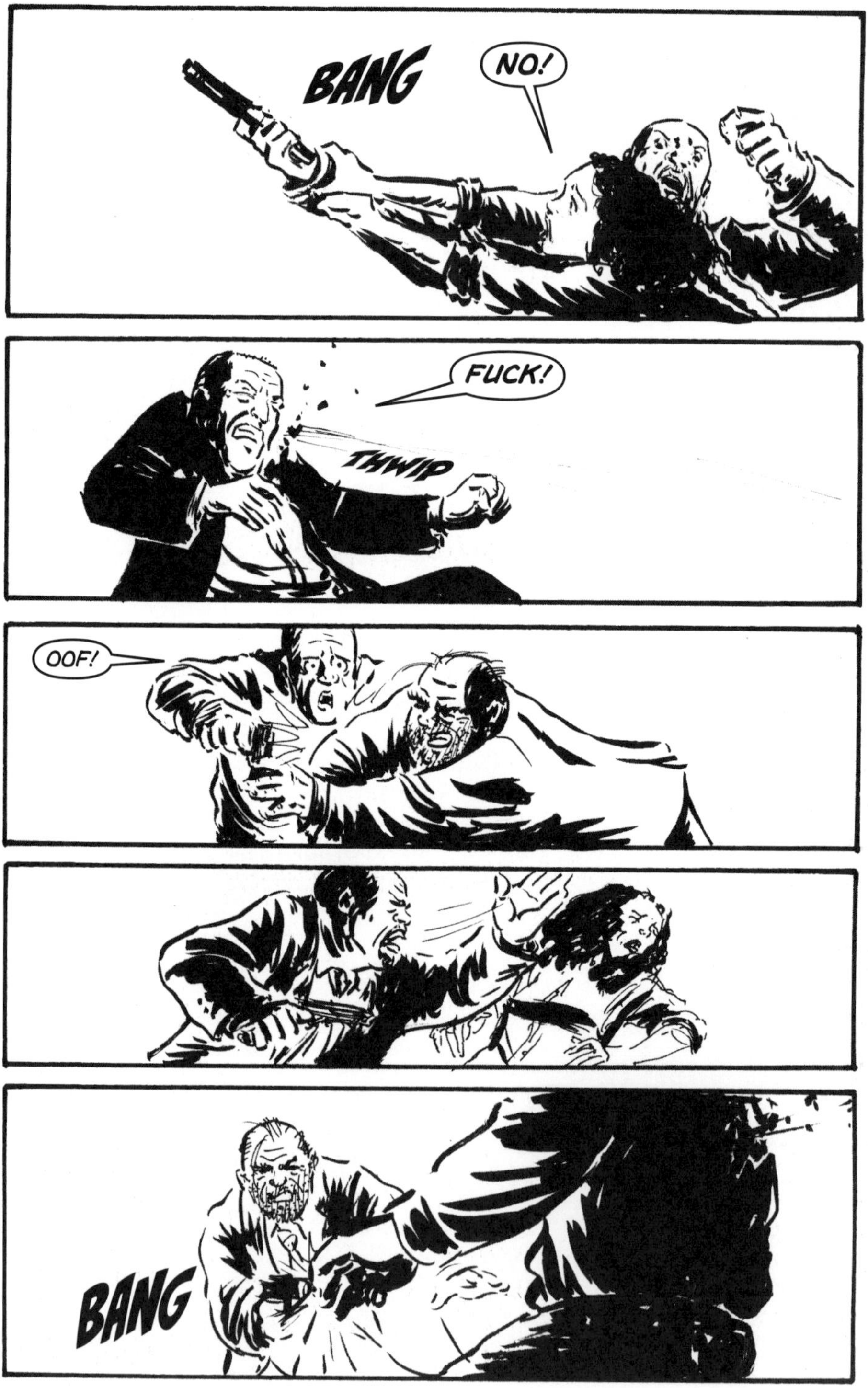
BANG
NO!
FUCK!
THWIP
OOF!
BANG

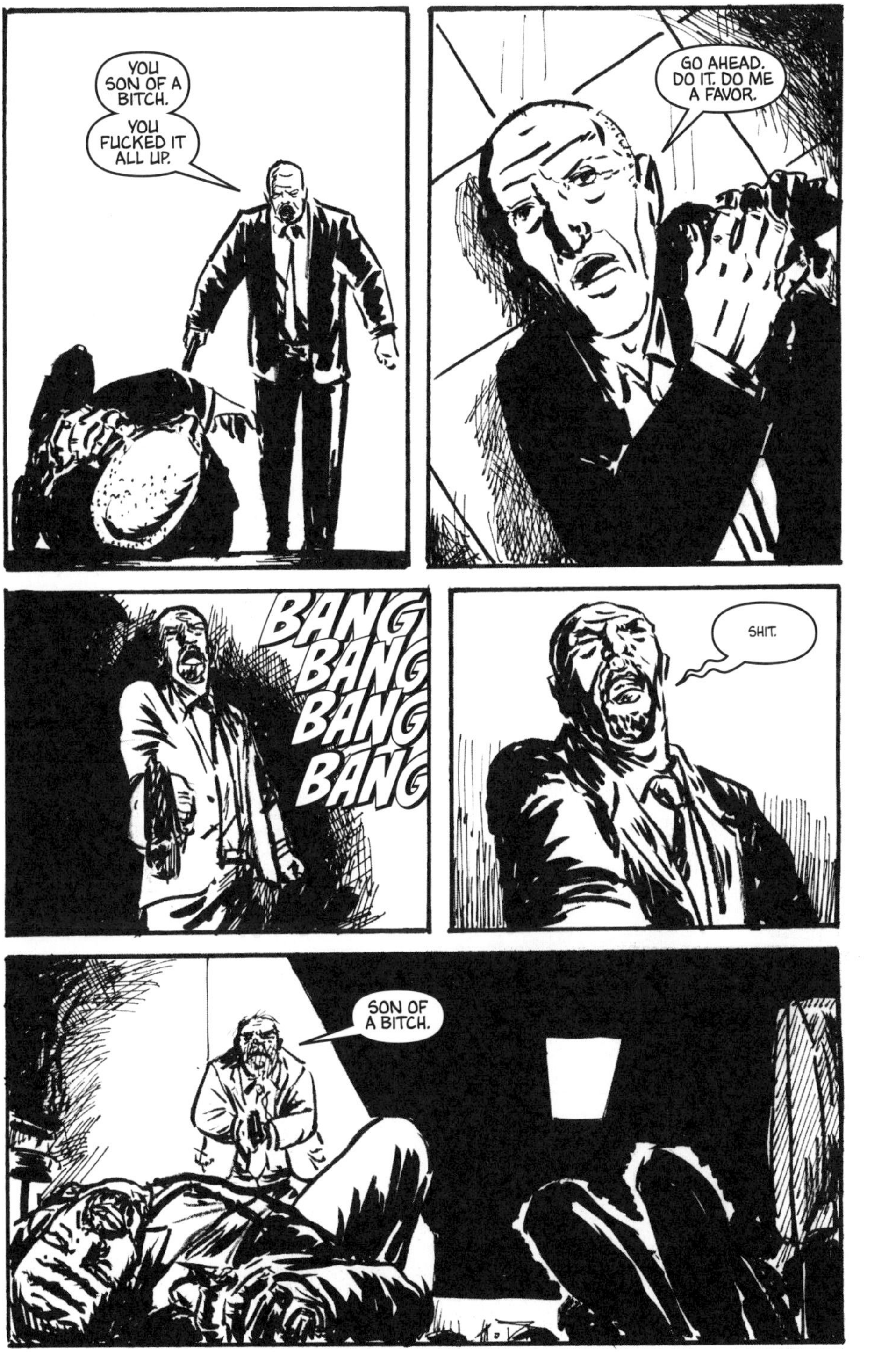
YOU SON OF A BITCH.
YOU FUCKED IT ALL UP.
GO AHEAD. DO IT. DO ME A FAVOR.
BANG BANG BANG BANG
SHIT.
SON OF A BITCH.

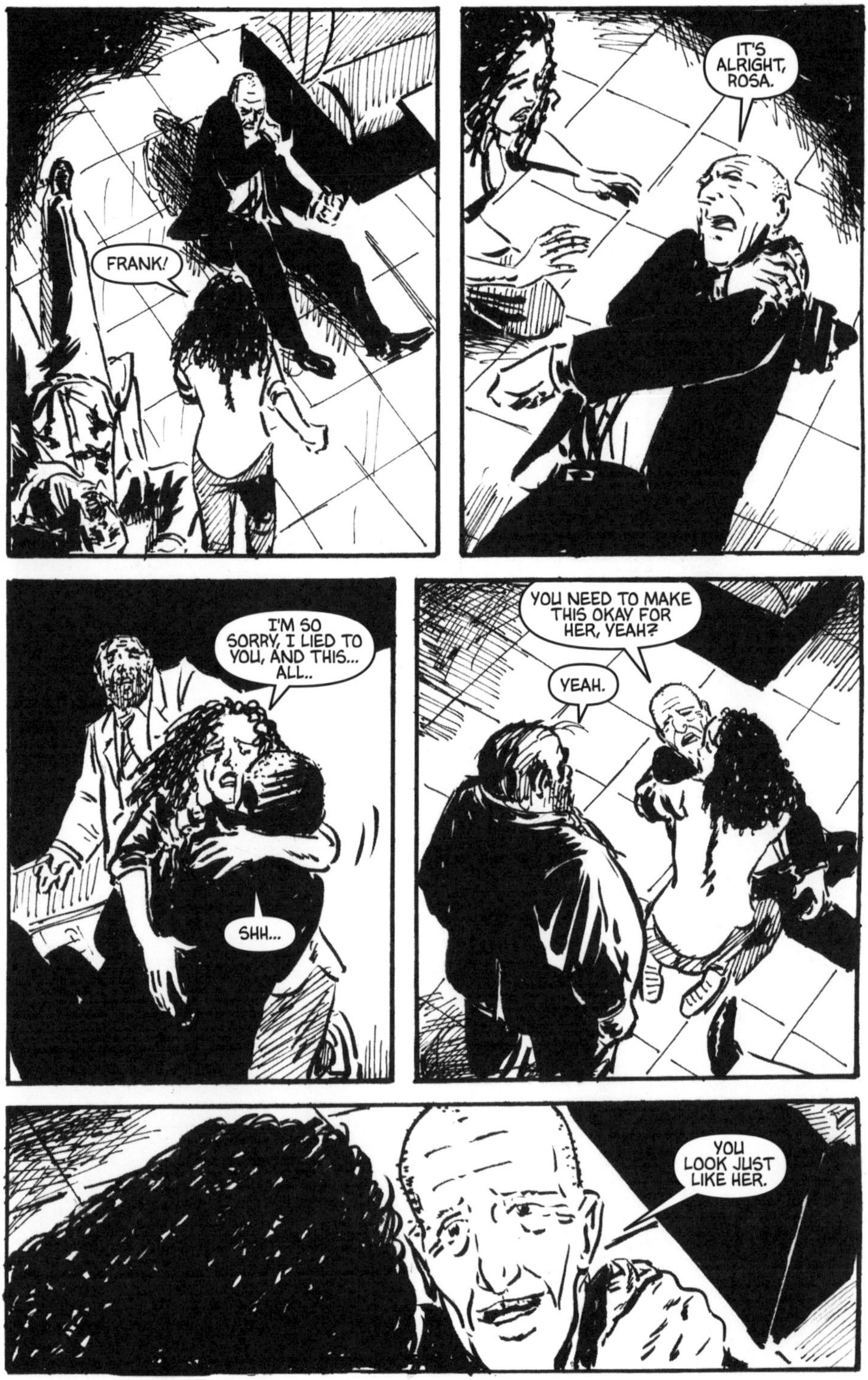
FRANK!
IT'S ALRIGHT, ROSA.
I'M SO SORRY, I LIED TO YOU, AND THIS... ALL..
SHH...
YOU NEED TO MAKE THIS OKAY FOR HER, YEAH?
YEAH.
YOU LOOK JUST LIKE HER.

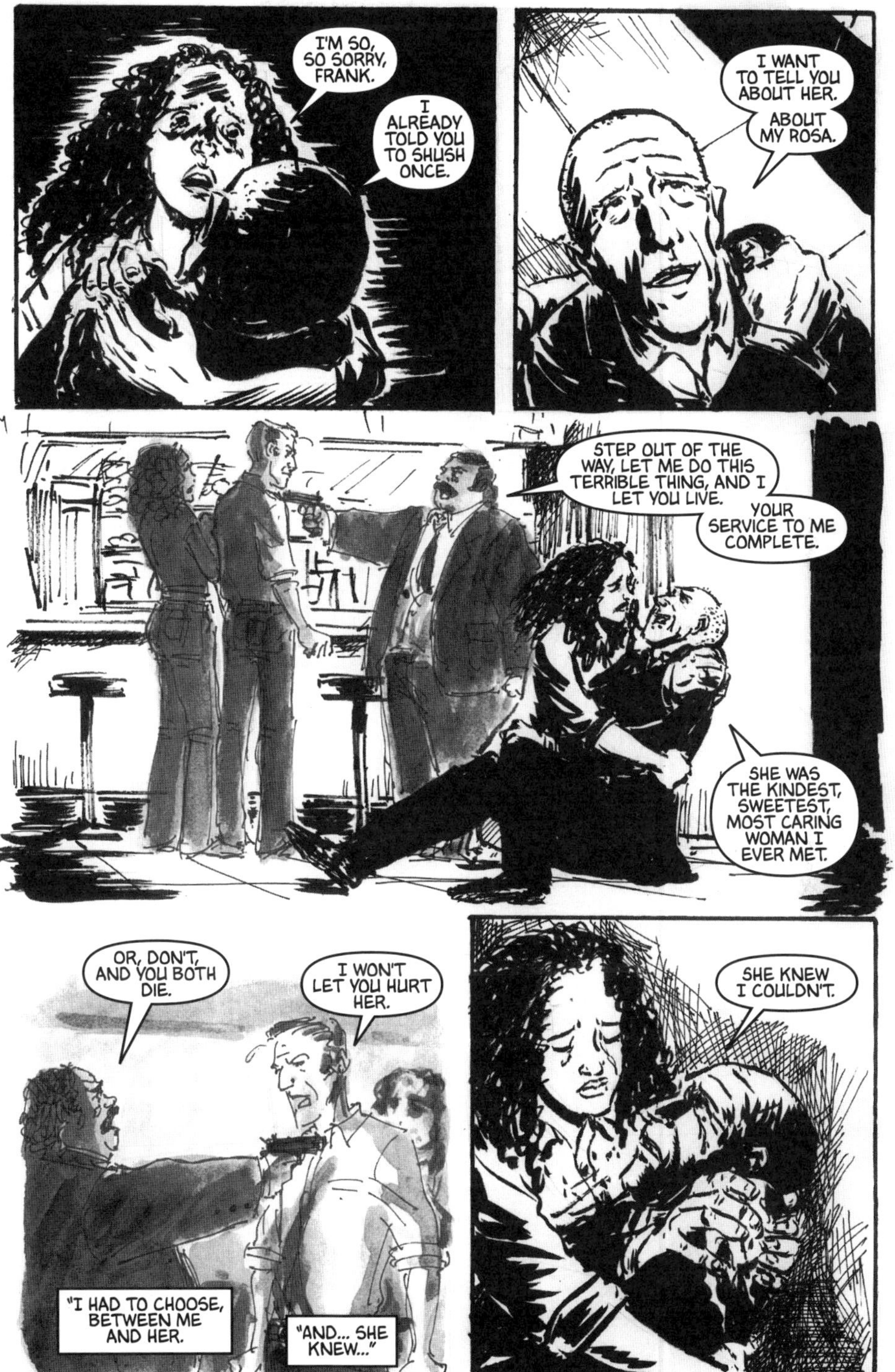

I'M SO, SO SORRY, FRANK.
I ALREADY TOLD YOU TO SHUSH ONCE.
I WANT TO TELL YOU ABOUT HER.
ABOUT MY ROSA.
STEP OUT OF THE WAY, LET ME DO THIS TERRIBLE THING, AND I LET YOU LIVE.
YOUR SERVICE TO ME COMPLETE.
SHE WAS THE KINDEST, SWEETEST, MOST CARING WOMAN I EVER MET.
OR, DON'T, AND YOU BOTH DIE.
I WON'T LET YOU HURT HER.
"I HAD TO CHOOSE, BETWEEN ME AND HER.
"AND... SHE KNEW..."
SHE KNEW I COULDN'T.

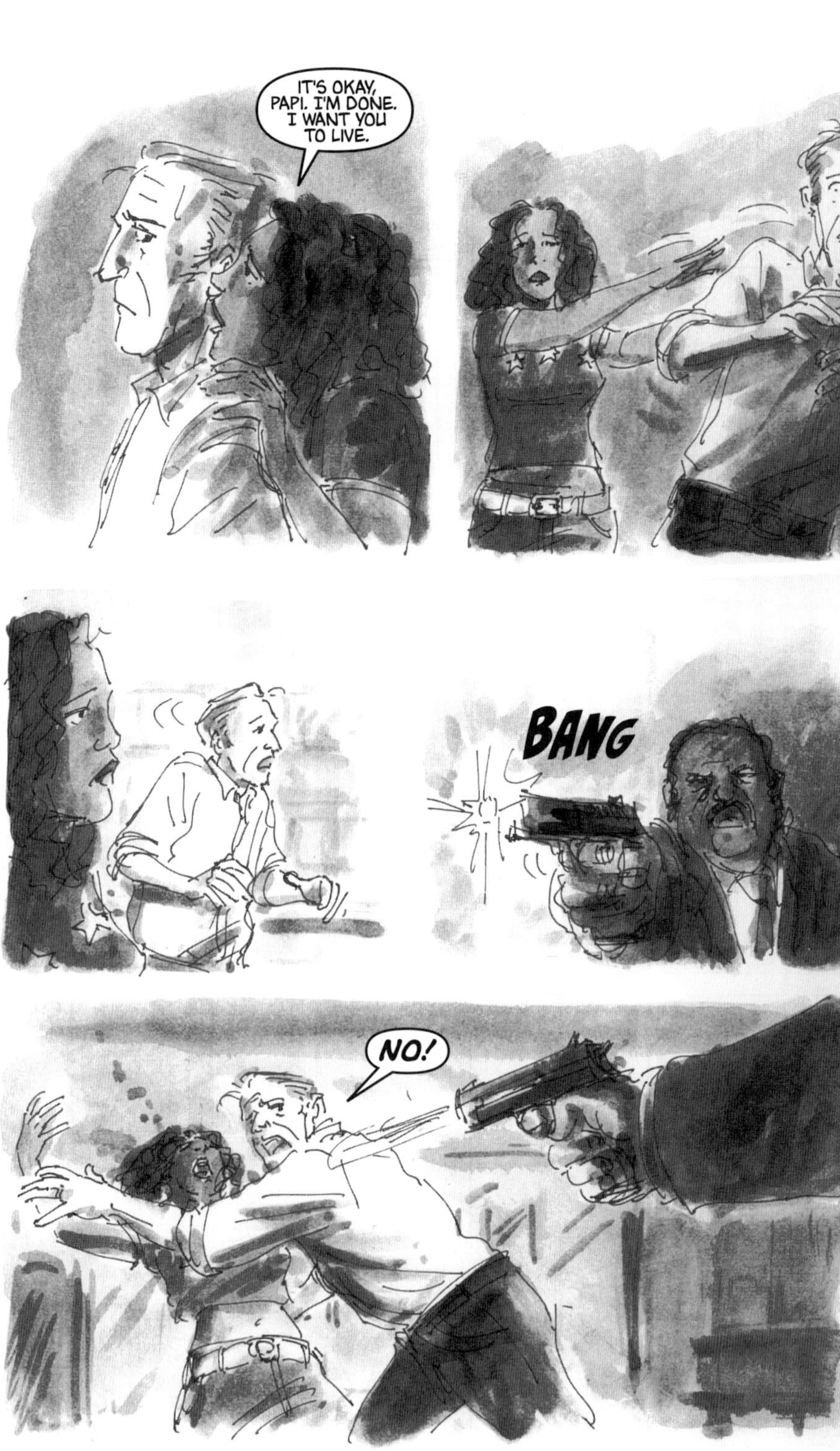
IT'S OKAY, PAPI. I'M DONE. I WANT YOU TO LIVE.
BANG
NO!

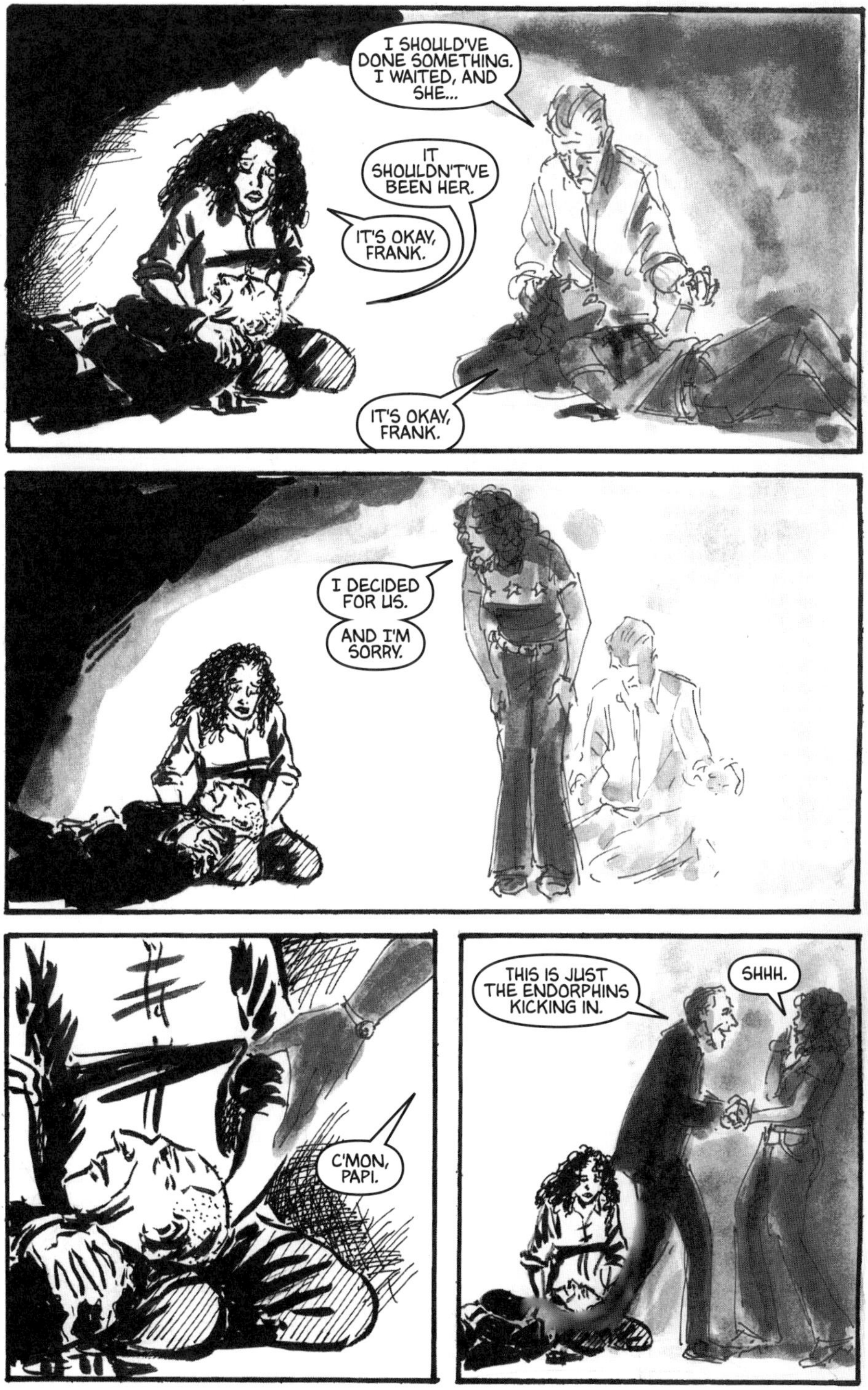
I SHOULD'VE DONE SOMETHING. I WAITED, AND SHE...
IT SHOULDN'T'VE BEEN HER.
IT'S OKAY, FRANK.
IT'S OKAY, FRANK.
I DECIDED FOR US.
AND I'M SORRY.
C'MON, PAPI.
THIS IS JUST THE ENDORPHINS KICKING IN.
SHHH.

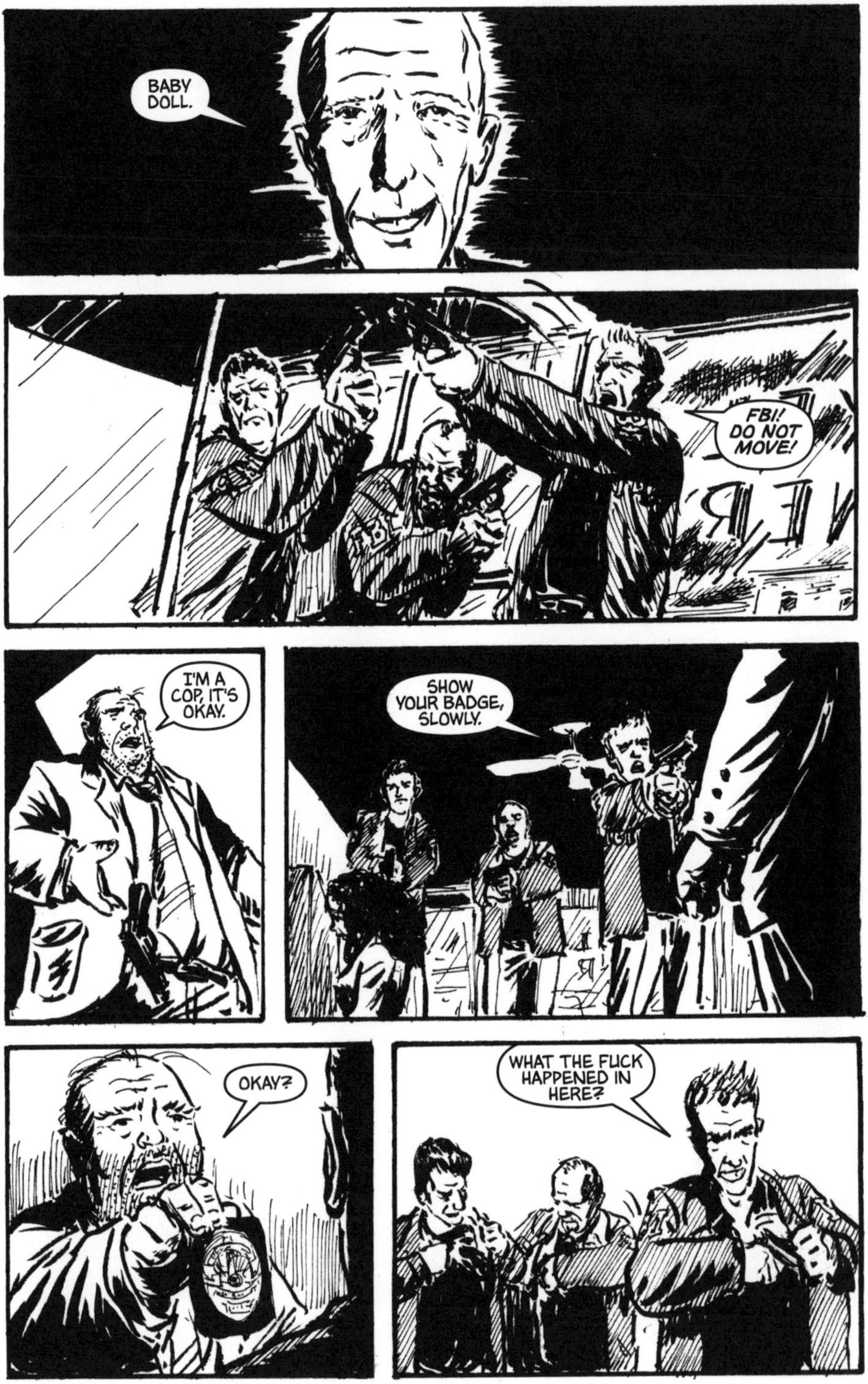
BABY DOLL.
FBI! DO NOT MOVE!
I'M A COP, IT'S OKAY.
SHOW YOUR BADGE, SLOWLY.
OKAY?
WHAT THE FUCK HAPPENED IN HERE?

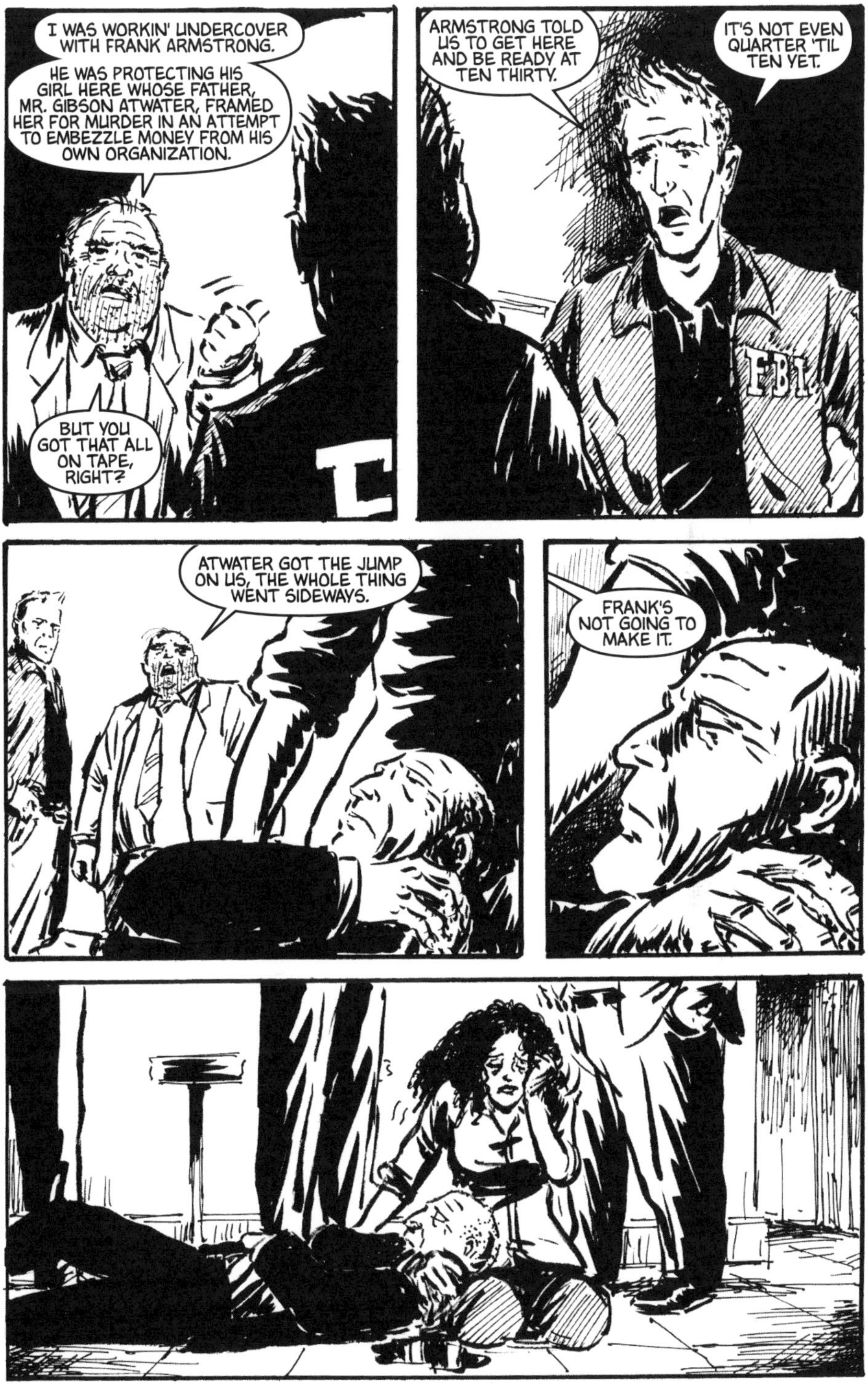
I WAS WORKIN' UNDERCOVER WITH FRANK ARMSTRONG.
HE WAS PROTECTING HIS GIRL HERE WHOSE FATHER, MR. GIBSON ATWATER, FRAMED HER FOR MURDER IN AN ATTEMPT TO EMBEZZLE MONEY FROM HIS OWN ORGANIZATION.
BUT YOU GOT THAT ALL ON TAPE, RIGHT?
ARMSTRONG TOLD US TO GET HERE AND BE READY AT TEN THIRTY.
IT'S NOT EVEN QUARTER 'TIL TEN YET.
FBI
ATWATER GOT THE JUMP ON US, THE WHOLE THING WENT SIDEWAYS.
FRANK'S NOT GOING TO MAKE IT.

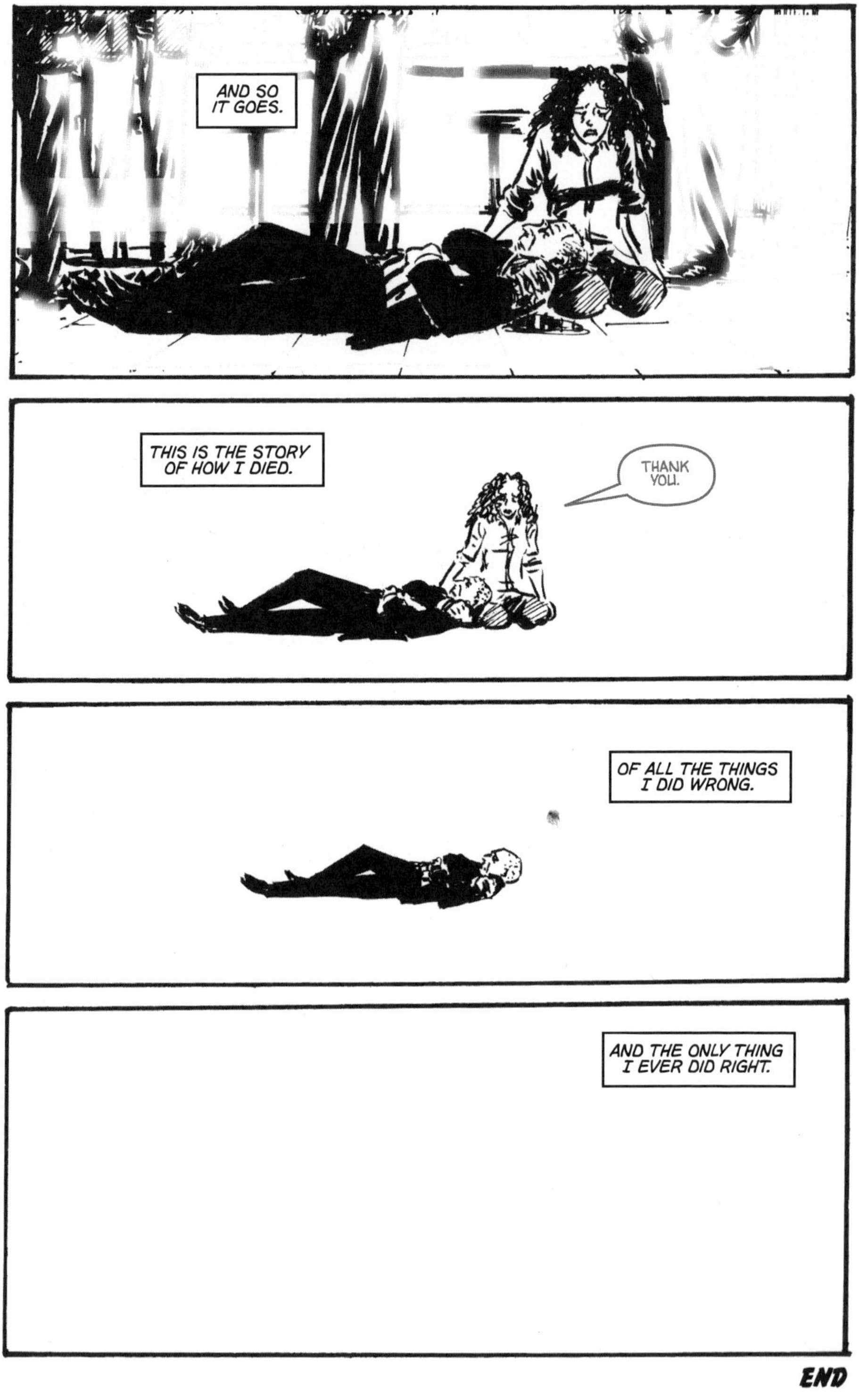
AND SO IT GOES.
THIS IS THE STORY OF HOW I DIED.
THANK YOU.
OF ALL THE THINGS I DID WRONG.
AND THE ONLY THING I EVER DID RIGHT.
END

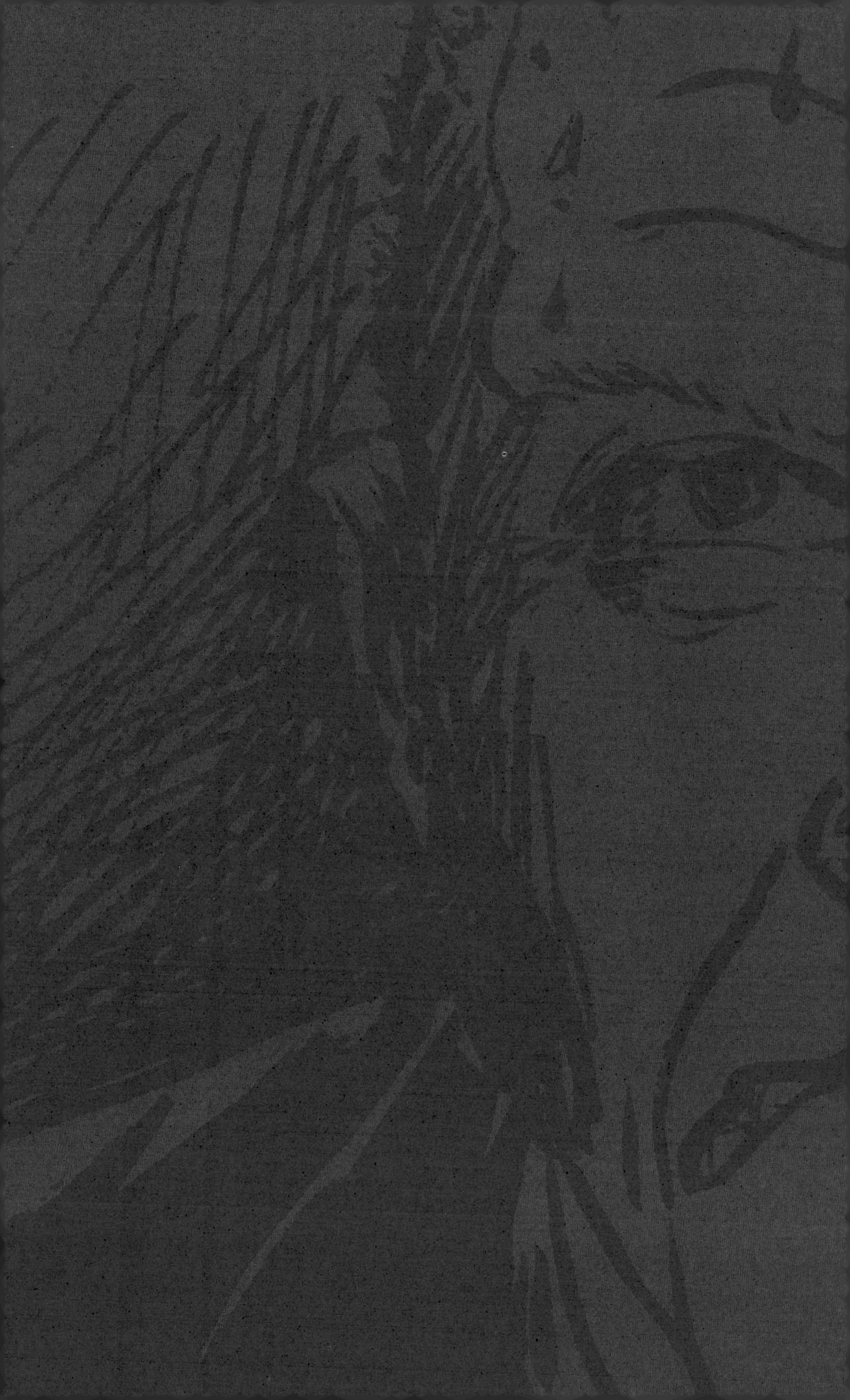

THE ORIGINAL PITCH

Fialkov & Tuazon's Early Concept for TUMOR

BY JOSHUA HALE FIALKOV & NOEL TUAZON

In the following pages you will find the original pitch document for *Tumor* created in 2006. In the years between conception and execution, a lot of the story changed, and a lot of it stayed the same. The two things that changed most drastically were the practical effects of the tumor (which changed thanks to my research and the invaluable input of Dr. Schiebel) and the method of Rosa's death. The original also had more of a Hitchcockian vibe, with much more mystery and much less personal history. The included art is some of my favorite work Noel has ever done. Unfortunately, enough changed between these pages and the final book that the art was unusable, but we're giving you a chance to check it out here. Hopefully this illustrates how far one goes on a project from conception to execution.

JHF

I should've known better than to take that damn missing girl case. But I haven't been thinking clearly... not with the headaches and the nausea. To add insult to injury, this morning I woke up in a bed that wasn't my own, with a woman I'd never met, and in clothes I've never worn. Happens to the best of us, right? Well, the difference is the bed was covered in blood, the woman was dead, and the clothes belonged to a man I'd shot dead twenty years ago.

The doctors tell me there's a ticking time bomb of a tumor in my head. Could go at any time. I've got to solve that missing girl case, find out who the dead blonde next to me is, and clear my name all before the tumor ruptures and I take the big sleep.

It's going to be one of those days.

Tumor is a 176-page original graphic novel from the award-nominated creative team behind the critically acclaimed *Elk's Run* (Villard Books, Random House Publishing Group). The book draws heavily from the Film Noir aesthetic but with a modern storytelling style combining Hitchcockian mystery and intrigue with a compelling first-person narrative in a style reminiscent of films like *Memento* and *Fight Club*.

Told using a shifting timeline, in which reality and Frank's shattered perception constantly blur, *Tumor* captures the inner-workings of a man being punished for a life he doesn't remember leading and for atrocities he doesn't remember committing.

Tumor follows Frank Armstrong, a past-his-prime Private Eye and former mob enforcer, who takes on a missing girl case tied to the mob, only to find connections to the murder of his own wife twenty years earlier. Now, he must find the girl before her fate is sealed. Oh, did I mention the much too late diagnosis of a massive brain tumor that is quickly killing Frank?

With literally days to live, Frank loses his senses one by one, his memories disappear, and his body fails. He's left to find the girl, solve his wife's murder, and, hopefully, avenge her death all before the tumor finally ends it all.

In the end, when all is revealed to him, the sad truth of his wife's death and his very active role in it is but a fleeting thought as he loses what little coherence he has left. He dies, he thinks, the way he's deserved to, in the arms of the woman he loves... even if he doesn't know who she is.

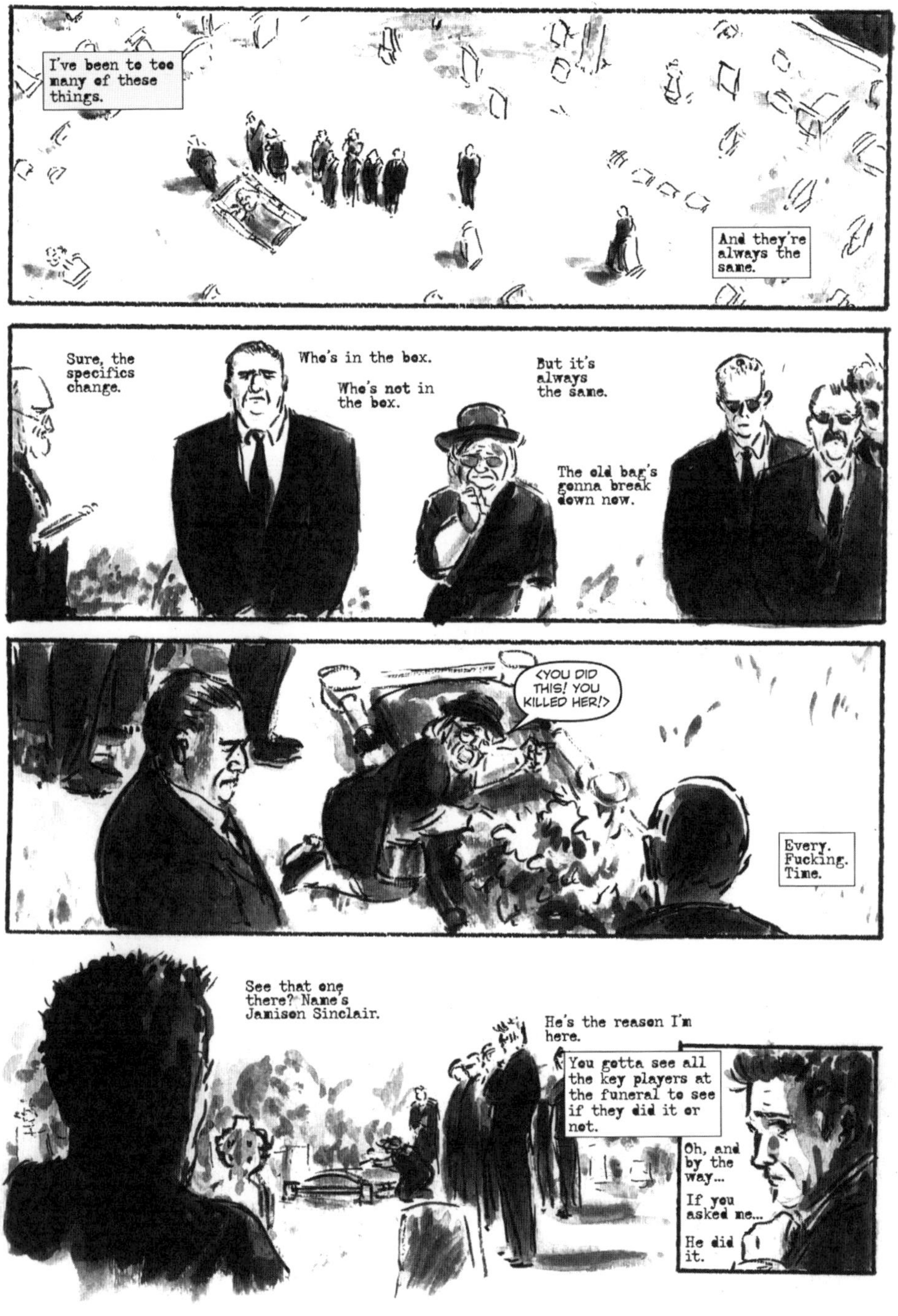
I've been to too many of these things.
And they're always the same.
Sure, the specifics change.
Who's in the box.
Who's not in the box.
But it's always the same.
The old bag's gonna break down now.
<YOU DID THIS! YOU KILLED HER!>
Every. Fucking. Time.
See that one there? Name's Jamison Sinclair.
He's the reason I'm here.
You gotta see all the key players at the funeral to see if they did it or not.
Oh, and by the way...
If you asked me...
He did it.

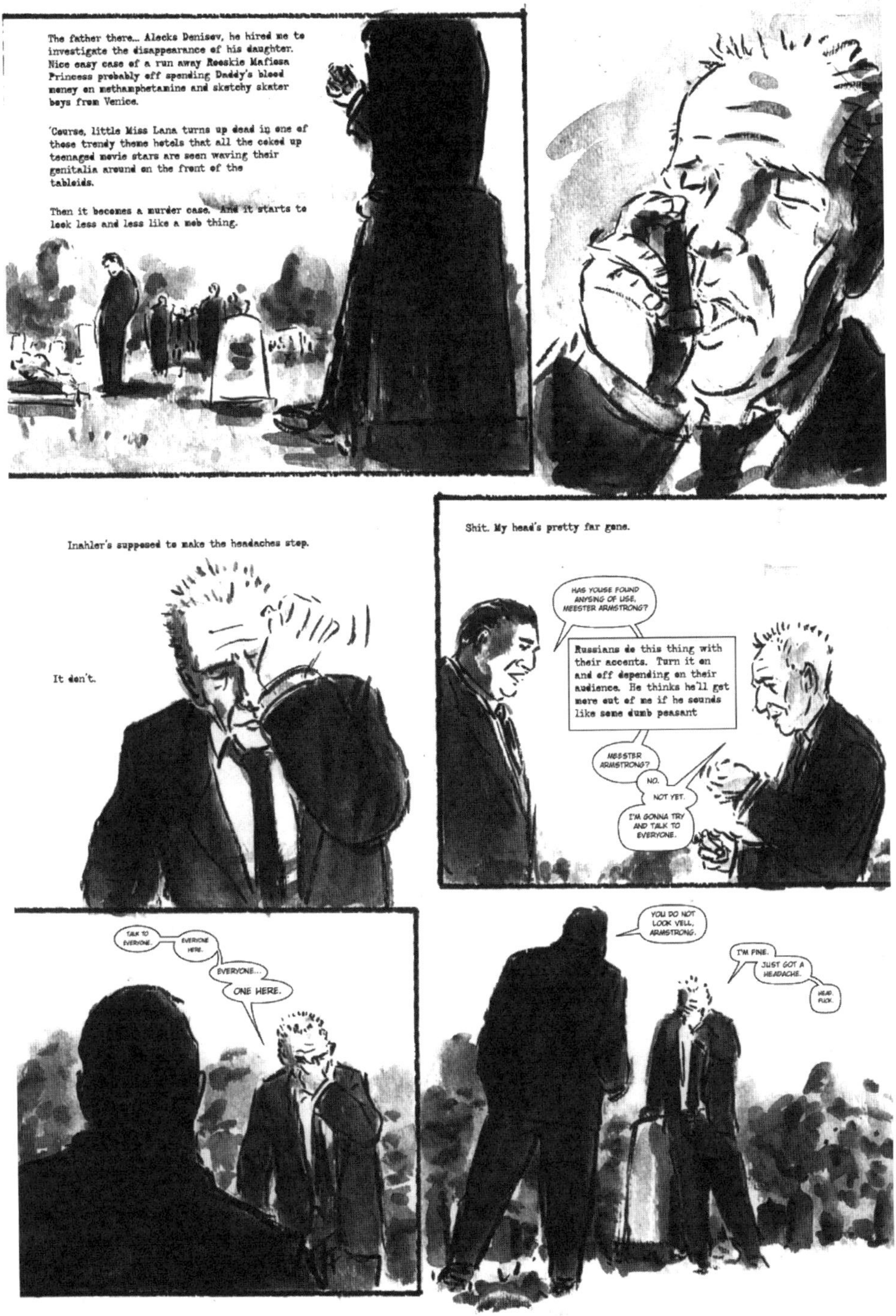
The father there... Alecks Denisov, he hired me to investigate the disappearance of his daughter. Nice easy case of a run away Rooskie Mafiosa Princess probably off spending Daddy's blood money on methamphetamine and sketchy skater boys from Venice.
'Course, little Miss Lana turns up dead in one of those trendy theme hotels that all the coked up teenaged movie stars are seen waving their genitalia around on the front of the tabloids.
Then it becomes a murder case. And it starts to look less and less like a mob thing.
Inahler's supposed to make the headaches stop.
It don't.
Shit. My head's pretty far gone.
HAS YOUSE FOUND ANYSING OF USE, MEESTER ARMSTRONG?
Russians do this thing with their accents. Turn it on and off depending on their audience. He thinks he'll get more out of me if he sounds like some dumb peasant
MEESTER ARMSTRONG?
NO.
NOT YET.
I'M GONNA TRY AND TALK TO EVERYONE.
TALK TO EVERYONE.
EVERYONE HERE.
EVERYONE...
ONE HERE.
YOU DO NOT LOOK VELL, ARMSTRONG.
I'M FINE.
JUST GOT A HEADACHE.
HEAD. FUCK.

Hours pass.

Maybe even days.

Time's become a little less regular than it used to be.

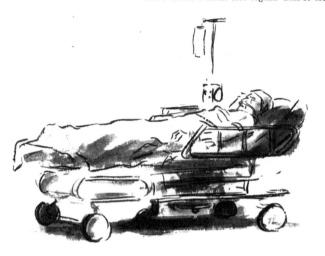

Where the
fuck am I?

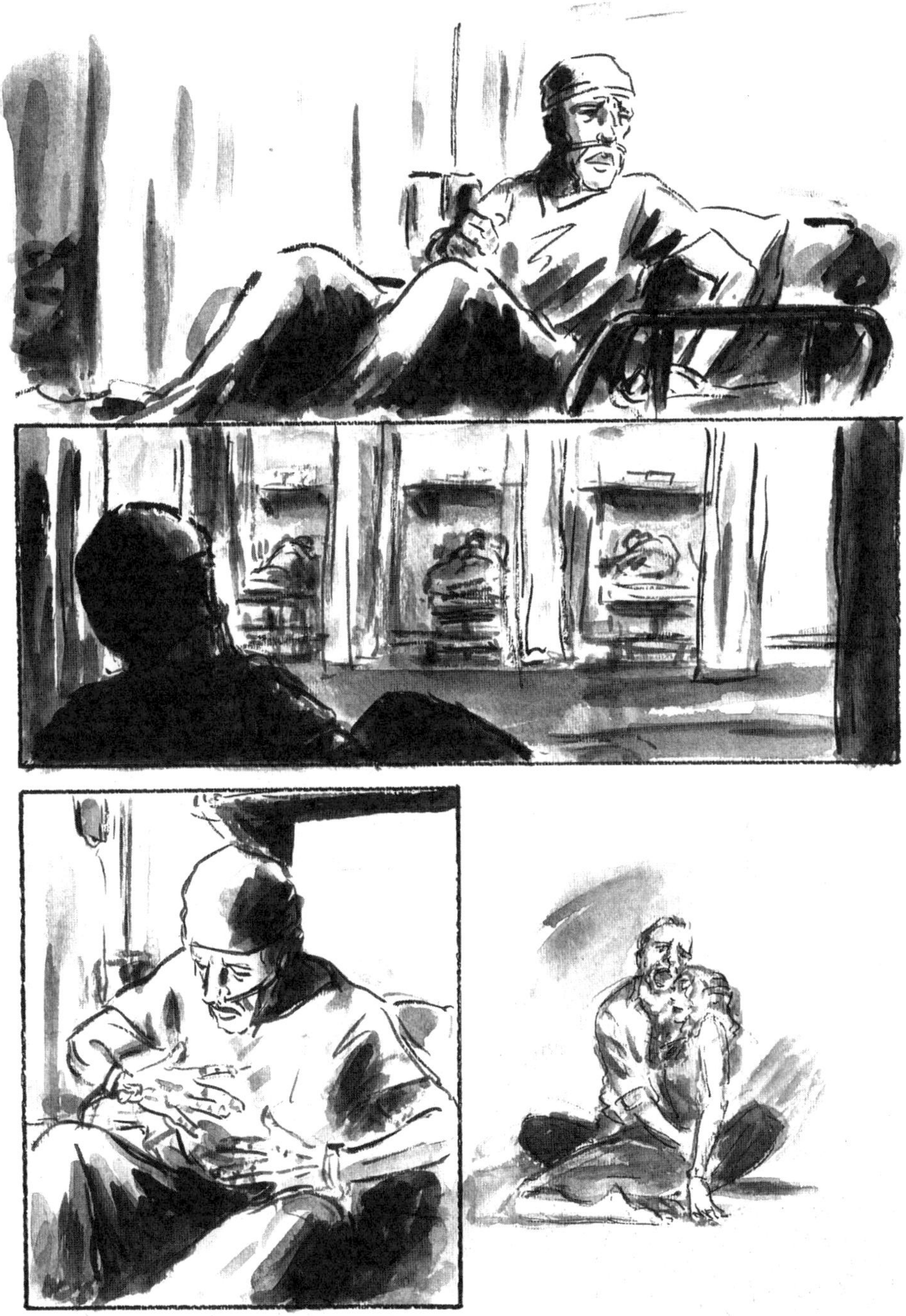

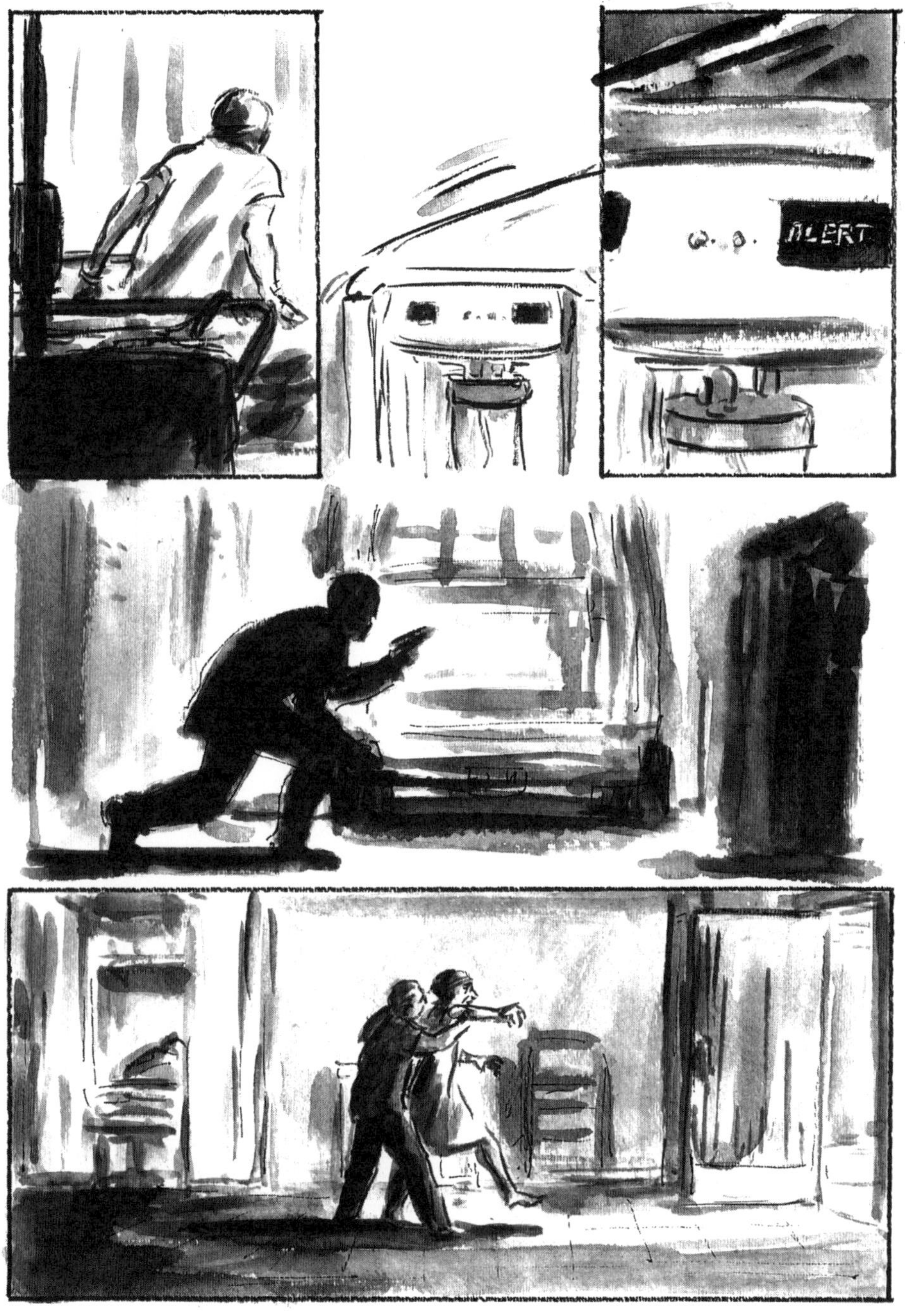
ALERT

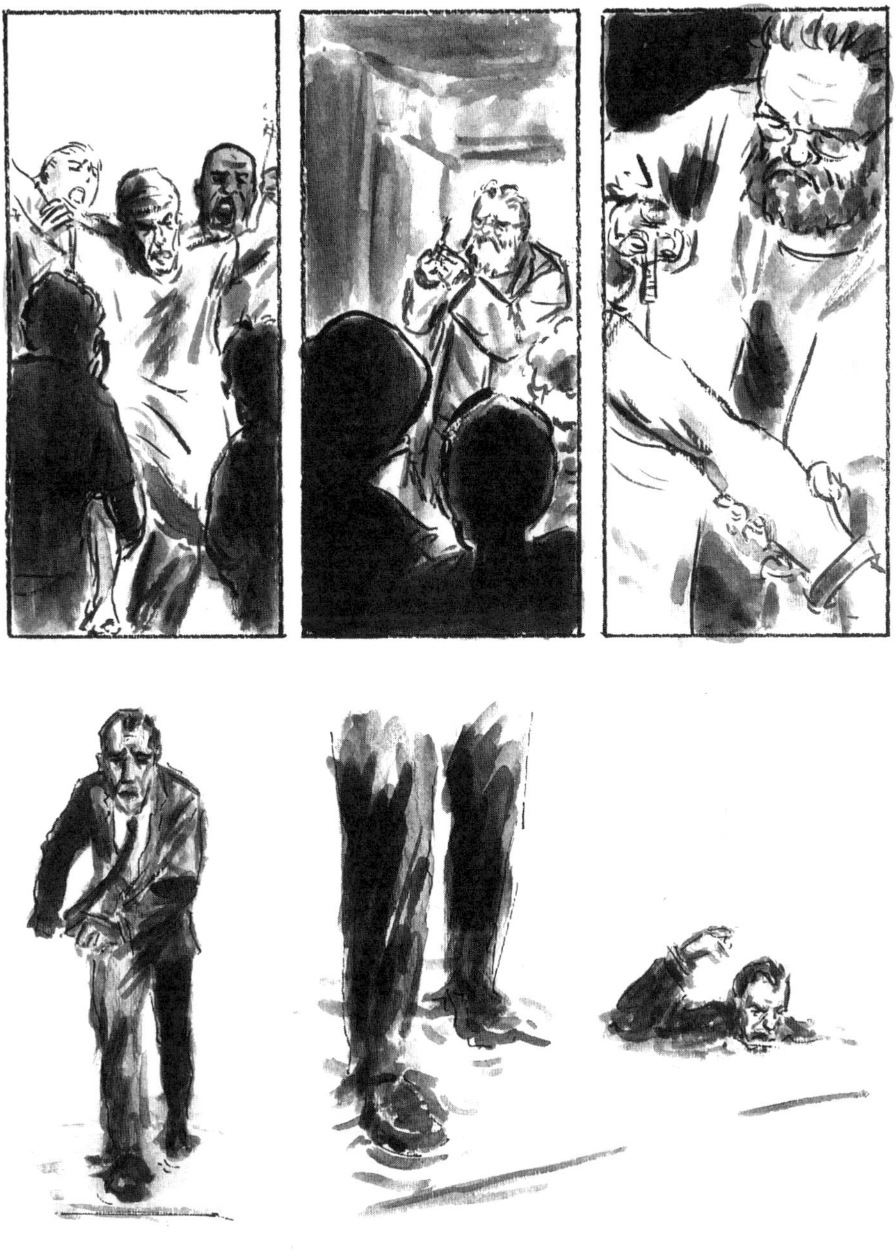

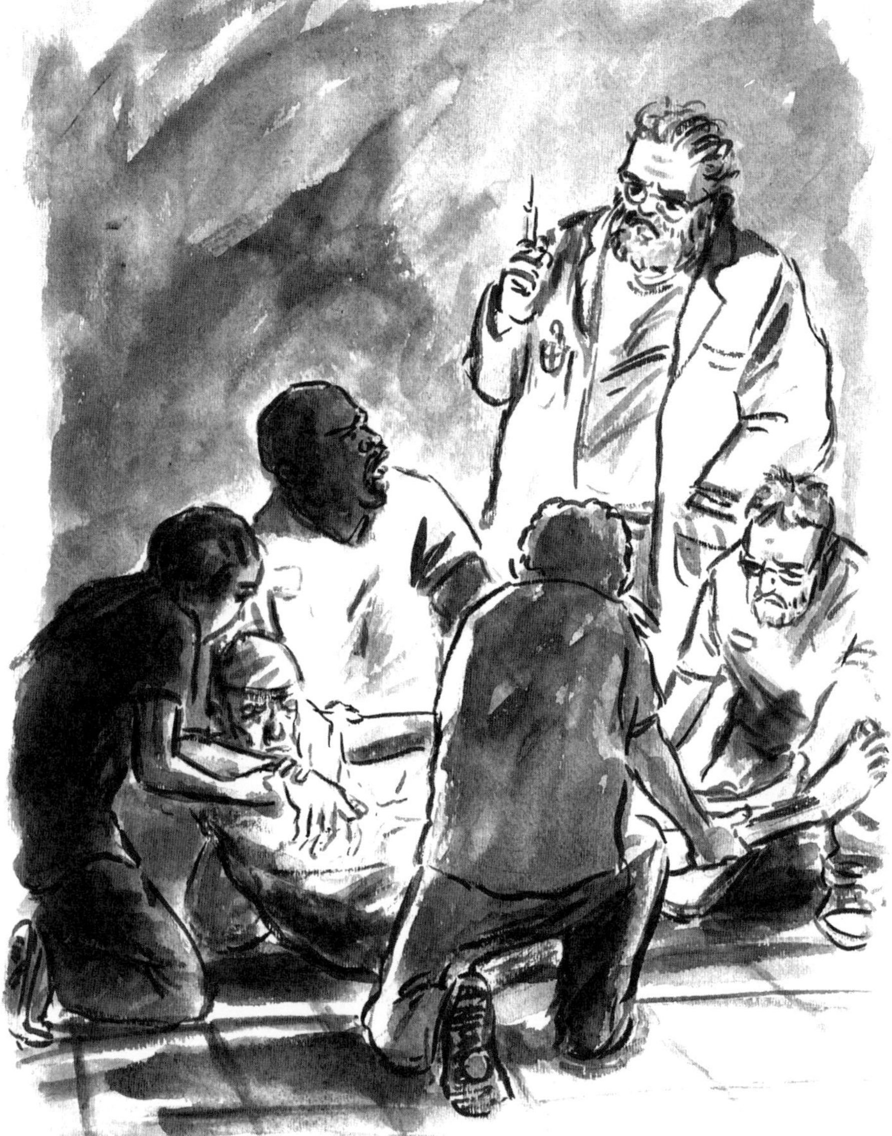

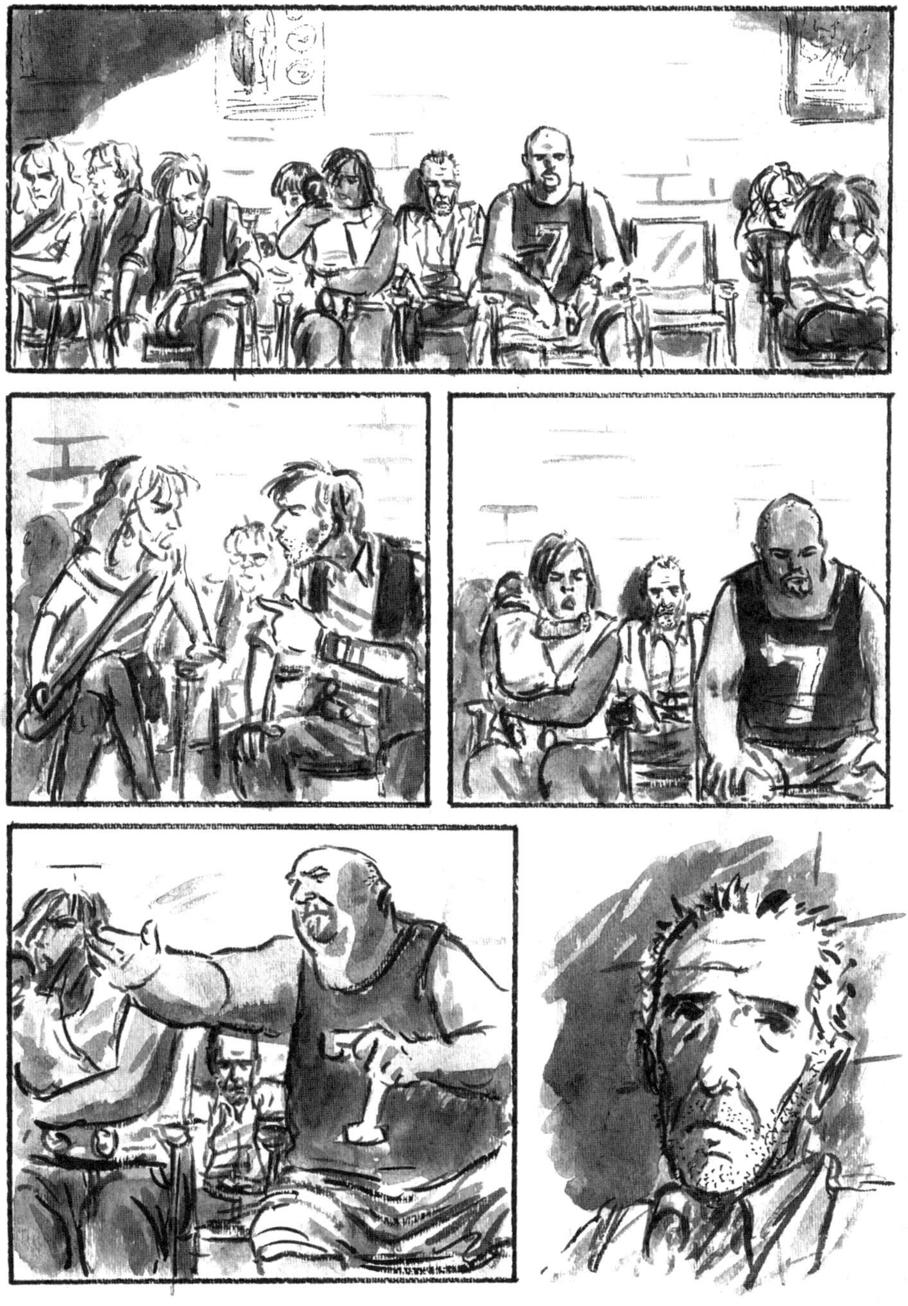

SKETCHBOOK

Early Concepts and Character Designs

BY NOEL TUAZON

In the past few years, Noel and I have learned how to communicate quickly and concisely on our projects together. Part of this comes from Noel's fast pen. We talk about concepts and then minutes later I have a rough version of what we're talking about. I've found that having Noel's sketches and imagery in front of me helps to guide the story and characters in a way that merely scripting the pictures in my head just can't do. Presented here are some examples of some of these images.

JHF

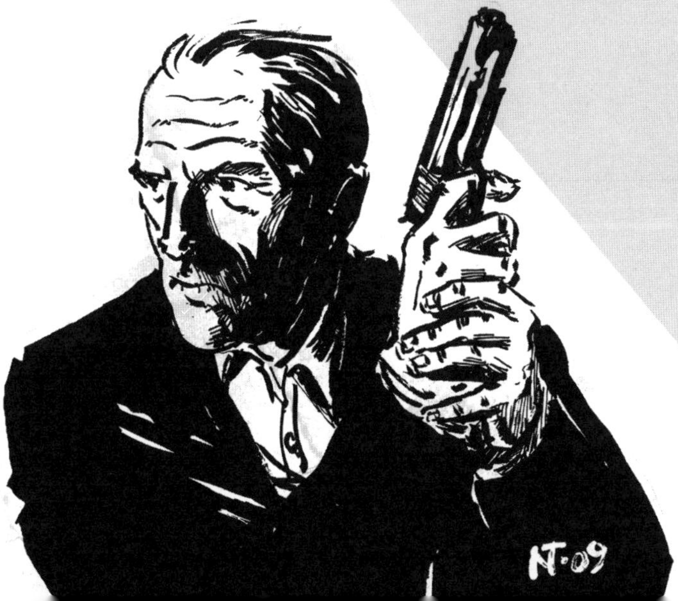
NT·09

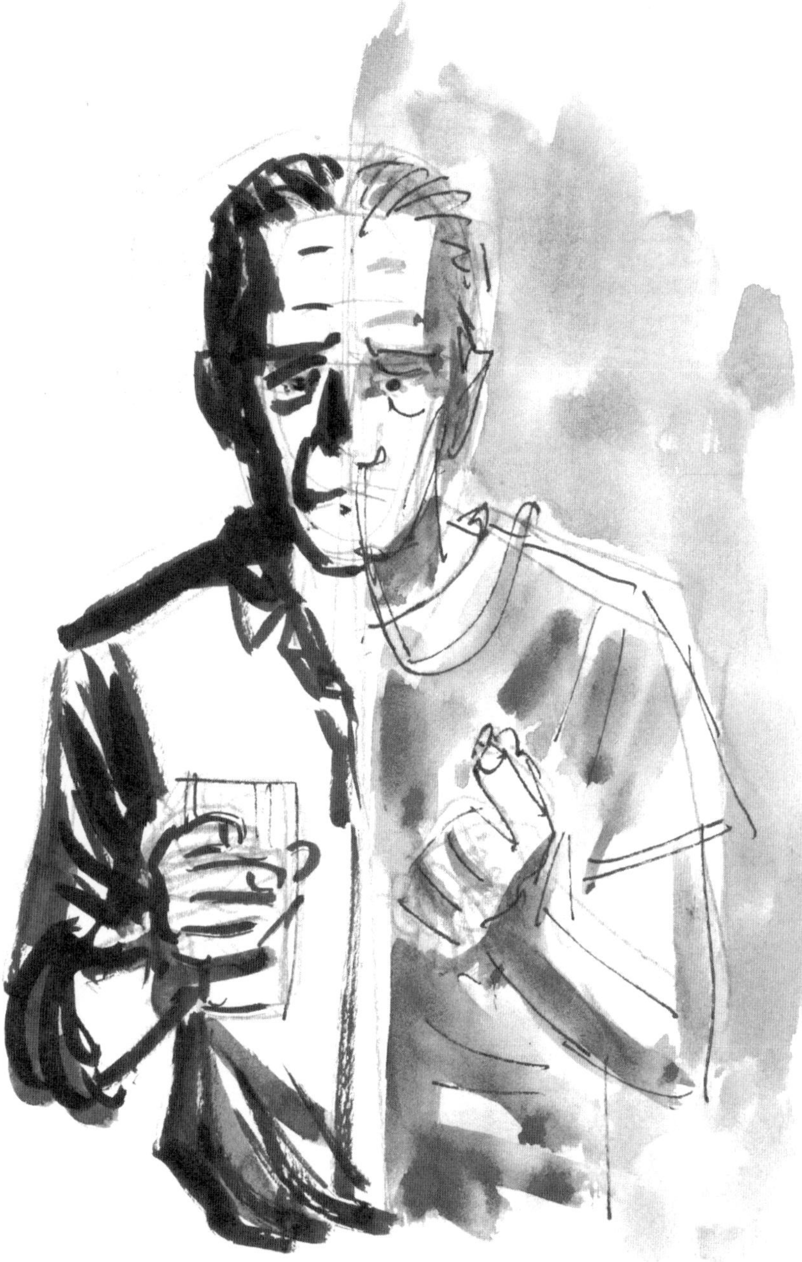

FRANK ARMSTRONG

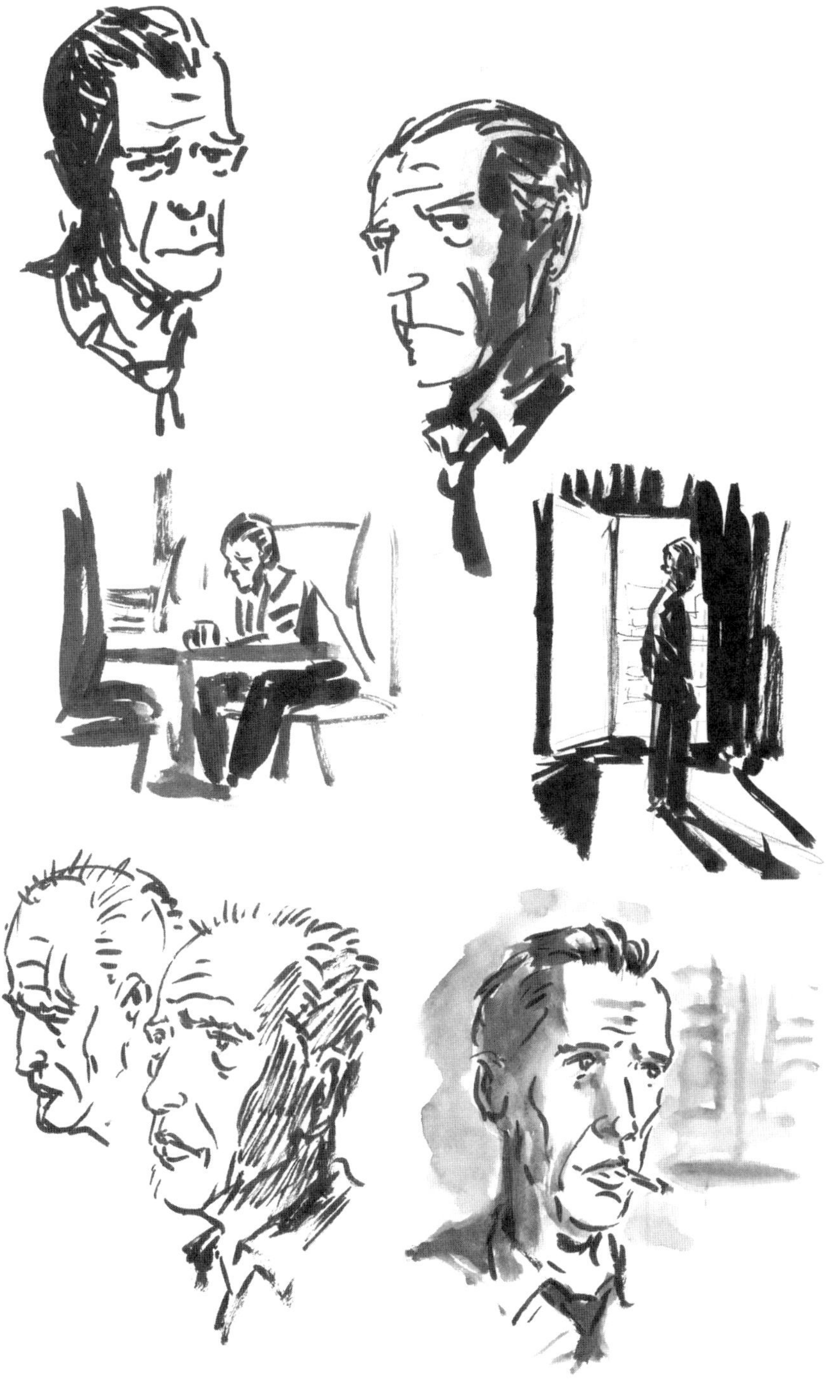

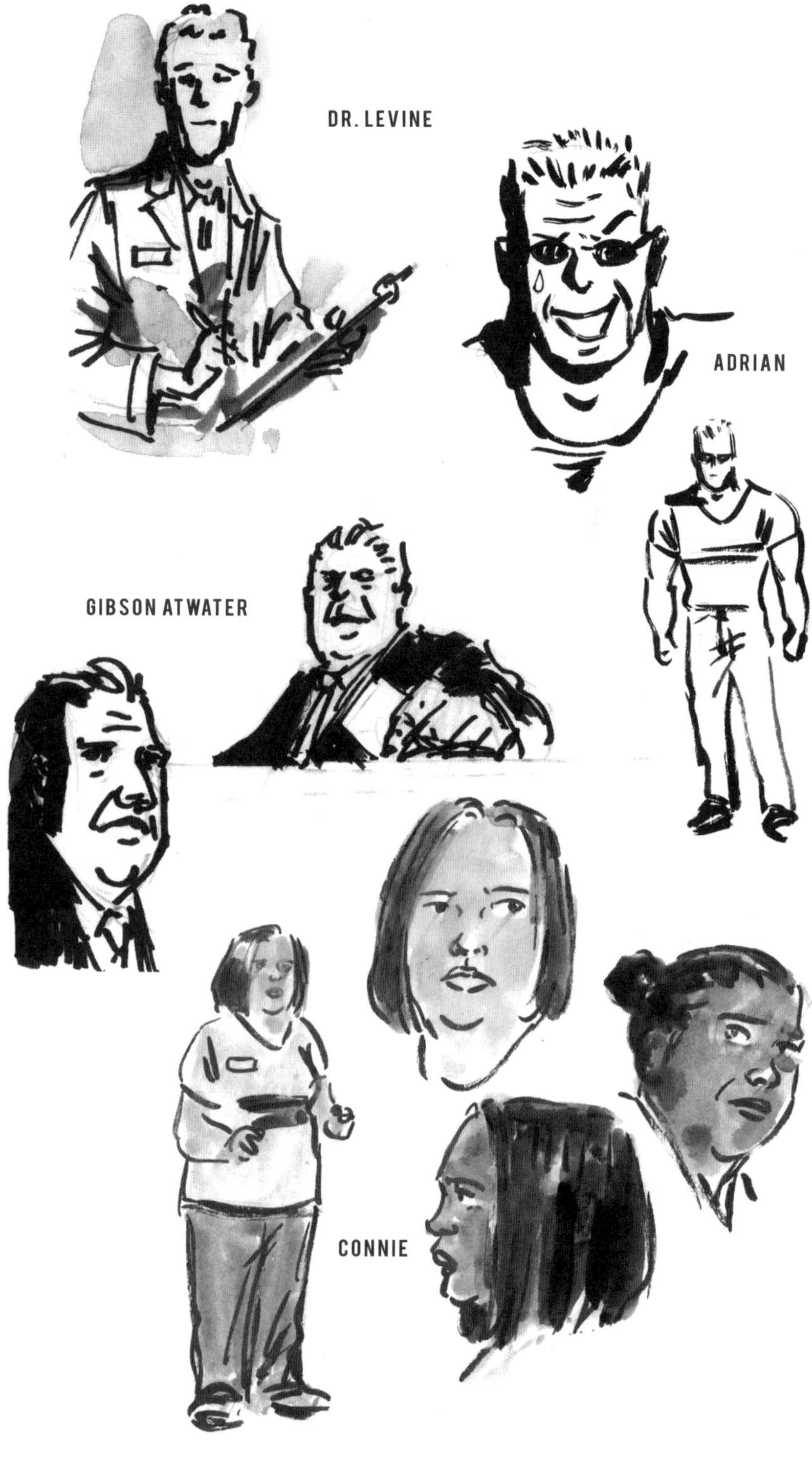
DR. LEVINE
ADRIAN
GIBSON ATWATER
CONNIE

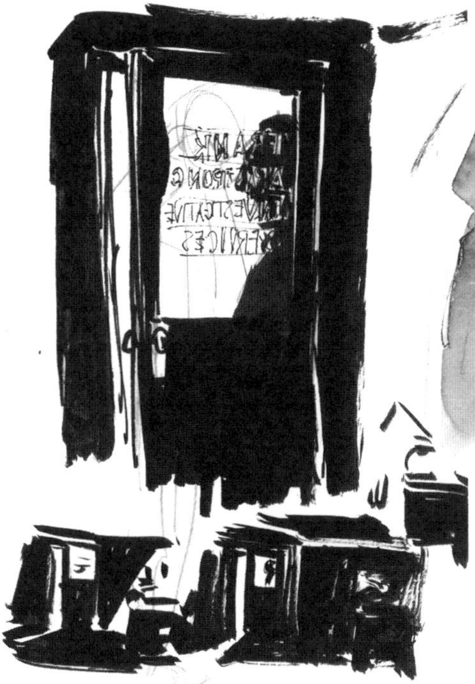

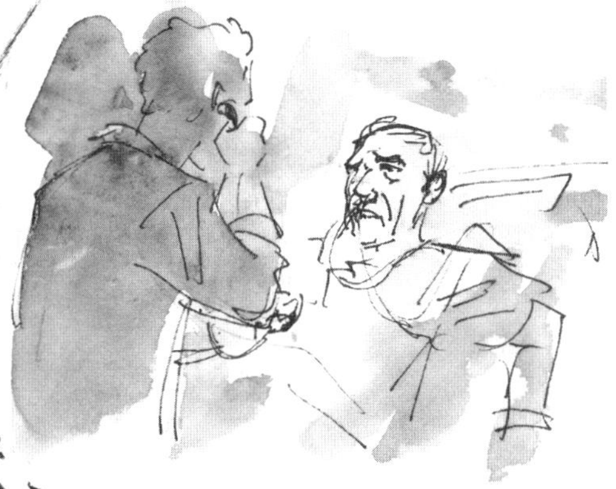

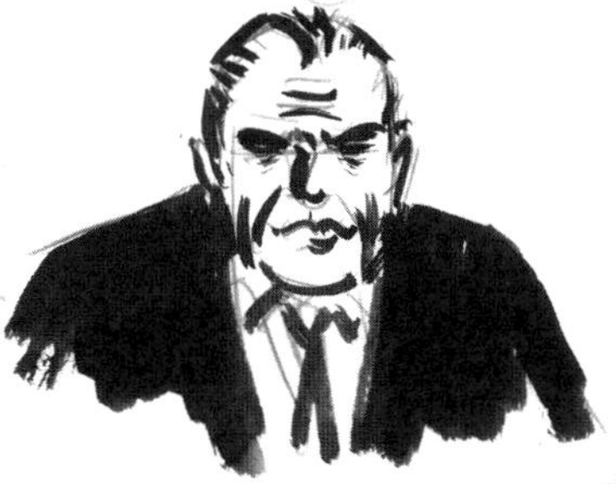

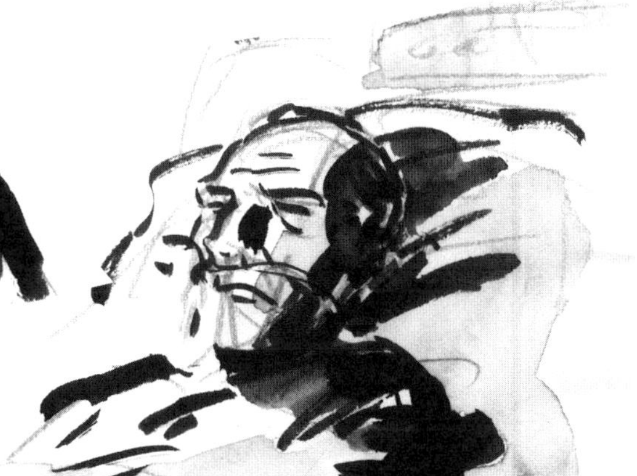

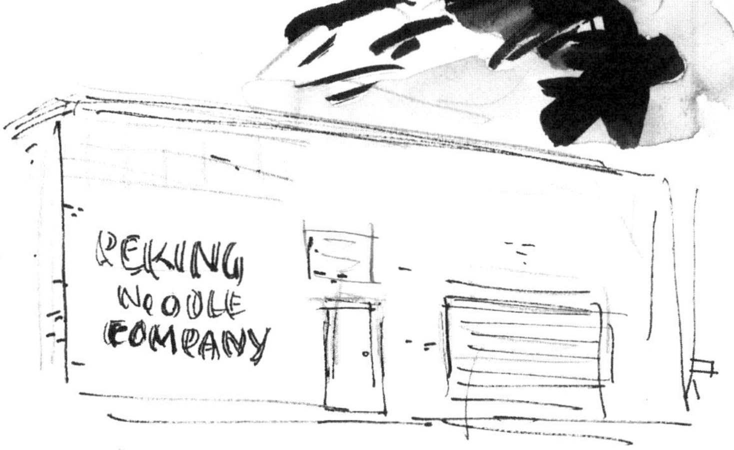
PEKING
NOODLE
COMPANY

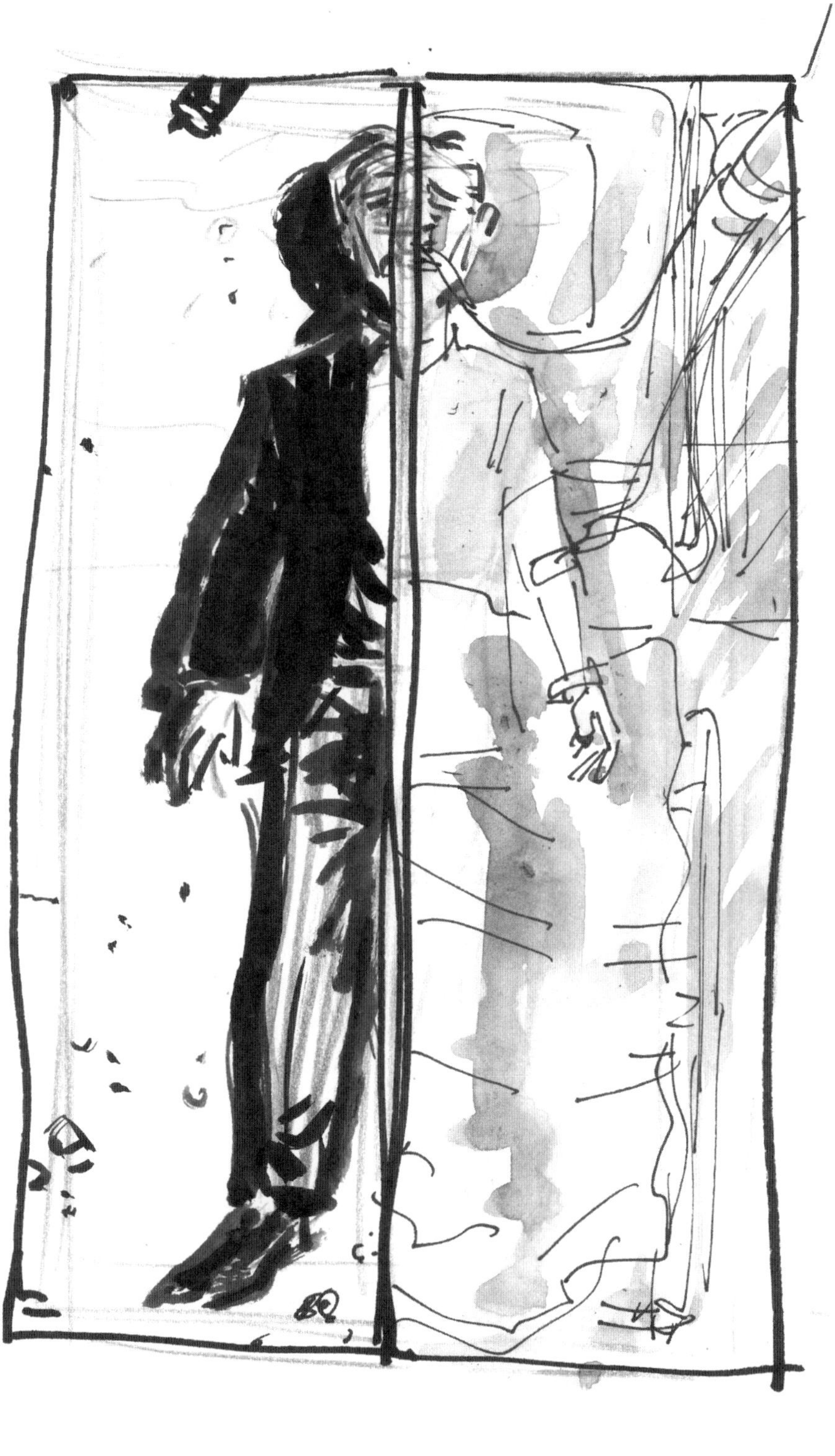

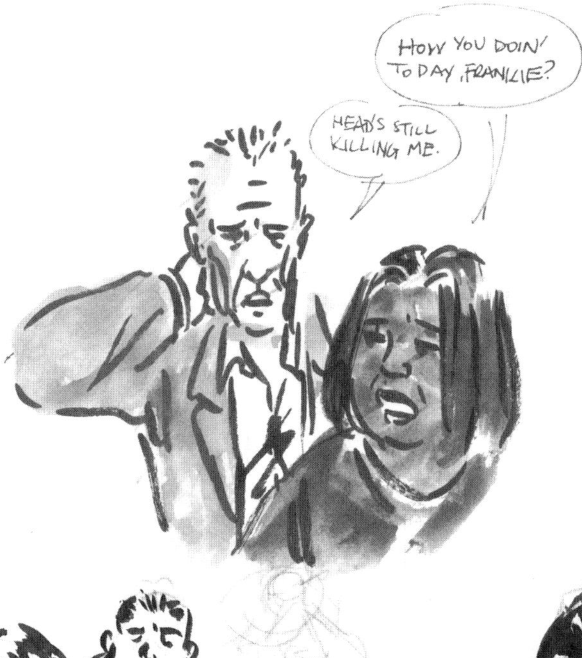
HOW YOU DOIN' TODAY, FRANKIE?
HEAD'S STILL KILLING ME.

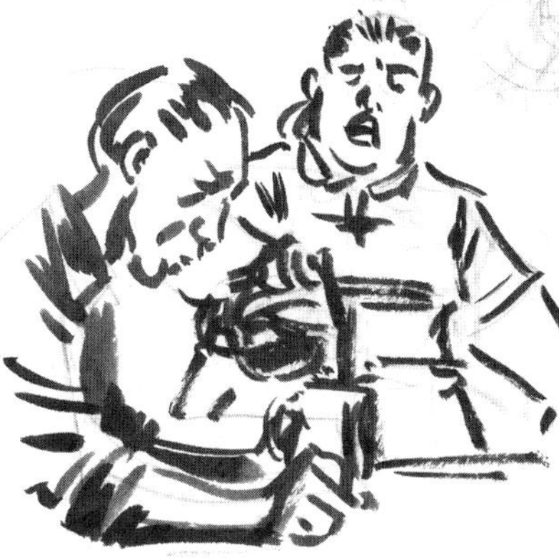

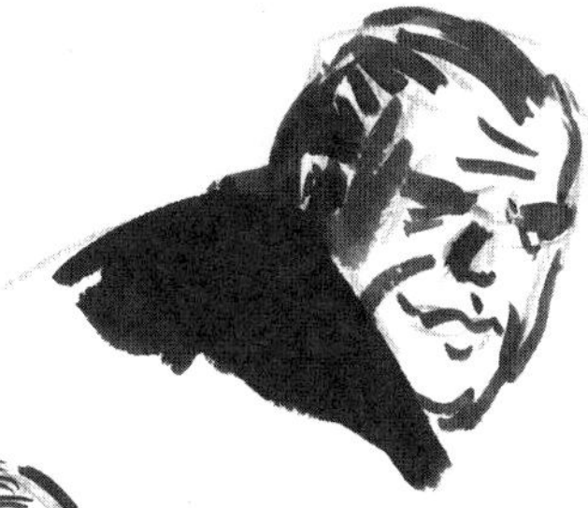

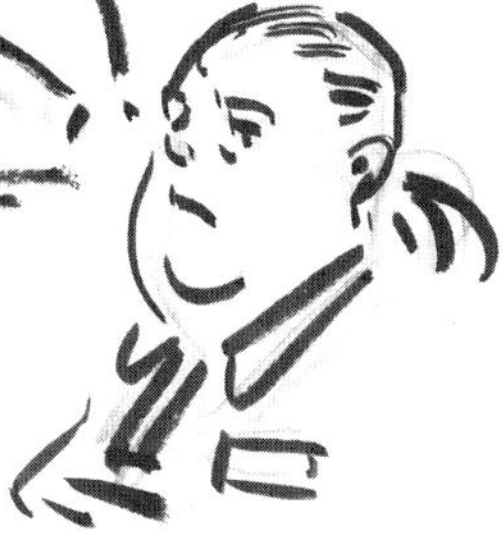

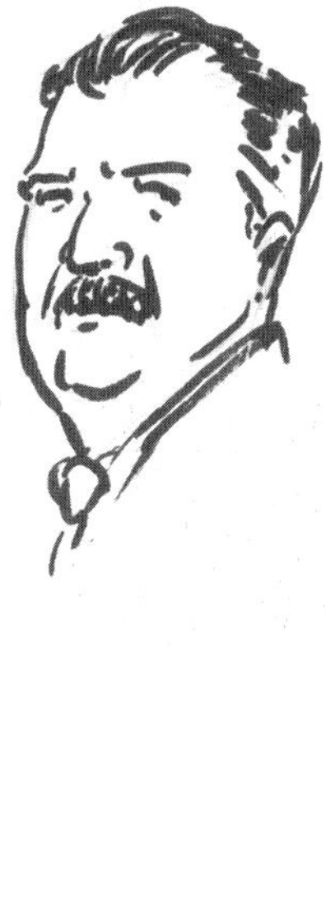

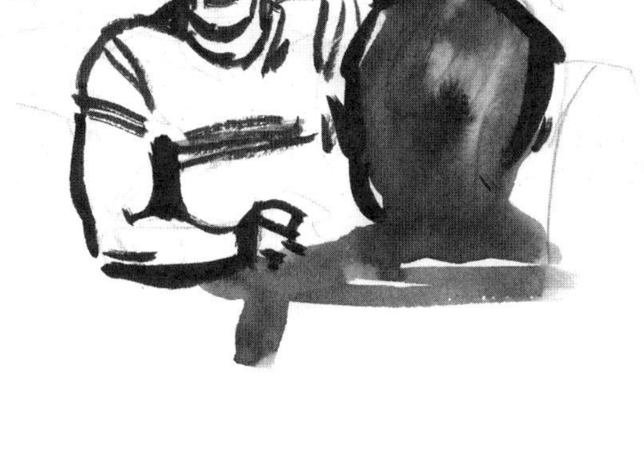

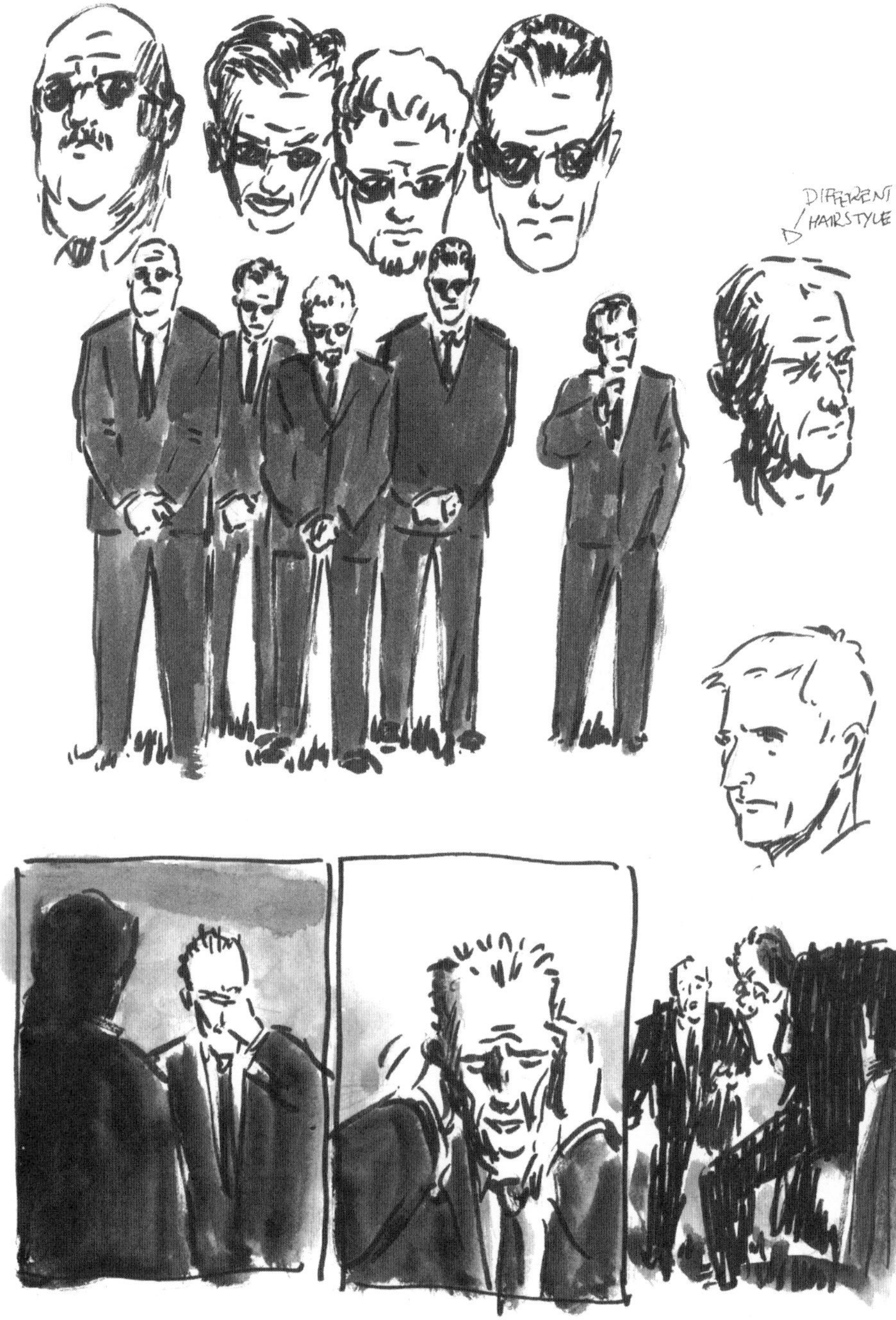
DIFFERENT HAIRSTYLE

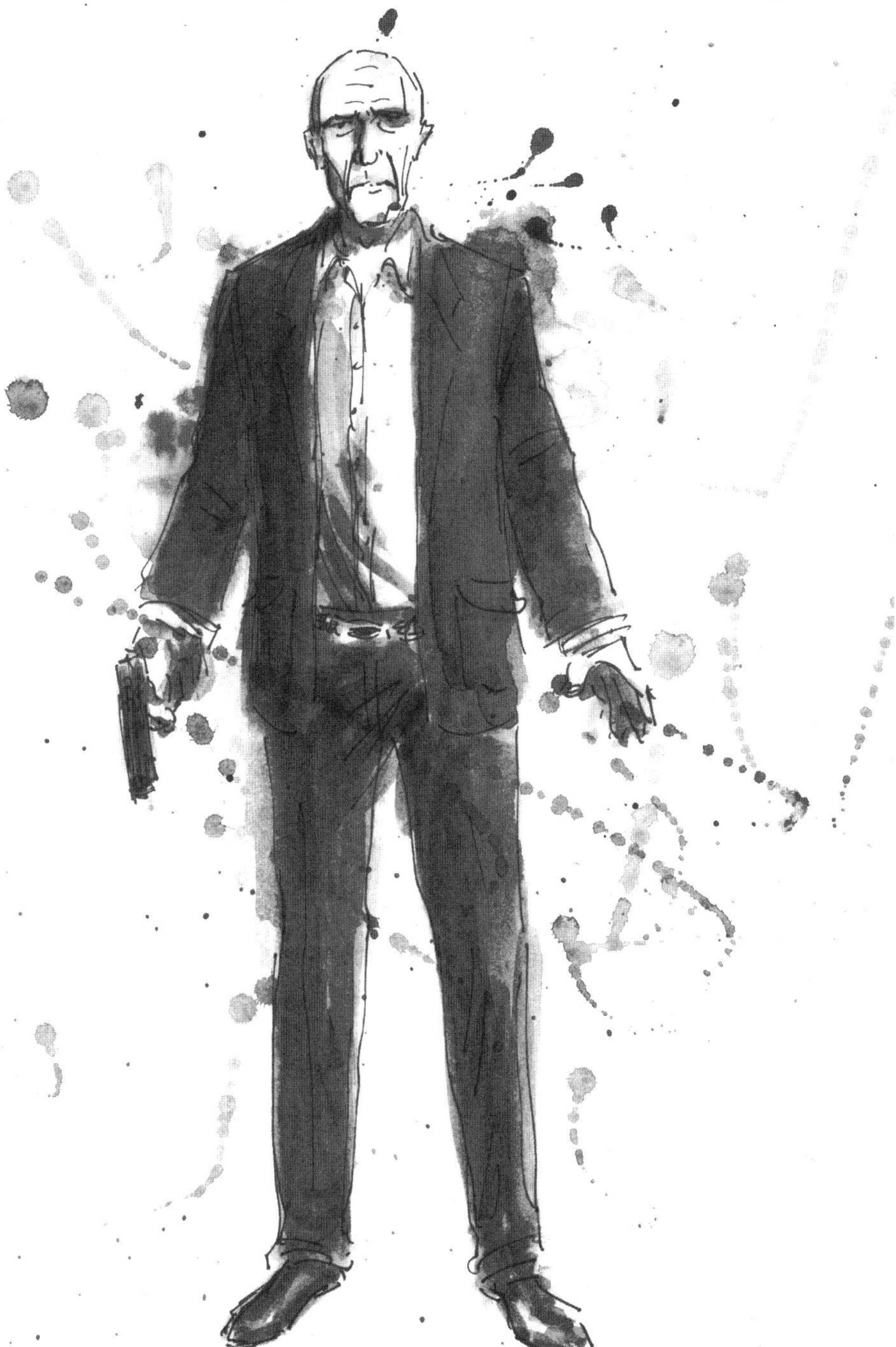

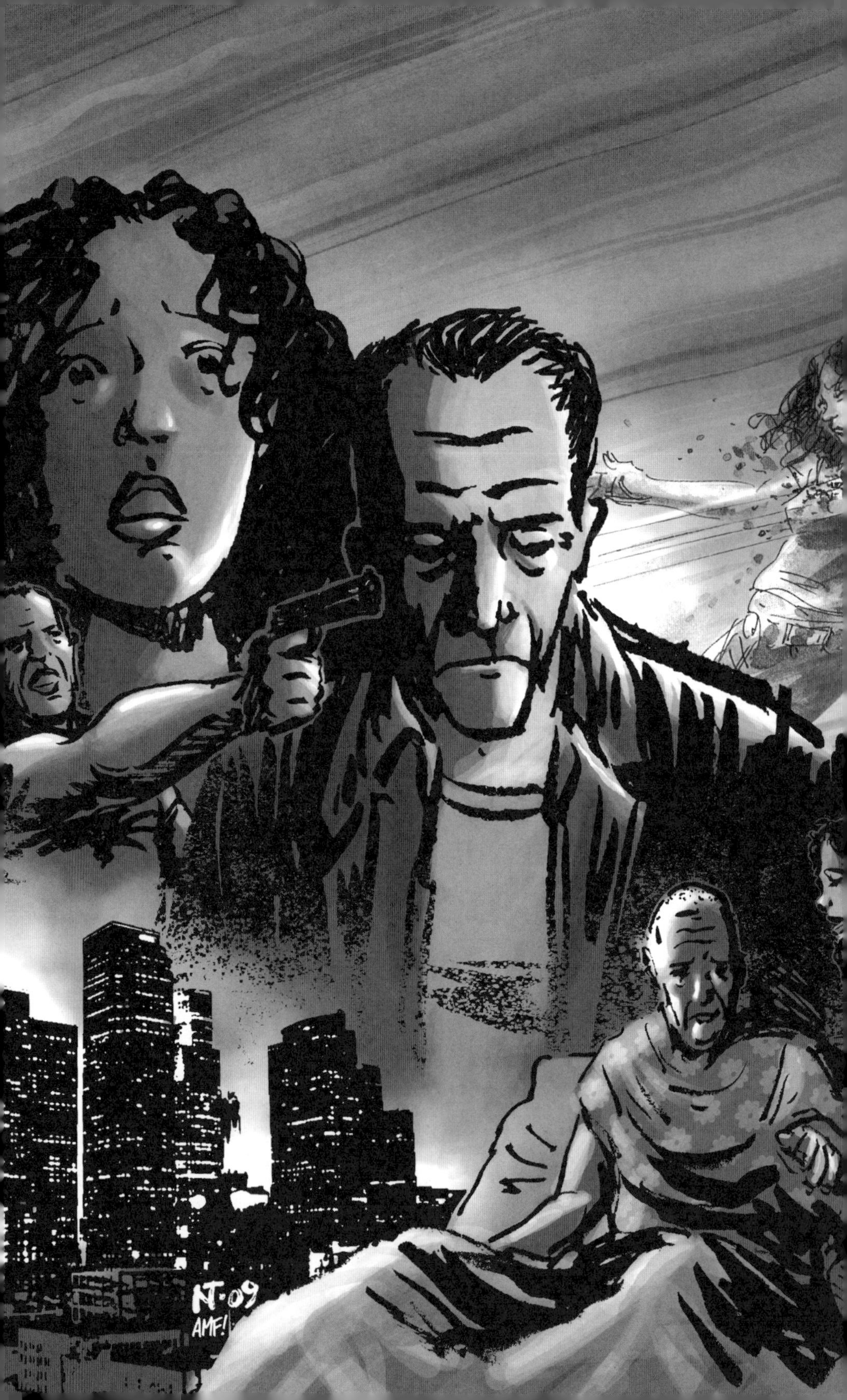
NT·09
AMF!

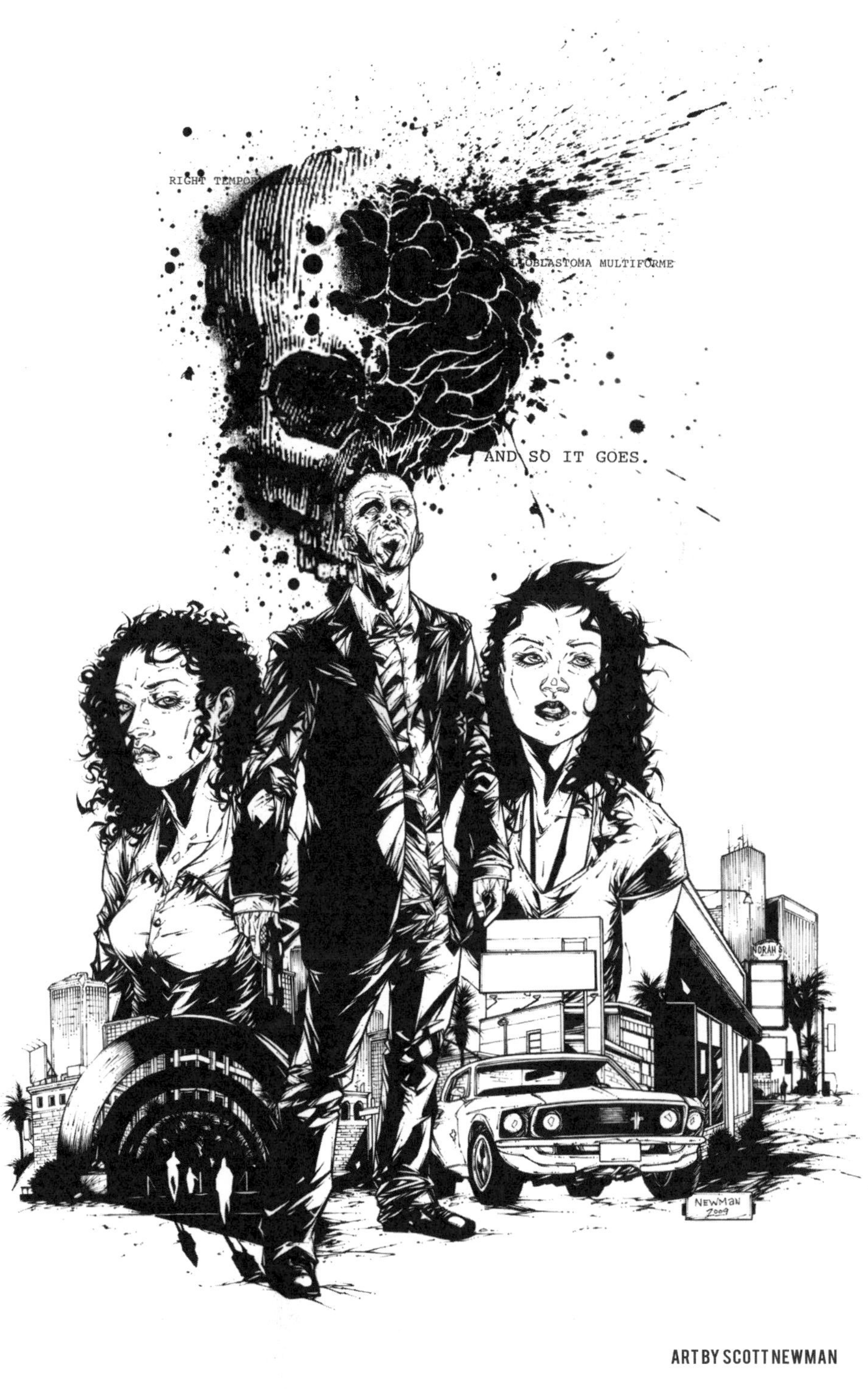
RIGHT
MULTIFORME
AND SO IT GOES.
NORAH'S
NEWMAN
2009

ART BY SCOTT NEWMAN

B & E

A Frank Armstrong Mystery

BY JOSHUA HALE FIALKOV

Thursday at the King Eddy is just like every other day. Except this Thursday is what they call Everybody's Payday. It's that rare month where disability checks, V.A. pension checks, and the last of the month fall on the same day. It might as well be Christmas Eve it's so busy in here. My usual stool's occupied, so I take up a small table in the corner and stare at the girl behind the bar so she knows what I want.

The past few months have been a blur of gin stains seeping through nicotine stains and sopping up into my skin. Camonte cut me loose after what went down, and I realized that aside from being a mediocre hitman, an errand boy for thugs and murderers, and a drunk, my prospects were nil.

And so it goes.

Drunk by ten thirty in the AM, wandering through downtown aimlessly from noon 'til five, then back to King Eddy's for the dinner rush. King Eddy's serves food, so between the booze, the cigarettes, and plates of one-dollar meatloaf, my life pretty much revolves around this place.

And the Nickel, around the corner. That's where my wife died. They also have a helluva good omelette and these bacon donuts, which sound revolting, but, man, they really hit the spot.

I'm proud to say I keep my schedule daily. If a man ain't got nothing else, at least he can be regular. So, like regular, Dennis from behind the bar walks over with my one-dollar plate of meatloaf and mashed potatoes, with a double of bourbon on the side.

"How you doin' Frank?"

"Same old."

"Some guy was here lookin' for you. Stocky, looks like a cop."

"You mind pointing him out without pointing me out?"

"Of course. Comes with the dinner."

Some fat ass cop is lookin' for me. Fantastic. Maybe Camonte's pinned Rosa's murder on me. Hell, maybe "pinned" isn't the right word. Turned me in, or gave me up. I didn't kill her, mind you, I just may as well have.

I hesitated. There was a single moment when I could've done something. I could've stopped him from shooting, or at least gotten in the way of the bullet.

I drink to forget.

It doesn't work.

I eat, I drink and I wait, 'til the stocky man who looks like a cop walks in. Dennis nods to me, but he doesn't have to. The guy might as well have a neon sign floating above his head. The entire bar quiets down when he walks in. I watch Dennis.

He does what he promised.

"He ain't here, officer."

"Yeah." The cop snorted as he walked straight for me. "You're Armstrong, right?"

Dennis started to cross from behind the bar to give me a hand.

"Look, man, you can't just come in here and hassle—"

"It's alright, Dennis. I'll talk to the man."

Dennis made eye contact. He's a good guy. Caring. That's why he still does the one-dollar meatloaf. For all us skid row rejects who're able enough to find a buck or two and not shit our pants. He's a good guy.

The cop pulls out the stool opposite me and takes a seat. He's jowly and balding, and while he's definitely a cop, I have a hard time believing he passed his entrance exam this decade. But the suit and the watch and the tie say that he's still on the street wearing blues if he's even allowed out from behind his desk.

"What can I do for you, officer?"

"Detective."

I keep eating my meatloaf. It tastes like shit if it gets cold.

"Look, I understand you're good at finding people."

I'm not.

He slides a folder in front of me with a wad of twenties paper-clipped to the front.

"You find him, you get another hundred."

I stop eating. I flip open the folder. It's a police file. Six rape-and-murders. They have a name, a social, an address, hell, even his shoe size.

"I don't get it. What do you need me for?"

"The witness who gave us all this, ain't no good. We tried for a warrant, but without the positive ID, we've got shit."

"Why can't you just sit on his place and wait?"

The cop downs the rest of his beer and turns to face the bar. Anita, Dennis's latest Mexican conquest is bent over just right cleaning off the bar.

"Hey, beautiful, how 'bout a draft of whatever you got?"

With tits like those in a place like this, it seems almost gentlemanly of him to talk to her like that.

"She's got a name."

"And a great set of tits." The cop smiles at his own witty repartee. "Look, we've been sitting on him for almost a week, and he just don't slip up. We see him go out, we tail him, nothing. Then, another rape, same M.O."

"Maybe you got the wrong guy."

"He's the right guy."

Tucked beneath the reports are pictures of his vics. Sliced across the throats and given makeshift caesareans that part them up to their belly buttons.

"He dangerous?"

"If you're a sexy twenty-year-old girl, you should quake in your boots."

"How do I know this is on the level?"

"You don't."

"I don't even know your name."

"I'm Detective James Polish. Call me Jimmy." He waves his finger in the air, beckoning for another as he finishes his current.

"Why me, Jimmy? Who sent you here?"

"You want the money or not?"

I paused just because if I didn't, I'd look desperate. Which I was.

"What do you want me to do?"

...

The address was in the canyons, and I don't have a car, so I catch a bus up to Hollywood and Laurel and hoof it the rest of the way. More and more people have been moving up here, to get out of the city and into the woods. Except, there's so many damn people that your neighbor can knock on your window to borrow a cup of sugar.

I'll never understand people's need to live up windy roads that are too narrow and on rock that likes to crumble when it rains. This used to be where all the hippie fucks lived, back when I was in my twenties and cared about that shit. We'd drive in from Glendora and try to find Jim Morrison's house.

For the record, it's the red one behind the little store a little ways up the hill.

He mentioned it in some song, which had we had half a brain we would've figured out. I always thought he was being deep.

But most of the freaks got driven out or became adults or whatever happens to rich kids with enough money to be total fuck-ups and not wind up on the streets.

The fact that this wacko lived up here didn't surprise me. There used to be plenty of places in the city to get a nice spread with a yard and a smidge of privacy. Now you have to go out to the suburbs or pay a fortune and a half to live on the beach. This guy would fit what I'd assume a serial killer would be.

Comfortable. White. A fucking deviant.

The hike up Laurel isn't so bad. It's going up the side streets that'll kill you. I stop for a cigarette every few minutes, and it only takes me thirty or forty minutes to get up to the house of Leonard Malle. From the file, I know that he's an attorney at one of these entertainment firms, probably working to get an extra stack of cash for some piece of shit actor who already has more money than every resident of my beloved Barclay Hotel will ever see combined. He moved out here from Texas at twenty-four, passed the bar the next summer, and got a job at the offices of Cohen, Davis, Greenblatt, and Cohen (no relation).

He quickly moved up, and when one of the other junior partners decided to split off, he went with, and they formed Malle and Stern.

This is what I read while I sit in a shrub waiting for the son of a bitch to make an appearance.

No wonder he got past the cops. They sit out front in a white Caddy with government plates. Masters of disguise, the Los Angeles Police Department. I chuck myself over the high wooden gate of Malle's next-door neighbors and make my way up the stone path to where the houses sit only a few feet apart. Jimmy swore up and down the place would be empty.

Somewhere nearby a dog barks and I suppose I should stop, but I never said I was smart. I pull myself up over the terraced concrete and lean over the fence, getting a clear view of Malle's living room. It's about what you'd expect. Nice, sparse, clean, unoccupied.

The dog barks again, and I shush it as quietly as I can, turning my head to look for it, half expecting it to bite my ankle off. Instead, my grip slips and I tumble over the fence and onto the concrete pathway not two feet from Malle's side window.

I freeze, praying to Christ no one saw me.

Nothing. A few minutes pass, still nothing. Jimmy swore Malle wouldn't be here when I was, but then, why is the white Caddy of fresh faced uni's still outside? I push my concerns down, 'cause that's what I do. Slowly I get up, keeping my head below the window line, just in case, and then head up towards the back of the house. There's a hill there covered in trees and underbrush. A real fire hazard. Hell, if the cops were serious about getting this guy, they should just drop a match and burn the fucker out.

His back door is double-pane glass, too thick to break, but I don't have to. A house with such a steep drop out back and a seven foot fence around the front doesn't need to worry about its back door. I slip inside the kitchen, and take a look around.

Not as nice as you'd hope. You live up here, you'd hope to get something a bit nicer than this plywood countertop, flimsy doored cabinetry-

"I've already called the cops, and I will shoot."

Click.

Yeah. I'm real bad at this.

...

I turn slowly to face Mr. Malle and see that he's shaking.

"Look, buddy, I don't want no trouble—"

"Shut up."

"I'm just gonna go out the way I came in."

"I'll fucking kill you. The cops'll be here in ten minutes and they'll-"

The front door crashes before he can finish his threat. The cops were right outside, and the two uni's are accompanied by Detective James Polish. Jimmy.

"DROP THE GUN! EVERYBODY HANDS UP!"

"This is my home, officer!"

"DROP THE WEAPON NOW!"

Malle tosses the gun on the ground, and I do my best to look like a common robber.

"What happened here?" Polish holsters his gun as he nods at one of the officers.

"This man broke into my—" his sentence is interrupted by the sound of the officers rummaging through his things.

"What the fuck is going on here?"

"Just making sure he doesn't have a partner, sir."

"Detective? You better come see this."

Polish cuffs me and drags me with him. In the front room, which is still just amazingly dinky, the uni's stand on either side of a piano bench which has been opened to reveal a stack of sheet music, and a bloody knife.

Polish pulls on a rubber glove he procures from his pocket, and picks the knife up.

"Mr. Malle, was it? This your bloody knife?"

"No... I never saw..."

They slap the cuffs on him as he struggles against them, but it's all for naught. They lead him out of his house and down to the waiting squad car.

I walk up to Polish, who lights a cigarette and smiles his ass off.

"You said he wouldn't be here."

"Yeah, I did. Oops."

"Was he really the guy?"

"How the fuck am I supposed to know? I mean, look, we found the bloody knife, right?"

"Why would he have kept a bloody knife? He would've cleaned it off, at least."

Jimmy snorts quietly to himself, and then uncuffs me.

"Look, you did good. Just like I told you, minus the gun to the head. If you want, I can give you more work."

"Like this?"

"Sometimes. Sometimes a bit more... straight."

He holds out the wad of bills, completing our little transaction.

I've had worse jobs, and I earned it. I take the money and say goodbye to Detective James Polish.

"We'll see each other again."

I don't tell him no.

...

INTERVIEW

Ain't It Cool News

BY MARK MILLER OF AICN

The following interview with writer Joshua Hale Fialkov originally appeared on *AintItCoolNews.com* on November 9th, 2009 and was conducted by Mark L. Miller.

MM: So for those who haven't been paying attention to this awesome miniseries, can you describe the premise of *Tumor*?

JHF: *Tumor* is a Los Angeles Noir about a P.I. who gets handed a huge money-making case to find and protect a missing girl on the same day that he's diagnosed with a terminal brain tumor. He decides that he's going to go out with a bang and do something right for the first time in his life. Of course, as he's protecting this girl, he's having the symptoms of a brain tumor, so he loses time, has seizures, hallucinates, and has violent mood swings.

MM: The book has been available through Amazon Kindle. Is this the first time a book has been released that way? How did this deal come about?

JHF: We're certainly the first original graphic novel on the device. There've been comics available for some time, but they're all reprints of previously published material. For the entirety of its release, *Tumor* Issue One has been the #1 comic on the Amazon Kindle, so that's been pretty exciting. The idea really just came out of a conversation between (Archaia bigwig) Stephen Christy and I about how much we love our Kindles, and how it really captures that feel of the pulps (the screen look and feel) and comics (the serialized distribution) perfectly.

MM: You had an extremely tough time releasing the final issues of *Elk's Run*, but *Tumor* seems to have run pretty smoothly and to have been released pretty consistently. What lessons did you learn in between the release of these two books?

JHF: That's what led me to digital comics, really. The fact is that the comics industry as a whole is not healthy enough to support most independent comics. The idea for me has always been that you use the individual issues as a loss-leader anyway, but, with the roadblocks of Diamond thresholds and the massive increase in printing costs, it's just not economically feasible for most indie creators to do the single issue format anymore.

With *Tumor*, we planned on the series being a book from day one. It was always intended to be released to the world as a beautiful and substantial hardcover. With the Kindle release we got the benefit of releasing individual issues, which is a marketing and "brand awareness" thing (look how douchey I sound!), without the financial risk. I also think that it makes people excited to finally get the book in print, both new readers and those who've followed the digital version. For me, digital first with a well designed, extras-loaded collection is the way of the future.

MM: At San Diego Comic-Con this year, there seemed to be a trend of a push to more digital comics released through iPhones and other computer avenues. How do you feel about this shift toward a more digital age of comics? Are printed comics going the way of the dinosaurs?

JHF: I think that Marvel and DC will be publishing monthly comics for a long while to come. But, you're going to start seeing less and less indie stuff delivered that way. The fact is that there's just not a lot of room in the market, or, frankly, a lot of interest for non-mainstream work. There are amazing retailers who've made it into their bread and butter, but, for the most part, most comic shops in this country subsist on the regular income of a well-scheduled mainstream event comics, and random independent books from— to them—B and C level creators just don't cut it.

MM: The themes of *Tumor* are definitely noir based. I detected a bit of a *Memento* vibe in this one. What influenced you for *Tumor*?

JHF: I probably owe the biggest debt to a film noir directed by Rudolph Maté from 1950 called *D.O.A.* (Which for the record, is not to be confused with the 80's remake or the creepy movie starring Jamie Pressley.) *D.O.A.* is about a man who's poisoned and has twenty-four hours to find his murderer. Yes, that's where *Crank* got it from. The other big influence was a TV miniseries by Dennis Botter for the BBC called *The Singing Detective* which follows a crime novelist with a debilitating skin condition who imagines the next novel in his series of books while hallucinating about his life leading up to the point we first meet him. It's probably the best six or so hours of television ever created, and like I said, it's a masterpiece worth stealing from.

MM: You really feel for Frank, the central character of *Tumor.* He is literally falling apart throughout this entire story and it's devastating to see his mind and body begin to fail due to the tumor. With such a deep emotional resonance to this story, one would assume that this is a highly personal story for you. Is this true or are you just that damn fine a writer?

JHF: I'll take the latter, please. Look, I've had some pretty fucked up health problems over the course of my life, and I suffer from a lot of things that made me paranoid that I had a brain tumor, so I just became fascinated with the way the human brain functions and how one's body reacts to that being tampered with.

A lot of my writing comes from my own worst nightmares, and losing my ability for cognitive thought is pretty damn far up the list. I think it's a recognizable fear for the reader as well because no matter what a person believes, at their core they know that their brain is who they are, and without it they're nothing.

MM: Your work with artist Noel Tuazon on this and *Elk's Run* have been a fantastic match of tone and content. I couldn't imagine those stories told from a different artistic hand. How did you go about finding and choosing him for these projects?

JHF: Noel and I worked together on *Elk's Run* prior to *Tumor,* and there's a chemistry between us that really works for me. Noel's art is certainly far from the mainstream of comics, but I think he draws with an energy that you see in the early 20th century's cartoonists. There's a rawness and an emotion that comes through in every panel.

His characters feel alive and vibrant in a way that an ultra-rendered or photo-real drawing can't. He manages to make the reader identify with the characters more because they fill in the lines with their own memories and characters from their lives.

MM: Now that *Tumor* is in the bag, what's next for you?

JHF: Noel and I have a couple more projects that have been percolating for quite a while, and we should be starting the next one in a month or two. In addition to that, I've got a new series that'll be coming out from Oni Press with art by Tony Fleecs sometime next year, and another crime comic I'm doing with Rahsan Ekedal who drew a book I did some work on last year for Dark Horse called *The Cleaners.* Plus assorted work-for-hire gigs, the one I'm most excited about is a new Western one-shot for Top Cow.

MM: Last chance, why should everyone order *Tumor* in this month's *Previews* and buy it when it hits the stands in... when does it hit the stands again?

JHF: I hear from people all the time who complain about event-driven superhero comics and how 'samey' so much of the medium has become. There's a lot of material that's totally different than everything else being released from the indie publishers, and, if you want the industry to change you have to take the chance and order them. That's the only way that the industry can change.

The book is available for Pre-Order from Diamond Comics right now (you can grab the order info from the official website here: http://www.tumorthecomic.com) and will ship in late January or early February. It's available right now for pre-order on Amazon.com as well. And, if you still aren't convinced, you can check out the entire book in a Flash-based reader over at www.tumorthecomic.com!

MM: Thanks for taking the time out for this interview. *Tumor* is a fantastic piece of work!

JHF: Thanks!

Mark L. Miller has been the editor and writer at AICN COMICS and AICN HORROR at Ain't it Cool News for 14 years. Mark also writes comics such as *Pirouette, Occupy Comics,* and *Jungle Book.* Find him on Twitter @Mark_L_Miller.

FRANK ARMSTRONG'S LOS ANGELES

A Tour of Frank's City and Its History

BY JOSHUA HALE FIALKOV

The story of *Tumor* and the death of Frank Armstrong is also the story of the ever-changing city of Los Angeles. Los Angeles is a city that's never rested on its laurels. In the ten years I've lived here, I've seen buildings erected and destroyed, classics restored, modern eyesores become familiar friends, and neighborhoods rise and fall. Neighborhoods that I've lived in less than five years ago look nothing like they did when I lived there. It can be a disorienting place, even when you have all of your faculties.

Los Angeles has a marvelous history, more than most cities founded within the past hundred and fifty years. As you drive around the city, landmarks are pretty much everywhere. Sure, there's the touristy stuff, but there's actual (and fictional) history here too. Chandler hung out in the back room of Musso and Frank's, occasionally venturing into the bookstore across the street, leading him to set Phillip Marlowe there for a mid-rain shower snog. Not a mile away is the building that once housed the Hayes Office, the home of film censorship that all of Hollywood learned to fear. Around the corner you'll find the building that the Black Dahlia herself lived in right around the time she was murdered.

Just above the 101 Freeway there's a huge marker on one of the walls, between the graffiti and billboards. It's The Fort Moore Pioneer Memorial, honoring the Mormon Battalion, the only religious unit in American military history. As you drive through Chinatown, you realize that it's not the original one, but in fact the third neighborhood of that name, as the first had been burned in a riot, and the second destroyed to make way for Union Station. Union Station, which I may add,

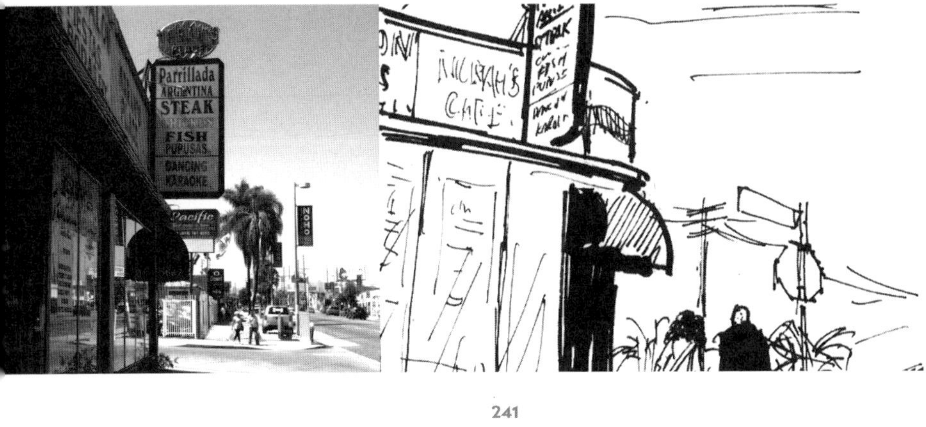
Parrillada
ARGENTINA
STEAK
FISH
PUPUSAS
DANCING
KARAOKE

sits directly across from the birthplace of the French dip sandwich. Either there, or a mile down the road in downtown, depending on which side you believe.

Then there's the boarded up Hall of Justice, which is where the Manson family was held, right around the corner from what was once Bunker Hill, an entire neighborhood of mansions, the kind you see in old movies, that was leveled to make way for some of the ugliest skyscrapers in America.

You make another few turns, and you find yourself on Broadway. Once one of the most concentrated strips of vaudeville and movie palaces in the country, it's now a strip of electronics, discount clothing, and tourist stores. Quite a few of them have been converted into churches. But here's where this all relates to *Tumor*. They didn't knock the theaters down. No, instead, the just moved the stores in, slapped some paint on the walls, and left the glorious neon and marquees still intact. You step inside and you see this is where the lobby was; this is where the theater itself was. A ghostly memory of what was once there stands lumbering over the present.

Frank is Los Angeles. He's unable to live in the now, because what's come before weighs so heavily on him. In constructing the plot and developing his character, what I came to realize is that the case and his relationship with Evelyn are a way of exorcising his past, to allow him for one single moment to have some peace. Unfortunately, that moment comes as he's once again passing onto a new stage.

For me, noir has its roots in Los Angeles because of this constant struggle. From its earliest founding, the city has struggled with its identity. We joke as modern

day Angelenos that the real estate market can't get any worse. Houses are so astronomical out here that unless you're approaching being a millionaire, you most likely rent or live so far out in the suburbs, you might as well just live in Detroit. But, from day one, this city has been just like that. It's been the American Dream to come out to the golden sunshine state and make your fortune since the mid 1800s. It's Manifest Destiny. It's every boy coming home from the war, and making a new life for himself with a wife and kids and a house with two cars in the garage.

But, that's myth. Los Angeles is a working-class city, filled with hard-working people doing their best to make a living in a city that's expensive, crowded, and with a history of corruption and crime that runs from the highest reaches of city hall to the guy selling tax-stampless cigarettes out of his car. This is the city that brought us both *The Shield* and *The O.C.* It's a city of contradictions and confusion, and we're all just living in it.

JOSHUA HALE FIALKOV

North Hollywood, CA

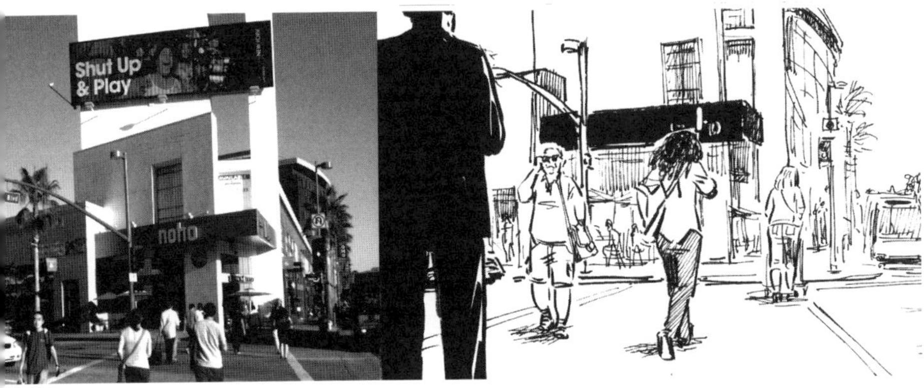

Shut Up & Play
noho

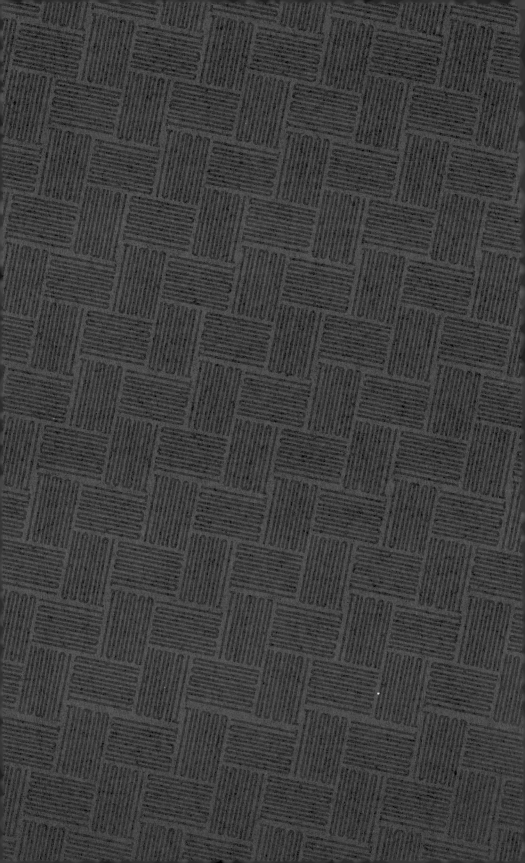

AFTERWORD

BY JOSHUA HALE FIALKOV

That mural? The one on the side of the Mexican restaurant Frank passes on his way to Polish's house. It's gone now. And the train stations? They do in fact require you to pay. (Well, sort of.) The scummy part of downtown that Frank lives in? It's now high-end luxury apartments. The bar Frank frequents got closed, and reopened as a sort of hipster recreation of the original bar. Gone are the $1 meatloaves. Angel's Flight, the funicular, has opened, and closed, and opened, (and, as of this writing) closed once more. Hell, plain old North Hollywood has become a destination, making the San Fernando Valley into more than just the punch line it's been for fifty years.

Tumor is a story about the lack of permanence. How everything we do, every place we go, every action we take, leaves ripples around it, but only for a moment. And what better place to set it than Los Angeles. A city that frequently forgets who it is, where it was, and how it had planned to get there. It's a story about the marks that are left on us and in us.

My wife was diagnosed with cancer not too long after this book came out. All of the research (an obsessional amount) that went into this book, trying to get it "right" and making it feel "correct" proved something to me. Words can't express the terror inherent in that six-letter word. And though she kicked cancer squarely in the balls, it's something that hangs over her, and us, every day of our lives.

To some degree, that cancer inspired her to do things she never had before. To be the person that she wanted to be, and to chase the dreams that were always just slightly after reach. She's written a book (or four or five), become an acclaimed author of Pony comics (the weird paths our lives go down), become the head of the Photo Collection at the LAPL, and been just about the best damn mom a person can be.

Somehow, like Frank, she didn't crumple under its weight. She stood stronger. Through not just the physical pain, but the emotional pain as well. She has a scar, hidden almost perfectly in the gentle fold of her neck, from the surgery. And I'm sure, deep down, she has scars from the experience. But, she fights. She remembers. But she doesn't mourn. She moves on.

I lied when I said this book was about the lack of permanence. It's about love. It's about how love can make you stronger.

More specifically, it's about how her love made me stronger.

So now, as before, this book is for my wife.

JOSHUA HALE FIALKOV
North Hollywood, CA
3-28-15

BIOGRAPHIES

JOSHUA HALE FIALKOV

Joshua Hale Fialkov is the Harvey-, Eisner-, and Emmy-nominated creator of graphic novels, including *The Bunker*, *Punks*, *Tumor*, *Echoes*, and *Elk's Run*. He has written *The Ultimates* for Marvel and *I, Vampire* for DC Comics. He lives in Los Angeles with his wife, author Christina Rice, their daughter, who will remain anonymous (and adorable), and their dogs Cole and Olaf.

NOEL TUAZON

Noel Tuazon lives in Toronto working a 9-5 job at Nelvana Animation. His comics output includes illustrating Joshua Hale Fialkov's *Elk's Run* and *Tumor*, Eric Hobbs' *The Broadcast* and *Family Ties* (NBM) and Brian Buccellato's *Foster* (OSSM Comics). His works can also be found in some comics anthologies, including Dark Horse's *Once Upon A Time Machine* and the indie *Monstrosity*, volumes one and two.

ALSO FROM JOSHUA HALE FIALKOV & NOEL TUAZON

ELK'S RUN
A TALE OF SMALL TOWN HORROR
New York Times Best-Selling Authors
JOSHUA HALE FIALKOV
NOEL TUAZON
SCOTT KEATING

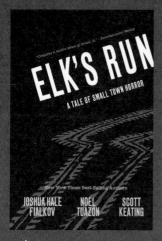

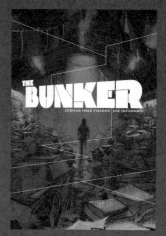

ELK'S RUN
10th ANNIVERSARY EDITION
By Joshua Hale Fialkov, Noel Tuazon, and Scott Keating
248 pages, hardcover, color
ISBN 978-1-62010-279-4

THE LIFE AFTER
JOSHUA HALE FIALKOV • GABO
1
10/10

THE LIFE AFTER, VOLUME ONE
By Joshua Hale Fialkov and Gabo
136 pages, softcover
color
ISBN 978-1-62010-214-5

THE BUNKER
JOSHUA HALE FIALKOV
JOE INFURNARI

THE BUNKER, VOLUME ONE
By Joshua Hale Fialkov and Joe Infurnari
136 pages, softcover
color
ISBN 978-1-62010-164-3

OTHER BOOKS FROM ONI PRESS

A BRAWN NOVEL
CAPOTE IN KANSAS
ANDE PARKS
CHRIS SAMNEE

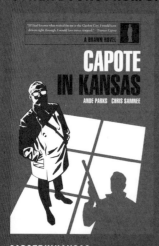

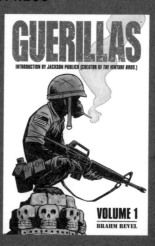

CAPOTE IN KANSAS
By Ande Parks & Chris Samnee
160 pages, hardcover
black and white
ISBN 978-1-934964-87-3

GUERILLAS
INTRODUCTION BY JACKSON PUBLICK (CREATOR OF THE VENTURE BROS.)
VOLUME 1
BRAHM REVEL

GUERILLAS, VOLUME 1
By Brahm Revel
168 pages, softcover
black and white
ISBN 978-1-934964-43-9

PETROGRAD
PHILIP GELATT • TYLER CROOK

PETROGRAD
By Philip Gelatt & Tyler Crook
264 pages, hardcover
two-color
ISBN 978-1-934964-44-6

For more information on these and other fine Oni Press comic books and graphic novels visit www.onipress.com. To find a comic specialty store in your area visit www.comicshops.us.

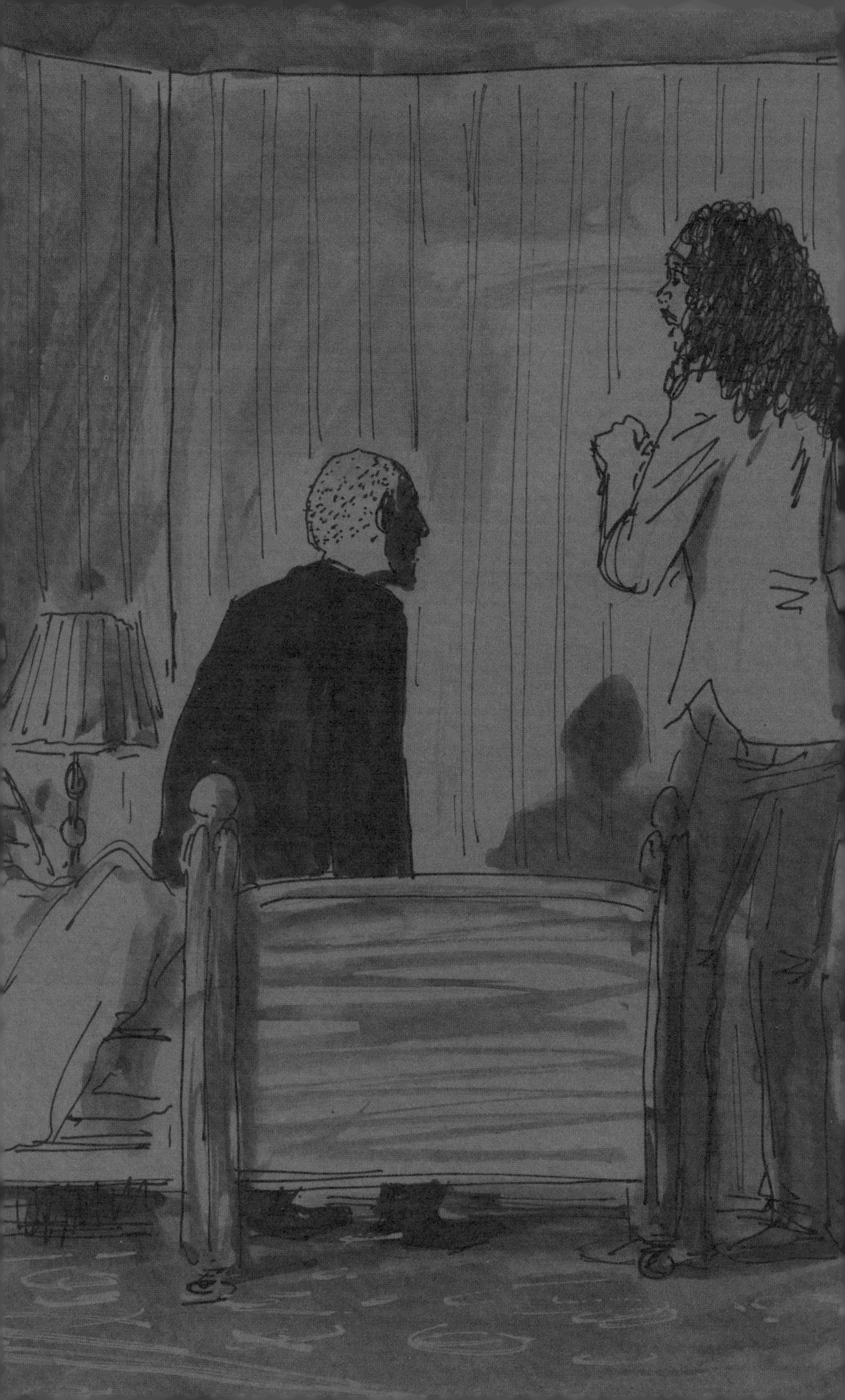